S0-BCL-339

Contested Governance in Japan

Contested Governance in Japan extends the analysis of governance in contemporary Japan by exploring both the sites and issues of governance above and below the state as well as within it. All contributors share a common perspective on governance as taking place in different sites of activity, and as involving a range of issues related to the norms and rules for the management, coordination and regulation of order, whether within Japan or on the regional or global levels. This volume discusses the contested nature of governance in Japan and the ways in which a range of actors is involved in different sites and issues of governance at home, in the region and the globe. Including chapters on global governance, local policymaking, democracy, environmental governance, the Japanese financial system, corruption, corporate governance and the family, this collection will be of interest to anyone studying Japanese politics and governance.

Glenn D. Hook is Director of the Graduate School of East Asian Studies and Professor of Japanese Studies at the University of Sheffield, UK.

Sheffield Centre for Japanese Studies/ RoutledgeCurzon Series

Series Editor: Glenn D. Hook
Professor of Japanese Studies, University of Sheffield

This series, published by RoutledgeCurzon in association with the Centre for Japanese Studies at the University of Sheffield, both makes available original research on a wide range of subjects dealing with Japan and provides introductory overviews of key topics in Japanese Studies.

The Internationalization of Japan
Edited by Glenn D. Hook and Michael Weiner

Race and Migration in Imperial Japan
Michael Weiner

Japan and the Pacific Free Trade Area
Pekka Korhonen

Greater China and Japan
Prospects of an economic partnership?
Robert Taylor

The Steel Industry in Japan
A comparison with the UK
Hasegawa Harukiyo

Race, Resistance and the Ainu of Japan
Richard Siddle

Japan's Minorities
The illusion of homogeneity
Edited by Michael Weiner

Japanese Business Management
Restructuring for low growth and globalization
*Edited by Hasegawa Harukiyo
and Glenn D. Hook*

Japan and Asia Pacific Integration
Pacific romances 1968–1996
Pekka Korhonen

Japan's Economic Power and Security
Japan and North Korea
Christopher W. Hughes

Japan's Contested Constitution
Documents and analysis
Glenn D. Hook and Gavan McCormack

Japan's International Relations
Politics, economics and security
Glenn D. Hook, Julie Gilson, Christopher W. Hughes and Hugo Dobson

Japanese Education Reform
Nakasone's legacy
Christopher P. Hood

The Political Economy of Japanese Globalization
Edited by Glenn D. Hook and Hasegawa Harukiyo

Japan and Okinawa
Structure and subjectivity
Edited by Glenn D. Hook and Richard Siddle

Japan and Britain in the Contemporary World
Responses to common issues
Edited by Hugo Dobson and Glenn D. Hook

Japan and United Nations Peacekeeping
New pressures, new responses
Hugo Dobson

Japanese Capitalism and Modernity in a Global Era
Re-fabricating lifetime employment relations
Peter C. D. Matanle

Nikkeiren and Japanese Capitalism
John Crump

Production Networks in Asia and Europe
Skill formation and technology transfer in the automobile industry
Edited by Rogier Busser and Yuri Sadoi

Japan and the G7/8
1975–2002
Hugo Dobson

The Political Economy of Reproduction in Japan
Between nation-state and everyday life
Takeda Hiroko

Grassroots Pacifism in Post-War Japan
The rebirth of a nation
Mari Yamamoto

Japanese Interfirm Networks
Adapting to survive in the global electronics industry
Ralph Paprzycki

Globalisation and Women in the Japanese Workforce
Beverley Bishop

Contested Governance in Japan
Sites and issues
Edited by Glenn D. Hook

Contested Governance in Japan
Sites and issues

Edited by Glenn D. Hook

RoutledgeCurzon
Taylor & Francis Group

LONDON AND NEW YORK

First published 2005
by RoutledgeCurzon
2 Park Square, Milton Park, Abingdon, Oxon OX14 4RN

Simultaneously published in the USA and Canada
by RoutledgeCurzon
270 Madison Ave, New York, NY 10016

RoutledgeCurzon is an imprint of the Taylor & Francis Group

© 2005 Glenn D. Hook editorial matter and selection;
individual chapters © the individual contributors

Typeset in Baskerville by Keystroke, Jacaranda Lodge, Wolverhampton
Printed and bound in Great Britain by MPG Books Ltd, Bodmin

British Library Cataloguing in Publication Data
A catalogue record for this book is available from the British Library

Library of Congress Cataloging in Publication Data
A catalog record for this book has been requested

ISBN 0–415–36419–1 (hbk)
ISBN 0–415–36498–1 (pbk)

Contents

Illustrations

Figures

Tables

Notes on contributors

J. Babb is Lecturer in Japanese politics at the University of Newcastle-upon-Tyne. Prior to going to Newcastle, he worked in Japan as both a part-time lecturer at Tokyo Metropolitian University and as a consultant to the National Institute for Research Advancement managed by the Economic Planning Agency of the Japanese government. He holds an MA and PhD from Stanford University, and a Certificate from the Inter-University Center for Japanese Studies in Tokyo. His major publications include *Business and Politics in Japan* (University of Manchester Press, 2001) and *Tanaka: the making of postwar Japan* (Longman, 2000).

Philip G. Cerny is Professor of Global Political Economy in the Center for Global Change and Governance, Rutgers University-Newark. His publications include *The Changing Architecture of Politics: structure, agency and the future of the state* (Sage, 1990), *Finance and World Politics: markets, regimes and states in the post-hegemonic era* (editor, Edward Elgar, 1993), *Internalizing Globalization: the rise of neoliberalism and the erosion of national models of capitalism* (co-editor, Palgrave, forthcoming 2005) and numerous other works including articles in *International Organization*, the *European Journal of International Relations* and the *Review of International Studies*.

Hugo Dobson is Lecturer in the International Relations of Japan in the School of East Asian Studies, the University of Sheffield. In addition to a number of articles and book chapters, his publications include *Japan's International Relations: politics, economics and security* (co-author, Routledge, 2001), *Japan and United Nations Peacekeeping: new pressures, new responses* (RoutledgeCurzon, 2004), and *Japan and the G7/8: 1975 to 2002* (RoutledgeCurzon, 2004).

Tom Gill is Associate Professor of Social Anthropology at the Department of International Studies, Meiji Gakuin University. His publications include *Globalization and Social Change in Contemporary Japan* (co-editor, Trans Pacific Press, 2000), *Men of Uncertainty: the social organization of day laborers in contemporary Japan* (SUNY Press, 2001), and numerous papers in English and Japanese. Home page: http://tomgill.homestead.com/TomGill.html

Hasegawa Harukiyo is Professor of Global Management and Human Resource Management at Doshisha Business School in Kyoto. His research interests are in Asian business and management. His publications include *An International Comparison of Business and Management* (Chūō Keizaisha, 1993, co-author, in Japanese); *Steel Industry in Japan: a comparison with Britain* (Routledge, 1996); *Japanese Business and Management: restructuring for low growth and globalization* (co-editor, Routledge, 1998); *The Political Economy of Japanese Globalization* (co-editor, Routledge, 2001). He is General Editor of the international journal, *Asian Business & Management* (PalgraveMacmillan).

Hatsuse Ryūhei is Professor of International Relations at the Faculty for the Study of Contemporary Society, Kyoto Women's University. His publications include *International politics: the trajectory of theories* (Dobunkan, 1993, in Japanese), *Ethnicity and Multiculturalism* (editor, Dobunkan, 1996, in Japanese), 'Regionalism in East Asia and the Asia-Pacific' in Yoshinobu Yamamoto (ed.) *Globalism, Regionalism and Nationalism* (Blackwell, 1999), and 'Japanese responses to globalization: nationalism and transnationalism' in Glenn D. Hook and Hasegawa Harukiyo (eds) *The Political Economy of Japanese Globalization* (contributor, Routledge, 2001).

Glenn D. Hook is Professor of Japanese Studies and Director of the Graduate School of East Asian Studies, the University of Sheffield. His research interests are in Japanese politics, international relations and security. His publications include *Militarization and Demilitarization in Contemporary Japan* (Routledge, 1996), *Japan's Contested Constitution: documents and analysis* (Routledge, 2001, coauthor), *Japan's International Relations: politics, economics, and security* (Routledge, 2001, coauthor) and *The Political Economy of Japanese Globalization* (Routledge, 2001, coeditor).

Lam Peng Er is a Senior Research Fellow at the East Asian Institute, National University of Singapore. He obtained his PhD in political science from Columbia University. His latest book is *Green Politics in Japan* (Routledge, 1999). He has published articles in journals such as *Pacific Affairs, Asian Survey* and *Japan Forum*.

Osawa Mari is Professor of Social Policy at the Institute of Social Science, University of Tokyo. She specializes in welfare issues, especially in relation to gender, and holds a PhD in economics from the same university. She works for the Council for Gender Equality under the Cabinet Office of Japan, as the Chair of the Committee of Specialists on Gender Impact Assessment and Evaluation of Public Policies. Her publications include *A History of Social Policy in Modern Britain: from Poor Law to the Welfare State* (University of Tokyo Press, 1986, in Japanese), *Beyond Corporate-Centered Society: a Gender Analysis of Contemporary Japan* (Jiji Press, 1993, in Japanese) and 'Government approaches to gender equality in the mid-1990s', *Social Science Japan Journal* 3, 1, 2000.

Miranda A. Schreurs is an Associate Professor in the Department of Government and Politics at the University of Maryland, College Park. She teaches courses on comparative politics, focused on Japan, East Asia, Germany, and the European Union as well as more specialized courses on environmental politics. She is author of *Environmental Politics in Japan, Germany, and the United States* (Cambridge University Press, 2002) and co-author of *Environmental Security in Northeast Asia* (co-author, Yonsei University Press, 1998) and the *Internationalization of Environmental Protection* (co-author, Cambridge University Press, 1997). She holds a PhD from the University of Michigan (1996) and an MA and BA from the University of Washington (1987, 1986).

J. A. A. Stockwin was Nissan Professor of Modern Japanese Studies and Director of the Nissan Institute of Japanese Studies at the University of Oxford between 1982–2003. He was also a Fellow of St. Antony's College. His degrees are from the University of Oxford (BA) and the Australian National University (PhD). Between 1964 and 1981 he taught in the Department of Political Science at the Australian National University, Canberra. His publications include *The Japanese Socialist Party and Neutralism* (Cambridge University Press, 1968), *Dynamic and Immobilist Politics in Japan* (editor and co-author, Macmillan, 1988), *Governing Japan* (Blackwells, 1999), *Dictionary of the Modern Politics of Japan* (RoutledgeCurzon, 2003) and the *Collected Writings of J. A. A. Stockwin: Part I, The Politics and Political Environment of Japan* (RoutledgeCurzon, 2004).

Takeda Hiroko completed her PhD at the School of East Asian Studies, the University of Sheffield. She previously taught at Cardiff Japanese Studies Centre, Cardiff University, and is currently a Lecturer in Japanese Studies in the School of East Asian Studies, the University of Sheffield. Her first book is *The Political Economy of Reproduction in Japan* (RoutledgeCurzon, 2004).

Preface and acknowledgements

This book is the fruit of a research project which grows out of a meeting held on 30 May 2001 between British and Japanese research funding bodies, other interested parties, and the British Association for Japanese Studies (BAJS). In the wake of the meeting, three research projects were identified as filling important gaps in the literature: governance in Japan; the 'Other' in Japanese literature; and modern and contemporary Japanese nationalism. It was agreed at a meeting of the BAJS council shortly thereafter that three members of council would act as project leaders, drawing on both members of the association and others in the field in order to find the best possible contributors to produce three edited books. This is the first of those three volumes, with the second being edited by Mark Williams and the third by Naoko Shimazu.

The members of these projects, and especially the project leaders and editors, owe an enormous debt of gratitude to the Great Britain–Sasakawa Foundation, and especially to Mike Barrett, its Chief Executive. If it had not been for the Foundation's generous support, and Mike's belief in us, these projects would not have been realized. We are also grateful to the Toshiba International Foundation and to BAJS for generous additional financial assistance and support.

Craig Folie at RoutledgeCurzon agreed to take on the three volumes as part of the Sheffield Centre for Japanese Studies/RoutledgeCurzon Series, subject to the standard international peer review. We are grateful for his enthusiastic support of these projects.

Finally, as far as this project is concerned, I would like to thank all of the contributors, most of whom were able to participate in a workshop to present drafts of their work in January 2003, for their chapters. Thanks are also due to the Chubu Electric Power Company for financial support, and to the anonymous referees, who made incisive comments on the chapters.

GDH

Note on the text

Following Japanese convention, the family name precedes the given name unless the author of a source publishes in English and does so using the reverse order. Long vowels are indicated by a macron, except in the case of common place and other names, such as Tokyo.

Abbreviations

AMF	Asian Monetary Fund
AOTS	Association for Overseas Technical Scholarship
APEC	Asia Pacific Economic Cooperation
APSF	Asian People's Friendship Society
ARF	Association of Southeast Asian Nations Regional Forum
ASA	ASEAN Swap Arrangement
ASEAN	Association of Southeast Asian Nations
ASEM	Asia-Europe Meeting
BOJ	Bank of Japan
BSA	Bilateral Swap Agreements
CASA	Citizens' Alliance for Saving the Atmosphere and the Earth
CCM	Capital Cost Management
CEFP	Cabinet Office's Council on Economic and Fiscal Policy
CEO	chief executive officer
CMI	Chiang-Mai Initiative
CPSU	Communist Party of the (former) Soviet Union
DP	Democratic Party
DVD	digital versatile disk
EAEC	East Asian Economic Caucus
EC	European Community
ESC	Economic Strategy Council of Japan
ETS	Emergency Temporary Shelter
EU	European Union
FCCC	Framework Convention on Climate Change
FRC	Financial Reconstruction Commission
FDI	foreign direct investment
FILP	Fiscal Investment and Loan Programme
FSA	Financial Supervisory Agency
FTA	Free Trade Agreement
GATT	General Agreement on Tariffs and Trade
GDP	gross domestic product
GLOBE	Global Legislators Organization for a Balanced Environment
GOCO	government-owned, contractor-operated

GSM	Global System for Mobile Communications
HRM	human resource management
IMF	International Monetary Fund
IPE	international political economy
IPO	Initial Public Offering
IR	international relations
IR	investor relations
ISO	International Standard Organization
IT	information technology
JCP	Japan Communist Party
JICA	Japan International Cooperation Agency
JITCO	Japan International Training Cooperation Organization
JSP	Japan Socialist Party (later Social Democratic Party (SDP))
JUSCANZ	Japan, United States, Canada, New Zealand
LDP	Liberal Democratic Party
M&A	merger and acquisition
MAFF	Ministry of Agriculture, Forestry and Fisheries
METI	Ministry of Economy, Trade and Industry
MEXT	Ministry of Education, Culture, Sports, Science and Technology
MHLW	Ministry of Health, Labour and Welfare
MHW	Ministry of Health and Welfare
MITI	Ministry of International Trade and Industry
MLIT	Ministry of Land, Infrastructure and Transport
MOC	Ministry of Construction
MOF	Ministry of Finance
MOFA	Ministry of Foreign Affairs
MOJ	Ministry of Justice
MOL	Ministry of Labour
MP	Member of Parliament
NAM	Non-Aligned Movement
NFRWO	Housewives Confederation and National Federation of Regional Women's Organizations
NGO	non-governmental organization
NIMBY	'not in my back yard'
NPO	non-profit making organization
NTT	Nippon Telegraph and Telephone Public Cooperation
OAS	Organization of American States
ODA	official development assistance
OECD	Organization for Economic Cooperation and Development
OPEC	Organization of Petroleum Exporting Countries
PARC	Policy Affairs Research Council
R&D	research and development
ROE	return on equity
SDP	Social Democratic Party
SEC	Securities and Exchange Commission

SSC	self-reliance support centre
SSM	Social Stratification and Social Mobility
SSS	Social Security Service
UK	United Kingdom
UN	United Nations
UNCED	United Nations Conference on Environment and Development
UNCTAD	United Nations Conference on Trade and Development
UNDP	United Nations Development Programme
UNHCR	United Nations High Commissioner for Refugees
UNSC	United Nations Security Council
US	United States
WEM	white-collar, employed, managerial
WHO	World Health Organization
WTO	World Trade Organization

Glossary

Japanese

ainori riding together.

amakudari 'descent from heaven'; practice of retired bureaucrats taking posts in industries, etc. that they used to regulate.

bakufu military government.

Daijūzeki the name of the stone weir built on the Yoshino river around 250 years ago.

daimyō feudal lords.

fukoku kyōhei 'enrich the country, strengthen the military.'

gaiatsu external pressures.

jiritsu shien sentā Self-reliance Support Centre (SSC).

keiretsu large conglomerates, often linking a variety of different sectors of the economy, which usually tie together large manufacturers and their suppliers.

kinkyū ichiji hinanjo Emergency Temporary Shelter (ETS).

kōenkai personal support machines at the constituency level.

Kōmeitō Clean Government Party.

mutōha non-party-affiliated voters.

naiatsu internal pressures.

Nikkei *Nihon Keizai Shimbun*.

Nikkeijin 'second-generation Japanese'; used here to refer to South-Americans of Japanese origin.

Nikkeiren *Nihon Keieisha Dantai Renmei* (Japan Federation of Employers' Associations).

seikatsu hogo livelihood protection; main form of general social welfare in Japan.

shakai fukushi social welfare.

shakai fukushi jimusho social welfare office.

shingikai advisory council.

shitei toshi 'designated city'; category for thirteen major metropolises (i.e. those with over 500,000 population though most have populations over 1,000,000) with higher level of autonomy than other cities.

sōgo shōsha general trading companies.

sokaiya racketeer.
Tennō Emperor.
yoseba a gathering place for day labourers.
zaibatsu pre-war industrial conglomerates.
zenecon general contractors in the construction industry.
zoku giin 'policy tribesmen'.

Non-Japanese

ASEAN 4 Association of Southeast Asian Nations members Indonesia, Malaysia, the Philippines and Thailand.
'big bang' range of measures taken to liberalize and deregulate the Japanese financial system.
'Dodge line' named after Detroit banker, Joseph Dodge, who in 1949 implemented a number of economic measures known as the 'Dodge line' in order to combat inflation and stimulate the Japanese economy.
G6 Group of six major industrialized countries; France, (West) Germany, Italy, Japan, United Kingdom and the United States.
G7 Group of seven major industrialized countries; Canada, France, Germany, Italy, Japan, the United Kingdom and the United States.
G8 Group of eight major industrialized countries; Canada, France, Germany, Italy, Japan, Russia, the United Kingdom and the United States.
G10 Group of Belgium, Canada, France, Italy, Japan, the Netherlands, Sweden, Germany the United Kingdom and the United States. Switzerland became the eleventh member, but the group is still called G10. G-7/G-8 and G10 are not related.
G77 Group of seventy-seven developing nations at the United Nations.
NIES 4 The Newly Industrialized Economies of Hong Kong, Singapore, Taiwan and South Korea.

Introduction

Contested governance in Japan: modes, sites and issues

Glenn D. Hook

Whilst a veritable avalanche of research has appeared in English on topics ranging from 'global governance' down to 'corporate governance' in different parts of the world, especially the Anglo-American world, the amount of work in the Japanese language is far more limited. Except for a burgeoning literature on corporate governance and to a lesser extent local governance, for the most part governance in Japan is simply viewed as what governments do, and, as the years since 1955 have been dominated by governments led by the Liberal Democratic Party (LDP), except for a brief period in the mid-1990s, governance has been viewed as predominately a question of how the LDP governs. Thus overwhelming interest has been focused on the balance between and amongst what are viewed as the key actors in the classic tripartite elite model of policymaking in Japan, the LDP, bureaucracy and big business, or how things have changed in the era of coalition governments in the 1990s and early 2000s. Other analysts have sought to broaden the understanding of how policy is formulated by examining actors outside of this triumvirate. This has expanded the range of actors seen to be involved in the policymaking process beyond the so-called 'iron triangle', as suggested by the term 'patterned pluralism' (Muramatsu and Krauss 1987), or 'bureaucracy-led, mass inclusionary pluralism' (Inoguchi and Iwai 1987: 5–7; also see Stockwin 1999: 221). Despite such a broadening in the way the actors playing a role in the governance of Japan is understood, however, the main focus has remained on how Japan is governed in terms of the actors involved in the policymaking process at the central government level.

This view of governance as a question of how the government and other actors govern Japan through the policies implemented is represented by the most recently available volume on governance in Japan published in English (Amyx and Drysdale 2003). The authors of *Japanese Governance. Beyond Japan Inc.* accordingly focus their attention on the policymaking process in Japan and do not attempt to examine the Japanese meaning of governance nor grapple directly with a definition of governance. Instead, their aim is to shed light on governance in the field of political economy, to go beyond 'Japan Inc.' as a metaphor for understanding the structures of governance in Japan, and to inquire into the changes, both political and economic, that have increased transparency and openness in the policymaking process. This view of governance is linked to the global, especially American, pressures on Japan to adopt more of a neo-liberal, market-based, mode of governance, and the authors tend to view Japan in the context of these types of yardsticks.

Hence, whilst the volume adds to our understanding of governance in relation to political economy and the policymaking process in Japan, it does not seek to question the specific political project promoting neo-liberal governance nor deal with the manifold meanings of the term 'governance' and governance of and by the Japanese more broadly. The chapters in the present volume aim to move the discussion of Japanese governance forward by going beyond an examination of the role of the government and other actors in the policymaking process at the national level, and to analyse the sites and issues of governance both above and below the state. Although the contributors approach governance differently depending on the topic addressed in their own chapter, all share a common perspective on governance as taking place in different sites of activity, and as involving a range of issues related to the norms and rules for the management, coordination and regulation of order, whether within Japan or on the regional or global levels. In other words, governance is seen as being practised both above and below the state as well as inside and outside of it. By adopting this approach, the book aims to draw attention to the contested nature of governance in Japan and the ways in which a range of actors is involved in different sites and issues of governance at home, in the region and the globe.

The purpose of this introductory chapter is to highlight a number of insights into governance in general, and then to proceed to a more detailed discussion of governance in Japan before introducing the chapters included in this volume. The aim is to identify different meanings of and approaches to governance as well as to examine how governance is understood in Japan. More particularly, if we accept the argument of certain broad typologies of capitalism (Coates 2000), such that governance in a late developmental state like Japan might well be different from governance under Anglo-American capitalism, then an important question to ask is what is distinctive about Japanese governance? In short, a central aim of examining governance in terms of sites and issues is to determine whether anything distinctive can be said about it.

Modes of governance

A useful starting point is an understanding of governance as involving a potential contestation between and amongst authority, legitimacy and competency in the management of political, economic and social order. This order can be achieved by three basic modes of governance – that by hierarchies, markets or networks (see Chapter 5). The balance between and amongst these three ways of governing differs over space and time, but the process of American-led globalization and the promotion of neo-liberal market answers to questions of economic growth and efficiency are creating a greater role for the market and networks, although often complemented by state-based hierarchies. The spread of pressures for de- or re-regulation and a small state has led commentators to pay increasing attention to how the state is making use of non-state private actors and quasi-governmental organizations as a means to achieve public goals. This changes the balance between the public and private spheres of activities and prioritizes a market-based or network-based mode of governance over hierarchical governance through the agencies of the state.

Essentially, this change in the balance between and amongst these three modes of governance reflects a re-ranking or re-ordering of the norms at the core of the governance of the state, economy and society. This changes the balance between governance through public or private actors, as can be seen in the increased involvement of non-state actors in carrying out erstwhile public tasks. The 'off-loading' of tasks by the British state, for instance, as seen in the way deregulation has created opportunities for non-state actors or quasi-governmental organizations to carry out tasks once the preserve of the state, as in health, education and the prison service, has thereby changed the mode of governance in the United Kingdom. The implication of the impact this has on the wider role of the state, however, is not clear-cut. Rhodes (1994), for instance, sees this change as leading to the 'hollowing out' of the state, whereas others, such as Pierrie (2000), view this rather as the state adopting strategies to ensure its continuing control (Bache 2003: 301). Whichever position is taken, however, it is clear that the hierarchical mode of governance characteristic of the state is being increasingly complemented by governance based on markets and networks.

Governance in Japan

The above discussion has provided a context for us to now move on to the case of Japan. Is there a particularly Japanese form of governance? The word for governance in Japanese is *tōchi*. As Naya has pointed out, however, the concept of *tōchi* gives a strong sense of 'actions to govern', as when the supreme court rules a matter such as the constitutionality of the Self-Defence Forces as the government's '*tōchi*' and not within the competency of the court to pass judgment, reflecting the dictionary definition of *tōchi* as 'the sovereign control of the land and people' (Naya 1997a: 194–5. Also see the Japanese dictionary, *Kojien*). It was precisely in order to try to provide a more nuanced meaning of governance, including the idea of 'autonomy or society forming a consensus, and participation in the development or shaping of order by these means', that Naya and Wessels proposed the term *kyōchi* (Naya 1997a: 201), 'governance' or, more precisely, 'co-governance'. Here governance is understood as 'the pattern of rule creation through the participation and cooperation of a variety of actors' (Naya 1997b: 9).

Rather than this neologism, however, the rendition of the English term 'governance' in the *katakana* script as, *gabanansu*, is increasingly being employed in Japan, as in the case of a new magazine concerned with local affairs, entitled *Gabanansu*. Thus, *tōchi* and *gabanansu* now exist side by side, with the latter expression tending to be used in order to capture this broader meaning of governance than seems possible by the use of *tōchi*, or to refer to specific sites or modes of governance, as in 'local governance'. In this latter case, as Yorimoto points out, the Japanese term *tōchi* does not convey the interrelationship between public and private bodies, with local authorities working together with non-governmental organizations (NGO), non-profit organizations, corporations and local citizens (Yorimoto 2004: 61). In this sense, *gabanansu* is being employed in order to capture this wider meaning of the term, although *kigyō tōchi* (corporate governance) continues to be used.

It seems clear from the above discussion that the Japanese '*tōchi*' is narrower in meaning than the English 'governance', which points to the need to pay attention to how governance is understood in different political cultures. Whilst a rational choice approach would no doubt wish to jettison this brief excursion into the linguistic differences in the meaning and usage of governance, in particular, and governance in the cultural context of Japan, in general, the approach taken here suggests instead the importance of looking beyond a view based on the maximizing interests of the individual, which leads to the expectation of a similar pattern of behaviour in the governance of Japan as in other polities. Thus, although Ramseyer and Rosenbluth find politicians in control in Japan by adopting a rational choice approach (Ramseyer and Rosenbluth 1993), this view is more congruent with the mode of governance found in the United States than the mode of governance in Japan (Curtis 1999: 59).The point is that, due to differences in the sphere of the public and private, the state, market and society, governance can and does indeed differ in Japan, though this is not to suggest that the Japanese mode of governance or indeed political culture are hermetically sealed from outside pressures.

The mode of governance adopted in Japan, therefore, results from a combination of both internal and external pressures. For instance, Chalmers Johnson, a strident critic of rational choice theory, has highlighted the dominant role of the bureaucrats not politicians, in line with his view of Japan as a 'developmental state' where the state's intervention in the market is viewed as legitimate (1982). This leads to a highly regulated political economy and, indeed, society, where governance takes place through informal as well as formal regulation based on a range of practices, as in the case of administrative guidance (*gyōsei shidō*). In short, governance does not rely on politicians or the market economy to function effectively but rather takes place in the context of a different relationship amongst the state, market and society and with a greater role for the state than under Anglo-American capitalism.

Rather than politicians being in sole charge, then, the actual power of those who have been elected to carry out 'actions to govern' is not as it may at first appear. Van Wolferen, for instance, talks about 'kings without power' (1990: 27), the lack of strong political leadership, and a system bereft of a political centre (1990: 49). However, this is a 'system' which 'almost always succeeds in bringing antagonistic groups within its fold' (1990: 49), indicating a range of different groups and networks are involved in governance. This is a view of 'governance from above' dominated by a hierarchical mode of governance under bureaucratic control – a view shared by others (Beeson 2003: 32–3). Haley, in contrast, sees the bureaucracy forced into negotiation and compromise with the politicians, where '[c]onsensus was necessary to achieve compliance and compromise was necessary to achieve consensus' (1987: 351). In this view, crucial to the Japanese system of governance is 'a separation of power from authority' where officials 'participate in the processes of governance as mediators, brokers, cajolers, and above all, presiding officials responsible for bargained-for, negotiated policymaking and implementation by reciprocal consent' (Haley 1991: 167). It is a view of governance which is quite different from governing 'in any Western sense of the word' (1991: 167): negotiation, rather than coercive power, is central to the mode of governance practiced in Japan.

Yet the above views of governance are in danger of placing too much emphasis on governance by consensus and ignoring the deep political divisions and contestation in Japanese society. As Stockwin has continued to point out, Japan remains a 'divided polity', as illustrated by the political battles of the 1960s and early 1970s, the factional clashes within the LDP during the rest of the 1970s, and divisions over the response to global pressures in the 1980s (Stockwin 1999: 3–7; 221). In the 1990s, despite the changes engendered by the short-term loss of power by the LDP, what emerged was not so much the end of a divided polity, but divisions engendered by a different coalescence of forces than at a time when the conservative and progressive forces were at loggerheads. Now, '[p]owerful sectional coalitions, combining political, bureaucratic, commercial, industrial and even religious interests confront other sectional coalitions made up of different combinations of similar elements' (Stockwin 1999: 221). In other words, conflict as well as consensus are at the basis of governance in Japan, and hence its contested nature.

What the above suggests is at least a different if not distinctive mode of governance in Japan, which appears to be more widespread in East Asia (Cheung and Scott 2003: 13–14), although there is a lack of agreement on the particular role of politicians and bureaucrats in governing at the national level. This mode of governance, with a central role for the state in the economy, has been under attack from supporters of the market-oriented, liberal model of capitalism. Indeed, whilst the closed nature of the Japanese political economy and the role of the state in the market has been at the heart of criticism by the United States from the 1960s onwards, and reached a peak during the 1980s, when trade conflicts and a burgeoning trade surplus put the Japanese model under attack, US-led globalization has increased pressure for convergence in the mode of governance along neo-liberal lines.

This has made governance in Japan a point of contestation in terms of how to govern the political economy and society at large. Although many in the LDP have resisted the thrust towards deregulation, privatization and a free-market model of the economy, a large number of policies supporting neo-liberal governance have been introduced from the 1980s onwards. Then, with the economic downturn following the bursting of the bubble at the end of the decade, the strong, interventionist state at the heart of the 'economic miracle' has been increasingly looked upon as inappropriate for a globalized economy. In this sense, Johnson's developmental state is viewed as being in crisis. Instead of the extensive development characteristic of the developmental state, a more intensive form, able to promote growth and maintain international competitiveness, is seen to be necessary in order to revive Japan's fortunes (Katz 1998: 2003). Whether American-style capitalism and Silicon-valley type networks of hi-tech entrepreneurs funded by venture capitalists are the salvation for the Japanese economy or not is a moot point (Werner 2004), but the domestic champions of reform are clearly aiming to dismantle many aspects of the developmental state and move in this direction. In short, economic stagnation has intensified questions about the model of development and governance Japan should pursue in a globalized political economy.

Thus, in the mid-1990s, following the administration of Japan New Party leader Hosokawa Morihiro, the LDP-dominated Hashimoto Ryūtarō coalition government and especially the first and second Koizumi Junichirō coalition governments have pushed ahead with 'structural reform' aimed at moving the political economy in a neo-liberal direction. Indeed, the November 2003 election was fought and won by Koizumi on the basis of his continuing commitment to reform. The Democratic Party emerged as the number two party, with many commentators viewing this as the sign for the future emergence of a two-party system in Japan. From the perspective of governance, a choice between the norms of efficiency and equity as the basis for a two-party system seems to be emerging, with the Koizumi administration seen as the champion of efficiency and the Democratic Party as the champion of equity. Although a gender analysis illustrates a more nuanced view of governance than a clear dichotomy between these two positions, as discussed in Chapter 6, the Koizumi reformist agenda is nevertheless viewed by critics as an attempt to change the relationship between the state and the market in favour of the market, whereas the Democratic Party, whilst supportive of the market, seems to place greater emphasis on equitable redistribution: equality of results over equality of opportunity. Thus, even though pressures from globalization and support for the norms of neo-liberalism may be driving Japan in that direction, such forces are being mediated by Japanese political parties, institutions and practices, thereby limiting the degree of convergence.

Sites and issues of governance

The above discussion of governance has focused on a review of the modes of governance especially at the national level in Japan, but the purpose of this book is to examine governance in the context of Japan's involvement in global and regional governance and the Japanese political economy and society more widely. By focusing on both the sites and issues of governance, moreover, we aim to provide the reader with a much broader and deeper understanding of the contested nature of governance in Japan than is presently available.

Thus, although the mode of governance may differ in terms of the sites of operation (Part I) and issues dealt with (Part II), the contributors provide a fuller picture of Japanese governance in these terms. Sites of governance may be contested, as when the competency to address a political, economic or social issue is located in one site of governance, but the authority, and with it the legitimacy, to deal with the issue is located in another site of governance; or, indeed, as when new issues of governance arise, social and political forces may contest 'siting' the problem as their own (e.g. as a way to gain resources) or someone else's (e.g. as a way to avoid responsibility for the problem).

Issues can be contested, too, in the sense of understanding them as issues of governance, rather than say of narrow issues of competency. For instance, when the competency to deal with a transborder issue of pollution is 'sited' at the level of a subnational political authority (city or prefecture), but the authority and legitimacy to negotiate internationally is 'sited' at the level of the state, then contestation between agents with competency and those with authority and legitimacy might well ensue: is competency sucked up, to the level of the state; is authority and legitimacy pushed down, to the subnational level; or, does the site of competency and the site of authority and legitimacy remain contested, and if so, what does that tell us about governance in Japan? An interest in questions such as these explains the structuring of the book in two parts, sites and issues.

Structure of the book

As seen above, Part I of the book focuses on governance in different sites of activity and Part II on issues of governance. The first site of activity dealt with is the metaphorically highest level of global governance, with a particular focus on Japan's role in the G7/8 summit. Here Dobson paints a mixed picture of Japanese activities, with the frequent change of political leaders limiting the effectiveness of Japan in shaping the mechanisms of G7/8 governance. However, the dominant image of Japan as a 'reactive state' (Calder 1988) does not capture the role policy-makers have gradually been able to play in the exercise of global governance. We thus find a more nuanced picture of the part Japan plays in governance in this site of activity through an examination of the way policymakers have influenced the summit process. Not only has Japan sought, albeit not always successfully, to expand the number and range of participants involved in G7/8 global governance, 'reaching out' to other states in East Asia as well as to NGOs, it has similarly brought issues of East Asian governance to the attention of the G7/8, as in the discussions revolving around the resolution of the Cambodian conflict during the 1980s.

The next chapter by Hook moves down a level to focus specifically on the region as a site of governance in East Asia. What is of interest here is how the 1997 financial and wider economic crisis has influenced the governance of the regional political economy and finance, and the implications of this for domestic governance in Japan. The International Monetary Fund's (IMF) response to the crisis high-lights how governance in East Asia is contested, with the IMF set on changing the domestic governance of the affected economies, eliminating 'crony capitalism' and promoting a neo-liberal mode of governance, despite local sentiment that the crisis was engendered by the rapid withdrawal of short-term foreign capital. Within Japan, those forces favouring a market economy are promoting neo-liberal norms and are working to change domestic governance, using such mechanisms as the Free Trade Agreement with Singapore to try to erode the power of those resisting reform. At the same time, Japanese policymakers have taken steps to maintain an East Asian model of governance with a central role for the state. Thus, efforts have been made to promote new sites of regional governance, as in the creation of the Association of Southeast Nations (ASEAN) Plus Three, as well as to institutionalize new mechanisms of financial governance in the wake of the New Miyazawa Initiative. In this chapter, too, Japan appears to be actively shaping governance in this site of activity.

In Chapter 3 Stockwin examines the national level of governance in Japan and asks why a system that was lauded from the 1950s to the 1980s is now found to be wanting. There are two different answers to this question: the first places emphasis on the need for the reform of the system of governance, suggesting that, due to domestic resistance from supporters of the old system, the sort of root-and-branch reform needed to revive the economy and enhance global competitiveness has not been carried out, partly as a result of weak political leadership from the top. In contrast, the second answer finds the problem precisely in tampering with a well-tested system: of course, governance under the '1955 system' may not have been transparent regarding the location of power, as seen in Van Wolferen's criticism touched on above, but it did perform relatively well in terms of governance functions, as seen in the fairly equitable distribution of the economic pie. In the face of these two contested approaches to national governance, Stockwin advocates the modernization of the old system in order to maintain its merits, such as the ability to create and distribute surpluses fairly equitably, but to respond to global pressures to eliminate the corruption it engendered and to make the system of governance more transparent. This issue of corruption is returned to in the second part of the book.

Local governance centring on the political economy of public works and pork-barrel politics has been facing increasing criticism from the voters at the local level in Japan, as Chapter 4 by Lam clearly shows. In the face of governance by pork, citizen movements have taken political action through the use of referenda, as in the case of protests against dam construction in Tokushima city. Local democracy through referenda and the promotion of greater transparency is being used to challenge public works projects and spur decentralized governance. At the same time, non-partisan voters at the grassroots level have used their voting power to upset the local political establishment by electing independent governors, as in the case of governor Tanaka Yasuo of Nagano prefecture. These governors are mounting a challenge to local pork-barrel politics where political leaders act as a conduit for public works, thereby stimulating the local economy, and winning re-election as payback. The contested nature of governance at the local level and the difficulties faced in seeking to bring about reform is well documented in this chapter, as seen in the case of Tanaka himself, who has been at loggerheads with the conservative members of the prefectural assembly. The resulting gridlock has clearly demonstrated how the forces of resistance remain powerful at the local level and impede the transformation of the system of governance in Japan.

Chapter 5 on finance examines how the domestic system of governance is being put under increasing pressure to change due to the spread of neoliberal, market-oriented economic globalization, on the one hand, and the failure of the government to stimulate a domestic economic revival following the bursting of the 'bubble economy' at the end of the 1980s, on the other. As the success of the Japanese developmental state was based on maintaining domestic barriers to full integration into the global economy at the same time as the internationally competitive corporations took advantage of global markets, such pressure is posing a fundamental challenge to the governance of the political economy. Cerny argues that the globalization of finance has put even greater pressure on the developmental state to move away from the credit-based system of finance at the heart of the Japanese model towards a market-based system. Whilst there are forces of resistance to the pressure for change arising from globalization as well as to the pressure for change brought about by the transformation in the structure of the domestic political economy, these forces may nevertheless be unable to counter these global and domestic pressures, especially as internationally competitive corporations are generally in support of change.

The final chapter in Part I discusses the welfare-employment regime in Japan and the impact this has on the family as a site of governance in terms of gender relations and the reproduction of human resources. As Osawa points out, with Japan facing issues of pension reform, an ageing population, and declining birth rates, the division of labour between the sexes is an important issue for the welfare employment regime. Many now recognize the need to examine the division of labour based on the 'male breadwinner model', that is, the male's participation in the labour market and the female's care for the members of the family through unpaid labour at home. What the new balance should be between the sexes and the government and the family, however, is contested. For instance, the Economic Strategy Council of Japan is keen to move the balance in the direction of neo-liberal, small government, believing in providing equality of opportunity more than equality of results. On the other hand, the author, herself the chair of a specialist committee of the government's Council for Gender Equality, places more emphasis on creating a gender neutral society in order to provide women with more choices, including the choice to be gainfully employed. How the Koizumi administration deals with these issues will exert a significant impact on the roles men and women play in the future governance of the domestic political economy.

Part II of the book focuses on key issues in the above sites of governance, from the 'higher' level site of the globe to the 'lower' level site of the family, with the chapters in the second part 'talking back' to the sites of governance in the first part of the book. To start with, Chapter 7 by Schreurs examines environmental governance on the global level. What this chapter demonstrates is the Japanese government's high degree of involvement in promoting global environmental governance, unlike in the 1960s when popular action was needed to galvanize action from a government reluctant to become involved in environmental issues at all. In the 1990s and early in the twenty-first century, in contrast, environmental governance is a central plank of Japanese foreign policy and both the government as well as NGOs are involved in the policymaking process, moving away from the highly bureaucratic policymaking of the 1980s. What Japanese policymakers have achieved over the years is a leadership role in providing official development assistance (ODA) for the protection of the environment and technology to control air pollution in especially developing East Asia. Its leadership role in global environmental governance can also be seen in the promotion of the Kyoto Protocol on Global Warming, although differences between the Europeans and Americans on the protection of the environment and the US's unwillingness to join the protocol means environmental governance at the international level remains highly contested. Nevertheless, Japan has sought to bring the two sides closer together, acting as an 'international broker' despite differences within the Japanese bureaucracy over how best to implement environmental governance.

Chapter 8 focuses on the issue of migration and foreign residents in Japan, drawing attention to the way migrants and non-national residents, both 'old' Asian residents from Japan's imperial past as well as 'new' residents from recent immigration, are treated. Hatsuse's chapter shows how the tension between the needs of the Japanese economy for labour and those of the state to control immigration and resident foreigners leads to contradictions in the way the immigration control regime actually functions as a tool of governance. We thus find the needs of the Japanese economy for particularly unskilled labour in contest with the needs of the state to control immigration. The end result is a system of governance which leads to foreigners over-staying their visas and becoming 'illegal' immigrants. What happens to the human rights of these illegal as well as legal 'old' and 'new' foreigners is a particular point of concern to a range of NGOs in Japan. The position of legal foreign residents has certainly improved as a result of the Japanese government joining a number of international human rights regimes, as with the decision to allow foreigners to live in public housing following the 1978 signing of the International Covenant on Economic, Social and Cultural Rights, but Japan has still not signed the International Convention on the Protection of the Rights of All Migrant Workers and Members of Their Families. In this situation, NGOs have become increasingly important as agents of governance, working to improve the rights and conditions of foreigners living in Japan.

The following chapter adopts a hermeneutic approach to investigate the contested issue of corruption in the governance of Japanese national politics. This approach leads Babb to trace the way corruption has been understood over history, examining the roots of the different terms used to refer to corrupt behaviour and how individual politicians view such 'corrupt' acts. What becomes clear from this analysis is that the general stance of the politicians who discuss the issue is not to see their own actions as corrupt, but rather as a means to protect weak groups in Japanese society, who in return provide political support for the politician. In short, Chapter 9 illustrates the contested moral stance of those who view the politicians as corrupt and the morals of the politicians themselves, who view their action as a perhaps necessary evil to get things done. The contest over what is and is not corruption is a particular point of concern in this chapter. Is the case of pork-barrel public works projects, for instance, systematic corruption, or a means of redistribution for the rural areas of Japan generating some of the same kinds of benefits as government policy aimed at supporting the rural population? Whilst rejecting cultural relativism, Babb seeks to avoid setting up an unnamed 'West' as somehow morally superior to Japan and examines how these practices are understood by the participants themselves.

Chapter 10 by Gill discusses the issue of Japan's homeless people as an issue of governance and illustrates how, despite a dominant image of Japan as a centralized state, the national government was unwilling, until the 1990s, to even deal with the issue, preferring instead to leave it in the hands of sub-national political authorities: prefectures, cities and local wards. The sheer increase in the number of homeless people following the bursting of the economic bubble, however, has meant that the central government has been forced to take action, albeit reluctantly, making governance of homeless people a contested issue between the local and national levels, with no one taking overall responsibility – there is no 'czar' for the homeless in Japan. As the issue of homelessness caught popular attention, the Ministry of Health and Welfare in 2000 adopted a national policy to deal with homelessness, but this has been implemented by a range of bodies, national as well as sub-national, with responsibility as diffuse as the different ministries, bureaux, prefectures, cities and wards involved in taking care of the homeless. The shelters that have been set up for homeless people do not necessarily respond to their needs, and they remain few and far between. In this sense, the contest over where to 'site' homelessness is likely to remain an outstanding issue between national and local actors in the governance of homeless people.

Chapter 11 on corporate governance deals with an issue of central concern to Japanese companies in an increasingly globalized political economy. Calls for transparency, the introduction of external monitors, and other mechanisms of corporate governance based on the Anglo-American model of capitalism are frequently heard in early twenty-first century Japan. Rather than accept these calls for the transformation of Japanese companies at face value, however, Hasegawa seeks to deal with them in the wider context of the need for capitalist rationalization and the contest between 'Anglo-American' and 'Japanese' modes of corporate governance. What this leads him to conclude is that, behind the corporate governance rhetoric, Japanese companies have in fact been pursuing large-scale restructuring. How companies have dealt with this issue is clarified by a number of case studies from both the manufacturing and service sectors of the economy, with the former seen as more subject to the pressures of globalization than the latter. Despite this difference, however, the case studies suggest 'good governance' in Japan is not so much viewed as a question of transparency and the role of external monitors, as in the Anglo-American type of corporate governance, but rather the healthy growth and profitability of the company. Given the wider contest between different models of capitalism, the author concludes that Japanese companies may not in fact converge along the lines of Anglo-American corporate governance.

The final chapter of Part II examines the governance of the family as an issue central to the maintenance of a healthy political economy. Casting aside the premise of the family as a private sphere of activity, Takeda shows how the public/ private spheres are contested, with the governance of the family taking place via the government and the economy. Chapter 12 illustrates the point by analyzing the way the management of the household economy is part of both the macro-economy of the nation as well as the micro-economy of the family. It provides a historical as well as contemporary discussion of household management, detailing the various efforts made by women to survive in different historical situations. At a time in the late 1990s and early twentieth century when couples often opt not to have off-spring, the low birth rate is forcing the government to rethink the governance of gender relations and the family in the context of the revival of the national political economy. What emerges from Takeda's analysis is not simply a picture of the way the government intervenes in family affairs, but also the way in which the family is potentially able to challenge the system of governance and make decisions on the reproductive activities at the centre of family and economic life.

In this way, *Contested Governance in Japan* draws on the expertise of both Japanese and outsiders to present a fuller picture of the different modes, sites and issues of governance in Japan.

References

Amyx, Jennifer and Drysdale, Peter (2003) *Japanese Governance. Beyond Japan Inc.*, London: RoutledgeCurzon.

Bache, Ian (2003) 'Governing through governance: education policy control under New Labour', *Political Studies* 51, 2: 300–14.

Beeson, Mark (2003) 'Japan's reluctant reformers and the legacy of the developmental state', in Anthony B. Cheung and Ian Scott (eds), *Governance and Public Sector Reform in Asia: paradigm shifts or business as usual?* London: RoutledgeCurzon, pp. 25–43.

Calder, Kent (1988) 'Japanese foreign economic policy formation: explaining the reactive state', *World Politics*, 40 (Summer): 517–41.

Cheung, Anthony B. and Scott, Ian (2003) 'Governance and public sector reforms in Asia: paradigms, paradoxes and dilemmas', in Anthony B. Cheung and Ian Scott (eds), *Governance and Public Sector Reform in Asia: paradigm shifts or business as usual?* London: RoutledgeCurzon, pp. 1–24.

Coates, David (2000) *Models of Capitalism: growth and stagnation in the modern era*, Oxford: Polity Press.

Curtis, Gerald L. (1999) *The Logic of Japanese Politics: leaders, institutions and the limits of change*, New York: Columbia University Press.

Haley, John O. (1987) 'Governance by negotiation: a reappraisal of bureaucratic power in Japan', *Journal of Japanese Studies* 13, 2: 343–57.

Haley, John O. (1991) *Authority without Power: law and the Japanese paradox*, Oxford: Oxford University Press.

Inoguchi, Takashi and Iwai, Tomoaki (1987) *Zokugiin no Kenkyū. Jimintō Seiken o Gyūjiru Shuyakutachi*, Tokyo: Nihon Keizai Shimbun.

Johnson, Chalmers (1982) *MITI and the Japanese Miracle*, Stanford: Stanford University Press.

Katz, Richard (1998) *Japan, The System That Soured: the rise and fall of the Japanese miracle*, New York: M. E. Sharpe.

Katz, Richard (2003) *Japanese Phoenix: the long road to economic revival*, New York: M.E. Sharpe.

Muramatsu, Michio and Krauss, Ellis (1987) 'The conservative policy line and the development of patterned pluralism', in Kozo Yamamura and Yukichi Yasuba (eds) *The*

Political Economy of Japan: the domestic transformation, Stanford: Stanford University Press, pp. 516–54.

Naya, Masatsugu (1997a) 'Kokusai "kyōchi" to anzenhosho mondai no kōzu', in Naya Masatsugu and David Wessels (eds), *Gabanansu to Nihon: kyōchi no mosaku*, Tokyo: Keisō Shobo, pp. 191–227.

Naya, Masatsugu (1997b) 'Kokusai kankei no naka no Nihon, Nihon no naka no kokusai kankei', in Naya Masatsugu and David Wessels (eds), *Gabanansu to Nihon: kyōchi no mosaku*, Tokyo: Keisō Shobo, pp. 3–22.

Pierrie, Jon (2000) *Debating Governance: authority, steering and democracy*, Oxford: Oxford University Press.

Ramseyer, J. Mark and Rosenbluth, Frances McCall (1993), *Japan's Political Marketplace*, Cambridge MA: Harvard University Press.

Rhodes, Rod (1994) 'The hollowing out of the state', *Political Quarterly* 65: 138–51.

Stockwin, Arthur (1999) *Governing Japan* (third edition), Oxford: Blackwell.

Van Wolferen, Karel (1990) *The Enigma of Japanese Power: people and power in a stateless nation*, New York: Vintage Books.

Werner, Richard A. (2004) 'No recovery without reform? An evaluation of the evidence in support of the structural reform argument in Japan', *Asian Business & Management* 3, 1: 7–38.

Yorimoto, Katsumi (2004) 'Synergistic-role responses to public-sphere issues and governance: partnerships amongst citizens, private enterprises and government administration', in Sadao Tamura and Minoru Tokita (eds) *Symbiosis of Government and Market: the public, the private and bureaucracy*, London: RoutledgeCurzon, pp. 55–72.

Part 1

Sites of governance

1 Global governance, the G7/8 summit and Japan

Hugo Dobson

This chapter comprises three sections that proceed from the general to the specific. With reference to the extant literature, the first section establishes a definition of global governance. With this definition in mind, the second section explores the changing nature of the G7/8 summit process – from an *ad hoc* and informal 'fireside chat' of international solons into an incremental, institutionalized, year-long process of negotiations that serves as one of the many mechanisms of global governance. It also locates where the G7/8 summit process fits in and functions as one of the sites of global governance alongside the United Nations (UN), International Monetary Fund (IMF), World Bank, Organization for Economic Cooperation and Development (OECD) and World Trade Organization (WTO). Finally, the third section explores the Japanese government and its people's role and contribution in shaping the structures and mechanisms of global governance, in particular through the G7/8 as one site of activity.

Global governance: definitions and discourse

During the 1990s, two phrases reached the level of ubiquity in the extant literature on international relations (IR): globalization and global governance. Despite, or possible because of, being so widely debated, both terms display a high degree of definitional fuzziness. The Commission on Global Governance does nothing to elucidate the confusion surrounding the latter term by stating that '[i]t is a broad, dynamic, complex process of interactive decision-making that is constantly evolving and responding to changing circumstances' (Commission on Global Governance 1995) – a definition that is about as easy to pin down as mercury is with a fork. The 'global' part of the term does not present too many problems; 'governance', in its broadest sense, has been defined as 'the sum of the many ways individuals and institutions, public and private, manage their common affairs. It is a continuing process through which conflicting or diverse interests may be accommodated and cooperative action may be taken. It includes formal institutions and regimes empowered to enforce compliance, as well as informal arrangements that people and institutions either have agreed to or perceive to be in their interest' (Commission on Global Governance 1995).

However, in spite of appearances, global governance does not refer to the amplification of a domestic national government to an international level in order to create a future world government based upon the UN, or any other global institution. Global governance is, rather, a process in reaction to both the positive and negative impacts of the decline in state sovereignty and the processes of globalization. As James Rosenau puts it:

> During the present period of rapid and extensive global change, however, the constitutions of national governments and their treaties have been undermined by the demands and greater coherence of ethnic and other sub-groups, the globalization of economies, the advent of broad social movements, the shrinking of political distances by microelectronic technologies, and the mushrooming of global interdependencies fostered by currency crises, environmental pollution, terrorism, the drug trade, AIDS, and a host of trans-national issues that are crowding the global agenda. These centralizing and decentralizing dynamics have undermined constitutions and treaties in the sense that they have contributed to the shifts in the loci of authority.
>
> (Rosenau 1993: 3)

Traditionally, governance has been an attempt to create order out of a system of anarchy and shape the actions of those governed. Within sovereign state borders, governments were able to provide this order through governance in a top-down, hierarchical fashion. Yet, with the opportunities, confusion and chaos created by globalization, governments are seen to have failed to provide order both in the international and domestic spheres. As a gamut of previously marginalized transnational issues vie for the attention of policymakers, it has become evident that traditional state structures of governance are unable to cope with this increased demand and have been forced to: (1) venture into new areas of governance tradi-tionally outside the remit of the state; (2) outsource responsibilities and duties to a range of state-centred and non-state organizations; and/or (3) have been usurped by these actors in the provision of governance. In this light, Rosenau argues that governance is not synonymous with governments and that 'it is possible to conceive of governance – of regulatory mechanisms in a sphere of activity which function effectively even though they are not endowed with formal authority' (Rosenau 1993: 5). Rather than a single, world government borne of the same state-centred thinking that dominated the discourse of IR in the Cold War period, global gov-ernance suggests an uneven mesh, or patchwork quilt, of state and non-state, national and transnational actors seeking a suitable division of labour in addressing a panoply of issues. Thus, we reach the idea of 'governance without government'. Rosenau suggests normatively that 'given the noxious policies governments pursue . . . governance without government is in some ways preferable to governments that are capable of governance' (Rosenau 1993: 5).

Nevertheless, care should be taken not to underestimate the lingering importance of traditional sovereign state actors and we may need to regard the appearance of new actors with suspicion. It is a standard rider in the literature, but the role of the state is still crucially important because, more often than not, it is the state to which non-governmental organizations (NGOs) direct their appeals and it is the state that will ultimately implement policy (Sally 2001: 56). Global governance only goes so far as to suggest that states' ability to cope with the issues engendered by globalization has diminished and provides few guarantees that the policies of the new actors will be any less ineffective or noxious. As the provision of governance on a global scale still requires the involvement of traditional state actors in addition to international organizations and regimes, social movements and non-governmental organizations, transnational organizations and corporations, a more accurate (although clumsy) sound bite may be 'governance not only with government'.

The G7/8

The G7/8 is one of many sites and mechanisms in this constantly evolving mesh of global governance and the focus now turns to an exploration of exactly what kind of entity the G7/8 is and how it contributes to the provision of global governance – a question far from readily agreed upon in the extant literature. The G7/8 first met as the G6 (France, Italy, Japan, United Kingdom [UK], United States [US] and West Germany) in November 1975 at the château of Rambouillet in France. This first meeting found its origins in an informal meeting of the French, German, UK and US finance ministers in the White House library in March 1973, later joined by Japan, to discuss the state of the international monetary system (Smyser 1993: 15–16). The impetus behind the meeting at Rambouillet was 'to recreate at the highest level the same sort of direct and informal exchange' (Hunt and Owen 1984: 658). Unlike traditional international organizations, which are the result of an international agreement or formal treaty, the G7/8 was ostensibly intended as an impromptu, never-to-be-repeated, informal meeting in reaction to both the 1973 oil crisis and the collapse of the Bretton Woods system of fixed exchange rates. However, the realization of this forum's utility as a unique meeting place for the world's leaders led to a second conference being held in San Juan, Puerto Rico in June 1976 at which Canada was added to form the G7. Since that time, other members, with varying levels of status, have joined – the European Community (EC)/European Union (EU) participated from May 1977 at London, and Russia's position has evolved from guest in 1991 through a range of statuses to a fully enfranchized member of the G8 by 2003. In tandem, the remit of discussion at the summit has expanded from chiefly economic issues to encompass political issues. In addition, the composition of summit delegations has developed from the original idea of solely the leaders, accompanied by foreign and finance ministers, to embrace regular ministerial-level meetings on education, employment, energy, the environment, justice and trade. As a result, the administration and preparation for the annual summit, directed by the leaders' personal representatives, or sherpas, in turn supported by *sous-sherpas*, who meet regularly during the year preceding a summit, has led to an ever-increasing bureaucratic load that has become one of the main rods with which to beat the summit process over recent years. Yet, this has also led to a reconsideration of the purpose of the summit process and numerous calls to return to the simplicity of informal meetings of prime ministers and presidents (Whyman 1995).

The G7/8 is neither an international organization in the traditionally understood sense, nor does it display the characteristics of a fully formed institution. It does not possess any of the 'clear organizational centers' of institutions. No permanent headquarters, flag, elected executive head, means of enforcement or secretariat to provide administrative support, and attempts to provide any degree of formality or bureaucracy have been strongly resisted (Hajnal 1999: 1; Hodges 1999: 69). Bayne has even gone so far as to state that '[t]he G7 summit is at the same time an institution and an anti-institution' (Bayne 1995: 494). Nevertheless, an instructive precedent for understanding the nature of the summit does exist in the form of the Concert of Europe that was utilized to varying degrees as part of great power diplomacy from the aftermath of the Napoleonic Wars to the outbreak of the First World War: both are extemporaneous groupings borne of crisis; both are founded on agreed principles – the Concert emphasized the right of the great powers to intervene in the affairs of smaller states, whilst the G7/8 has reiterated in its communiqués its own principles, chiefly the promotion of democracy and the free market economy; both are able to address broader issues in an iterative fashion but also capable of adding issues of the day to the agenda; both are groupings flexible and amorphous enough to respond to changes in the balance of power; both emphasize the role of the individual and their success depends upon the ability and cooperation of the individuals involved; both groupings only work when core national interests are sacrificed or left untouched; both essentially preserve the right of the powerful – in 2001 the summit members accounted for roughly two-thirds of global gross domestic product (GDP) (World Bank 2002) – to take decisions on behalf of the rest of the world.

In this light, the G7/8 clearly represents a point at which actors' expectations converge over a given issue – an attempt to navigate through the choppy waters of an increasingly globalized world and provide 'the control tower of global governance' (*gurōbaru gabanansu no shireitō*) (Takase 2000: 176). It seeks to set the agenda, tone or mood for global governance whilst conscious of its position in relation to other mechanisms of global governance. If anything it is the international community's mouthpiece, a global catalyst and consciousness-raiser, and ultimately the world's biggest think-tank. In other words:

> The G7/8 is a forum, rather than an institution. It is useful as a closed international club of capitalist governments trying to raise consciousness, set an agenda, create networks, prod other institutions to do things that they should be doing, and, in some cases, to help create institutions that are suited to a particular task.
>
> (Hodges 1999: 69)

Thus, the G7/8's position in the patchwork quilt of global governance can only be truly understood in relation to other institutions and mechanisms of global

governance. The G7/8 recognizes 'that strong and effective international institutions . . . help . . . to resolve the tensions of globalization, between domestic and
international pressures' (Bayne 1995: 500), and it was to this end that French
President Jacques Chirac proposed inviting the executive heads of the UN, IMF,
World Bank and WTO to the 1996 Lyon Summit (Bayne 2001: 5).

The main diplomatic tool and mouthpiece of the summit used to coordinate
these institutions is the summit communiqué and related documents (for a detailed
review of the summit's promotion of international organizations through communiqués and declarations, see Hajnal 1999: 45–55). For example, the work of the
UN has been repeatedly praised and encouraged in the final summit communiqués,
which have sought to galvanize its functions by encouraging: (1) reform of its
institutions (Bayne 2000: 125); (2) the evolution of a concerted anti-terrorist policy
(Belelieu 2002); and (3) preventive diplomacy and its peacekeeping functions
(Inoguchi 1994: 27–8). In addition to this 'gentle prodding', the G7/8 has replaced
the UN at times as the international institution of choice. It was the G8, not the
UN, which played a central role in coordinating Germany and Japan's financial
support of the Gulf War of 1991, in addition to ending the Kosovo conflict of 1999.
Furthermore, it has been argued that the G7/8 is more representative than the
UN Security Council (UNSC) due to the inclusion of Germany and Japan (Smyser
1993: 19–20). However, rather than being a zero-sum game, the G7/8 and the
UN can be seen to complement each other – the G7/8 was intended to provide
an opportunity for national leaders to meet informally and discuss chiefly economic
issues; whereas the UNSC is a highly formalized meeting of ambassadors concerned
chiefly with security issues. In this light, proposals have been put forward for a
much closer dialogue between the members of the two groupings.

Equally, the G7/8 has sought to promote both the work of and coordination
with other international institutions. At the 1995 Naples Summit and the 1996
Halifax Summit, the summit agenda focused on international financial issues and
recommended a number of reforms in the functioning of the IMF, especially in
early-warning mechanisms, and the World Bank, in particular the concentration
of resources on poorer countries. Within the framework of the G7/8, institutional
depth is also evident: for instance, a significant achievement was the creation of the
Group of 20 finance ministers and central bank governors (G20) in September 1999
as a permanent grouping including several important developing countries to
address financial and monetary reform in cooperation with the IMF and World
Bank (Kirton 2001a). This again suggests that the G7/8 has not eclipsed other
international institutions, but rather created a mutually reinforcing division of
labour, and that G7/8 member states have sought 'to protect the existing system
and make it work better' rather than pursue radical reform (Putnam and Bayne
1984: 141). To this end, the G7/8 has unwaveringly supported the work of the
General Agreement on Tariffs and Trade (GATT) and the WTO by: (1) regularly
emphasizing in its communiqués the rapid conclusion of ongoing (or the inception
of new) multilateral trade negotiations – an issue the Japanese government and its
people have been particularly supportive of; and (2) creating the Trade Ministers'
Quadrilateral (more commonly known as the 'Quad') at the 1981 Ottawa Summit

to meet three to four times a year. These initiatives have been credited with some success, particularly in exerting pressure on the conclusion of the Uruguay Round (Hajnal 1999: 35; Bayne 2001: 11). In addition, formal and informal techniques have been used to link the G7/8 with the OECD, the most salient example being the practice from 1976 of holding the OECD Council just prior to the annual summit meeting (Bayne 2000: 53–4).

Regional organizations, such as the Association of Southeast Asian Nations (ASEAN) and the Organization of American States (OAS), have also taken up the guidance and political will displayed by the G7/8 in combating issues, such as terrorism (Belelieu 2002: 24–5). Other participants brought into the summit process have included business groups such as the International Chamber of Commerce, the Business and Industry Advisory Committee and the Trade Union Advisory Committee of the OECD (Bayne 2000: 217). Moreover, not only state actors but also the participation of NGOs has been sought. At the 1995 Halifax Summit, the G7 recognized the importance of both an active civil society and the NGOs that constitute it, and thereafter instituted a policy of 'outreach' to include these groups. This interest has been reciprocated and the 1998 Birmingham Summit was billed by Jubilee 2000 (an NGO dedicated to resolving debt issues in developing nations) as the People's Summit in an attempt to construct a system of global governance from the bottom up, rather than from the top down.

What the G7/8 does best is offer a blueprint for global governance through its communiqués and declarations in order 'to provide political will and direction' (Hunt and Owen 1984: 659), and thereafter delegates to more traditional international institutions to furnish the necessary specialization and implementation. Ultimately, most observers seem to agree that that the G7/8 represents 'a recognition of the growing need for coordination of policy and behavior on a number of fronts' (Falk 1995: 216–17). If the formal institutions of global governance can be regarded as spinning plates, the G7/8 is best thought of as the showman who keeps them all spinning in unison.

Japan and the G7/8

The G7/8 has completed four cycles of seven summits, each hosted by the original seven member states – France, the US, the UK, Germany, Japan, Italy and Canada. In 2002, the fourth cycle of rotation came to an end and in June 2003 the fifth cycle began at Evian-les-Bains in France, the instigator of the original G7 meeting. However, this time Russia is factored into the cycle and is scheduled to host its first summit in 2006. Not only through directly hosting of the summit, but also through regular participation since its inception, the Japanese government has been in a position to contribute to both the functioning of the G7/8 process specifically and global governance in general, although it has not always instrumentalized this position effectively. The purpose of the remainder of this chapter is not to examine the importance of the summit to Japan or the economic, political and social issue-areas it has promoted or addressed in this forum, as has been the focus of much research (Sakurada 1988; Saitō 1990; Inoguchi 1994; Watanabe

1999; Katada 2001; Dobson 2004a). It can be taken for granted that the G7/8 is important to the Japanese government in providing both access to a high-level, multilateral grouping, and recognition of its position as one of the contemporary great powers. Rather, the focus is placed upon Japan's contribution to the structure and functioning of the summit as a site of global governance. Sir Nicholas Bayne, the master grader of G7/8 summits, has annually evaluated the success of each summit using the following criteria: leadership, effectiveness, durability, accept- ability and consistency. In this light, the factors considered here as facilitating the successful functioning of the summit process are: membership as a means of securing legitimacy; leadership through the participating personnel; the ability to set a relevant summit agenda; the efforts made as chair and host nation to ensure a successful summit; and compliance with the G7/8's pronouncements as a manifestation of their effectiveness and acceptability.

Membership

Membership of the summit, alongside the remit of its agenda, is one of the core issues that divides opinion on the merits and legitimacy of the summit process. The non-invitation of Canada, Italy and Japan (despite being G7 members) to the special Guadeloupe summit of January 1979 to discuss European security issues demonstrates the sensitivity and pride that goes with membership of this executive club (*The Japan Times*, 16 January 1979; Putnam and Bayne 1987: 104–5). Thus, the current and future issue commanding attention is whether to expand the number of participants. Many regard an expanded G7/8 as a betrayal of the original spirit of the summit that it should be an informal forum for discussion between the top political leaders (Bayne 1995; Weilemann 2000: 19). As touched upon above, the summit was intended to be a 'personal encounter of the leaders of the world's most powerful economies' (Bayne 2001: 3). Others bemoan its exclusivity and regard expansion of the membership as a necessary condition to providing legitimacy and effective global governance (Smyser 1993). To this end, Russia and China's membership have been most controversial, but also the participation of middle powers like Australia and representatives of the Non- Aligned Movement (NAM), such as Indonesia, have been discussed, in addition to the potential role of business groups and civil society.

G7/8 leaders are wary of expanding the membership of the summit and membership has been contested for fear that its meaning and utility will be diluted and the process will end up replicating the UN. Yet they have sought to supplement the core membership by sporadically inviting specific representatives. To this end, the Japanese government was extremely supportive of including Canada to form the G7 at the 1976 San Juan Summit, having given the Canadian government a detailed report of discussions at Rambouillet the previous year (Kirton 1998: 306–7). Furthermore, it has actively used its position as chair and host of the summit to sponsor the participation of other Asia-Pacific states, namely Australia and Indonesia in the Tokyo Summits of 1979 and 1993 respectively, and China, India, Indonesia and South Korea in the Okinawa Summit of 2000. Coupled with the encouragement extended to NGOs to participate, this has been cast as part of the policy of 'outreach' to non-G8 countries as outlined in the Okinawa Communiqué (Kojima 2001: 102). Although in many of these cases it was ultimately frustrated and had to shape a compromise, this is one aspect of the Japanese government's greater objective of attempting to use its position in the summit to 'bat' for Asia and promote wider 'Asian issues'.

The Japanese government's attempts to invite Australia to the 1979 Tokyo Summit were met with European opposition. In the case of Indonesia, Japanese policymakers responded to a request from President Kemusu Argamulja Suharto to attend the 1993 Tokyo Summit (Eguchi 1993: 42–3); but similarly in the end capitulated to European protests and invited Suharto, as chair of the NAM, not to the summit itself but to a pre-summit meeting on 5 July 1993 with President Bill Clinton and Prime Minister Miyazawa Kiichi at which he expressed dissatisfaction with the progress of the Uruguay Round and the G7's handling of debt relief (*Far Eastern Economic Review*, 15 July 1993; Kirton and Kokotsis 1997–8: 52).

In the case of China, the Japanese government used the 1989 Paris Summit in the aftermath of the Tiananmen Square massacre in order to prevent China's isolation from the international community through overly severe sanctions (Takagi 1995). Prior to the Okinawa Summit, Prime Minister Obuchi Keizō declared that 'China is a major power in Asia and therefore I would like to have China's voice reflected in the summit' (Kirton 2001b: 189). To this end, a concerted effort along-side German Chancellor Gerhard Schröder was made to approach the Chinese government. On the Japanese part, this effort to invite China either officially or unofficially was led by government coalition partner and Kōmeitō leader Kanzaki Takenori (*The Japan Times*, 16 February 2000). Yet, despite debate as to the pros and cons of inviting China to join (Hajnal 1999: 30–2), the Chinese leadership demonstrated little interest in an invitation as demonstrated in its rejection of the proposed wording of the ASEAN Regional Forum (ARF) statement welcoming the successful conclusion of the Okinawa Summit (Soeya 2000). Eventually, the Japanese government was keen not to alienate any of its summit partners by unilaterally inviting China and the issue was dropped.

There are three crucial problems in embracing Chinese participation: (1) the democratic principles of the G7/8 would be compromised as within the G7/8 'there is a deep, tacit consensus that China does not play by the rules of democracy and free trade' (Kirton and Kokotsis 1997–8: 51); (2) the existence of other candidates with economic clout and democratic systems that are able to provide deeper regional coverage in the summit's membership and, therefore, legitimacy (for example, Brazil or India); and (3) the G7/8 has never expelled or downgraded a member state and it is unclear how it would go about doing so if, say, an incident similar to the Tiananmen Square massacre were to occur. However, at the outset of the fifth cycle of summitry, China's traditionally antagonistic attitude towards the summit process began to alter. Chinese President Hu Jintao was extended, and readily accepted, an invitation to participate in an enlarged dialogue meeting between the leaders of G8 and developing nations on the first day of the 2003 Evian Summit. Although this limited participation was officially welcomed by the

Japanese government, China's possible full participation in the G8 and the creation of a future G9 pose a number of additional problems to those mentioned above and could threaten Japan's traditional role of representing Asia (Dobson 2004b).

A similar contradiction can be witnessed in the Japanese government's attempts to include a variety of other participants in the summit process. On the one hand, the Japanese government has introduced a number of successful initiatives: for example, arranging a meeting before the 2000 Okinawa Summit in Tokyo between most G7/8 leaders, representatives of the World Bank, World Health Organization (WHO), United Nations Development Programme (UNDP) and the leaders of a range of developing countries (Bayne 2001: 14; Kojima 2001: 102). Equally, whilst preparing the information technology (IT) agenda for this summit, the Japanese government enlisted the participation of a number of multinational corporations and Prime Minister Mori Yoshirō held a roundtable discussion with international business leaders in Tokyo three days prior to the summit (Bayne 2001: 14; Ullrich 2001: 235). Finally, at this summit the opinions of a range of NGOs were sought and the government constructed an NGO centre to provide these groups with necessary facilities, symbolic of the first time that the importance of NGOs had been recognized by the host prime minister. Both NGOs and businesses were involved in the follow-up to the summit including the creation of a Digital Opportunities Taskforce (DOT force) to address the 'digital divide', another task force on renewable energy and a programme to combat infectious diseases (Bayne 2001: 15). Thus, the Japanese government has recognized that governance cannot simply be furnished by the most developed economies and has sought to supplement their efforts through a policy of 'outreach' to the governmental and non-governmental institutions that constitute the patchwork quilt of global governance.

However, on the other hand, the sincerity of the Japanese government's attempts to 'reach out' has been doubted. In particular, its management of the above-mentioned NGO centre was characterized as coercive. The centre was under-used possibly because it was a considerable distance from the press centre from which the NGOs were barred, cost ¥10,000 (US$91) per NGO to use, and involved registration procedures such as submitting individual photographs and registering individuals' details such as address and height, implying Japanese government surveillance (*The Japan Times*, 25 July 2000; Toyoda 2000: 21). Moreover, many of the preparatory meetings conducted in the run-up to a summit with various groups, especially the opposition parties, have been cosmetic and perfunctory at best. Furthermore, the Japanese government has also sought actively at times to limit membership of the summit. In the 1990s, it came close to alienating its G7/8 partners over the issue of the reconstruction of the former Soviet Union after initial reluctance to extend aid to Russia and include it as a summit member; Japan was even cited as *the* major obstacle to G7 support for President Boris Yeltsin by German Foreign Minister Klaus Kinkel (Miyashita 2001: 51). On the one hand, the Japanese position was that 'Russia is not an advanced economy [and should not join the G7]' (*Far Eastern Economic Review*, 16 July 1992). On the other hand, the Japanese government would not contemplate extending either aid or summit membership to Russia until the Northern Territories' dispute had been resolved (the Northern Territories are a group of islands – Etorofu, Kunashiri, Shikotan and Habomai – off the northern tip of Hokkaidō occupied by the Soviet Union in the last days of the Second World War, see deVillafranca 1993; Kimura and Welch 1998). Thus, although a policy of 'outreach' is, in general, clearly visible, the Japanese government has not been consistent in realizing this key strategy for legitimizing the summit process.

Personnel

> Let me just quickly – because I know time is important – point something out. Sitting at that table in this Summit were the representatives – the heads of state – of nations that not too many years ago were deeply engaged in a hatred-filled war with each other. And here we are, sitting as closely as we're sitting with a really warm, personal friendship that had developed between us, but more than that, with a friendship between our peoples.
>
> (Ronald Reagan after the 1983 Williamsburg Summit
> (quoted in Hajnal 1989: 250))

The connection between the role of the individual, fostering an *esprit de corps*, and the successful outcome of the summit is probably more amplified in the G7/8 process than in any other mechanism of global governance. However, as mentioned above, the steady institutionalization of the summit process led to an expansion in its remit and participation that, in the eyes of some, compromised the original goal of the summit process: the creation of an informal and intimate forum for policy coordination. In an attempt to streamline the work of the summit and return it to these roots, at the 1998 Birmingham Summit UK Prime Minister Tony Blair separated the ministerial meetings from the leaders' meeting and was widely applauded for focusing the minds of the summit leaders on that year's agenda. The Japanese government continued this trend in 2000 when the foreign ministers' meeting took place in Miyazaki, the finance ministers' meeting in Fukuoka, and the leaders' meeting in Okinawa.

However, within a concert-like mechanism of global governance as heavily personalized as the summit, both having to conduct diplomacy in a foreign language and the domestic political system of Japan – with its emphasis on consensus and the kind of political leaders thereby selected – have tended to exert a negative influence on the Japanese government's ability to play a proactive role at the summit. The Japanese government, like the German government, has added to the increasing number of personnel involved in the summit by dispatching its trade minister on occasions to accompany the finance minister. In addition, the nature of factional politics in Japan (and coalition politics in Germany) has been suggested as one reason why solely the prime minister, without attending ministers, was not invited to the summit in the first place and, thus, the summit process expanded in remit. Another way in which Japan has inadvertently contributed to the expanded number of personnel involved in summitry is through the high turnover rate of Japanese prime ministers compared to other countries. Admittedly, Japan has been more unfortunate than other states in the longevity of its leaders – both Prime Minister Ōhira Masayoshi and Obuchi passed away not long before summit meetings (Foreign Minister Ōkita Saburō replaced Ōhira only ten days before the 1980 Venice Summit, whereas Mori was in place more than two months before the 2000 Okinawa Summit). Yet this is problematic in that the summit was intended to be an intimate forum. In contrast to German Chancellor Helmut Kohl who attended sixteen summits from Williamsburg (1983) to Birmingham (1998), Prime Minister Nakasone Yasuhiro holds the Japanese record by attending a total of five consecutive summits from Williamsburg (1983) to Venice (1987). During this time a level of camaraderie was created amongst the world leaders due in part to his active participation and the perception of him as the least Japanese of Japanese prime ministers (Saitō 1990: 80). It is this consistency in personnel that has been widely credited with facilitating any successful working of the summit process (Bergsten and Henning 1996: 78–9). However, both before and after Nakasone and up until the end of the millennium, the Japanese prime minister was regarded as a transient figure, 'the odd man out, tongue-tied if not completely speechless', on the sidelines of the official summit photograph (Hook *et al.* 2001: 19).

Another obstacle to successful participation in the summit from the Japanese point of view has been the language barrier. The *lingua franca* of the summit is first and foremost English, and thereafter French. One Japanese newspaper speculated with reference to the Guadeloupe Summit that '[i]f our Prime Minister [Fukuda Takeo] had attended this conference wearing a polo shirt, he would have had to discuss the whole range of world problems in English, with only a notebook or two in his hands. It is easy to imagine what would have happened. Perhaps it was fortunate that he had not been invited' (*The Japan Times*, 16 January 1979). Furthermore, Fukuda Takeo described participation at the 1978 Bonn Summit as 'a trying experience . . . [and] . . . not as easy an exercise in diplomacy for him as it must have been for his colleagues from America and Europe' (*The Japan Times*, 16 January 1979). Miyazawa Kiichi stands out as the exception due to his proficiency in English, and possibly Nakasone Yasuhiro having used French at the summit in conversation with French President François Mitterand.

Although this is an accurate representation up to a point, there is one way in which participating Japan delegations have demonstrated consistency in their personnel; namely, most Japanese prime ministers have attended the summit before at the ministerial level. Take the example of Miyazawa Kiichi again, who attended the first summits in Rambouillet (1975) and San Juan (1976) as foreign minister, then the Venice (1987) and Toronto (1988) summits as finance minister, Munich (1992) and Tokyo (1993) as prime minister, and then Cologne (1999) and Okinawa (2000) as finance minister again. Few of the western participants can boast such a veteran of the summit process. Other individuals have attended a number of summits in various capacities, for example Hashimoto Ryūtarō (seven times), Takeshita Noboru (six times) and Abe Shintarō (five times). Moreover, in June 2004, Prime Minister Koizumi Junichirō attended his fourth summit at the Sea Island resort in the US and looks set to equal, if not better, Nakasone's record.

More importantly for the G7/8, in the new millennium it has achieved an unprecedented level of consistency in its membership with only one change (Paul Martin replacing Jean Chrétien as Canadian prime minister) since the 2001 Genoa Summit.

Agenda-setting

As regards the agenda of each summit and its expansion into political affairs, the Japanese government was initially reluctant to see the summit used in this way; for example, it contested the discussion of terrorism at the 1978 Bonn Summit (Belelieu 2002: 10). Nevertheless, this attitude has been shed over the years and often as the host nation the Japanese government has shown the ability and influence to promote topical and relevant issues or policies in regional, international and bilateral terms.

In particular, the Japanese government has specifically set out to bring Asian issues to the attention of the international community and the prime minister of the day has regularly visited other Asian leaders prior to the summit in order to sound them out as to the topics they wish to see discussed. Thus, a number of 'Asian issues' credited to Japan's insistence have regularly appeared in the final communiqués, political declarations or chairman's summaries issued by the summit: Indo-Chinese refugees were discussed at the 1979 Tokyo Summit and the 1980 Venice Summit; Cambodia was a regular topic at the 1981 Ottawa, 1988 Toronto and 1989 Paris Summits; the importance of the Asian Pacific region was stressed at the 1986 Tokyo Summit; aid to the Philippines and the hosting of a successful Olympic Games in South Korea were called for at the 1988 Toronto Summit; in the aftermath of the East Asian economic and financial crisis of 1997, Japan promoted a new international financial architecture (Katada 2001); and deep concern was expressed over North Korea's nuclear programme at the 1999 Cologne Summit. In addition, the Japanese government has acted as more than a simple mouthpiece and has sought to connect the summit process more closely with the region. Thus, Foreign Minister Sonoda Sunao succeeded in persuading US Secretary of State Cyrus Vance to jointly attend an ASEAN dialogue meeting after the 1979 Tokyo Summit (Saitō 1990: 64–5).

At the 2004 Sea Island Summit and with the focus placed on Iraq, Japan's role as a 'bridge' between regions was expanded to embrace the Middle East. Regarded by representatives of the region as ' . . . the only [G8] leader who can listen to the opinions of both the United States and the Arab World' (*International Herald Tribune/The Asahi Shimbun* 4 June 2004), Koizumi successfully inserted expressions of respect for 'uniqueness' and 'diversity' in the G8's statement on social and economic reform in the Middle East and North Africa (MOFA 2004).

The Japanese government has also attempted to demonstrate its commitment and contribution to international society more broadly through shaping the G8's agenda. Okinawa was, for better or worse, remembered as the IT summit that tried to address the 'digital divide' – a personal proposal of Obuchi before his sudden death, and subsequently taken up by his successor Mori. However, this did not go to plan. Despite the efforts mentioned above to embrace NGOs, their reaction was not wholly positive to the results of the Okinawa Summit and the NGO Jubilee 2000 symbolically burned a laptop computer in protest at the perceived vacuity of the IT-led agenda, the lack of attention paid to debt issues in the developing world, and the cost of the summit, stating that: ' . . . the Japanese misjudged public opinion. They thought information technology was a sexy new theme for the year 2000' (*The Gazette*, 23 July 2000). Despite the opprobrium heaped upon the Japanese government, the digital opportunity task force initiative was followed through at subsequent summits, in similar fashion to Nakasone's Human Frontier Science Programme announced at the 1987 Venice Summit, and has been accorded a degree of praise.

Finally, the Japanese government has demonstrated a readiness to instrumentalize the G7/8 as a multilateral site to promote bilateral issues, although ultimately with little success. Although its G7 colleagues responded to Japanese lobbying and expressed support for the rapid resolution of the above-mentioned Northern Territories' dispute at three consecutive summits (Houston 1990, London 1991 and Munich 1992), the bilateral territorial dispute remained the thorn in the side of Russo-Japanese relations. Undeterred, at the 2003 and 2004 summits, the Japanese government continued to instrumentalize this multilateral forum to secure successfully G8 support for another intrinsically bilateral issue: the resolution of the issue of Japanese citizens abducted by the North Korean government (see Dobson 2004a: 84–96; Dobson 2004b).

Hosting

After the 'battle of Seattle' at the WTO meeting in December 1999 and the terrorist attacks of 9/11, providing security for the summit and the choice of venue have become increasingly important. The Japanese government has always taken its hosting of the summit very seriously as a sign of its commitment to international society and it has been credited by the University of Toronto's G8 Research Group as the only host of consistently successful summits (Dobson 2004a: 180–1). Japan's ability in hosting the summit has been captured in a diplomatic quip that rather than rotating the summit venue every year, Japan should simply be allowed to host it every year (*The Financial Times*, 23 July 2000). This importance of the summit to Japan was manifested in the fierce resistance displayed by Hashimoto in reaction to Yeltsin's attempt at the 1998 Birmingham Summit to wrest the role of host for the 2000 summit from Japan (Bayne 2000: 155). The domestic impact of the summit is also significant and the impact of a successful summit upon a prime minister's electoral chances has never been underestimated. Thus, being seen in the eyes of both the Japanese electorate and the world to have hosted a successful summit, more than promoting the summit as an effective and central mechanism of global governance, is a strong motivation for the Japanese government.

Japan has hosted four summits, three in Tokyo (1979, 1986 and 1993) and one in Okinawa (2000). Okinawa is the exception and deserves greater attention as this summit ' . . . was in retrospect more notable for the fact that it was held in Nago

[City, Okinawa] than for anything it decided' (McCormack and Yonetani 2000). Despite being regarded as a clear outsider in the bidding for the host venue due to the lack of infrastructure and the difficulty in providing security (it should be remembered that rocket attacks by left-wing Japanese radicals on US military bases and the summit venue itself had taken place at previously Japanese-hosted summits in 1986 and 1993), Okinawa was eventually chosen at the end of April 1999, allegedly as the personal preference of Obuchi (*The Japan Times*, 29 April 1999). It has been argued that Okinawa was chosen as a potent reminder of both the Second World War and Japan's diversity, a chance to publicize the inequitable burden shouldered by the prefecture in hosting the continuing presence of US bases in a post-Cold War world, a geo-political crossroads of Asia illustrative of Japan's role in the region, and finally as an attempt to expedite the issue of the relocation of the US airbase in Futenma and quash any opposition (Yonetani 2001).

One result of choosing Okinawa was that extra expense was incurred to the tune of ¥81.4 billion (US$750 million) in order to provide the island with the infrastructure to host an international summit. Thus, the Okinawa Summit became the most expensive summit in the history of the process, roughly 100 times more expensive than its predecessor, the 1999 Cologne Summit. Preparations included the construction of a new conference centre, a press centre, and the above-mentioned NGO centre. The cost of the summit and the heavy security presence came in for a great deal of criticism as did Mori's pre-summit gaffes and these issues tended to overshadow the content of the summit's discussions and final communiqué. In addition to the expense, the Okinawa Summit was characterized by a high degree of festivity: a competition to design the summit's logo made open to the public, a new ¥2000 banknote carrying an image of Shuri Castle located in Naha, the penning of a summit theme song for the first time and an unnecessary focus upon the food to be served at the formal summit banquets (Abe 2000; Nishikawa 2000). All this served only to trivialize the summit into nothing more than a frivolity in the eyes of some observers and thereby soil its reputation as an effective mechanism of global governance.

Compliance

Compliance with G7/8 statements and pledges is one indicator of the influence of the summit process and has the effect of legitimizing its work. With specific reference to the Okinawa Summit, a cartoon in a Japanese newspaper hinted at the difficulties Mori might encounter in honouring pledges made at the summit by depicting him as a mountaineer finding the way down from the summit peak more difficult than the ascent (*Asahi Shimbun*, 25 July 2000). However, in the aftermath of this summit, a number of meetings of G8 and non-G8 members were held before the end of the year in both Tokyo and Okinawa to promote the discussions conducted and pledges made at the summit on the 'digital divide', disposal of Russian weapons-grade plutonium, drugs, infectious diseases and transnational organized crime, helping to make Okinawa 'the most credible G7/8 summit ever held' (Kirton *et al.* 2002: 269).

In more general terms, the Japanese delegation has never threatened to walk out of the summit as the French did over multilateral trade negotiations at the 1985 Bonn Summit (Sakurada 1988: 102). According to the G8 Research Group, Japan's performances in the summit from 1996 to 2002 have been averaged as a 'B plus', ranking it above Italy and Russia and on a par with Canada, the EU, France, Germany, the UK, and the US (G8 Research Group 2004: 219). In addition, Japan's level of compliance with G7/8 pledges has been rated as a middling power. Its level of compliance in the G7 from 1975 to 1989 was rated at 26.2 per cent – ranked fifth out of the seven summit members, above France and the US and below the average compliance score of 30.7 per cent. From 1996 to 2001, its level of compliance had risen to 48 per cent – still ranked fifth out of the now eight summit members, above France, Germany and Russia, but also above the average compliance score of 45 per cent (Kirton *et al.* 2002: 272). Although Japan lost ground to France in the compliance assessments after the 2003 Evian Summit, this can be understood as France responding actively to its role as host, and Japan's continued role as a middling power in terms of upholding G8 pledges is still evident (Kirton and Kokotsis 2004: 3).

Conclusion

As Fred Halliday argues, the pressing question is how our systems of global governance can be made 'more effective, more just, and more responsive to the changing international situation' (Halliday 2000: 19). In light of this question and what we know about the G7/8's position as a site of governance in this patchwork quilt of global governance, what has the Japanese government done to facilitate its effective functioning? As regards the legitimacy of the summit as manifested in its membership, the Japanese government has attempted to 'reach out' and include a variety of state and non-state actors from Japan and East Asia in line with the broadening range of actors involved in the provision of global governance. However, as seen above, in the case of the NGOs that constitute civil society, the degree of sincerity has been questioned; and, in the case of Russian participation, a long-running bilateral dispute, rather than the international public good, meant the participation was contested. As regards fostering intimacy amongst summit personnel – almost akin to a founding principle of the summit process – the Japanese government, hampered by regularly changing prime ministers, has contributed little to the intended camaraderie of summit proceedings. In fact, in a forum where the role of the executive head is pivotal, Japan has been decidedly handicapped despite a few notable exceptions. As regards agenda-setting, Japan has been more successful in responding to an East Asian norm, 'batting' for the region at the summit and introducing an expanded range of timely and pressing issues for the summit's consideration. As regards hosting the summit, it has been stated that the Japanese government 'considers staging a successful summit to be a matter of such national pride that the event has assumed remarkable domestic political significance . . . ' (*The Financial Times*, 24 July 2000). This, alongside a mixture of individual actors' preferences and East Asian, bilateral and internationalist norms, shaped the decision to hold the summit in Okinawa. Yet, as a result of near obsession with hosting a successful summit the Japanese government has done a great deal, with Okinawa as emblematic, to reinforce the image of the summit as a moribund political show, and very little to communicate the achievements and meaning of the summit to the world as an important mechanism of global governance. Finally, as regards compliance, the Japanese government has demonstrated the importance it places on the G7/8 through a middling, but increasing, willingness and ability to honour its summit pledges.

In its thirtieth year, the summit process is now an established and central mechanism of global governance. At the 2004 Sea Island Summit a record-breaking number of commitments, mandates and funding projects were announced. In short, the summit appears to be in good health. It has been argued that within the G7/8, 'both Japan and Canada have shared a strong interest in having it and its associated institutions develop as the *primary* instrument through which to pursue their foreign policy priorities and to shape international order' (Kirton 1998: 292, emphasis added). However, notwithstanding the unique and important position the G7/8 occupies in Japan's foreign policy, it is unlikely to ever assume a position of primacy. Equally, although Japan's commitment to the summit process is much clearer than, say, the fickle relationship the US has with this multilateral forum, in reality and as demonstrated above, it has a decidedly mixed record of ensuring the effective functioning of the summit as a site of global governance.

Acknowledgments

I would like to thank the Japan Foundation Endowment Committee (grant number 173) and Hōsei University in Japan for support provided under the Hōsei International Fund Fellowship in researching and writing this chapter.

References

Abe, Yasushi (2000) 'Samitto "bansankai" tenyawanya', *Bungei Shunjū* Special Issue, (September): 134–41.

Bayne, Nicholas (1995) 'The G7 summits and the reform of global institutions', *Government and Opposition* 30, 4: 492–509.

Bayne, Nicholas (2000) *Hanging in There: the G7 and G8 summit in maturity and renewal*, Aldershot: Ashgate.

Bayne, Nicholas (2001) 'Decision making in the G7/G8 system', *Paper for ECPR Workshops*, Grenoble (April): 1–24. Available on-line at:
http://www.essex.ac.uk/ECPR/events/jointsessions/paperarchive/grenoble/ws12/bayne.pdf, accessed 23 June 2003.

Belelieu, Andre (2002) 'The G8 and terrorism: what role can the G8 play in the 21st century', *G8 Governance* 8 (June): 1–35. Available on-line at:
http://www.g8.utoronto.ca/governance/belelieu2002-gov8.pdf,
accessed 23 June 2003.

Bergsten, C. Fred and Henning, C. Randall (1996) *Global Economic Leadership and the Group of Seven*, Washington: Institute for International Economics.

Commission on Global Governance (1995) *Our Global Neighbourhood: the report of the Commission on Global Governance*. Available on-line at: http://www.cgg.ch/contents1-2.html, accessed 13 November 2002.

deVillafranca, Richard (1993) 'Japan and the Northern Territories' dispute: past, present, future', *Asian Survey* 33, 6: 610–24.

Dobson, Hugo (2004a) *Japan and the G7/8, 1975–2002*, London: RoutledgeCurzon.

Dobson, Hugo (2004b) 'Japan and the G8 Evian Summit: bilateralism, East Asianism and multilateralization', *G8 Governance* 9 (February): 1–17. Available on-line at: http://www.g7.utoronto.ca/governance/dobson_g8g.pdf, accessed 11 June 2004.

Eguchi, Yūjirō (1993) 'Samitto to tojōkoku ni taisuru seisaku kadai: Ajia Taiheiyō chiiki no chūshin ni', *Kokusai Mondai* 402 (September): 34–45.

Falk, Richard (1995) *On Humane Governance: toward a new global politics*, Cambridge: Polity Press.

G8 Research Group (2004) 'Performance assessment, by Country, 1996–2002', in John J. Kirton and Radoslava N. Stefanova (eds) *The G8, the United Nations and Conflict Prevention*, Aldershot: Ashgate, p. 219.

Hajnal, Peter I. (ed.) (1989) *The Seven-Power Summit: documents from the summit of industrialized countries, 1975–1989*, Millwood, New York: Krauss International Publications.

Hajnal, Peter I. (1999) *The G7/8 System: evolution, role and documentation*, Aldershot: Ashgate.

Halliday, Fred (2000) 'Global governance: prospects and problems', *Citizenship Studies* 4, 1: 19–33.

Hodges, Michael R. (1999) 'The G8 and the new political economy', in Michael R. Hodges, John J. Kirton and Joseph P. Daniels (eds) *The G8's Role in the New Millennium*, Aldershot: Ashgate, pp. 69–73.

Hook, Glenn D., Gilson, Julie, Hughes, Christopher W. and Dobson, Hugo (2001) *Japan's International Relations: politics, economics and security*, London: Routledge.

Hunt, John and Owen, Henry (1984) 'Taking stock of the seven-power summits: two views', *International Affairs* 60, 4: 657–61.

Inoguchi, Kuniko (1994) 'The changing significance of the G7 summits', *Japan Review of International Affairs* 8, 1: 21–38.

Katada, Saori (2001) 'Japan's approach to shaping a new international financial architecture', in John J. Kirton and George M. Von Furstenberg (eds) *New Directions in Global Economic Governance: managing globalisation in the twenty-first century*, Aldershot: Ashgate, pp. 113–26.

Kimura, Masato and Welch, David A. (1998) 'Specifying "interests": Japan's claim to the Northern Territories and its implications for international relations theory', *International Studies Quarterly* 42, 2: 213–44.

Kirton, John J. (1998) 'The emerging Pacific partnership: Japan, Canada, and the United States at the G7 summit', in Michael Fry, John J. Kirton and Kurosawa Mitsuru (eds) *The North Pacific Triangle: the United States, Japan and Canada at century's end*, Toronto: University of Toronto Press, pp. 292–313.

Kirton, John J. (2001a) 'The G20: representativeness, effectiveness, and leadership in global governance', in John J. Kirton, Joseph P. Daniels and Andreas Freytag (eds) *Guiding Global Order: G8 governance in the twenty-first century*, Aldershot: Ashgate, pp. 143–72.

Kirton, John J. (2001b) 'The G7/8 and China: toward a closer association', in John J. Kirton, Joseph P. Daniels and Andreas Freytag (eds) *Guiding Global Order: G8 governance in the twenty-first century*, Aldershot: Ashgate, pp. 189–222.

Kirton, John J. and Kokotsis, Ella (1997–8) 'Revitalizing the G7: prospects for the 1998 Birmingham meeting of the eight', *International Journal* 53, 1: 38–56.

Kirton, John J. and Kokotsis, Ella (2004) *2003 Evian Final Compliance Report*. Available on-line at:
http://www.g7.utoronto.ca/evaluations/2003evian_comp_final/2003evian_final.pdf, accessed 11 June 2004.

Kirton, John J., Kokotsis, Ella and Juricevic, Diana (2002) 'Okinawa's promises kept: the 2001 G8 compliance report', in John J. Kirton and Junichi Takase (eds) *New Directions in Global Political Governance: the G8 and international order in the twenty-first century*, Aldershot: Ashgate, pp. 269–80.

Kojima, Akira (2001) 'The G8 summit and Japan', *Asia-Pacific Review* 8, 1: 99–106.

McCormack, Gavan and Yonetani, Julia (2000) 'The Okinawan summit seen from below', *JPRI Working Paper* 71 (September). Available on-line at:
http://www.jpri.org/WPapers/wp71.html, accessed 23 June 2003.

Miyashita, Akitoshi (2001) 'Consensus or compliance? *Gaiatsu*, interests and Japan's foreign aid', in Akitoshi Miyashita and Sōichirō Satō (eds) *Japanese Foreign Policy in Asia and the Pacific: domestic interests, American pressure and regional integration*, Basingstoke: Palgrave, pp. 37–61.

MOFA (2004) *Partnership for Progress and a Common Future with the Region of the Broader Middle East and North Africa*. Available on-line at:
http://www.mofa.go.jp/policy/economy/summit/2004/partner.pdf,
accessed 11 June 2004.

Nishikawa, Megumi (2000) 'Shunōtachi no shokutaku shurijō no kyōen: "sekai no chōwa" o mezashite', in 'Samitto no subete ga wakaru hon', *Gaikō Fōramu* 147, Special Issue (October): 110–19.

Putnam, Robert D. and Bayne, Nicholas (1984) *Hanging Together: the seven-power summits*, Cambridge: Harvard University Press.

Putnam, Robert D. and Bayne, Nicholas (1987) *Hanging Together: cooperation and conflict in the seven-power summits*, London: Sage.

Rosenau, James N. (1993) 'Governance, order and change in world politics', in James N. Rosenau and Ernst-Otto Czempiel (eds) *Governance without Government: order and change in world politics*, Cambridge: Cambridge University Press, pp. 1–29.

Saitō, Shiro (1990) *Japan at the Summit: Japan's role in the Western Alliance and Asian Pacific cooperation*, London: Routledge.

Sakurada, Daizō (1988) *Japan and the Management of the International Political Economy: Japan's seven power summit diplomacy*, Country Study Number 6, Centre for International Studies: University of Toronto. Available on-line at:
http://www.g7.utoronto.ca/scholar/sakurada1988, accessed 23 June 2003.

Sally, Razeen (2001) 'Looking askance at global governance', in John J. Kirton, Joseph P. Daniels and Andreas Freytag (eds) *Guiding Global Order: G8 governance in the twenty-first century*, Aldershot: Ashgate, pp. 55–76.

Smyser, W. R. (1993) 'Goodbye, G7', *Washington Quarterly* 16, 1: 15–28.

Soeya, Yoshihide (2000) 'No view from the summit', *Look Japan* 46, 535: 23.

Takagi, Seiichirō (1995) 'Human rights in Japanese foreign policy: Japan's policy towards China after Tiananmen', in James T. H. Tang (ed.) *Human Rights and International Relations in the Asia-Pacific Region*, London and New York: Pinter, pp. 97–111.

Takase, Junichi (2000) *Samitto: shuyō shunō kaigi*, Tokyo: Ashi Shobō.

Toyoda, Naomi (2000) 'Okinawa kara mita "Okinawa samitto"', *Gekkan Shakai Minshū* 544 (September): 16–25.

Ullrich, Heidi K. (2001) 'Stimulating trade liberalization after Seattle: G7/8 leadership in global governance', in John J. Kirton and George M. Von Furstenberg (eds) *New*

Directions in Global Economic Governance: managing globalisation in the twenty-first century, Aldershot: Ashgate, pp. 219–40.

Watanabe, Kōji (1999) 'Japan's summit contributions and economic challenges', in Michael R. Hodges, John J. Kirton and Joseph P. Daniels (eds) *The G8's Role in the New Millennium*, Aldershot: Ashgate, pp. 95–105.

Weilemann, Peter R. (2000) 'The summit meeting: diplomacy at its highest level', *NIRA Review* 7, 2: 16–20.

Whyman, William E. (1995) 'We can't go on meeting like this: revitalizing the G7 process', *Washington Quarterly* 18, 3: 139–65.

World Bank (2002) 'World development indicators database'. Available on-line at: http://www.worldbank.org/data/databytopic/GDP.pdf, accessed 23 June 2003.

Yonetani, Julia (2001) 'Playing base politics in a global strategic theater: Futenma relocation, the G8 summit and Okinawa', *Critical Asian Studies* 33, 1: 70–95.

2 Japan's role in emerging East Asian governance

Regional and national implications

Glenn D. Hook

The purpose of this chapter is to elucidate Japan's role in the governance of the East Asian political economy. Its main focus is on the Japanese role in subregional institutions, particularly the Association of Southeast Asian Nations (ASEAN) plus Three as an emerging site of governance, as well as on the policies the government has adopted in the wake of the 1997–8 East Asian financial and wider crises. As it stands, a number of articles have appeared on the Japanese policy response to the crises (e.g. Hughes 2000; Hook *et al.* 2002), but work on Japan's role in East Asian governance is particularly sparse (Kikuchi 2003), with attention tending to be directed at the impact of the crises on national governance within the affected economies (e.g. Jomo 1998; Kim 2000; Haque 2002).

Thus, whilst much has been said about the way the crises exposed weaknesses in the affected economies' national systems of governance, this chapter focuses rather on how the crises have strengthened the impulses towards establishing a system of governance on the East Asian level and the implications for the governance of the Japanese political economy. The central argument can be summarized in three points: first, the demands placed on the affected economies by the International Monetary Fund (IMF) in the wake of the crises – namely, trade liberalization, deregulation, privatization and the general shrinking of the role of the state in the national economy – was part of a political project to promote a neo-liberal system of governance in East Asia. Second, in reaction to the IMF's national prescriptions, Japanese policymakers have in a number of ways contested this system of governance and sought to promote a new system of governance at the level of the subregional political economy (on subregionalism, see Hook and Kearns 1999). And third, the policies these officials have promoted at the subregional level have national as well as international implications, suggesting a close connection between the governance of the regional and national political economies of East Asia.

Before turning directly to examine Japan and East Asian governance, however, let us first elucidate the meaning of governance, *per se*, as this will facilitate our understanding of the different ways in which Japan is playing a crucial role in the governance of the East Asian subregion.

What is governance?

As intimated above, a useful distinction can be made between theories aiming to explain governance, on the one hand, and a political project championing a specific system of governance, as with the IMF's and World Bank's promotion of 'good governance' and 'global governance', on the other (Payne 2005). When examining governance in East Asia, then, attention needs to be paid to the political role played by particular projects of governance in reshaping actual systems of governance as well as the Japanese role in them. Given our interest in both regional *and* national governance, we here regard governance as a form of regulatory 'system' for maintaining *order* through different mechanisms of 'steering' and 'control' at both the regional and national levels (Payne 2005; Rosenau 1997).

In seeking to achieve order, governance entails both material and normative regulation. In terms of material power, military capability is at the heart of a system of regional governance based on the balance of power, even though threats to its stability can emerge from outside the system, as with terrorism. In governance of the national political economy the state may still maintain the authority to respond to cross-border activities, as with the authority to control intrusions across a border, but often lacks the competency to do so: it may be lacking or have moved out of the hands of the state into those of other actors, above the state as in the European Union (EU), below the state, as in the expanded role of local governments in international affairs, or 'sideways' to corporations and non-governmental organizations (NGOs) (Breslin and Hook 2002; Rosenau 2000: 23). In this way, the state may no longer enjoy the ability to deploy its material capabilities in order to exert control over a range of outside actors.

In terms of norms, governance as the codification of binding rules of normative preferences in law is seen as a key element of governance by some commentators (Young 1994), but compliance does not necessarily rely on law. Indeed, noncodified norms can and do emerge based on non-binding forms of interaction and cooperation, that is, new rules of governance emerge to replace other rules of governance as well as to co-exist with them. In the case of the balance between the private and the public sphere in a system of governance for the orderly conduct of national or regional economic affairs, for instance, the spread of neo-liberal norms placing greater weight on the role of market principles has challenged norms supporting a dominant role for the state in the economy. In this way, systems of governance are subject to change at both the international and national levels.

This brief discussion suggests that, in examining governance on both the regional and national levels of analysis, we need to bear in mind difference between governance projects and the analysis of governance, the role of both state and non-state actors, and the material as well as normative aspects of governance as a system.

Governance in East Asia: from Cold War to post-Cold War

During the Cold War era, the material elements of East Asian governance were symbolized by the US–Japan alliance and the 'hub and spokes' security system the

US set in place through the regional deployment of military power following the defeat of Japan in the Second World War. This was a classic 'balance of power' system of governance aimed at maintaining order and preventing the expansion of communism. It was at the heart of a system of governance which allowed the capitalist, authoritarian regimes of East Asia to develop economically, taking advantage of the liberal trading order maintained by the US's 'hub and spokes' alliance system. For Japan, which the US established as the bastion against communism in the Far East, this system provided the stability needed in order to rebuild the economy and emerge as the most important economy in East Asia: on the one hand, it imported resources from Southeast Asia and further afield; on the other, it pursued an export-oriented trade policy dependent on access to especially US markets.

Politically and militarily, respective Japanese governments supported the US's global and regional strategies by providing the bases the former occupier required in order to be able to deter or prosecute both conventional and nuclear wars, acquired weapons from the US, and gradually built up the Self-Defence Forces (SDF) into a highly sophisticated military establishment. From the end of the 1970s, moreover, the government additionally started to provide financial support for US deployments in Japan through 'sympathy payments' (host-nation support) and over the years increasingly took on a military role in the region as part of the wider confrontation with the communist threat. This is illustrated by the 1981 decision of Prime Minister Suzuki Zenkō to take on responsibility for patrolling the sea lines of communication up to 1,000 nautical miles from Japan. In this way, the Cold War era split the regional political economy between the capitalist and communist camps, with the system of governance maintained overtly by military power under a 'balance of power' system, with Japan playing a crucial supportive role in this US-dominated order.

The norms at the base of this system of governance supported an understanding of the world as composed of two antagonistic camps, the communist East and the capitalist West, and the need for the US deployment of military forces to maintain order in the region. Within this externally maintained system of governance, the East Asian region was criss-crossed with a web of relationships, in political economy and, to a lesser extent, security and culture. The division of East Asia between East and West and the anti-Japanese sentiments arising from the legacy of the war acted as structural impediments to the emergence of a new system of sub-regional governance during the Cold War period. Nevertheless, as a result of the Japanese government's policy of separating politics and economics (*seikei bunri*), the division of the region was not as complete as the balance of power system implied. Whilst the Cold War stand-off limited the amount of trade carried out with communist countries, for instance, Japan was still able to make strategic use of war reparations and official development assistance (ODA) elsewhere, and this provided opportunities for Japanese companies to develop a range of economic links with the developing East Asian economies. With the rise in the value of the yen following the Nixon shocks in the early 1970s, and the Plaza Accord in the mid-1980s, Japanese manufacturers moved increasingly offshore, particularly to

East Asia, gradually knitting the region together as a cross-border production system. In this way, Japanese firms, first in textiles, later in automotives, electronics and electrical goods, moved offshore in order to maintain international competitiveness, taking advantage of cheaper factors of production, such as the cost of labour, available in developing East Asia, as well as the rise in the value of the yen. This created the basis for the emergence of greater regional cooperation, but the history of Japanese imperialism meant that, until the end of the Cold War, the government faced resistance, both on the policymaking and mass levels in East Asia, to any type of leadership role in the region. The role of Japan's conservative political leaders in resisting the demands for an apology for the war was crucial in this respect (Wakamiya 1995).

Cold War's ending

With the ending of the Cold War, the potential for deeper economic cooperation and integration, and the potential to supplement a system of governance reliant on an external power with a greater role for the states in the region, started to emerge. The regionalization of Japanese capital and production which occurred during the Cold War period had provided a base for the strengthening of intra-regional trade relations between Japan and the other East Asian economies in the years following the end of the Cold War. This can be seen from the import and export figures for the period 1991–2000: East Asian (NIES 4, ASEAN 4 and China) exports to Japan rose from 9.7 per cent to 11.6 per cent of the total, and exports from Japan to East Asia grew from 30.2 per cent to 37.9 per cent. Illustrative of intra-industry trade and the close ties between manufacturers, parts made up 42.9 per cent of the total exports in 2000 (JETRO various years). This regionalization of Japanese manufacturing production strengthened the need for a system of governance for the East Asian political economy beyond the architecture set in place through the US–Japan security treaty and the wider US military presence in the region.

From the perspective of the emergence of new sites of governance in East Asia, the ending of the Cold War provided an opportunity for Japanese policymakers to move forward with the institutionalization of regional level meetings of East Asian states. Especially in the early post-Cold War years, however, the boundaries of the region remained contested, with proposals made to establish regional institutions linking Asia and the Pacific, on the one hand, and those to establish East Asian subregional groupings, on the other. As seen in the role Japan played in establishing a forum for economic dialogue, the Asia Pacific Economic Cooperation (APEC) forum (Krauss 2000), Japanese policymakers sought at first to join together the Asian and Pacific wings of the Cold War order, thereby supplementing the system of governance set in place by the US during the confrontation with communism. Over the years the Japanese and US attitudes towards APEC have differed, however, particularly in regard to two points: its function and the opening of domestic markets. Whereas Japan and many other East Asian states prefer APEC to play a role as a loose forum for building consensus on issues, the US has increasingly sought to institutionalize APEC as a forum for negotiating the liberalization of trade and finance and introducing market principles to the region (Ravenhill 2002).

Indeed, especially after the 1993 meeting of APEC in Seattle, when the US took on more of a leadership role, the forum has gradually emerged as the core regional organization for promoting neo-liberal economic policies and norms, with the US seeking to lower barriers to trade and more generally promote the principles of the free-market economy in East Asia. Japanese policymakers, along with those of many other East Asian states, have nevertheless resisted opening up their domestic markets in internationally non-competitive sectors, especially agriculture, as seen at the November 1998 meeting of APEC in Kuala Lumpur, when Japan baulked at US pressure to open its markets in fish and forestry products. Thus, whilst Japanese policymakers remain engaged with APEC, the goal of achieving complete liberalization of trade and services for Japan and the other developed members of the organization by 2010, has continued to meet with strong resistance from agricultural interests in Japan and elsewhere in East Asia. The enormous sums involved in agricultural public works projects has meant that, whereas some sections of the Japanese state favour opening up the domestic market, others remain opposed. Indeed, the consolidation of interests among agricultural voters, the Liberal Democratic Party, and the Ministry of Agriculture, Forestry and Fisheries (MAFF), makes the agricultural lobby a formidable obstacle to the reform of the national system of governance in Japan.

At the same time as a new organization linking Asia and the Pacific was being established, however, moves were afoot to establish an East Asian regional grouping of states. As seen in the 1991 proposal by Prime Minister Mahathir Mohamad of Malaysia to establish the East Asian Economic Grouping, later East Asian Economic Caucus (EAEC), the ending of the Cold War had also provided an opportunity for East Asian states to take the initiative in establishing a subregional grouping of East Asian states, linking ASEAN with the Northeast Asian states of China, Japan and South Korea (for details, see Hook 1999). The US, along with Australia and New Zealand, were explicitly excluded from the EAEC proposal, whereas Mahathir viewed Japan as the potential 'voice of Asia' in global institutions. Whilst certain elements in the Japanese government were more sympathetic to the Malaysian proposal than others, fear of damaging the US–Japan relationship remained the overriding concern of key policymakers in the Ministry of Foreign Affairs, making the government initially unwilling to support the Malaysian proposal. In the intervening years, however, Japan has come to accept, and even play an active role in promoting, an East Asian grouping of states, the ASEAN plus Three. In all but name, this grouping of states can be regarded as the institutionalization of the Malaysian proposal for the EAEC.

As the announcement of this proposal makes clear, the resistance to a greater Japanese role in the region had waned considerably by the end of the Cold War. In the interim, Japanese policymakers have increasingly come to play a key role in representing East Asia outside of the region, as in G7/8 meetings or meetings in international institutions, as discussed in Chapter 1. The launch of the first Asia-Europe Meeting (ASEM) in 1996, moreover, gave substance to the EAEC proposal in terms of developing an 'East Asia' to meet with the 'Europeans' (Gilson 2002). In short, ASEM has served a normative function in providing a forum for shaping an East Asian identity, which appeared concretely in the need to negotiate a common 'East Asian' position for dialogue with the members of the EU.

The institutionalization of the ASEAN plus Three meetings from 1997, which took on increasing importance in the wake of the East Asian financial and wider crises, now provides a forum to supplement, if not directly contest, the system of governance set in place during the Cold War. Certainly, the US was central to the governance architecture set in place during this period, and even with the Cold War's ending, it remains as the core of the 'hub and spokes' security system. In the realm of political economy, however, the East Asian financial and wider crises have provided the impetus for East Asian states to question the role of outside actors and to search for regional answers to regional questions.

East Asian crisis

Whilst the changes in the system of financial governance at the global level represented by the move to the floating exchange rate in the early 1970s, the rise in the value of the yen following the Plaza Accord in the mid-1980s, and the ending of the Cold War at the end of the 1980s all served to engender changes in the Japanese role in the regional political economy, the Japanese response to the East Asian crises has more fundamentally transformed Japan's role in the regional system of governance. To start with, the East Asian crises made Japanese policy-makers clearly aware of the close links Japanese business had developed with East Asia, especially during the previous decade, on the one hand, and the importance of maintaining regional stability and order, on the other. It served to highlight the degree to which the Japanese economy was intertwined with others in the region and that, despite the existence of the US 'hub and spokes' security system, the stability of the region could be threatened in non-military ways, as illustrated by the spread of the financial crisis to the non-financial sectors of East Asia's economy and society.

To summarize briefly (for details see Pempel 2000), the East Asian crises started with the collapse of the Thai baht in July 1997, and spread to other East Asian economies, with Indonesia, Malaysia and South Korea being especially affected. The dramatic fall in the value of local currencies against the dollar, to which they were in effect pegged, brought chaos to local banking and business, with many banks unable to service their foreign loans and corporate debt rising rapidly. Foreign investors, once assured of the security of their assets by the close link between local currencies and the dollar, responded to the crises by withdrawing their short-term holdings, compounding the problem. What started as a currency crisis soon developed into a wider financial and economic, and especially in Indonesia, social and political crises. As a result of the severity of these crises, indeed, the 'miracle' economies of East Asia touted by the World Bank (1993) now seemed to have gone from being a 'miracle' to needing one (McLeod and Garnaut 1998).

Responses to the crisis

The failure of APEC to pursue a regional answer to the problems faced by the East Asian economies underlined the weakness of this institution as a site of governance for dealing with *East Asian* problems. The response to the crises instead came most significantly from the IMF and Japan, with the 1997 meeting of APEC in Vancouver, held just after the outbreak of the currency crisis, simply endorsing the IMF rescue package for the affected economies. In essence, the IMF viewed the crises as resulting from the nature of the political economies of the East Asian states. Its response thus included pointed criticism of macroeconomic policies as well as weaknesses in the financial system, but most importantly focused on the close relationship between government and business. In short, the IMF viewed the close-knit links between government and business, lack of transparency, and the central role of the state in the economy, as the fundamental causes of the crises.

Its recipe for the affected East Asian economies can be understood in a variety of ways, but here let us focus on the role of the IMF as a vehicle for promoting a governance project; that is, a political project with both material and normative elements aimed at changing the system of governance in the affected East Asian political economies. The IMF's remedy was to offer loans and other material support to help the affected economies out of the crises, but to do so based on 'conditionalities'. These in effect disciplined the affected East Asian economies in terms of neo-liberal norms, changing the balance between the public and private sectors of the domestic political economy. The pressure to conform to international (US) norms meant that the issue of governance emerged in relation to the nature of governance *within* regional states, with 'crony capitalism' viewed as an issue of corporate governance and the balance between the public and private sector or, more broadly, 'good governance'. That is, a governance *project* to change the nature of the model of capitalism pursued by the East Asian states and reform the systems of governance in these states, was introduced by the IMF as part of the rescue package. In this way, the normative issue of 'good governance' was put at the centre of the material crisis the East Asian economies faced, illustrating the earlier point we made about understanding governance as a political project.

The IMF adopted a stabilization programme that called for the restructuring of the national political economies of Indonesia, Thailand and South Korea, whereas Malaysia refused to seek IMF assistance. It included a wide range of measures such as the introduction of 'global standards' for the banking industry, which led to the collapse of a number of institutions and the creation of an environment for takeovers to be launched by outside financial institutions from the US and elsewhere. A significant rise occurred in the interest rates charged to corporate clients, which forced many to restructure or fail. Helped by the drafting of new legislation to deal with the problem of workers being laid off as part of corporate restructuring, large numbers of employees moved from positions of secure employment to temporary work or even to the dole queues of the unemployed. With the general cutting back of the state, which fundamentally limited the amount of public provision for those in need, along with the privatization of public services, the IMF's measures fundamentally altered the balance between the state and the market within the affected economies.

Its intervention in East Asia was symbolic of the IMF's role in the governance of the international financial system. To put it another way, the mechanisms of governance for dealing with the East Asian financial and wider crises were 'sited' at the global, not regional, level. The measures it took to combat the East Asian crises, however, cannot be understood simply as a means to restore order to the financial system, but need to be understood more broadly as a way to bolster a specific system of governance in the affected economies. Thus, the policies adopted in response to the crises implied the greater consolidation of a neo-liberal system of governance for the affected economies through deregulation and the implementation of a range of corporate, administrative and structural reforms. In essence, the IMF's policies implied pushing East Asia away from the state-centric system of governance championed by Japan, with the heavy hand of the state felt in the industrial and financial systems, and replacing it with one favouring the market. This policy accelerated the move within the national political economies towards a market-led mode of governance.

The IMF's response to the crises was a clear challenge to the role Japan had been playing in the regional political economy in both a material and normative sense. As a wide range of research testifies, Japan has been pivotal in knitting the regional political economy together, through ODA, foreign direct investment (FDI) of approximately US$15 billion between 1986–90 and the creation of subregional and microregional cross-border production systems, especially in the automotive, electronics and electrical industries (Bernard and Ravenhill 1995; Hatch and Yamamura 1996; Hook 2002). In this way, the affected economies had been able to stave off the 'structural adjustments' (trade liberalization, deregulation, privatization) the IMF and the World Bank had been imposing on Latin America and elsewhere (Bello 1998).

Whilst investments from elsewhere, especially US pension funds, helped to replace the decline in Japanese FDI which followed the bursting of the Japanese 'bubble economy' in the 1990s, these were mainly short-term portfolio investments and were not for the creation of production bases as in the case of much Japanese investment. Not only did Japan play a role in a material sense, but also normatively: the Japanese model of catch-up development, with a key role for the state in the industrial and financial sectors of the economy as well as a focus on export-orientated growth, had been followed to varying degrees by policymakers in other parts of East Asia. Whilst from the perspective of the IMF this model was seen to give rise to a problem of governance in the national political economy, from the perspective of Japan the model's more important element was East Asia's role as part of the 'flying geese' pattern of development. This provided a normative framework for understanding the governance of the regional political economy as hierarchical, and centring on Japan.

In the flying geese model, originally proposed in the 1930s by Akamatsu Kaname and developed by disciples such as Kiyoshi Kojima (2000) (Korhonen 1994), Japan is viewed as the lead goose in a v-shaped flock of geese, followed by the NIES 4 of Hong Kong, South Korea, Singapore and Taiwan, then the ASEAN four of Indonesia, Malaysia, the Philippines and Thailand, and finally China (for problems with the model, especially related to Japan's current economic difficulties, see Ozawa 2001). The idea is that, as the lead goose loses comparative advantage in the production of a particular product, the follower goose next down the v-shaped flock takes up that production. Even with the change in the site of production and the emergence of Japan's role in a range of cross-border production systems, where Japanese multinational corporations have established production sites and processes in other parts of East Asia, this normative mapping of the governance system remains central to Japanese policymakers' views of the region.

The IMF's role in promoting a neo-liberal answer to the East Asian financial and wider crises acted as a catalyst for Japanese policymakers to take a more proactive role in introducing, shaping and seeking to control the regional system of financial governance with the aim of achieving medium- and long-term stability. Given that the threat to regional stability emerged in the financial, rather than the real, sector of the economy, Japanese efforts have been made first and foremost to prevent a re-occurrence of financial turmoil. The regional system of financial governance gradually being set in place does not replace the architecture of governance established during the Cold War period under the US–Japan security system, nor challenge fundamentally the role of the IMF, but it does represent the emergence of a new site of governance with the potential to supplement if not replace the role of outside actors in the overall governance of the East Asian regional political economy.

More specifically, in the wake of the crises Japanese policymakers faced a twofold question: materially, how to ensure the essential ingredients for sustaining the development of the Japanese economy, such as energy, raw materials, markets, and sites for capital investment in East Asia; and, normatively, how to ensure support for a Japanese or, more broadly, East Asian model of capitalism, with a continuing interventionist role for the state and the continued flight of the follower 'geese'. As argued elsewhere (Hook *et al.* 2002), the Japanese response to the crises evolved in a number of stages. To start with, Japan had already, in July 1996, hosted the first Executives' Meeting of East Asia-Pacific Central Banks (EMEAP), suggesting a growing awareness of the need to develop financial dialogue with regional partners. The group excludes the US, but as its eleven members do include representatives from Australia and New Zealand, the membership is not coterminous with the ASEAN plus Three. It functions as a forum for officials from central banks and monetary authorities to hold dialogue on regional financial issues, especially the operation of central banks and wider economic policy. Although by the time of the first official meeting in Tokyo Japan had made agreements to supply liquidity to a number of the economies affected by the crises, the final decision remained in the hands of the central government, not the central banks. In terms of governance the crucial point is that, unlike the IMF, EMEAP cannot impose discipline on member economies through conditionalities. In the end, however, the EMEAP did not play a direct role in combating the crises.

More significantly, Japanese policymakers put forward a proposal to establish an Asian Monetary Fund (AMF). Although the AMF was not realized due to US and IMF as well as Chinese opposition, the proposal is a clear illustration of the pro-active role Japan is attempting to play in shaping regional financial governance. Of particular concern to the US and IMF was the potential for the AMF to establish different 'rules of the game' in offering assistance to the affected economies, as in allowing softer conditionalities than the IMF for those receiving material assistance. Despite this initial set back, and following Japan's cooperation with the US in establishing the Manila Framework – a surveillance mechanism harking back to the AMF proposal – Finance Minister Miyazawa Kiichi in October 1998 announced the 'New Miyazawa Initiative' package of bilateral financial support for the affected economies to the tune of $US30 billion. As these funds did indeed offer softer conditionalities than the IMF, they in effect served to support the domestic system of governance in the affected economies. This is clearly illustrated by Japanese financial assistance to Malaysia, which had challenged neo-liberal orthodoxy by clamping down on the free flow of short-term capital and refusing IMF assistance. In this way, Japanese policymakers, whilst not contesting it directly, did adopt policies at odds with the ones pursued by the IMF.

ASEAN plus Three as an emerging site of governance

Thus, faced with the IMF's challenge to the governance of their national political economies, which seemed to put the interests of outsiders above those of the region, East Asian policymakers sought a way to deal with any future crisis without having to rely as heavily on the IMF. The failure of APEC to offer an effective response to the East Asian crisis, along with concern over the way the IMF medicine would impact nationally, highlighted the importance of Japanese material and normative support in dealing with future crises. In a sense, the weakness of APEC in the face of the crisis acted as a spur for the further integration and institutionalization of the region as 'East Asia'.

Following the East Asian crises, a new system of governance is gradually being put in place as a means to control or steer the regional political economy. Intra-regional cooperation, with Japan strengthening its links with other parts of East Asia, has been manifest most concretely in terms of the closer cooperation between Southeast and Northeast Asia symbolized by the ASEAN plus Three meetings. As FDI remains as an essential tool for the relocation of Japanese manufacturers, a system of governance to ensure financial stability in the region remains crucial to Japan. In effect, East Asian policymakers need to find a means to protect their economies from the sort of turmoil experienced at the time of the 1997–8 crises.

As a regional grouping bringing together the developed and developing economies of Asia *and* the Pacific (APEC) was unable to respond effectively to the crises, the need to establish an East-Asia wide subregional grouping became increasingly recognized among policymakers. What has surfaced in the intervening years is indeed a subregional grouping centring on East Asia, as envisioned by

Mahathir's proposal for EAEC. Its institutionalization started with the attendance of the leaders of China, Japan and South Korea at the annual summit of ASEAN leaders in Kuala Lumpur in November 1997. Annual summit meetings of the ASEAN plus Three leaders have taken place since then: in Hanoi in December 1998, in Manila in November 1999, in Singapore in 2000, in Brunei in November 2001 and in Phnom Penh in 2002. What is more, as illustrated by the first meeting of the Agriculture and Forestry Ministers in Sumatera (Indonesia) in October 2001 and the fifth meeting of finance ministers in Shanghai in May 2002, ASEAN plus Three meetings are taking place among a range of East Asian policymakers. In this way, the institutionalization of regular meetings among the leaders and other officials of East Asia suggests how, in the context of the need to combat the negative influences generated by outside forces following the crises, the ASEAN plus Three is emerging as a new site of governance for addressing a range of issues at the subregional level of East Asia.

The actions Japan has taken in the years after the crises have been particularly important as steps towards strengthening financial governance in East Asia. To start with, following the failure of the proposal to establish the AMF and the announcement of the Miyazawa Initiative, Miyazawa announced the Chiang-Mai Initiative (CMI) at the 2000 ASEAN plus Three meeting of finance ministers in Chiang-Mai, Thailand (MOF 2002). The CMI aims to strengthen and expand the ASEAN Swap Arrangement (ASA), established among members of ASEAN in 1977. The new Bilateral Swap Agreements (BSAs) set in place will be used in particular to tackle difficulties in balance of payment and short-term liquidity and more generally to prevent a future systemic crisis. Although the BSAs have been the main focus of attention in the CMI, it also set in motion the systematic exchange of data on short-term capital movement, which can act as an early warning system for potential crises. Similarly, the CMI aims to train personnel in fiscal, financial and banking areas, with South Korea and China, but most importantly, Japan, centrally involved in providing the technical training needed to upgrade Southeast Asian human resources.

The ASEAN plus Three finance ministers, who meet annually in order to exchange views, particularly in regard to economic development and financial cooperation, have taken the lead role in moving the CMI forward. At the Shanghai meeting in 2002, for instance, the ministers discussed issues related to implementing the CMI, noting that by that year seven countries – Brunei, Indonesia, Japan, South Korea, the Philippines, Thailand and Vietnam – had begun to share data on short-term capital flows on a bilateral basis. As far as the BSAs are concerned, the Japanese government has taken the lead in signing agreements, and had by 2002 set in place BSAs with the following five countries: a US$2 billion won swap with South Korea agreed in July 2001, which builds on the US$5 billion swap arrangement made under the New Miyazawa Initiative; a US$3 billion baht swap with Thailand agreed in July 2001; a US$3 billion peso swap with the Philippines agreed in August 2001; a US$1 billion ringit swap with Malaysia in October 2001, which is further to the US$2.5 billion arrangement made under the New Miyazawa Initiative; and a US$3 billion yen–renmin swap with China agreed in March 2002.

In addition, the Japanese government is negotiating swap arrangements with Indonesia and Singapore. Finally, other swap agreements have been made or are under negotiation by other members of the ASEAN plus Three, as in the case of the agreement made between China and Thailand.

In essence, the Chiang-Mai Initiative has bolstered the ability of the East Asian economies to respond to any future crisis without the need to rely totally on the IMF. As it stands, only 10 per cent of a swap can take place without an IMF agreement being in place or being negotiated, which in effect means the IMF is still in a position to establish the conditionalities for the swaps to take place. Despite the earlier rejection of the AMF proposal, moreover, the IMF has become more sympathetic to East Asian cooperation and now regards the emergence of this regional mechanism as 'useful' (*Far Eastern Economic Review*, 25 July 2002: 24). It is nevertheless important to note that, irrespective of the potential for the IMF to continue to play a central role in the financial governance of East Asia, the BSAs represented a significant change in the potential role of East Asian states in another crisis.

To start with, the ability of an affected economy to call on a number of BSAs simultaneously (or one after the other), together with its rights under the original ASAs, means that once all BSAs have been negotiated a substantial sum, upwards of US$35 billion, will be available through the combination of ASAs, the New Miyazawa Initiative and the BSAs. Second, as can be illustrated by the case of Thailand, the combined borrowing can amount to more than four times the sum available through its IMF quota of US$1.36 billion, with other East Asian countries also being able to draw on amounts several times their IMF quota. And third, once the BSAs are formally in place, the amounts can be readily changed, as has happened in swap agreements between members of the G10 (Institute of International Economics 2002: 11–13).

Finally, whilst the future of the CMI remains unclear, it is important to note the potential for these new BSAs to be linked, thereby creating a system of financial governance in East Asia similar to Japan's original AMF proposal. There is also the possibility that, in an actual crisis situation, the ASEAN plus Three will move away from IMF conditionalities and establish its own conditions for the swaps. At the very least these new financial arrangements are 'pathbreaking' and 'provide a focus for concrete negotiations, periodic reviews among officials within the region, and the basis for building serious policy dialogue' (Institute of International Economics 2002: 19). In this way, the ASEAN plus Three is emerging as a new site of governance for the regional political economy, with the ASA, New Miyazawa Initiative and the CMI providing the basis for strengthening multilateral, regional cooperation, enhancing the ability of East Asian economies to withstand a future crisis without relying as heavily on the IMF.

The impact of free trade agreements on governance

At the same time as Japan is using the ASEAN plus Three as an emerging site of governance at the regional level in East Asia, the signing of a Free Trade Agreement

(FTA) with Singapore in January 2002, and the ongoing negotiations to sign FTAs with Mexico, South Korea and others now taking place (Dent 2003), symbolize how Japanese policymakers are deploying international agreements to reshape the governance of the regional *and* national political economies. The 'Agreement Between Japan and the Republic of Singapore for a New-Age Economic Partnership', as the FTA is formally known, was the first FTA signed by Japan, and represents a major change from the previous policy of promoting multilateral trade under the General Agreement on Tariffs and Trade and its newly created successor, the World Trade Organization (WTO). Singapore and Japan are important trade partners, with Japan standing as Singapore's third most important partner in 1999, and Singapore ranked as Japan's ninth most important partner in 1999, suggesting the FTA is expected to strengthen these links even further. Given that Singapore is not a significant exporter of agricultural products, the FTA has only limited implications for the agricultural sector, with a small increase in Japan's commitments to zero-tariffs above those made under the WTO. As Munakata (2002) argues, however, the inclusion of agriculture is nevertheless significant:

> In essence, the Singapore deal created a 'pinhole' for Japan's policymakers in the barriers surrounding Japan's agricultural 'sanctuary'. Traditionally, the Japanese farm lobby would never have allowed any concessions on agriculture, no matter how small.
>
> The goal was clear: the Japanese negotiators wanted to establish a principle that entire sectors of the economy can no longer be placed off limits by domestic interests fundamentally opposed to free trade agreements.

Specifically, the Japan–Singapore FTA aims to bring down barriers to economic interactions and to facilitate trade in goods, eliminating all tariffs on Japanese exports to Singapore and tariffs on 94 per cent of Japan's imports from Singapore; facilitate the movement of people, in business, science and tourism; develop human resources; facilitate trade in services, moving beyond the two countries' commitment under the WTO; facilitate the flow of capital and information, including investments, intellectual property (e.g. patents), financial services, information and communication technology; and the development of cooperation among small and medium size enterprises. As the above makes clear, the agreement is a comprehensive attempt to develop a wide range of economic relationships between the two countries (MOFA 2002b).

MOFA suggests Japan gains both economic and political advantages by signing FTAs (MOFA 2002a):

(1) Economic advantages
FTAs lead to the expansion of import and export markets, the conversion to more efficient industrial structures, and the improvement of the competitive environment. In addition, FTAs help reduce the likelihood of economic frictions becoming political issues, and help expand and harmonize existing trade-related regulations and systems.

(2) Political and diplomatic advantages

FTAs increase Japan's bargaining power in WTO negotiations, and the results of FTA negotiations could influence and speed up WTO negotiations. The deepening of economic interdependence gives rise to a sense of political trust among countries that are parties to these agreements, expanding Japan's global diplomatic influence and interests.

Similarly, Keidanren (the Japan Federation of Economic Organizations), which has played a particularly active role in promoting FTAs, points to a number of advantages for Japan in signing FTAs. As illustrated by the organization's, 'Urgent Call for Active Promotion of Free Trade Agreements' issued in July 2000, Keidanren sees FTAs as useful to expand business opportunities, eliminate the competitive disadvantage suffered by Japanese companies compared to those of Europe and North America, promote intraregional competition and domestic reform in Japan, and complement WTO trade and investment liberalization and rule-making (Keidanren 2000). As pointed out in Keidanren's earlier 'Report on the Possible Effects of a Japan–Mexico Free Trade Agreement on Japanese Industry (Keidanren 1999), moreover, Japan's exclusion from membership in the North American Free Trade Agreement (NAFTA) and the EU disadvantages Japanese firms: whereas North American firms as a result of NAFTA and European firms as a result of the FTA between Mexico and the EU can export both products to the Mexican market and parts to production plants for export from *maquiladoras* to the North American and wider world market, Japanese firms face substantial tariff charges on parts and finished products (10–20 per cent for automobiles and household electrical appliances), making them less competitive internationally. Thus, eliminating such disadvantages is a major goal of the proposed FTA with Mexico. Even if Japan does not succeed in signing an FTA with Mexico, however, the FTA with Singapore may provide the possibility of entry into Mexico for Japanese firms, as Singapore and Mexico have already signed an FTA. In other words, if the opposition to opening up the Japanese agricultural market cannot be overcome in negotiating the agreement with Mexico, depending on the origins of the product in question, the FTA with Singapore might serve as a means to transform the island state into a regional export hub for Japanese manufacturers in Southeast Asia targeting the Mexican market or supplying parts to Japanese production sites in Mexico for export to the North American and wider market.

As far as the implications for the governance of the regional and national political economies are concerned, two points deserve mention. First, as Keidanren recognizes in the above report, 'Urgent Call for Active Promotion of Free Trade Agreements', FTAs provide an opportunity for Japan to 'disseminate Japanese standards internationally'. In the agreement with Singapore, for instance, the move to promote e-commerce between the two countries, as seen in the mutual recognition of digital signatures, is a step towards institutionalizing a Japanese standard for e-commerce in East Asia. The spread of Japanese standards will provide the basis for the creation of common regulatory procedures and the governance of aspects of the regional economy based on Japanese 'global standards' rather than

American 'global standards'. At the least, the regional dissemination of Japanese standards will strengthen Japan's negotiating position in any contestation over 'ruling making' at the WTO and in agreeing global standards in international negotiations.

As far as the governance of the national political economy is concerned, MOFA is clearly aware of the role FTAs can play in promoting efficiency and competition, suggesting its support for moving Japan in the direction of a greater role for market principles. The same Keidanren report similarly recognizes the utility of FTAs for promoting deregulation, restructuring and the promotion of market competition in Japan. Given the strength of the agricultural lobby, the proposed FTAs with Mexico and South Korea may not succeed. Nevertheless, the role that FTAs are seen to play in promoting deregulation and market principles demonstrates how both state and non-state actors view them as a means to help to change the balance between the state and the market in the governance of the national economy. In short, Japan's recently acquired interest in FTAs illustrates the close connection between the governance of the regional and the national political economies in East Asia.

Conclusion

The above discussion of Japan's role in emerging East Asian governance has sought to clarify how Japanese state and non-state actors have been involved in reshaping the governance of the East Asian and Japanese political economies. The regional and national implications of the discussion can be summarized as follows.

First, as far as the regional level is concerned, whilst the role of the IMF at the time of the 1997–8 crises demonstrates how material assistance from an international institution was accompanied by the promotion of neo-liberal norms as the longer term answer to East Asia's problems, both state and non-state actors have in the intervening years taken action to contest the IMF formula and sustain a pivotal role for Japan in the region, in both a material and normative sense. More specifically, not only has the financial assistance under the New Miyazawa Initiative contributed to restoring the health of the East Asian 'miracle' economies, with the affected economies by 1999 enjoying comfortable GDP growth rates – South Korea 10.9 per cent, Malaysia 6.1 per cent, Thailand 4.4 per cent (Takahashi 2003: 132) – policymakers have also placed Japan at the centre of the ASEAN plus Three, as seen in the proactive role the government has taken in signing the new BSAs. Whilst the ASEAN plus Three's importance should not be exaggerated, the potential for the BSAs to be linked together demonstrates a regional answer to East Asian problems may emerge in future as a direct challenge to the conditionalities of the IMF. At the least, this new 'East Asian' grouping of states can be expected to play an increasingly important role as an emerging new site for the governance of the regional political economy.

As far as the national level is concerned, the above discussion has demonstrated how both MOFA and Keidanren are clearly aware of the potential for FTAs to play a role in restructuring the Japanese political economy. The signing of the FTA with Singapore can thus be viewed as integral to the attempt to undermine the power of the agricultural lobby as part of the reshaping of the system of national governance in Japan. It is true that, in the case of Singapore, only a small amount of trade in agricultural products takes place, but as we have seen a small increase in Japan's commitment to the elimination of agricultural tariffs has been made with the signing of the agreement. The extent to which FTAs can be effectively used to undermine the power of the agricultural lobby and promote national restructuring will become clearer if the other FTAs presently under negotiation with Mexico and South Korea are completed. Thus, whilst resistance to new FTAs can be expected, especially from the agricultural lobby, the role of both state and non-state actors in either promoting or contesting the institutionalization of neo-liberal norms suggests Japan remains split over the role of the state and the market in the political economy, as illustrated by the contrastive case of MOFA and MAFF. But whatever the outcome of the struggle over national reform, the balance between the role of the state and the market in the governance of the Japanese political economy will be struck not only in the national, but also the regional, context. In this can be seen the close connection between the international and national levels of governance in East Asia.

References

Bello, Walden (1998) 'The end of a "miracle". Speculation, foreign capital dependence and the collapse of the Southeast Asian economies', *The Multinational Monitor*, 19 (1 and 2). Available on-line at:
http://www.hartford-hwp.com/archives/54/124.html, accessed 10 December 2002.

Bernard, Mitchell and Ravenhill, John (1995) 'Beyond product cycles and flying geese: regionalization, hierarchy, and the industrialization of East Asia', *World Politics* 45, 2: 171–209.

Breslin, Shaun and Hook, Glenn D. (2002) *Microregionalism and World Order*, Basingstoke: PalgraveMacmillan.

Dent, Christopher M. (2003) 'Networking the region? The emergence and impact of Asia–Pacific bilateral free trade agreement projects', *The Pacific Review* 16, 1: 1–28.

Gilson, Julie (2002) *Asia Meets Europe: inter-regionalism and the Asia–Europe meeting*, Cheltenham: Edward Elgar.

Hatch, Walter and Yamamura, Kozo (1996) *Asia in Japan's Embrace: building a regional production alliance*, Cambridge: Cambridge University Press.

Hook, Glenn D. (1999) 'The East Asian Economic Caucus: a case of reactive subregionalism?' in Glenn D. Hook and Ian Kearns (eds) *Subregionalism and World Order*, Basingstoke: Macmillan, pp. 223–45.

Hook, Glenn D. (2002) 'The Japanese role in emerging microregionalism: the Pan-Yellow Sea Economic Zone', in Shaun Breslin and Glenn D. Hook (eds) *Microregionalism and World Order*, Basingstoke: PalgraveMacmillan, pp. 95–114.

Hook, Glenn D. and Ian Kearns (1999) *Subregionalism and World Order*, Basingstoke: Macmillan.

Hook, Glenn D., Gilson, Julie, Hughes, Christopher W. and Dobson, Hugo (2002) 'Japan and the East Asian financial crisis: patterns, motivations and instrumentalisation of Japanese regional economic diplomacy', *European Journal of East Asian Studies* 1, 2: 177–98.

Haque, M. Shamsul (2002) 'Globalization, new political economy, and governance: a Third World viewpoint', *Administrative Theory & Praxis* 24, 1: 103–24.

Hughes, Christopher W. (2000) Japanese policy and the East Asian currency crisis: abject defeat or quiet victory? *Review of International Political Economy* 7, 2: 219–53.

Institute of International Economics (2002). Available on-line at: http://www.iie.com/publications/files/chapters_preview/345/3iie3381.pdf, accessed 12 December 2002.

JETRO (Japan External Trade Organization) JETRO *Bōeki Hakusho*, Tokyo: JETRO (annual).

Jomo, K. S. (ed.) (1998) *Tigers in Trouble. Financial governance, liberalization and crises in East Asia*, London: Zed Books.

Keidanren (1999). Available on-line at: http://www.keidanren.or.jp/english/policy/pol099.html, accessed 14 December 2002.

Keidanren (2000). Available on-line at: http://www.keidanren.or.jp/english/policy/2000/033/proposal.html, accessed 14 December 2002.

Kikuchi, Tsutomu (2003) 'Regionalism and regional governance in Northeast Asia', in Fu-Kou Liu and Philippe Regnier (eds) *Regionalism in East Asia. Paradigm shifting?* London: Routledge, pp. 100–18.

Kim, Hyuk-Rae (2000) 'Fragility or continuity? Economic governance of East Asian capitalism', in Richard Robison, Mark Beeson, Kanishka Jayasuria and Hyuk-Rae Kim (eds), *Politics and Markets in the Wake of the Asian Crisis*, London: Routledge, pp. 99–115.

Kojima, Kiyoshi (2000) 'The "flying geese" model of Asian economic development: origin, theoretical extensions, and regional policy implications', *Journal of Asian Economics* 11: 375–401.

Korhonen, Pekka (1994) *Japan and the Pacific Free Trade Area*, London: Routledge.

Krauss, Ellis (2000) 'Japan, the US, and the emergence of multilateralism in Asia', *The Pacific Review* 13, 3: 473–94.

McLeod, Ross H. and Garnaut, Ross (1998) *East Asia in Crisis: from being a miracle to needing one?* London: Routledge.

MOF (Ministry of Finance) (2002). Available on-line at: http://www.mof.go.jp/english/if/chiangmai.htm, accessed 12 December 2002.

MOFA (2002a) Available on-line at: http://www.mofa.go.jp/policy/economy/fta/strategy0210.html, accessed 14 December 2002.

MOFA (2002b) Available on-line at: http://www.mofa.go.jp/region/asia-paci/singapore/agree0201.html, accessed 14 December 2002.

Munakata, Naoko (2002) Available on-line at: http://www.brook.edu/views/articles/fellows/munakata_20020710.htm, accessed 14 December 2002.

Ozawa, Terutomo (2001) 'The "hidden" side of the "flying geese" catch up model: Japan's *dirigiste* institutional set up and a deepening financial morass'. Available on-line at: http://www.gsb.columbia.edu/japan/pdf/wp193.pdf, accessed 12 December 2002.

Payne, Anthony (2005, forthcoming) 'The study of governance in a global political economy', in Nicola Phillips (ed.) *The Globalisation of International Political Economy*, Basingstoke: MacmillanPalgrave.

Pempel, T. J. (ed.) (2000) *The Politics of the Asian Economic Crisis*, Ithaca, New York: Cornell.

Ravenhill, John (2002) *APEC and the Construction of Pacific-Rim Regionalism*, Cambridge: Cambridge University Press.

Rosenau, James N. (1997) *Along the Domestic–Foreign Frontier: exploring governance in a turbulent world*, Cambridge: Cambridge University Press.

Rosenau, James N. (2000) 'The governance of fragmegration: neither a world republic nor a global interstate system', *Studia Diplomatica* 53, 5: 15–40.

Takahashi, Wataru (2003) 'The East Asian economies after the financial crisis: a role for the Japanese yen?' in Hugo Dobson and Glenn D. Hook (eds) *Japan and Britain in the Contemporary World: responses to common issues*, London: RoutledgeCurzon, pp. 131–49.

Wakamiya, Yoshibumi (1995) *Sengo Hoshu no Ajiakan*, Tokyo: Asahi Shimbunsha.

World Bank (1993) *The East Asian Miracle: economic growth and public policy*, New York: Oxford University Press.

Young, Oran R. (1994) *International Governance*, Ithaca: Cornell University Press.

3 Governance, democracy and the political economy of the Japanese state

J. A. A. Stockwin

A political system and mechanisms of governance that appeared to work well – even spectacularly well – from the 1950s to the 1980s are now widely castigated as the source of Japan's economic malaise and other policy problems.

There are, however, two different approaches to an understanding of what has happened. The first, and most widely canvassed, argument is that attempts from the early 1990s to reform the system have not been sufficiently followed through, essentially because of resistance from vested interests, and lack of leadership. The second, by contrast, says that policy failures from the early 1990s result from the partial breakdown of the existing governance system, rather than from a failure to reform it. According to this view, the old system contained within it a great deal of flexibility in its ease of communication throughout the system. Even though the location of ultimate responsibility within the system may not always have been evident, decisions taken were on the whole reasonably sensible and far-sighted. The allocative mechanisms may not have been ideally transparent, accountable or fair, but they facilitated dynamic and often effective outcomes for the Japanese political economy as a whole.

In the course of this chapter my aim is to tease out the contested and contrasting – though to some extent also overlapping – logic of these two positions. They are not, of course, merely descriptive analyses, since they suggest equally contrasting prescriptions for how such a system of governance might be beneficially reformed.

Describing the Japanese political system

Many attempts have been made to describe analytically the Japanese political system, and any comprehensive account will contain substantial abstraction from a complex and changing reality. Most descriptions start with an account of the formal, constitutional structures and proceed to delve into the workings of politics in practice – with particular emphasis on the location of power. Moreover, without giving a historical understanding of the evolution of the system, any attempt to describe it is likely to be too static and formal (for recent accounts, see Curtis 1999; Stockwin 1999; Neary 2002; Stockwin 2003: especially xii–xxi).

The formal constitutional structures that emerged from the Allied Occupation (1945–52) were constructed in reaction against the structures embedded in the

Meiji Constitution of 1889, but also embodied certain continuities with it. The two principal aspects of the 1889 Constitution that were targeted for revision were executive dominance (particularly the institution of the *Tennō*, or Emperor), and lack of democratic accountability. The second of these two problems had been compounded by a conspicuous lack of civilian control over the military, a phenomenon sometimes referred to as 'dual government'. The 1946 Constitution therefore sought to strengthen the role of a parliament (National Diet), directly elected by universal suffrage, and to entrench the institution of cabinet government, essentially on the Westminster model. Although the *Tennō* institution had been a source of great power, and the focus of a cult of personality, under the 1889 Constitution, the *Tennō* had been only marginally a personal ruler. After the war, however, Japan became a constitutional monarchy, and both the person and the institution were deprived of all political power, leading to a system where the key site of governance was different from that under the Meiji Constitution.

Under the 1946 Constitution, the electorate elects members of the House of Representatives and the House of Councillors, the former essentially determining the shape of the ensuing government and the latter having important powers of scrutiny and veto. In Japan, as in Britain, the vast majority of members of parliament belong to political parties. Parliament elects the prime minister, normally from the party holding a majority of seats. The prime minister appoints members of cabinet, who are in charge of the ministries of government, and under article 66 the prime minister and all other ministers of state must be civilians. This constitutes a major difference from the pre-war days, when the military predominated.

Up to this point, the system closely resembles the British model of cabinet government. In practice, however, it has come to differ from it in two crucial respects. First of all, from 1955 political party competition settled into a pattern of single-party dominance, with the broad-church conservative Liberal Democratic Party (LDP) winning every election for both houses of parliament until 1989, and from 1994 (after a few months out of office) remaining the dominant party in coalition governments of varying composition. As with the dominant party in other single-party-dominant systems, the LDP evolved into the central focus of patronage networks that eventually encompassed a great part of the political economy. Second, and in part for historical reasons, the central ministries of government retained substantially more power of policy initiative than is normally the case in systems based on the Westminster model. The result was the emergence of what in American parlance are called 'iron triangles', in the Japanese case linking powerful networks of influence that embrace sections of the ruling party, ministries of the bureaucracy and associated interest groups. Perhaps the most famous example of such a triangular relationship is to be found in the area of agriculture (George Mulgan 2002) but they exist to a greater or lesser extent throughout the political economy.

An important area of continuity between political practice under the 1889 and 1946 constitutions was precisely this close linkage between the political centre, the government bureaucracy and interest groups (particularly business interest groups).

The cooperation between them had become particularly intense during the 1930s, stimulated by the government's need for procurement of munitions. After a short break during the early Occupation period, this was revived from the late 1940s in the interests of facilitating and promoting rapid economic growth. Most observers would agree that, in terms of results, this worked spectacularly well between the 1950s and the 1970s, the period of Japan's 'economic miracle', suggesting that the system of governance set in place in the post-war period was able at least to deliver on the economy.

The disadvantages of this system, however, were becoming apparent even during the earlier post-war period, when political argument between the party in power and parties in opposition was couched in highly ideological terms, focusing in particular on the peace clause of the 1946 Constitution (article 9) and on the security relationship with the United States. These were indeed most important issues, but it seems arguable that undue concentration on matters of this kind had the effect of de-emphasizing national policy debate on fundamental economic and other issues between cohesive, policy-oriented political parties. Parties themselves became patronage organizations rather than competitive policy aggregators. This tendency was accentuated by a feature of the electoral system for the House of Representatives that pitted candidates of the same party against each other in the same multi-member electoral districts. Factional divisions (not only for this reason) were entrenched within at least the larger parties, and locally-oriented candidate-centred campaigning became the norm, to the detriment of party-centred, policy-oriented campaigning. Largely because of the patronage aspect, elections were also inordinately expensive for candidates and their backers. Revision of the lower house electoral system in 1994 has only partially solved this problem (Stockwin 2003: 49–57. For a more optimistic view, see Reed 2003).

The ways in which politics is conducted in Japan in the early twenty-first century are not entirely the same as they were up to the end of the 1980s. Economic stagnation that set in during the 1990s has subjected the political system as a whole to considerable strain. Moreover, the ideological polarization of the past gave way to party fragmentation, even though to a considerable extent the LDP has managed to retain its cohesiveness. What had been the principal party of opposition, the Japan Socialist Party (later Social Democratic Party), split in 1996 and was reduced to the status of a minor party. Apart from the communists, parties of opposition were either joining in coalitions with the LDP or actively positioning themselves so that the coalition option might come their way. The Democratic Party, formed in 1996 and the principal party of opposition from 1998, was both internally divided and ambiguous in its attitudes to the LDP. Policy-based competition between evenly matched parties each contending realistically for power remained as far away as ever. This might not have mattered so much had the economy been in a healthy state, but neither did the LDP-based government appear able to mount effective policies to lift the economy out of its stagnation, nor did opposition policies have a realistic chance of replacing it in power. This was partly because of the strength of LDP patronage networks, but also because no opposition party could come up with convincing alternative economic strategies.

On the other hand, the lower house general elections of November 2003 produced the best result for a single opposition party since the formation of the LDP in 1955. The Democratic Party, strengthened by its recent amalgamation with the Liberal Party led by Ozawa Ichirō, won 177 out of 480 seats, on the basis of 36.9 per cent of the total vote. While the Democrats were still far short of winning a majority (or even a plurality) of seats, they had improved their performance at every general election since their foundation. On the other hand, the party's 'Representative' (leader), Kan Naoto, had to resign in May 2004, having missed paying pension contributions some years previously, so that the immediate future of the Democratic Party seemed uncertain (*Asahi Shimbun*, 11 May 2004).

The 'failure of reform' argument

The 'failure of reform' argument is generally quite specific in prescribing changes to make governance and decision making substantially more accountable. Thus central leadership must be strengthened and lines of responsibility clarified. Specifically, the role of the prime minister should be enhanced, with the central power position of the British prime minister (Margaret Thatcher or Tony Blair) seen as a desirable model. Specifically also, the lines of responsibility should be made clearer. The prime minister and cabinet should be answerable to the electorate through elected politicians. In other words, the role of politicians within the system ought to be enhanced *vis-à-vis* the role of government officials. The way politics works should be restructured to create a situation in which government officials *implement* decisions taken by politicians with the backing of the electorate, rather than shaping or determining, in large part, the decisions themselves. This is a view which places emphasis on the need for reform to create accountability and transparency throughout the decision making process. *Perestroika* requires *glasnost*.

If the principal purpose of reform is to make politics more accountable and more transparent, a closely linked purpose is to make the economy more subject to the competitive rigours of the market. As Macpherson (who liked neither liberal democratic politics nor a capitalist economy) pointed out several years ago, you cannot have the one without the other (Macpherson 1972: 4). It has become fashionable among some observers to describe the contemporary Japanese politico-economic system as 'quasi-socialist', as in the case of David Pilling (*Financial Times*, 7 January 2003), so that the kinds of prescription earlier applied to Eastern European systems are now applied to Japan. According to this view, Japan is at a crossroads: 'It must now decide whether it wants to be like a European welfare state, with everyone getting an equal share of a gradually shrinking pie; or whether it wants to be like the US or the UK, more unequal but more dynamic, with a pie that is growing' (Mark Chiba, of UBS Warburg, Tokyo, quoted in Pilling *ibid.*).

The principal complaints of liberal-capitalist reformers concerning the Japanese system boil down to the following:

1   There is too much concern with equality, and with the strong protecting the weak. Japan is one of the most equal countries in the world in terms of income and wealth distribution, even though the inequalities may be somewhat increasing.

2   There is over-reliance on group solidarity, whereby group effort is privileged over individual effort. For instance the Nobel Prize for Chemistry was recently awarded to a mid-ranking employee of a company that did not appear to recognize his individual talents (Pilling *ibid.*). But some change is emerging, in part because of the example of foreign firms operating in Japan, including those linked with Japanese companies.

3   Competition only operates within restricted limits. In particular the 'convoy system' ensures that many companies are allowed to survive that should go to the wall if true capitalist competition were applied. The banks have played a crucial role in this system's perpetuation, lending to companies whose long- term prospects may in hard-nosed terms be dubious. (In fact, of course, the convoy approach to regulation is now far less prevalent than before, even though banks have presented a serious obstacle to radical change in this practice.)

4   Companies traditionally 'hoard' workers, many of whom are on permanent or semi-permanent contracts, and are reluctant to release them when economic times are bad. As a result, unemployment has been low and company solidarity has been remarkably high. But increasing economic pressures are making this system more difficult to sustain.

5   In politics, there has been a diffusion of responsibility and it is often difficult to ascertain where decision making is actually taking place.

6   Central power (especially the power of the prime minister) needs to be strengthened to enable the blocking position of manifold vested interests to be effectively combated. Koizumi Junichirō, the present prime minister, has had some limited success in achieving this, but on many issues entrenched vested interests are proving too powerful for him to overcome (for an elegant exposition of this view, see George Mulgan 2002).

7   Among the most significant concentrations of power constituting a barrier to political accountability are the well organized and internally loyal policymaking machines of government ministries. The apparently radical reorganization of the ministries that took place in January 2001 substantially reduced the numbers of ministries, but had rather limited effect on the strength and scope of bureaucratic power.

The long recession in the economy, which has persisted for much of the period since 1991, has tarnished the lustre of the Japanese system of political economy. The much more rapid growth of the Chinese economy over the past two decades has created a sense internationally that China is 'dynamic' whereas Japan is 'static' or 'stagnant' economically. Even though this may be belied by the continuing strength of foreign investment in Japan, concern both with failings in the Japanese system of political economy and with long-term demographic trends in Japan (the 'ageing society') have tended to create a general sense of pessimism about economic prospects.

'Good old system' arguments

The Japanese system of governance, however, used to be regarded with respect and admiration by observers outside Japan as well as within it, during the periods in which it was seen to be succeeding.

Perhaps the best known example of this kind of literature was Ezra Vogel's *Japan as Number One: Lessons for America*, published in 1979. In retrospect, it seems likely that a principal motivation for writing the book was to provide a 'wake up call' for the United States, demoralized by defeat in Vietnam and suffering from a sluggish economy. If there is one perception that appears to underlie the argument of the book, it is that the Japanese approach to political economy is better organized, and more consciously thought through, than that of the United States. The following extract makes this clear:

> Japan, unlike Western countries, has consciously examined and restructured all traditional institutions on the basis of rational considerations. America's political system was designed almost two hundred years ago for a pre-modern agricultural society, and it has not undergone any consciously designed major reorganizations since then. New organizations have grown up piecemeal, with no overall conceptualization of their desirability. Japanese institutions have undergone two major explicit reexaminations in the past 110 years to determine which institutions are desirable. . . . no country is more experienced in evaluating the effectiveness of existing institutions and in creating or reshaping institutions by rational planning to meet future needs.
>
> (Vogel 1979: 4–5)

Vogel recommends that the United States adopt a similar approach, and it is instructive to note which Japanese institutions he thinks (or thought in 1979) the US might take on board. In his concluding chapter, he lists four of these:

1 *An industrial and trade policy*. In Vogel's view: 'Japan accepts the ultimate value of market forces, but aims to hasten institutional adjustment to long-term trends while easing the human readjustments necessitated by changing economic forces' (Vogel 1979: 232).
2 *A small core of permanent high-level bureaucrats*. He argues: 'Great issues require long time horizons and great continuity before solutions are found; it is not possible to pursue long-term policies when all key personnel change every two to four years . . . bright, noncareer outsiders . . . cannot match a small core of highly able, dedicated professionals . . . who have been given the best possible training, have been exposed to the most progressive thinking of private and governmental groups . . . and have been seasoned as junior officials working on problems they will face as they acquire greater responsibilities' (Vogel 1979: 233).

3   *A communitarian vision.* Inveighing against excessive application of adversary relations and regulation by outside bodies lacking responsibility for the organizations they regulate, he argued: 'The Japanese have been in the forefront of making large organizations something that people enjoy. Americans tend to think of the organization as an imposition, as an outside force restraining the free individual. Japanese from an early age are taught the values of group life' (Vogel 1979: 235).

4   *Aggregation of interests.* He admires the ways in which interests in Japan cooperate with each other. As he puts it: 'Aggregation of interests works well when representatives of different groups meet frequently without immediate business in order to build up friendship and trust which become invaluable at the time of difficult negotiations. . . . When various groups send representatives to negotiate, they do not use attorneys but 'go-betweens', intermediaries who are known for their capacity to gain the trust and confidence of all groups because of their personal reputation and social position. . . . Americans may more easily win an argument, but the Japanese more easily win an agreement' (Vogel 1979: 237).

With the benefit of hindsight, certain comments, positive and negative, seem relevant to Vogel's four favoured Japanese characteristics. On the first, his advocacy of industrial and trade policy has become deeply unfashionable since the 1980s, but we should remember how powerful it seemed in its day. British experience since 1997 suggests that there may be innovative ways of combining market economics with government-led planning for key national aims. On the second, since Vogel wrote, high profile scandals and policy failures have dented the prestige of the Japanese bureaucracy. Even so, sections of it have been impressive by most international comparisons. Replacing officials every time that the central government changes is a characteristic of the US system, but not of the British, which is based on the practice of a permanent civil service. Even this, however, has recently suffered erosion with the introduction of short-term and contract positions, and a great increase in the number of separately appointed ministerial advisers. The advantages of a permanent civil service, professionally equipped to serve governments of different ideological colouring, have come to be underestimated, and are due for renewed appreciation. The problem with the Japanese civil service has been its symbiotic relationship with a single ruling party, and the network of interests it represents. The most powerful stimulus to bureaucratic efficiency is the knowledge that the political masters may really be replaced as the result of elections, and that a new government, with new thinking and a clear mandate from the electorate, will be examining critically the performance of its civil servants.

Vogel's third and fourth recommendations are less persuasive from our current perspective, but not entirely without merit. Concerning the third, there is a core of truth in his argument that organizational dynamism rather than self-centred individualism drive performance in Japanese organizations, and that the system works. This model, however, has suffered some erosion in the past two decades. The view that large organizations in Japan are 'enjoyable' is given a jaundiced examination by Kamata, in his account of life in a car factory (Kamata 1983). There is some truth even now in his fourth recommendation, about aggregation of interests, but even he admits that minority groups, women, foreigners and non-conformist Japanese citizens tend to lose out in such a system (Vogel 1979: 238–45).

A number of other scholars have seen merit in the political economy of Japan as it emerged from the late 1940s to the late 1980s. One of these is David Williams, who in his book *Japan: Beyond the end of history* (1994), argued that the Japanese system was both theoretically and in practical terms distinct from that of any Western state. He traced it back to the ideas of the nineteenth-century German writer, Friedrich List, who argued that the state had a vital role to play in the promotion of development. Japan, Williams maintained, had put into practice the Listian prescriptions with spectacular success.

The Japanese model, however, was more than just a successful version of a state-led political economy. In Ronald Dore's terms, whereas in an American-type system transactions are mostly contract-based, in Japan contracts are less important since transactions tend to be 'relational'. Dore went so far as to see advantages in the practice of *dangō* (usually translated into English as 'rigged bidding'), whereby local authorities would award contracts to bidders favoured because of long personal relationships. This was because, at least in a society that carefully fostered relationships, transactions emerging from the rich soil of personal contact and knowledge were likely to be more satisfactory than those based on cold contract or impersonal scrutiny of sealed bids (Ronald Dore, Lecture, Oxford, 8 November 2001).

Dore's view has much in common with the arguments of Bouissou and Pombeni, comparing the political systems of Japan and Italy. They argue that in both countries a dominant party has shared the benefits of economic growth among 'historically closed sectors of society'. They call this 'redistributive regulated party-rule', and argue that in both countries such a system has contributed to economic growth and to social cohesion (Bouissou and Pombeni 2001: 545–67).

Both Dore and the Bouissou/Pombeni duo admit that the system is either changing, or is likely to change, in the direction of contract and 'Western-style' accountability. But they separately admit this with a tinge of regret for a system they believe was both original and had merit.

Many contemporary observers, influenced by the US-based globalization model, are inclined to dismiss such views as anachronistic. Indeed, scathing commentary on the proponents of any kind of socialistic or corporatist model of political economy (e.g. Jospin in France or Schröder in Germany) has become extremely widespread (see Vernon Bogdanor, obituary of Roy Jenkins, *Observer*, 12 January 2003. Bogdanor sees Tony Blair and Charles Kennedy as contenders for Jenkins' mantle of modernized liberalism, which he appears to admire). On a recent stay in Tokyo the present writer was told by a senior university political scientist that any scheme of political reform in Japan needed to be 'adjusted to an American standard' (Itō Daiichi, private conversation, September 2002).

'Unnecessary (and botched) reform' arguments

It is therefore interesting to note the appearance of a contesting set of views, holding that rather than the failure of reform, it is the partial breakdown of the old system that is to blame for current problems. On the face of it, it might seem that this is merely an exercise in reactionary conservatism, motivated by nostalgia or by loss of advantages caused by undesired change. The argument, however, has some substance, and may be broken down into the following elements:

1   The era of coalition government since 1993 has created political instability and rendered party politics less comprehensible to the electorate. In an unstable political situation many politicians have been clearly revealed as venal, opportunistic and self-serving. This in turn has contributed to increasing political apathy and declining turnout at elections. The era of LDP monopoly of governmental office at least had the advantage of presenting the electorate with clear choices between parties with differing policy perspectives and backers, even though many electors voted on personality, rather than party, lines.

2   The reform of the House of Representatives electoral system put in place in 1994 has been largely a failure in terms of its aims. The numerically predominant single-member constituencies were expected to give the electorate a clear choice, based on party policy rather than personality and pork-barrel. Policy aggregation, centred on large parties having a national and clearly articulated vision, would contest elections. *Kōenkai* (personal support machines at constituency level) would be a thing of the past. The residual seats elected by proportional representation from regional blocs, would permit representation from minority parties, but without allowing them to overwhelm the system. In practice, little of this has been realized. The new system has not produced competitive party politics of the type envisaged, as parties other than the LDP have found effective policy aggregation largely beyond them. Elections continue to be fought on personality grounds and if there is a reduction in money politics (in any case an uncertain proposition) it is more a result of tightened anti-corruption laws than of single-member electoral districts. *Kōenkai* remain as prevalent as ever, and have increased in size with the need to gain at least a plurality in order to win in a single-member constituency. Attempts have been made to preserve the interests of sitting members by making it possible for the results in proportional representation blocs to depend on candidates' scores in single-member districts (for details, see Stockwin 1999: 130–1). Finally, even though in the redrawing of constituency boundaries the notorious malapportionment problem had been addressed, the discrepancy in the value of votes remains substantially more than two to one at the extremes, seriously disadvantaging the cities over the countryside.

3   Under the old system the opposition parties had little chance of coming to power (though there was a window of opportunity during the 1970s), but despite their many weaknesses and divisions, they contrived to present an

alternative vision of society that was recognizable by the electorate. In particular, they succeeded over a long period in elevating issues of peace and security to a central position in political debate. While they could not exercise political power as such at central level, they were able to exert significant veto power over constitutional revision, and at times over other policy initiatives emanating from government. In 1994, however, Murayama Tomiichi, the first socialist prime minister since 1948, abandoned his party's opposition to the Self-Defence Forces and the Japan–US Mutual Security Treaty, as well as to the compulsory use of national symbols (anthem and flag) in schools. After 'selling the pass' on these issues, the socialists then disintegrated and re-formed in such a fashion that it was difficult to distinguish any of the non-communist opposition from the LDP.

4   The weakening of the government bureaucracy was billed as necessary in order to enhance political accountability by placing more power in the hands of politicians. During the 1990s, however, it actually led to a reduction in policymaking efficiency in some areas of policy. With the political confusion prevalent in that period, communication between the LDP and government ministries ran less smoothly than previously, without a concomitant improvement in the policymaking capacity of ruling party politicians (Hori 2003). On the other hand, since the amalgamation of ministries into 'super-ministries' in January 2001, and the formation of the Koizumi administration in April of the same year, communication between politicians and bureaucrats has further evolved, arguably towards greater efficiency.

Taking these arguments together, they add up to a general sense that the economic and other difficulties faced by Japan since the early 1990s may plausibly be attributed to the efforts made to reform the system rather than to the failure of such reform efforts. In this view, it would have been better to stick to the old system, fine tuning it rather than seeking to scrap it and start again according to new principles (for instance, Dore, *ibid.*, although Dore does not subscribe to all elements in this picture. See also Bouissou and Pombeni 2001). In this reading of the 'old' political system, its key elements were single-party dominance, bureaucratic initiative, dispersed leadership combined with continuous and intensive efforts to seek consensus, and a complex network of inter-relationships linking politicians, government officials and interest groups of all kinds. The principal role of opposition was not to provide an alternative government but to keep a check on government excesses through the use of veto power. In terms of political economy, government played a role of strategic guidance in an economy characterized by a combination of fierce competitiveness and readiness to conform. By a variety of mechanisms (cross-shareholding, exclusive sub-contracting relations, etc.), the private sector behaved in ways reminiscent of a controlled economy, but with the crucial difference that commitment to the firm and competitive drive were relentlessly fostered.

Among these characteristics, single-party dominance is one that has proved most difficult to change. Even though the Democratic Party did well at the November

2003 elections, its ascent is fragile, and being severely tested as of May 2004. Whatever the reality may be, the assumption that it is advantageous for the health of the polity for one large catch-all party to remain continuously in power over long periods is deeply entrenched. Related to this is the perceived advantage that long-term tenure of office creates dynamic synergies throughout the politico-economic system. Government ministries, knowing that they can rely on essentially the same set of politicians being in power up to and beyond any realistic planning horizon, can arguably construct plans envisaged for years and even decades ahead. Interest groups, knowing that the structure of politics is unlikely to change, readily understand where to plug into the system, and can plan accordingly. Given the dynamic elements in the economy (loyalty to the organization, an intense drive to maximize market share, etc.), dangers of systemic sclerosis are allegedly minimized. It must be added, however, that the preservation of such a system always depended on the LDP remaining firmly in power. When the LDP was out of office briefly in 1993–4, it found some of its parliamentarians moving to other parties, and civil servants had little difficulty in establishing links with the non-LDP politicians that were (temporarily) in power. Civil servants were also busy making contact with the Democratic Party after the November 2003 general elections.

On the other hand, there is a serious weakness inherent in such a set of arrangements. Long-term planning may be facilitated by stability and predictability in the domestic system, but may be thrown off course by unexpected changes in the external (international) environment. Although precise causal connections are difficult to establish, it seems highly plausible that the ending of the Cold War and collapse of the Soviet Union around the beginning of the 1990s constituted a change in external circumstances that upset some of the long-term planning mechanisms and expectations of government. Among other things it led to a marked increase in the international dominance (both economic and strategic) of the United States, leaving Japan more exposed and less able to project her own model of political economy. The Gulf crisis and war of 1990–1 was a famous example of Japanese government failure to respond adequately (according to international expectations) to a significant change in the external environment. To some considerable extent the breakdown in the established party system that occurred from the early- to mid-1990s took place as a result of the disappearance of the Soviet 'enemy' and the inadequacy of the Japanese response to international demands over the Gulf conflict. The thinking of Ozawa Ichirō was deeply affected by his reflections on the Gulf conflict experience, although domestic political issues and factional conflict within the LDP were of great importance also in explaining his group's defection from the ruling party in 1993. More recent examples include the panic induced in 1998 by the firing of a North Korean missile across Japan, political pressures in 2002–3 brought about by the prospect of a North Korean nuclear weapons programme, and widespread policy paralysis in the face of increasingly insistent globalizing trends. Response to the impact of a resurgent Chinese economy may also perhaps be significant.

Other writers have convincingly argued that the various attempts at reform so far have been rather inadequate and ineffectual, where not actually misguided

(George Mulgan 2002). The reforms since Koizumi became Prime Minister in April 2001 have attracted widespread interest, but they actually follow on from reforms initiated during the time in office of his predecessors Hashimoto Ryūtarō and Obuchi Keizō. The result is that the Prime Minister and Cabinet have somewhat enhanced capacity to affect policy, the bureaucracy has been reshuffled with mixed results, but the political opposition, despite the advance of the Democratic Party in November 2003, is still remote from office, with the two parties constituting the coalition government having established an effective system of electoral pacts to sustain their collective parliamentary majority. Moreover, decision making within a coalition government is more complex than in the period of single-party rule.

A proposal for reform

How, then, might the Japanese politico-economic system be reformed so as to overcome the problems of recent years, and what might these reforms imply for governance?

The following proposal may possibly be seen as idealistic, but is put forward as an attempt to describe the outlines of a modernized and essentially liberal system, adapted to a Japanese context and maintaining the positive aspects of Japanese political economy as it has developed in modern times (but especially since 1945). The perspective underlying this proposal rejects the globalizing principle of 'one size fits all', while at the same time being disinclined to accept the more radical propositions of Japanese exceptionalism. If exceptionalism, in the shape of *Nihonjinron*, was a favourite butt of criticism in the self-confident 1980s, it may be globalization as applied to Japan that merits concerted critical scrutiny in the problematic 2000s.

There are, of course, clear advantages in a strategy of conforming to globalizing trends, or testing proposals 'to an American standard'. The efficiencies and dynamism associated with clear lines of political accountability, strong leadership by individual political leaders, free market economics, Schumpeter's principle of 'creative destruction', free trade across international boundaries, flexible hiring and firing of labour, and so on, are impressive. (It has to be admitted, however, that not even the United States follows all of these principles all of the time.).

On the other hand, it needs to be recognized that in Japan we are not dealing with a Soviet-style system of state monopoly of the means of production, with ubiquitous central control over people's lives. Policies were nowhere near as socialistic as, for instance, in India. The Japanese system had socialist and corporatist features, and was also in its heyday impressively dynamic, competitive and socially responsible. It managed to combine rapid economic growth with a capacity to distribute the fruits of that growth in an equitable fashion. It combined loyalty to the goals of the enterprise with a high level of job security. Provision of social welfare and education presented problems, but came to compare well with that of many other industrially advanced countries. For the most part job security (especially among the 'shock troops' of permanently employed workers and managers in large firms) did not erode – perhaps even enhanced – economic dynamism. This appears to be contrary to the precepts of classical economics, but this was the kind of dynamic that operated. The system was indeed ruthless in certain ways (for instance in relation to casual workers and to firms in exclusive sub-contracting relationships with larger firms), but in terms of creating an economic surplus over a sustained period it was highly successful.

We therefore accept that merits existed (and exist) in the Japanese system of political economy, but also find a pressing need to modernize it, taking into account globalizing pressures. Whereas most commentary hitherto has taken a stand either for or against 'reform to an American standard', we suggest that the way forward is to combine features of both. The following are our specific proposals:

1   A capable, professional, self-confident, even elitist, government bureaucracy has been one of the strengths of the Japanese system, and though it needs to be made more accountable, it should not be emasculated. Its reputation since the 1990s has been harmed by a number of corruption scandals and by manifest policy failures, particularly in relation to the banking system. Parts of it suffer from too close (sometimes corrupt) relationships with interest groups, resulting in colossal waste of public funds on such things as construction projects and subsidies for inefficient industries, firms and farming enterprises. Plainly, a scalpel needs to be taken to such problems, and wielded effectively, though there may be areas here where the social welfare aspect should be taken into account. It seems unlikely that the scalpel will be wielded to much effect by an LDP-dominated government, which will take us to our fourth proposal.

2   An important aspect of the system has been networks of interests throughout the system. These may have at times a corrupt aspect, but at the same time they have been rapid and effective transmitters of information and ideas. As creators of consensus between different groups and interests (including government interests) they play an extremely valuable role. On the other hand, they sometimes come together to form obstructive nodules of veto power against needed reform. Networks, in other words, can be highly valuable and constructive, but adequate countervailing power to their excessive influence needs also to be fostered in order to contest any veto power (Amyx 2004).

3   For this reason, among others, central leadership needs to be strengthened, including in its capacity to overrule obstructive interest networks. To some extent this is happening under Koizumi, with his enhancement of the powers of prime minister and cabinet. On this point we strongly support the efforts of the reformers, though accountability is also crucial, and this can best be provided by the prospect of a change of party or parties in power.

4   This is perhaps our most controversial proposal, though some, even in Japan, would see it as a natural progression. Against the views of much elite opinion in Japan at the present time, we believe that the era of single-party dominance (even in coalition arrangements) ought to be brought to an end. The most valuable contribution of the LDP to the health of the Japanese political economy would be to dissolve itself. Rather than a competitive political party,

the LDP over its decades in power has become an entrenched political machine with its tentacles extending throughout the system. It is a permanent 'guiding force' in politics, rather on the model of the Communist Party of the former Soviet Union (CPSU). Even though the nature of the political economy is such that it controls far less than did the CPSU, it is widely regarded as *the* political power centre. Perhaps the greatest missed opportunity of recent Japanese politics is the premature resignation of the Hosokawa Cabinet in April 1994. With the LDP out of power, it suffered a spate of defections by its parliamentarians, and to its horror, government officials were quick to establish links with the parties of the Hosokawa coalition government. In retrospect it seems clear that had the Hosokawa cabinet lasted for, say, three to four years, with the LDP kept out of power, that would have resulted in the gradual atrophy of its machine. Starved of the oxygen of power, it would have lost members, lost enthusiasm and perhaps split.

The most problematic part of this package is its final item. What would (or should) replace a system of governance based centrally on LDP single-party dominance? In broad terms our answer is that it should be replaced by a system that would readily permit the substitution of one set of politicians by another. Rather than saying 'alternating party politics', the idea of sets of politicians able to replace each other in power encapsulates the essence of the proposal. This could be a system centred on two major parties competing with each other, or it could be alternative coalitions (for the complexities of LDP alliance politics, see George Mulgan 2003: 172–4). It should not be the current situation where minor parties join with the single major party (LDP) as marginal participants in power, and where there are occasional shifts in the identity of these participants.

What is the rationale for such a package? It would be designed to ensure two desiderata: on the one hand, continuity and long-term planning (in which a reformed bureaucracy would play a key role, but with proper political direction), and on the other accountability and renewal. By building on the long-established skills of the government bureaucracy, a long-term vision and essential systemic stability would be preserved. By revamping the party system into one where changes of party or parties in power were not only possible but also expected by the electorate, the current power holders would be constantly on notice that they had to perform effectively and accountably or the electorate would collectively decide to replace them in power. Thus the strengths of the bureaucracy would be harnessed to parties whose tenure of office could not be expected to be permanent, thus inhibiting the formation of stagnant (and sometimes corrupt) linkages.

The second and third prerequisites – maintenance of smooth communication networks, and effective central leadership structures – would be necessary conditions to make the first and fourth items work. We need to recognize, however, that they are not easy to achieve. A party (or parties) in power on a limited expected tenure would need access to strong central leadership structures to effect its programme, for which it would be responsible and accountable in a real, as well as a legal, sense. In order to put its programme into practice it would need to use effective communication channels with the bureaucracy, interests and society in general. For the most part, these channels and networks exist already, but have often been misused for corrupt or semi-clandestine purposes.

The final question is a practical one: what might be an effective strategy for realizing this package, and especially for creating a realistic likelihood of alternative sets of politicians replacing each other in power? This is a difficult and perplexing question. Japan, since 1945, has seen repeated failure of efforts to create a viable party of opposition or coalition of opposition parties (for the best analysis of these efforts, see Johnson, 2000). For many years the Japan Socialist Party (later Social Democratic Party) was much the largest party of opposition to the LDP, but after its heyday in the late 1950s when briefly it seemed it might break the mould of politics, it stagnated and showed little sign of really working to come to power at national level. In the 1990s the most promising attempt to form a viable party of opposition was the New Frontier Party (*Shinshintō*), formed by Ozawa Ichirō in December 1994, which appeared to be mounting a serious challenge to the LDP in 1995. But it was merely a coalition of disparate elements, including the former Clean Government Party (*Kōmeitō*), which never fully merged its organization into this composite party. Riddled by internal contradictions and personality squabbles, it flew apart at the end of December 1997. Since then the Democratic Party has in some senses replaced what used to be the JSP/SDP (though this is a slight simplification of a more complex situation). It has made substantial electoral progress, as we have seen, but it suffers from internal difficulties and has a way to go before it could replace the LDP. The Japan Communist Party (*Nihon Kyōsantō*), is a constant element on the political scene. Its great advantage is that it has a platform that is clearly distinct from that of the major parties, including the LDP, and is a generator of policy ideas. But it continues to be supported by less than 10 per cent of the electorate, so that in so far as it will not join coalitions with other parties (an attitude that may be changing), it does not constitute a viable alternative. It suffered a severe reverse at the general elections of November 2003.

The LDP, aided by the electoral system for the House of Representatives, continues to win close to a majority of seats, which it can then supplement by the addition of those of its minor coalition partners, to form a clear majority. This situation seems unlikely to change, barring some catastrophe. Therefore, the best chance to arrive at a system based on the possibility of changing the party or parties in power would be a major split in the LDP. Manifestly, the LDP is a coalition of disparate interests and views. The Koizumi regime has deeply split the party between Koizumi-style reformers and protectionist conservatives. The possibility of Koizumi being frustrated in his reform programme by the conservatives and breaking away to form a new party together with elements from other parties has been present since the start of his government. The fact that it has not happened may reflect the fact that he thought he could realize his programme by dominating the existing LDP, or it may reflect a lack of wholehearted commitment to reform. Koizumi has consolidated his leadership since September 2003, so that splitting the LDP seems an unlikely option for the near future.

More generally, it would be important that the new parties that emerged from a radical party realignment should reflect genuine divisions on policy and on type of electoral backing. Most of the current parties are as much divided internally as they are between themselves and other parties. The types of division most easy to envisage are between cities and the countryside, between open economy and protectionism, between redistribution to create equality and allowing the market free rein on distribution, between what Ozawa calls a 'normal state' defence policy (similar to that of European NATO members) and pacifism/defence of the 1946 Constitution, and between young and older age groups. The male/female divide could hardly constitute the basis of a division between major parties, but it no doubt correlates with divergence of attitude on some of the issues mentioned above. Feminism emerges sporadically as a force in Japanese politics, particularly in circumstances of substantial unemployment and economic recession. The popularity of the outspoken Tanaka Makiko, for instance, led to her appointment as foreign minister in the first Koizumi cabinet, although scandals and policy misjudgements produced her dismissal.

The strongly personalistic machine politics that has characterized much electioneering practice since the war is an obstacle to the kinds of outcome adumbrated above. This is also a part of the explanation for both intra-party factionalism and for the inherently fissiparous nature of parties, particularly those out of power. This, however, may perhaps give us a clue to the secret of creating the politics of alternation in power. It is one of the paradoxes of Japanese politics that whereas until the early 1990s opposition parties fragmented and proliferated with little apparent sense of the advantages of solidarity, the LDP, despite organized internal factionalism, scarcely ever split. The splits of 1993 changed that situation, but it suggests that power is a great unifier, in Japanese political conditions.

Perhaps the creation of rough electoral parity between two parties (or close coalitions of parties) would impose the kind of discipline of power (or discipline of the anticipation of power) that would be needed for the creation of a stable party system having a real possibility of alternation. Admittedly, political history since 1993 is not particularly encouraging in this regard, but the transformation of conservative politics after the LDP was formed in 1955 might suggest the potency of power possession in stabilizing a party. The 2003 amalgamation of the Democratic and Liberal parties may be significant in this regard.

The current paradox of Japanese politics is that disillusionment with the LDP (as distinct from its current leader) is widespread, but the assumption that it will remain in power is still strong. But while it stays in power in its present form, the prospects for a healthy reconstruction of Japanese politics, and still more, of the political economy, are dim. The Republic of Korea and the Republic of China (Taiwan) have both experienced changes of party in power since they established democratic politics in the late 1980s or early 1990s. Discussions between the present writer and senior members of the Kuomintang (KMT) of Taiwan, and the Hannaradang (Grand National Party) of South Korea, in 2001 and 2002, showed that they scarcely regarded their having being removed from power in a general election as a natural part of the political process! Nevertheless, if these two young democracies, similar in their political culture to Japan, can achieve this, why cannot Japan, a much more mature democracy, follow their example?

References

Amyx, Jennifer (2004), *Japan's Financial Crisis: institutional rigidity and reluctant change*, Princeton, NJ: Princeton University Press.

Bouissou, Jean-Marie, and Paolo, Pombeni (2001) 'Grandeur et décadence de la "partitocracie redistributive régulée": L'évolution du système politique au Japon et Italie depuis la guerre', *Revue Française de Science Politique* 51, 4 (août): 545–67.

Curtis, Gerald L. (1999) *The Logic of Japanese Politics*, New York: Columbia University Press.

George Mulgan, Aurelia (2002) *Japan's Failed Revolution: Koizumi and the politics of economic reform*, Canberra: Asia Pacific Press.

George Mulgan, Aurelia (2003) 'Agricultural policy and agricultural policymaking: perpetuating the status quo', in Jennifer Amyx and Peter Drysdale (eds), *Japanese Governance: beyond Japan Inc.*, London: Routledge, pp. 170–93.

Hori, Harumi (2003) 'Changes in the Japanese political system after 1993: incapacitated cooperation between the Liberal Democratic Party and the Ministry of Finance', unpublished doctoral dissertation, University of Oxford.

Johnson, Stephen (2000) *Opposition Politics in Japan: strategies under a one-party dominant regime*, London: Routledge.

Kamata, Satoshi (1983) *Japan in the Passing Lane: an insider's account of life in a Japanese auto factory*, Boston: George Allen and Unwin.

Macpherson, Crawford B. (1972), *The Real World of Democracy*, New York: Oxford University Press.

Neary, Ian (2002), *The State and Politics in Japan*, Cambridge: Polity Press.

Reed, Steven R. (ed.) (2003), *Japanese Electoral Politics: creating a new party system*, London: Routledge.

Stockwin, J. A. A. (1999), *Governing Japan*, Oxford: Blackwell.

Stockwin, J. A. A. (2003), *Dictionary of the Modern Politics of Japan*, London: Routledge.

Vogel, Ezra (1979), *Japan as Number One: lessons for America*, Cambridge, MA: Harvard University Press.

Williams, David (1994), *Japan: beyond the end of history*. London: Routledge.

4 Local governance

The role of referenda and the rise of independent governors

Lam Peng Er

The rise of referenda and the new wave of independent governors have ushered in greater contestation among the sites of governance in Japan (national, prefectural and city/village), and also enhanced local democracy. This trend of referenda and independent governors threatens to strike at the very heart of Japan's political economy: the struggle over the appropriate site of authoritative decision making, especially over massive public works. At issue are the competing modes of local governance in Japan today.

Hitherto, the dominant mode of governance has been traditional machine politics where governors, mayors and conservative Diet members act as brokers to obtain public works funding from the political and bureaucratic centre in Tokyo to stimulate the local economy, reward their supporters with business contracts and jobs, and win re-election. Building a 'pipe' from the locality to the centre was deemed necessary because local governments could raise around only one-third of their own tax revenues. Construction companies would provide jobs to retired bureaucrats (*amakudari*) and funds, organizational and manpower support to the election campaigns of pro-public works politicians. Many conservative politicians would also become 'policy tribesmen' (*zoku giin*) in the construction division of the ruling Liberal Democratic Party's (LDP) policymaking body, the Policy Affairs Research Council. These politicians would forge close ties with bureaucrats for influence and information, and lobby for construction companies and public works in their electoral districts.

Especially pervasive is the practice of *ainori* (riding together) where all non-communist political parties support a single candidate for governor or mayor, become the local ruling coalition and renege on their 'checks-and-balance' roles in the local assemblies. While *ainori* often ensures a smooth relationship between local executives and legislatures, it has also led to collusion, structural corruption (see Chapter 9) and political alienation among citizens.

Challenging this traditional mode is the advent of local referenda and governors who rely on grassroots, non-party partisan support. These local executives and activists are often self-conscious about their roles in transforming their localities and then Japan through a decentralized, bottom-up approach. Simply put, they are contesting and hope to change national governance by first changing local governance. While direct democracy (referenda) and independent governors have revitalized grassroots democracy, they have also resulted in tension and gridlock in local governance. Local assemblies and mayors of cities and villages are often suspicious of local referenda and populist governors whom they perceive as threats to the system of representative democracy.

This chapter will first explain why the phenomena of referenda and non-partisan governors have emerged. Next, it will examine two case studies: (1) the anti-dam movement of Tokushima city that not only won a referendum but also co-opted the city mayor and governor of Tokushima to take a stance against the central government, and (2) Governor Tanaka Yasuo of Nagano and his struggle against the majority of mayors and prefectural assembly members in Nagano, thereby bringing into focus two different systems of governance: centralized, on the one hand, decentralized, on the other. Following that is an assessment of the battle sites where governance is contested: Have new modes of contestation resulted in additional gridlock in local and national governance? Has local democracy been enhanced? In essence, the chapter examines the extent to which these two phenomena have challenged a deeply rooted domestic political economy based on wasteful public works spending that keep the LDP in power at the national level, and create jobs to benefit interest groups, bureaucrats/ex-bureaucrats and voters.

My central argument is that the advent of referenda and the wave of independent governors are challenging the prevailing mode of local governance based on *ainori* and the pork barrel politics of public works. However, challenges to collusive governance in certain prefectures do not necessarily lead to a checks-and-balance mode of local governance between the governor and the prefectural assembly but 'fragmented governance', as evidenced by the Nagano and Tokushima cases, when confrontational politics between governors and local assemblies have led to political gridlock. Nevertheless, political disharmony and friction are not necessarily bad when they block pork barrel projects which lead to fiscal distress for the national and local governments, not to mention environmental destruction.

A new wave of independent governors

These independent governors have sought to change Japan by first changing governance in their prefectures. They include: Asano Shirō (Miyagi), Kitagawa Masayasu (Mie), Hashimoto Daijirō (Kōchi), Fukuda Akio (Tochigi), Ishihara Shintarō (Tokyo),[1] Dōmoto Akiko (Chiba), Tanaka Yasuo (Nagano), Ōta Tadashi (Tokushima) and Matsuzawa Shigefumi (Kanagawa). They appear as harbingers of political change in Japan. The title of Governor Dōmoto Akiko's political autobiography reflects this bottom-up approach to governance and change in Japan – *Revolution of the Non-Party Affiliates: Change Chiba, change Japan* (Dōmoto 2001). The distribution of governors according to their political affiliation immediately after the April 2003 Local Elections was: *ainori* (26), ruling parties (7), opposition parties (2) and independents (11). The governorship of Tokushima was vacant in April 2003 (*Sankei Shimbun*, 15 April 2003).

Just after the April 1991 local elections, the distribution of governors was: *ainori* (18), exclusively LDP (5), coalitions including LDP (14), exclusively left and coalitions including left parties (5) and independents (5) (*Asahi Shimbun*, 9 April 1991). A comparison between these two local elections over twelve years reveals that both *ainori* governors and independents have actually increased since the early 1990s.

Independent governors tend to share at least three characteristics. First, they reject support from the established political parties and attract voters who do not otherwise support any established parties. Second, they emphasize transparent local governance where residents have access to information disclosure. Third, they reject the political economy of wasteful public works in their prefectures.

While unique local issues, the charisma and the policies of these independent governors might have contributed to their rise, they also benefited from two trends among Japanese voters since the 1990s. Just after the 1995 local elections, the media highlighted the rising phenomenon of non-party affiliated voters (*mutōha*), many of whom were well educated and interested in public policies (*Asahi Nenkan* 1996: 234). Moreover, the national and local governments' attempts to spend their way out of Japan's lingering economic stagnation since the early 1990s through massive public works projects led to a ballooning fiscal problem. Many non-party affiliated voters were attracted to independent candidates who opposed wasteful public works which would lead to a looming fiscal crisis and environmental destruction.

Governors and mayors not associated with the ruling LDP are by no means a recent phenomenon in Japan. Some of them emerged as early as the 1960s and appealed to voter demands for environmental protection and social welfare. Known as 'progressive' governors or mayors, they received support from the socialist and communist parties. However, the new wave of governors disavowed endorsement from established parties and are known as governors of the non-party aligned voters.

A forerunner of this new wave is Governor Asano of Miyagi who was first elected in 1993. In that year, both the governor of Miyagi and the mayor of Sendai (the prefecture's capital) were arrested for corruption. Not surprisingly, this event enraged local residents. Some politicians, local residents and activists then approached Asano (then a section chief with the then Ministry of Health and Welfare) to run for election. His clean image, and association with social welfare and services for the disabled, appealed greatly to a disillusioned local electorate.

Asano's election for governor and the policies he adopted for his administration became the prototype for the new wave of governors. He conducted an inexpensive election campaign and relied on volunteers, ordinary citizens and the *mutōha* for campaign support rather than on interest groups, political machines, and the network of national and local politicians (Satō, 1998; author's interview with Asano, 24 May 2002). His '100 yen' campaign established itself based on contributions from local residents and he refused financial support from business groupings and other interest groups. Once in office, he advocated a clean government and full disclosure of public information to citizens whenever requested. Asano also abolished the practice of local government bureaucrats regularly wining and dining central government bureaucrats in order to garner political support.

Asano also formed horizontal links with other prefectures to strengthen local governance. In June 2002, for instance, the governors from Miyagi, Iwate, Mie, Wakayama and Fukuoka, and Keio University established *Bunken kenkyūkai* (Association for the Decentralization of Authority) to promote local autonomy and decentralization. These prefectures are committed to assigning their local bureaucrats to the association in order to study issues including centre-local relations, reform of the tax structure, public works, welfare and education (*Kahoku Shimpō*, 23 May 2002).

Although non-party affiliated governors like Asano and Hashimoto had already won their elections in the early 1990s, it was the victories of independent governors in the most populated areas of Japan that caught the nation's attention. In the 1995 local elections, Aoshima Yukio and Yokoyama Knock, buoyed by the support of non-party affiliated voters, captured the governorships of Tokyo and Osaka respectively. Less than a year and a half after the elections of these two independent governors, another political milestone was made when the very first referendum took place in Japan.

Local referenda

The first referendum was held in the town of Maki, Niigata prefecture in August 1996 where residents voted overwhelmingly against the building of a nuclear facility in their village (*Niigata Nippō Hōdōbu* 1997). In rapid succession, local referenda were conducted on a range of controversial issues: the construction of rubbish incinerators and nuclear facilities, American bases and a proposed military heliport in Nago city, Okinawa, and massive public works, especially dams (Imai 1997; Shindō 1999; Ishikawa 2003). The Tokushima city referendum in January 2000 was the tenth plebiscite in Japan and the first that canvassed the views of local residents about the desirability of public work projects (Jain 2000).

Why did local referenda remain a latent instrument of grassroots democracy until 1996? A few plausible reasons spring to mind. The system of referenda was originally imposed from above by the US Occupation authorities based on the American model. Until the Maki referendum, there were no Japanese precedents; activists and voters in Japan were unfamiliar with the procedures and political benefits of launching a referendum. Once the Maki referendum set a precedent and amidst widespread coverage by the national media, a 'referenda contagion' took place in various localities. Citizens are encouraged to use referenda to express their political preferences and shape policies that impact on them. If the momentum of citizens resorting to referenda were to continue, this mode of direct democracy will surely impact on governance in Japan, local and national.

Hitherto, social movements have relied on local elections, opposition parties especially the Japan Socialist Party (JSP), demonstrations, and law suits to exert political pressure. By the 1990s, around half of Japanese voters neither identified with nor supported any established party, the JSP faced oblivion, and law suits remained a protracted process. Not surprisingly, non-partisan local activists believed that referenda offered them a viable alternative to pursue their goals.

Initially, a referendum did not appeal to activists because it appeared politically toothless. Conservative politicians in the Diet watered down the system of referenda in 1948 (*The Japan Times*, 1 January 1999). First, the local assembly must approve an ordinance for a referendum. Even if a majority of voters support a referendum, the local assembly can still reject their petition for a referendum. Second, the results of referenda are legally non-binding in Japan. Even if citizens were to overwhelmingly vote against a proposition, the local and national governments are not legally obliged to honour the results. Nevertheless, referenda do carry political weight because local and national politicians might lose reelection if they were to reject the preferences of the citizens, and fierce criticism from the media. Conservative politicians, to maintain their hold on power and to prevent local anti-pollution movements from coalescing into national ones, responded promptly and effectively to local concerns by introducing a tougher regime of anti-pollution laws since the early 1970s. Such responsiveness to local concerns helped to obviate the use of a referendum among social movement activists in the 1970s and 1980s.

Another reason for the absence of referenda until 1996 was the Herculean efforts required to organize them. Activists must surmount many hurdles in the political process before a referendum can be held. The first hurdle is organizing a signature campaign. While the law requires at least 2 per cent of total eligible voters to sign a petition for a referendum to be held, activists in various referenda movement sought to obtain at least 50 per cent of total eligible voters to strengthen their bid politically and morally.

The next hurdle is to seek a majority of assembly members to support an ordinance for a referendum. This is by no means an easy task, especially when many assembly members believe that referenda undermine representative democracy and simplistically cast governance into a stark yes or no proposition. If the mayor and local assembly members are uncooperative, the activists pushing for a referendum will face the difficult task of either launching a recall or nominating their own candidates for mayor and assembly seats against entrenched politicians in the next local election.

Even after forging a majority in the local assembly to approve an ordinance for a referendum, the activists must next mobilize a high turnout of voters in support of their preference. At the final hurdle, they need to secure the sympathy of the mass media, national public opinion, the main opposition parties and even groups within the ruling parties to make the referendum result politically binding.

Tokushima city referendum

At issue in this referendum is the construction of a dam spanning 720 metres across the Yoshino, the third longest river in Japan. The dam, to be located 13 kilometres from the Yoshino river mouth, has dual functions: a road spanning the dam, and also ten electronically controlled sluice gates to prevent massive flooding. Costing an estimated 103 billion yen (around US$950 million) to build, the proposed dam will replace Daijūzeki, the name of the stone weir built around 250 years ago during the Tokugawa Shogunate.

According to the Ministry of Construction (MOC, from January 2001 part of the Ministry of Land, Infrastructure and Transport), Daijūzeki is already worn out and needs to be replaced as it is no longer able to prevent a massive flood that is predicted to occur once every 150 years. If the anticipated flood were to take place before the new dam is built, lives and property would be lost. However, the anti-dam activists pointed out that the new dam is a waste of taxpayers' money and will damage the environment including the Yoshino's water quality, wetlands, endangered species and migratory birds. The activists argued that Daijūzeki has served Tokushima well for two and a half centuries and is also a cultural heritage that should not be destroyed. The activists believed that repairing the old weir and strengthening the embankments will be adequate to prevent any serious flooding, and that it is unnecessary to build a dam for an imaginary flood that is supposed to occur only once in 150 years. Besides the 103 billion yen to construct the new dam, it will cost 700 million yen annually to maintain the dam. Moreover, citizens who would be affected by the new dam have no say in the policymaking process for building the dam.

In 1982, the MOC deemed it necessary to repair Daijūzeki. Six years later, it conducted research on the old weir. In 1992, the MOC announced a totally new plan: a new dam with a road atop would replace Daijūzeki. In 1995, the MOC established an advisory council (*shingikai*) comprising a panel of experts to examine the feasibility of the plan and its impact on the environment. The panel, handpicked by the MOC, declared in July 1998 that the plan for the new dam was appropriate.

This triggered off a signature campaign by Tokushima city residents to seek an ordinance for a referendum on the new dam. By January 1999, a group of non-party affiliated citizens (Daijūzeki jūmin tōhyō no kai/Association for Daijūzeki referendum) spearheaded the signature campaign and collected 101,535 signatures or 48.8 per cent of Tokushima city's eligible voters in favour of a referendum. However, in the following month, the Tokushima city assembly turned down the request for a plebiscite.

The founding father and leader of Daijūzeki jūmin tōhyō no kai was Himeno Masayoshi. He was born in a village next to Tokushima city, educated at Chūō University and was a student activist against the Vietnam War and the US–Japan Security Treaty in 1970. In 1992, Himeno noticed that the MOC had set aside a budget for the proposed dam at Yoshino (author's interview: 28 June 1999). In 1993, he formed the Yoshinogawa Symposium to seek greater information disclosure and citizen participation in the MOC's deliberations on Yoshino (*Kankyō Shimbun*, 26 August 1998). Himeno subsequently organized the Daijūzeki jūmin tōhyō no kai on a horizontal network style based on amateurs and volunteers who were *mutōha*; almost two-thirds were women. Although the group had interaction with other referenda groups in Maki, Kobe, Mitake and Nago, it was independent from all other organizations.

In the April 1999 Local Elections, the pro-referendum group sponsored five candidates for city assembly and succeeded in winning three seats. This was sufficient to tilt the balance of power within the city assembly to twenty-two in favour and eighteen against the referendum. In the Tokushima city assembly, the

Democratic Party (DP), Social Democratic Party (SDP) and the Japan Communist Party (JCP) were against the dam and in favour of a referendum; *Kōmeitō* (Clean Government Party) supported both dam and referendum while the LDP-affiliated conservatives supported the dam and opposed a referendum.

In June the same year, the Tokushima local assembly passed an ordinance for a referendum but no timetable was specified, much to the dismay of the pro-referendum citizens. In a separate memorandum of understanding, the pro-referendum groups in the assembly agreed to meet within six months after the ordinance was in place and the timing of the plebiscite would be decided by the majority of those in favour of the move. They met in December 1999 and fixed a date in January 2000. The assembly also attached a condition that was unprecedented in Japanese referenda. If voter turnout were less than 50 per cent of all eligible voters in Tokushima city, the votes (yes or no) would not even be tallied. This was no easy task. In the last mayoral election held in February 1997, voter turnout was only 30.68 per cent (*The Japan Times*, 13 January 2000).

Nevertheless, the voter turnout was 55.00 per cent and 91.6 per cent of voters cast their ballots against the new dam. Mayor Kōike Masakatsu of Tokushima city made a turnaround and declared that he would abide by the referendum's anti-dam results. He was previously an MOC official and, as mayor, had supported the dam. Himeno earlier had reflected on the significance of the referendum: 'If the majority of residents opposed the scheme, then the MOC's claims that the project stems from the strong appeal of the locality will be shattered' (*Asahi Shimbun*, 8 December 1999). Himeno also intimated that Kōike changed his stance because the mayor was probably afraid that the pro-referendum group might launch a recall against him (Author's interview, 28 June 1999).

In February 2000, Prime Minister Obuchi Keizō, in Diet interpellations with opposition leaders Hatoyama Yukio (DP), Fuwa Tetsuzō (JCP) and Doi Takako (SDP) concerning the Tokushima city referendum, remarked that the residents lacked understanding and cautioned against making referenda legally binding (*Tokushima Shimbun*, 10 February 2000). In May the same year, Construction Minister Nakayama Masaaki retracted his promise to meet the residents of Tokushima to discuss the Yoshino issue. His excuse was that he had no desire to meet the head of the anti-weir group who was arrested as a student during protests against the Vietnam War. (Nakayama was probably referring to Himeno because he intimated that the leader had attended his same alumni, Chūō University.) The mentality of Obuchi and Nakayama revealed the mode of top-down, centralized governance which they deemed suitable for Japan.

Nevertheless, the Tokushima referendum acted as a catalyst for the national government's rethinking on public works to ensure its electoral interests: 'The referendum prompted a decision later in the year by the three central government ruling parties that the government "go back to the drawing board" on the project in a sweeping review of all big public work projects' (*Asahi Shimbun*, *Asahi.com*, 13 June 2002).

In July 2000, the LDP established a committee to radically review public works projects (Jimintō Kōkyō Jigyō Bappon Minaoshi Kentōkai). In the next month,

Kamei Shizuka, the LDP Policy Affairs Research Council (PARC) Chairman, led a team comprised of policymakers from the three ruling coalition parties to visit Tokushima and study the Yoshino issue. Apparently, the LDP sought to improve its image after suffering heavy losses in metropolitan Japan at the June Lower House Elections (*Sankei Shimbun*, 29 August 2000 and 25 October 2000, *Daily Yomiuri On-line*, 5 August 2000). Amidst prolonged economic stagnation, disgruntled urban voters had become more critical of their tax money being wasted on pork-barrel projects in rural Japan (*Mainichi Shimbun Interactive*, 14 July 2000). Reviewing the new dam at Tokushima along with other planned public works was a strategy to ensure that the LDP would not be punished again at the 2001 Upper House Elections (*Asahi Shimbun, Asahi.com, editorial*, 9 August 2000). The decision to review public works was also made against the backdrop of the Mori Yoshirō administration's plunging popularity, and the LDP's desire to win back the *mutōha* with conservative tendencies.

In August 2000, the committee recommended that the national government should cancel 233 public works projects,[2] and that plans for a new dam at Yoshino be sent back to the drawing board. Originally, the decision was to cancel (*chūshi*) the dam but after intense lobbying from the pro-dam supporters (Tokushima Governor Endō Toshio, the LDP Tokushima prefectural chapter and local politicians), the eventual decision was to freeze (*tōketsu*) the project (*Tokushima Shimbun*, 25 August 2000). An ambiguity was ensured when the expression '*hakushi ni modori*' (return to a clean slate) was used to address the Yoshino issue (*Tokushima Shimbun*, 12–14 September 2000). The anti-dam activists wanted the new dam proposal to be unequivocally scrapped based on the referendum results while the proponents of the new dam insisted that their pre-existing plan must still be considered. The MOC remained adamant that the new dam proposal is the best option. To the MOC, public works is the ministry's *raison d'être*. It also creates jobs for retiring MOC bureaucrats in construction firms.

A LDP member from the Tokushima Prefecture Chapter remarked: 'It is strange to abandon the dam in Tokushima just because the LDP is worried about losing the Upper House Election' (*Tokushima Shimbun*, 17–20 August 2000). Ironically, abandoning the dam was precisely what the Tokushima LDP Prefecture Chapter did after losing the Tokushima mayoral election in February 2001 (*Tokushima Shimbun*, 18 March 2001). Mayor Kōike, who won a landslide victory, soon established a window in a city government office to accept alternative plans to dam construction from the local citizens (*Tokushima Shimbun*, 13 March 2001). This was his approach to promote democratic and local governance, and win the support of Tokushima voters. Indeed, both the local LDP and the mayor of Tokushima were driven by electoral considerations to stop championing the dam.

In April 2002, Ōta Tadashi won his election to become governor of Tokushima prefecture after his predecessor Endō Toshio was indicted for accepting bribes over public works project. Ōta's victory was a turning point in Tokushima's political history because it ended half a century of conservative executive rule (*Tokushima Shimbun*, 29 April 2002). Ōta's core supporters in his election campaign were the anti-dam, pro-referendum activists. The new governor then pledged to scrap the controversial plan to dam the Yoshino after his victory. Less than two and a half years after the Tokushima city referendum, the anti-dam activists finally succeeded in coopting both mayor and governor to oppose the MOC's plan for a dam.

While the central government and MOC have not officially scrapped the dam, the proposal appears politically dead though not buried (*Asahi Shimbun, Asahi.com*, 13 June 2002). The shift in the national mood against mega public works projects, which have exacerbated Japan's fiscal crisis, and the ascendance of Prime Minister Koizumi Junichirō, who insisted on capping the budget for public works, make it unlikely that a dam will be built across the Yoshino.

The Tokushima city referendum has indeed raised a number of issues concerning local governance. These include: the tension between representative democracy and direct democracy, bureaucratic/technocratic governance versus democratic governance, differences among local governments, and between the national and local governments.

Prior to the referendum, the Tokushima city and prefectural assemblies had already passed resolutions supporting a new dam. In addition, the local assemblies of another two cities and eight villages along the Yoshino supported the plan. Critics argued that the referendum challenged the decisions of the local assemblies whose members have been duly elected by the people. Then LDP Secretary General Mori Yoshirō said: 'If every decision is based on the outcome of a referendum, then there will be no need for legislatives' (*The Age*, 29 January 2000). Moreover, why should one city veto the interests of other pro-dam cities and villages in a referendum? Proponents of the dam also collected 316,003 signatures from residents living along the Yoshino (but beyond Tokushima city too) who were in favour of the new plan to bolster their claims of representing the people's will.

The MOC also sought to rationalize its plans on the basis of its scientific and technical expertise. An MOC official in Tokushima remarked: 'The appropriateness of public works cannot be judged by amateurs' (*Asahi Shimbun*, 18 December 1998). The MOC manager in charge of public works in Tokushima opined: 'In general, local residents lack analytical ability, and tend to be swayed by the emotions of the moment rather than reason, and because they are moved by feelings, there is a danger that they will produce an irrational result' (TBS News 23, 16 February 1998).

Then Construction Minister Nakayama Masaaki also said that the dam for Tokushima is not suitable for a plebiscite because decisions on such projects require technical and scientific knowledge (*The Japan Times*, 13 January 2000). After the referendum results were known, Nakayama remarked that the Tokushima referendum was representative of the 'flaw of democracy'. He also praised the mayor of Nago who ignored his city's referendum results for doing the right thing (*Tokushima Shimbun*, 14 January 2000). The Minister then backtracked after facing criticism of his comments on referenda: 'For an elected politician, votes are like a revelation from God' (*Mainichi Shimbun*, 26 January 2000).

Both pro- and anti-dam groups would marshal 'scientific' data from different sets of simulations to support their positions. The press reported: 'According to simulation, the water level would exceed the safety level of the embankments by

42 cm at a point 16 km from the mouth of the river, according to the ministry. Dam opponents argue that the ministry's simulation over estimates the levels and that the proposed dam would only lower the water level by a mere 50 cm which is not sufficient to deal with major floods' (*The Japan Times*, 18 April 2000). Convinced of its own bureaucratic expertise, the MOC would not budge from its position that the dam is best even after the referendum. The ministry repeatedly said that it would seek the understanding of local residents that the dam is necessary. Implicit in the MOC's concept of governance is the need to educate the people; it is the understanding of the masses and not the ministry that has to change.

Conceivably, the Environment Agency (from January 2001 Ministry of Environment) and the 1997 New River Law could have shaped decision making towards the Yoshino. But the reality was that the Environment Agency did not even play a peripheral role in the Yoshino case. This reveals the bureaucratic weakness of the Environment Agency *vis-à-vis* the MOC. The New River Law has two key features: the views of residents in the river's vicinity should be considered in decision making and that the impact of public works on the environment must be examined. Between July 1998 (when the MOC *shingikai* rubber-stamped the plan for a new dam) and August 2000 (when Policy Affairs Research Council Chairman Kamei Shizuka visited Tokushima city), there was virtually no mention of the New River Law by the national and local governments. Apparently, the MOC believed that the governor, mayors and assembly members represented the voices of the people while the anti-dam activists insisted that local residents must be directly consulted (*Daily Yomiuri on-line*, 12 December 2001). Moreover, experts from the pro- and anti-dam groups have conflicting opinions about environmental damage. It appears that the 1997 New River Law was legally binding only when the central and local governments chose to honour it. While the intent of the New River Law was laudable, the legislation was subjected to different interpretations. It was really grassroots activism that stopped the proposed dam at the Yoshino and not an ambiguous piece of legislation. The implication for governance in Japan is that policy outcomes are often framed by political contests and local resistance rather than a formal piece of legislation.

After the referendum, decision making concerning the Yoshino became dead-locked among local governments, and between local and national governments. When mayor Kōike switched his position to an anti-dam stance, the city of Tokushima was pit against Governor Endō and the prefectural assembly, and the national government (the ruling LDP and the MOC). Then Prime Minister Obuchi affirmed that the dam project will proceed despite the referendum results (*Mainichi Shimbun Interactive*, 25 January 2000). After Ōta became governor, Tokushima's executive and legislature split over public works and an investigation into public works corruption. The prefectural assembly refused to endorse Ōta's nominee for Vice-Governor and forced him to abandon some of his campaign pledges including a review of public works projects around Tokushima airport.

In March 2003, the prefectural assembly passed a motion of no-confidence against Ōta and he was forced to resign. (Tokushima was politically rudderless, especially when there was no Vice-Governor to stand in until the election for a new

Governor. In the absence of a Governor, as well as a Vice-Governor and Chief Treasurer, the prefectural government was run by a bureaucrat [chief of the planning and general affairs department] as a stop-gap measure.) Supported by civic groups, Ōta announced that he would seek re-election in May the same year. In the April 2003 local elections, Ōta's supporters in the Tokushima prefectural assembly made gains. The political cleavage in the 42-seat assembly was: 16 pro-Ōta members versus 26 anti-Ōta members. By controlling more than 40 per cent of the assembly, the supporters of Ōta would be able to defeat a second no-confidence motion (which needs more than 32 votes to pass) if Ōta were to capture the governorship again (*Daily Yomiuri Online*, 15 April 2003).

Unfortunately for Ōta and his grassroots supporters, he lost his reelection bid in May 2003 by a small margin: 47.7 per cent to LDP-supported Iizumi Kamon's 49.7 per cent. Ironically, Ōta actually won 197,732 votes, far more than the 160,656 he won in April 2002 (*Daily Yomiuri Online*, 22 May 2003). The national LDP mobilized its entire organizational apparatus to support Iizumi, a former home affairs ministry official, and sent forty-five Diet members (including ministers and party chiefs) to Tokushima to drum up support for him, particularly among businesses. Moreover, Iizumi had strong support from many mayors and other local politicians in the prefecture.

The *Asahi Shimbun* noted: 'Concerned about the growing opposition to public works projects and stung by a series of lost governorships, as in Nagano, the LDP pulled out all the stops to win in Tokushima' (*Asahi Shimbun, Asahi.com*, 20 May 2003). Moreover, Tokushima's construction companies, which were hit by some arrests in connection with the Endō bribery case, openly campaigned for Iizumi this time after laying low in 2002 (*Asahi Shimbun*, editorial, 19 May 2003). Iizumi did not support building a dam across the Yoshino during his campaign and also pledged that he would respect the findings of a committee established earlier by Ōta to investigate public works corruption in Tokushima. Thus Iizumi shrewdly avoided any major policy differences with Ōta. Further controversies on the dam issue and public works scandals during the campaign might well have cost Iizumi some votes and tipped the electoral victory over to Ōta.

Iizumi's main appeal to many Tokushima voters was his promise to restore normalcy to governance in the prefecture. An Iizumi victory would mean a smoother relationship with the conservative-dominated prefectural assembly; an Ōta victory would surely guarantee fragmented governance in the prefecture. Even if Ōta had won his reelection with sufficient legislative support to defeat another no-confidence motion, he would still have faced difficulties implementing his campaign promises because a majority of assembly members remained hostile to him.

After winning his governorship, Iizumi ruled out reviving the controversial project to build a dam across the Yoshino. The new governor proposed to repair the existing old weir on the river instead and remarked that he has no right to overturn the results of the Tokushima referendum (*The Japan Times*, 20 May 2003, *Asahi Shimbun, Asahi.com*, 18 May 2003). However, the saga of Tokushima's public works controversy does not end with the election of Governor Iizumi. Once the corruption investigation panel Ōta appointed has presented its report, a number of local politicians might well be implicated in various scandals leading to further political turmoil and voter alienation in the prefecture. Although the pro-referendum activists at the heart of Ōta's campaign were deeply disappointed by the election result, they pledged to watch the new Iizumi administration and affirmed that this setback would not fundamentally change the new epoch of citizen-centered democracy in Tokushima.

Despite Ōta's loss, the anti-dam activists benefited from two further developments. First, in the November 2003 Lower House Elections, the DP's manifesto fiercely criticized the proposed dam at Tokushima as a prime example of the LDP's wasteful public works policy. (The DP did well in that election to the extent that many analysts believe that a two-party system is emerging in Japan.) Second, Governor Iizumi in March 2004 requested the MOC to consider other options first rather than to build a sluice-gate dam on the Yoshino. The media noted: 'In an apparent change of heart, Iizumi hints that the project should be abandoned – although he stopped short of clearly stating so, probably in fear of stepping on central government toes and losing the support of local proponents of the project' (Editorial, *Asahi Shimbun*, 6 April 2004).

Tokushima prefecture was led by three governors in less than two years. Governance over public works in the prefecture was also robustly contested by local and national politicians, bureaucrats from the MOC, interest groups (especially construction companies) and pro-referendum activists. Against the backdrop of a prolonged economic stagnation and a local administration saddled with accumulated debts of more than 800 billion yen, Governor Iizumi would have to consider carefully whether Tokushima can still depend on public works to boost the local economy (*Daily Yomiuri Online*, 22 May 2003). The term 'fragmented governance' might well be apt to describe the decision-making process towards public works in Tokushima. This concept of fragmented governance is also applicable to our next case study: Governor Tanaka Yasuo's anti-dam policy in Nagano.

The Nagano model of local governance

Just before the Tokushima referendum took place, the local media reported that novelist Tanaka Yasuo came to Tokushima city to bring out the votes (*Tokushima Shimbun*, 10 and 16 January 2000). Obviously, widely known for his novel *Nan to naku kurisutaru* (*Somewhat Like Crystal* which described the hedonistic lifestyle of young Japanese in a materially affluent society) he was a national celebrity even before he became governor of Nagano the same year. Tokushima's media also mentioned that Tanaka was prominent in the signature campaign to launch a referendum against the construction of an airport in Kobe city. Subsequently, Tanaka as governor would consider initiating a referendum to canvass the views of Nagano's residents on the desirability of constructing new dams (*Sankei Shimbun*, 13 November 2002).

Before Tanaka became governor in October 2000, Nagano prefecture was continually led by only two governors (who were ex-bureaucrats and vice-governors) for 41 years and both sought to handpick their vice-governors (also ex-bureaucrats) to become their successor. However, a number of local residents, including the president of Nagano's largest local bank (Hachijūni), local businessmen, intellectuals and civic groups, were against the practice of another bureaucrat occupying the office of governor. They chose instead to look for an attractive alternative candidate.

Moreover, they were also unhappy with the local administration over the corruption surrounding the 1998 Nagano Winter Olympics, the massive fiscal deficit the Olympics placed on Nagano citizens, and the local economic downturn after the Olympic bubble economy in Nagano had burst. Citizens were also enraged when the Olympics organizing committee burnt their accounts to prevent citizens from auditing them for misappropriation of funds. Opponents to Nagano's traditional bureaucratic governance picked Tanaka (who lived in Nagano for many years as a student) as their candidate.

When Tanaka agreed to run for election, many local residents volunteered to campaign for him. The only established organizational support he received was from Rengō, a trade union in Nagano. Running against him was a candidate supported by almost all the established parties, mayors and prefecture assembly members. Campaigning on environmental protection and greater transparency in local government, Tanaka chalked up a victory with over 100,000 votes over his rival.

Even though most prefectural assembly members and many local bureaucrats supported his political opponent, Tanaka was not deterred. Drawing support from an unprecedented 91.3 per cent support in December 2000 (*Shinmai Nenkan*, 2002: 30) from Nagano's residence, he launched his Nagano model of local governance (Nagano ken 2001; author's interview, 22 May 2002). The features of this model included:

- a glass office for the governor that can be viewed by the public to symbolize transparency and closeness to local residents;
- e-governance where the governor and his staff welcome and answer e-mails from residents;
- regular town hall meetings (*kuruma shūkai*) with citizens in different areas of Nagano;
- an anti-dam declaration committing Nagano not to accept wasteful public works (Uchiyama 2001);
- dismantling the press club system in Nagano to rid the prefecture of information cartels; and
- a weekly press conference by the governor with question and answer sessions.

The national media gave wide-spread coverage to Tanaka's anti-dam declaration which challenged the political economy of public works and governance in Japan. An editorial noted: 'Nagano Governor Tanaka Yasuo's announcement of a no dam policy opened the floodgates to a torrent of debate on dams throughout Japan' (*Mainichi Interactive*, 17 April 2001).

Fragmented governance in Nagano

Armed with only a popular mandate, Governor Tanaka had to face a hostile prefectural assembly, and other city and village governments that support public work projects. With the exception of the communists, every single political party in Nagano was against his anti-dam declaration (*datsu damu sengen*). Even the DP, the main opposition party at the national level, joined the LDP assembly members to oppose the governor. Apparently, many DP local politicians were former LDP members who left with ex-Prime Minister Hata Tsutomu when he joined the Shinshintō (New Frontier Party) and then the DP.[3] In this regard, many DP politicians in Nagano shared the same conservative background and values as the LDP. Ironically, the DP at the national level officially opposed wasteful public works.

Prefectural assembly members blasted Tanaka for being dictatorial in his style of governance. They questioned the appropriateness of Tanaka unilaterally stopping the construction of dams without seeking an understanding with the prefectural assembly and other city and village governments. To circumvent the governor's anti-dam policy, the prefectural assembly passed a budget that included money for public work projects that Tanaka had opposed, and passed an ordinance to set up a committee to consider whether more dams should be built in Nagano.

When Tanaka announced the cancellation of the Asakawa and Shimosuwa dam projects on 25 June 2002, Nagano's prefectural assembly soon passed a no-confidence motion against him on 5 July 2002. This act was unprecedented in the history of post-war, local governance in Japan. Never before had a prefectural assembly sought to dismiss a governor over policy disputes (there was only one prior case of a prefectural assembly passing a no-confidence motion against a governor for corruption). Tanaka had two choices: either dissolve the prefectural assembly for new elections or run for reelection as governor. Tanaka opted to let the citizens of Nagano decide on his suitability as governor.

In September 2002, Tanaka won a landslide victory. Running as an independent again, he garnered 822,897 votes while his main contender (supported by most assembly members, and city, town and village mayors) obtained only 406,559 votes. Despite his overwhelming victory, Tanaka still is confronted by a hostile prefectural assembly. It is difficult to break the impasse between the executive and legislature in Nagano prefecture unless citizen groups supportive of Tanaka succeed in winning seats in the prefectural assembly or Tanaka were to step down as governor.

In the April 2003 local elections, Tanaka and his supporters had hoped to put at least fifteen pro-Tanaka assembly members in office, a number large enough to veto any future no-confidence motions against the governor in the 58-seat assembly. The result was a grave disappointment for Tanaka: only ten pro-Tanaka assembly members were elected. Even though an *Asahi Shimbun* exit poll found 67 per cent of those who voted in Nagano's 2003 Elections proclaimed support for Tanaka, the governor's own popularity does not necessarily extend to the candidates he supports (*Asahi Shimbun, Asahi.com*, 16 April 2003).

Another obstacle to Tanaka's leadership is an unsupportive local bureaucracy with a vested interest in public works. Bureaucratic hostility towards Tanaka is evidenced by the arrest of some local bureaucrats who broke election laws when they campaigned for his rival, and also the notorious 'business card bending' incident. This incident occurred when Tanaka gave his business card to the division chief of public works during his first day as governor. The bureaucrat defiantly folded Tanaka's business card in front of the media and the public. Outraged by the bureaucrat's rudeness and insubordination, 25,000 residents phoned the prefectural office to criticize his behaviour (*Shinmai Nenkan*, 2002: 30).

The high indebtedness of Nagano prefecture and the stagnant economy of both prefecture and country are further obstacles to Tanaka's vision of local governance. The prefecture has a debt of US$12.5 billion, about half of it stemming from the Olympics (*International Herald Tribune*, 22 May 2001). Indeed, Nagano's level of indebtedness is the second worst among all prefectures in Japan. The governor is against pump-priming of the local economy based on wasteful public works. However, it remains unclear what the environmentally friendly policies are that could possibly revitalize the economy of Nagano.

Assessing the battle sites of local governance

The phenomena of referenda and the new wave of independent governors have taken place even in rural Japan, a bastion of conservative rule. A key reason why some rural prefectures have become contested battle sites of local governance is the issue of wasteful public works and environmental destruction in those localities. (Public works are less critical to boosting the economy of and vote gathering in metropolitan Japan.) In a number of pitched battles, non-partisan activists had routed their seemingly entrenched conservative opponents. While victories in localities like Tokushima and Nagano might seem dramatic and impressive, the reality is that referenda in Japan are no easy task and independent governors still remain a minority among their counterparts in the nation's 47 prefectures.

Have referenda been a boon or bane to local governance? Referenda have certainly given ordinary citizens the opportunity to directly voice their preferences in public policy issues. From a democratic, ethical point of view, national and local governments should not go against the people's will when they formulate and implement policies. Though plebiscite is relatively new to Japan, ordinary citizens have clearly embraced the spirit of referenda. According to public opinion polls, the Japanese support referenda as a guide to local and national governance (see Tables 4.1 and 4.2).

However, critics have pointed out that local referenda often focus on issues that have ramifications beyond their immediate vicinity. Is it appropriate for the little town of Maki to decide on nuclear facilities which impact on national energy policy? Should Okinawa prefecture and Nago town decide on US military bases which are central to the US–Japan alliance? After all, foreign relations are the responsibility of the central government. Why should Tokushima city override the preferences of Tokushima prefecture, two cities and eight villages along the Yoshino?

Table 4.1 Referendum and local governments

Question: Do you think local governments and local assemblies should follow the results of a local referendum, they should respect the results as much as possible, or should the results be only used as a reference?

Responses	Per cent
Should follow the results	23
Should respect the results as much as possible	58
Use the results as a reference	13
No response/others	6

Table 4.2 Roles of referenda

Question: Which of the following opinions about local referenda is close to your own?

Responses	Per cent
Local referenda should be held often in order to reflect local residents' opinion in local politics	61
Local referenda should be held only when there is a serious issue	29
Local referenda are not necessary because they can be replaced by local assemblies	5
Others/no responses	5
$N = 1,567$	

Asahi Shimbun, 16 February 1999, J-Poll: US-Japan Foundation & Roper Center for public opinion research.

While the phenomena of local referenda and the new wave of independent governors have enhanced grassroots democracy, such trends have also led to fragmented governance in certain localities of Japan. In the cases of Tokushima and Nagano, there were gridlocks among village, city, prefecture and national governments over public work projects. Governors Ota and Tanaka were confronted by hostile prefectural assemblies. As mentioned above, however, fragmented governance may not necessarily be bad if it blocks wasteful and environmentally destructive public works. Smooth governance among governors, mayors, prefecture, city, town, village assemblies, the national bureaucracy and ruling parties is not necessarily good if it merely promotes pork barrel politics and corruption,[4] and excludes local residents from policymaking that impacts directly on their lives and environment.

To what extent have these twin phenomena of referenda and independent governors challenged the political economy based on wasteful public works spending? Despite fragmented governance in Tokushima and Nagano, massive

Table 4.3 Public works as percentage of GDP

	1990	1997
Japan	6.6	7.8
US	3.5	2.8
France	3.3	2.8
UK	3.2	1.6
Germany	2.3	1.9

Source: Bank of Japan, International Comparative Statistics in *Social Science Japan*, December 1999.

dam projects have been checked by grassroots democracy. The media have paid much attention to the anti-dam movements in Tokushima and Nagano. They have also highlighted the extent to which Tokyo's relentless construction of dams runs against the grain of other developed countries' dam policies (*Asahi Shimbun*, 20 May 2001 and 21 November 2002). Indeed, the US is proceeding to destroy some dams to allow rivers to flow naturally and fish to spawn again. Increasingly, the national mood is shifting against the construction of dams and other public works after Japan's attempts to spend its way out of economic stagnation have failed.

A ballooning fiscal problem and perhaps another decade of economic stagnation will probably place tremendous stress on Japan's political economy of the construction state (*doken kokka*) and LDP rule (*Social Science Japan*, December 1999). Japan is already the biggest spender on public works among the G-7 countries (Table 4.3). The episode of PARC Chairman Kamei visiting Tokushima city and *jūdaizeki* in August 2000 captured the dilemma and contradictions of LDP rule. The party sought to appease the urban voters by ostensibly scaling back on some public works projects in rural Japan but was severely criticized by its politicians and supporters in rural Japan who have grown dependent on public works. How is the LDP going to square the circle by placating both urban and rural voters at the same time?

Conclusion

Local governance based on the political economy of public works may still be business as usual in many prefectures. Nevertheless, it is probably not sustainable in the long run. Cognizant of this, Prime Minister Koizumi Junichirō's administration has rejected the hitherto approach of massive public works spending to stimulate economic recovery. This seems to suggest that Koizumi's anti-public works stance and the stance of anti-reform local politicians and bureaucrats are in contestation. While Koizumi has boosted his mass popularity by adopting a reformist image, we should be reminded that the electoral successes of Tanaka and the new wave of reform-minded independent governors contributed to the sense of crisis among LDP rank and file and party chapters which led to an unprecedented grassroots party revolt which catapulted Koizumi into power. The shifting national mood against wasteful public works and Koizumi's structural reforms which emphasize fiscal austerity and a cap on public works have given greater legitimacy and a political boost to local anti-public works movements including referenda.

An editor asked: 'Is Tanaka's insistence that we consider the burdens public work projects impose on society a manifestation of a revolt whose impact will be felt only in Nagano or has he started a revolution that will eventually spread throughout the country?' (*Mainichi Interactive*, 24 February 2001). Trying to tap into Governor Tanaka's popularity, the DP appointed him to its shadow cabinet as minister in charge of decentralization just before the November 2003 Lower House elections.

The anti-dam movements in Nagano and Tokushima might well become a catalyst for other local challenges to a centralized system of governance based on public works and pork-barrel politics. Conceivably, these challenges would intensify if referenda were to become legally binding. While there is a nationwide network that advocates legally-binding plebiscite, the national ruling parties are unlikely to strengthen the system of referenda (*The Japan Times*, 2 June 1999). The economic rise of China (which has contributed to the hollowing out of industries in various localities of Japan), a looming fiscal crisis for both national and local governments, weak coalition governments at the national level and voter dealignment from political parties will pose major challenges to both national and local governance in Japan. Amidst such ferment, local referenda and independent governors might well play a larger role in governance in the next decade than might appear at first sight.

Moreover, the rural vote has become less than solid for the LDP especially in areas where referenda and the new wave of governors have emerged. In 1998, Tokushima prefecture received 550 billion yen (US$4.41 billion) from the national coffers, the second most generous outlay among Japan's 47 prefectures (*Asian Wall Street Journal*, 2 July 2001). That Tokushima, the second largest beneficiary of the central government's public works largesse, could turn against Tokyo confirms that there is a greater contestation among the sites of governance and that cracks are appearing in the very structure of local and national governance in Japan.

Interviews

Governor Asano Shirō, 24 May 2002.
Himeno Masayoshi, 28 June 1999.
Governor Tanaka Yasuo, 22 May 2002.
Hata Jirō, 23 December 2002.

Acknowledgements

In June 1999, I had a home stay with a family which belongs to the pro-referendum movement in Tokushima city. I wish to thank the pro-referendum activists who shared their insights with me. My fieldwork to Tokushima was made possible by a Rikkyo University Visiting Fellowship. I also benefited from interviews with Governors Asano of Miyagi and Tanaka of Nagano. These interviews were made possible by funding from the Shibusawa Foundation.

Notes

1 Ishihara may not fit comfortably into this group because he is a right-wing nationalist; most of the other independent governors are not. Nevertheless, he does not depend on the established parties for support. Besides Governor Tanaka, he is the only governor to hold a weekly question and answer session.
2 'However, most of the projects mentioned in the report had already been suspended by the relevant government ministries for a variety of reasons' (*Asahi Shimbun, Asahi.com*, 29 August 2000). A scholar noted that in reality less than 0.5 per cent of the 8,000 development projects examined have been cancelled (McCormack 2002).
3 Hata Tsutomu was the LDP bigwig in Nagano. According to his son and personal assistant, Hata Jirō, the local DP in Nagano was not necessarily against Tanaka's anti-dam policy but his style of governance (Author's interview, 23 December 2002). However, the media did report a split between the national DP and the Nagano DP over the issue of dam construction. Moreover, Tokushima DP and Nagano DP have different orientations towards dams. It also shows how incoherent the main opposition party is, a feature which contributes to its inept image and inability to displace a ruling party in decline, the LDP.
4 The collusion between the LDP and the construction industry can be seen from the fact that two Ministers of Construction were indicted for bribery in recent years: Nakamura Kishirō in 1994 and Nakao Eiichi in 2000. Nakao belonged to the Kamei faction whose leader, Kamei Shizuka, sought to refurbish the LDP's image as a party that does not support wasteful public works. Nakao's corruption case was linked to the Yamaguchi gumi, the largest Yakuza group in Japan.

References

Dōmoto, Akiko (2001) *Mutōha Kakumei: Chiba ga kawareba Nihon ga kawaru*, Tokyo: Tsukiji Shokan.

Imai, Hajime (1997) *Jūmin Tōhyō: 20 seikimatsu ni mebaeta Nihon no shin rūru*, Osaka: Nikkei Osaka PR.

Ishikawa, Shunichi (2003) *Jūmin Sansei Seido*, Tokyo: Gyōsei.

Jain, Purnendra (2000) 'Jumin tohyo and the Tokushima anti-dam movement in Japan', *Asian Survey* 40, 4 (July/August): 551–70.

McCormack, Gavan (2002) 'Breaking the Iron Triangle', *New Left Review* 13, January–February: 5–23.

Niigata Nippō Hōdōbu (1997) *Genpatsu o Kobanda Machi: Makimachi no min i o ou*, Tokyo: Iwanami Shoten.

Satō, Yutaka (1998), *Miyagi no ran: Asano chiji asshō no himitsu*, Sendai: Hon no Mori.

Shindō, Muneyuki (ed.) (1999) *Jūmin Tōhyō*, Tokyo: Kyōsei.

Shinmai Nenkan (2002) Nagano.

Social Science Japan (1999) 'Public Works in Japan' 17 (December).

Uchiyama, Takurō (2001), 'Tanaka Yasuo Nagano ken chiji no shin shikō to kōkyō jigyō', *Sekai* (April): 138–50.

5   Governance, globalization and the Japanese financial system

Resistance or restructuring?

Philip G. Cerny

The governance of the financial system in Japan – especially the relationship between governments and banks – has been at the core of the way the developmental state has worked over the past half-century. In the age of 'Japan, Inc.', how money, especially investment capital, was allocated between different uses involved a largely closed shop of bureaucrats, politicians, banks, stock markets and firms, insulated from international financial markets and locked into government-backed, quasi-oligopolistic competition at home. However, with increasing international economic interdependence and openness – especially the huge upsurge in international capital mobility since the 1970s and the global integration of financial markets and price sensitivity across borders – that closed shop is being contested from both outside and inside. Financial governance in Japan has been on the threshold of fundamental restructuring for at least a decade, probably two or three. Yet, despite a wide range of particular measures having been adopted since the 1970s, particularly the 'big bang' reforms of the mid-1990s, that restructuring is still to a large extent on hold while academics, politicians, bureaucrats, the media and a range of interest and pressure groups debate how, and how far, to change long-entrenched practices and relationships focused on both the site and mechanisms of financial governance.

Specific changes over the past ten years or so include:

- interest rate deregulation;
- opening financial markets to international integration;
- financial innovation;
- restructuring key aspects of the banking system;
- reshaping financial control structures of both financial and non-financial firms;
- reforming corporate governance arrangements;
- introducing new forms of arm's-length prudential regulation to replace earlier forms of direct bureaucratic interventionism; and
- reforms to the tax system, and much more.

Nevertheless, analysts are agreed that these changes do not yet add up to the kind of full-scale system reform that would be required to drag the Japanese financial system – and the Japanese economy – into the twenty-first century. Whether, if, and how such fundamental restructuring might take place is at the core of debates about governance in Japan. More than that, however, what is at stake is not merely what happens in Japan but involves the centrality of finance and money to governance in general, combined with the dramatic impact of financial globalization everywhere. Fundamental change in Japan would indicate that globalization is reshaping governance even in the most deeply embedded 'developmental state' in the contemporary world.

The concept of governance cuts across the familiar antinomies of 'government' and 'society', of 'state' and 'market', of formal institutions and informal practices, to focus on fundamental modes of structuring power and outcomes on both sides of the public/private divide, enmeshing the two in a multidimensional system of allocating values and resources. The three core 'modes' of governance are (1) *hierarchies*, where outcomes are the result of power and authority organized vertically, (2) *markets*, where outcomes are determined through horizontally organized economic exchanges between autonomous buyers and sellers setting mutually acceptable prices, and (3) *networks*, where ongoing, interdependent social interactions over time create habits, norms and accepted ways of doing things ('practices') that often seem to trump both hierarchies and markets (see Thompson *et al.*, 1991).

The so-called 'Japanese model', while formally capitalist in economic terms and liberal democratic in governmental terms, has involved a strong predominance of both formal and informal hierarchies and networks – although in different admixtures depending on the author, with Chalmers Johnson (1982), for example, emphasizing hierarchies and Karel van Wolferen (1990) emphasizing rather convoluted networks. In both of these authors' views, however, a mix of hierarchy and network is in control – *rather than* market forms of governance as such. This is true for both economic markets – where competitiveness rather than cartels, profitability rather than market share, transparency rather than behind-the-scenes deals, and price-setting in the market rather than by fiat are seen to be both necessary and desirable for economic efficiency – and political markets – where pluralism, accountability, transparency and competitive democracy, rather than vague consensus, corporatism, cronyism and one-party control, are seen to be crucial to 'good governance' and effective public policy.

Nowhere is this more important than with regard to the financial system. For as John Zysman (1983) has argued (see also Cerny 1994), the creation and allocation of money and credit are the underlying elements that make other activities and outputs possible. They determine who has the resources to 'get what, when and how' (the 'medium of exchange'), they permit the comparative measurement of value (the 'unit of account'), and they create the possibility of future investment and growth (the 'store of value'). Indeed, the financial system is the heart and circulatory system of the Japanese model. In the 1970s and 1980s, the Japanese model – or 'developmental state' (Johnson 1982) – was thought not only to be a uniquely successful, exceptional approach to the problems of advanced capitalist society, but also to embody a different *potential* approach for others to copy in the future – one which might indeed be applicable to one extent or another not only in various Asian 'tigers' but also to the 'British disease', the American 'rust bowl' and other cases where the post-long boom recession was undermining the postwar settlement.

Since that time, however, a combination of the post-1989 crisis of the Japanese economy and polity along with the further expansion of neo-liberal, market-oriented economic globalization has undermined what is now seen as the myth of Japanese prowess and caused some key Japanese policymakers increasingly to attempt to pursue basic structural reforms. The core of this uneven and underdeveloped process concerns the Japanese financial system – which lies at the heart of the Japanese model – despite huge entrenched barriers to such reform. In contrast, today's international financial system is often seen as involving the extension of actual market structures and extrapolation of market-like practices across the world. With financial liberalization, pro-market re-regulation and the reduction of capital controls, it is no longer primarily governments that determine what states and economic actors are able to do in the way of allocating capital, although they may play a facilitating role. Nor is it the cosy insider trading cliques of old-style banks and stock markets nor the collaboration of neo-corporatist social partners that determines prices and market outcomes. Rather, it is changing, globally linked financial market governance structures themselves which constitute the principal steering mechanism of the new international financial architecture (Cerny 2002).

The structural challenge: from institutions to markets

The postwar Japanese model was predicated on two things: on the ability of Japan to resist the kind of competitive marketization, globalization and neoliberal *laissez faire* that was later to be embodied in Thatcherism and Reaganism; and on the ability of Japanese firms, backed up by the state, to *exploit* that very globalization and marketization in order to expand their world market shares. The combination of these two factors permitted Japanese firms to use others' openness to their own advantage by exporting or establishing overseas operations while not having to face foreign competition at home. At the core of the model was the financial system, the 'infrastructure of the infrastructure', which seemed capable of squaring the circle. At the beginning of the twenty-first century, however, a combination of ongoing domestic financial crises within Japan plus the spread of globalizing financial market practices is currently leading to the partial collapse and extensive restructuring of the Japanese financial system. The globalization of finance – itself a combination of accelerating international capital flows, growing cross-border price sensitivity, and the restructuring of the financial services sector around a market-based model – impinges upon and penetrates national models everywhere, forcing fundamental changes which must be absorbed and integrated into national institutions and practices if economies are to keep up with the evolving practices of the Competition State (Cerny 2000) and the 'post-Fordist', 'new economy'-based Third Industrial Revolution.

In this context, financial globalization is a particularly powerful and pivotal process in driving political as well as economic change. More specifically, some national economic systems are a priori more open and vulnerable to the 'imperatives' of financial globalization than others. Some systems, especially those of the United States and the United Kingdom, can be classified as *financial market economies* (Coudrat 1986; Loriaux 1991). In such systems, the key to money and finance lies in how 'negotiable' financial instruments known as 'securities' – such as stocks, shares, bonds, and, more recently, a multiplicity of innovative instruments including 'derivatives', 'asset-backed securities', and so on – are *traded* amongst relatively autonomous buyers and sellers. Governments in these systems – if they wish to promote the expansion of financial markets in the name of general economic growth and development, and therefore if private market actors are effectively to provide capital to the economic system as a whole – must therefore keep themselves at arm's length from the ostensibly sacrosanct market relationship between buyers and sellers. Of course, such relationships are open to abuse, as the Enron and other recent scandals in the United States have reminded us. Indeed, pro-market regulation – i.e., regulation intended to make markets more competitive and transparent and less collusive, for example traditional anti-trust legislation and prohibitions on insider trading – has always been at the core of the financial market model. Those sorts of regulation are meant to make markets work better, to 'commodify' rather than to 'decommodify' economic activities (Cerny 1990).

Financial globalization, too, is driven by just this sort of financial market trading and therefore raises the same sort of regulatory issues on a wider, transnational level. This is the case precisely because governments, while they can and do regulate such markets – i.e., set the rules of the game and shape basic aspects of market design – are far less able to shape and control the actual *outcomes* of market transactions. They instead attempt to make the system as a whole work more smoothly by providing nurturing environmental conditions such as 'sound' monetary and fiscal policy, an effective legal system to adjudicate disputes, a market-friendly set of regulatory institutions and processes, and so on. International finance is thus particularly able to escape the clutches of the state in significant ways, especially through 'regulatory arbitrage' or the playing off of different regulatory jurisdictions against each other to get the best, most international-finance-friendly, deal (Cerny 1993: 51–85; Lütz 2002). Regulatory arbitrage, it must be emphasized, like policy responses to perceived 'footloose capital' in general, is not merely the product of specific firms pressurizing governments by shifting (or refusing to shift) their capital around; rather, it usually involves a wider process of policy transfer triggered by policymakers' anticipation of a need for regulatory change in response to 'global realities' (Evans 2004). Thus the whole 'big bang' programme of the mid-1990s can be seen as an attempt by the Hashimoto government to attract reluctant international investors and financial firms into Japan.

Many late nineteenth- and twentieth-century national financial systems such as that of Japan, however, were based on very different structures and practices. Several key nation-states were 'late industrializers', wishing not to see capital flowing freely across borders, but rather to keep it at home. While protecting domestic infant industries from destructive foreign competition, such countries in addition adopted what are called *credit-based* financial systems (Zysman 1983) – also called 'debt-based economies' (Renversez 1986) or 'overdraft economies' (Loriaux 1991). Such systems were aimed at (1) keeping capital at home in order to promote the development of the domestic economy in order to escape the financial market dominance of London and (later) New York, and (2) ensuring that investment flowed to industries that would come to constitute an autonomous, even self-sufficient, economic base for rapid 'catch-up' with (a) earlier industrializers (i.e. Britain) and/or (b) countries with large, practically self-sufficient domestic resources and large-scale domestic markets (mainly the United States).

In finance as in other sectors of these economies (and, indeed, closely interlinked with those sectors), governments fostered the development of monopolistic or oligopolistic cartels. In other words, they promoted systematic attempts to *prevent* too much competition amongst producers and traders in order to resist external domination. Regulated competition was the norm at home. Relations between firms were organized around not competition but market sharing and price fixing. Investment capital in such systems is normally provided not through open market transactions between buyers and sellers, but from negotiated – usually called 'inter-mediated' – relationships between closely intertwined institutions, with the amount of capital provided, and its cost (mainly the rate of interest paid by borrowers) based on collaboration and bargaining amongst institutional actors and not on prices determined through trading on relatively open markets. In this case, it has generally been governments, using resources taken from taxes and/or borrowing, that have provided key backing.

This backing has taken a number of forms, especially in terms of raising investment capital: whether directly by providing subsidies to firms; indirectly through guarantees and the subsidization of interest rates and payback conditions for bank loans to industry; or even more indirectly through anti-competitive regulations and supportive practices which often permit or even encourage firms and cartels to manipulate financial markets themselves in order to ensure a substantial and liquid supply of capital at rigged prices. Development came through the provision of this kind of cheap, long-term capital (sometimes called 'patient capital'), especially in the context of Second Industrial Revolution-type develop-ment where extremely large investments were needed in order to achieve viable economies of scale and scope (Chandler 1990). This approach enabled Germany, Japan and at (a later stage) France and East Asian economies such as South Korea, Malaysia and Thailand to develop rapidly. It also fostered the development of political coalitions, interest group collaboration and bureaucratic practices which gave these governments at various times a potential *strategic* role in promoting development – what Zysman (1983) called the 'strategic state' and Chalmers Johnson (1982) the 'developmental state'.

This is not to say that such systems did not possess capital markets as such, but rather that the *dominant* mode of capital provision and price-setting was through banks – especially those banks with close, entrenched linkages with par-ticular firms and sectors as well as with key government ministries and agencies.

Financial markets played a secondary role – for example in Japan, by providing a forum wherein established financial and industrial firms could carry out deals amongst themselves in order to manipulate the supply and cost of capital through prearranged share transactions. Intermediaries sought to manipulate, and/or authoritatively to restrict the growth of, competitive, shareholder-oriented financial markets – especially where it was felt that foreign capital needed to be kept out in order to focus on domestically generated priorities. But at the same time banks (and the state) had to provide enough finance for the massive investments required for Second Industrial Revolution firms, something financial markets were often unwilling or unable to do except in the United States with its huge domestic market (Chandler, 1990; Chernow, 1990). Large investments required large institutions with deep pockets, whether private or public.

The Japanese intermediary-led system under pressure

Nowhere was the cartellized, intermediary-led model more fully imposed and entrenched than in Japan. It has been at the heart of the post-Meiji approach in the nineteenth century; it was entrenched in the private sector through the big *zaibatsu* trading companies (the forerunners of today's *keiretsu*); it was forcibly imposed by the military regime prior to and during the Second World War; it survived the American Occupation; and it formed the basis of the Japanese developmental state model until recent years. Katz (2003) argues strongly that this sense of historical continuity is largely a myth manipulated and reshaped in the mid-twentieth century. Nevertheless, the way the Japanese financial system has been governed over a long period of time, took on a particular form in the 1960s–1980s, and is solidly 'embedded', as institutional analysts say, through several interlocking foundations – the following six in particular (Johnson 1982; Zysman 1983; Horne 1985; Suzuki 1987; Wright and Pauli 1987; Brown 1994 and 1999; Vogel 1996 and 1999; Hartcher 1997; Katz 1998 and 2003; Carlile and Tilton 1998; Pempel 1998a, 1998b; Morishima 2000; Malcolm 2001; Mikuni and Murphy 2002). These dimensions vary over time, of course, and analysts disagree about details, but their broad parameters are well known and are merely summarized here.

The first foundation was the insulation of the system itself from outside capital. Both the availability of foreign exchange and its use were closely regulated *and rationed* by the government, particularly by the Ministry of Finance (MOF). Dependence on domestic bank financing has thus been the major method by which public–private networks and influence relationships have been signed and sealed. Nevertheless, the restructuring process since the mid-1990s has to a large extent been driven by a combination of a crisis of domestic institutions and an influx of foreign financial firms and investors, increasingly welcomed even by sectors of the government and bureaucracy. The cartellized financial system may not yet be fully open to foreign capital – market share abroad is still widely seen as the key measure of Japanese economic strength – but it is increasingly so, and sometimes in quite spectacular fashion in particular instances. Despite major withdrawals of foreign firms in 2000–2, foreign investors have been the overwhelming (indeed almost the only) driving force of the stock market rebound in mid-2003 (*International Herald Tribune*, 9 July 2003; *Financial Times*, 11 July 2003).

The second foundation was the rationing of domestic capital, too, through both direct and indirect control by MOF. Large loans, especially those above ceilings set by MOF, had to be approved, and MOF (and other ministries) kept a close watch on their uses to ensure that they went to the appropriate infant industries, especially the competitive and highly promoted export sector. Such loans were also usually at discounted, non-market rates in order to keep capital costs low and encourage investment; in this the Japanese model was extremely successful, and it is here that the country gained its reputation as 'Japan Inc.'. These private sector loans were supplemented by public sector financing funded primarily by savings held in the postal savings system (*zaito* funds) and carried out via the MOF's purchase of private sector bank debentures (as well as public sector debentures) through the Fiscal Investment and Loan Programme (FILP; see Wright 2001).

However, as Katz (1998 and 2003) and Carlile and Tilton (1998) argue, from the 1970s onwards such low cost, long-term loans went increasingly not to successful export sector firms, but to the non-competitive, protected sector. Competitive firms found their own sources of capital from export profits. Indeed, much of today's 'bad loans crisis' is said to result from banks having *too much* to lend in recent decades, leading to a sharp increase in 'nonperforming' loans, i.e. to bad (and under-supervised) credit risks (see also Mikuni and Murphy 2002). The ability of banks to obtain guarantees, regulatory approval, rediscounting facilities and the like for such loans has not only ensured their availability but also implied state approval for the activities subsidized. This second characteristic was exacerbated from the 1970s onwards as the special interest politics fostered by the Tanaka government drew the Liberal Democratic Party more closely into a much wider range of quasi-corrupt, clientelistic cartel arrangements mainly for electoral purposes (Pempel 1998a).

A third foundation, much debated in the literature (contrast Hartcher 1997; Brown 1999; and Mikuni and Murphy 2002), has been so-called 'administrative guidance'. Administrative guidance refers to a mix of formal and informal practices whereby banks and other firms regularly consult with their supervising ministries (broadly speaking, the MOF for financial institutions, the Ministry of Economy, Trade and Industry for the competitive exporting sector, the Ministry of Public Management, Home Affairs, Post and Telecommunications for the telecoms sector, the Ministry of Land, Infrastructure and Transport for the construction sector, etc.) and are basically told how to run their businesses, at least at certain times and in ways deemed important by the bureaucracy and (some) politicians. Mikuni and Murphy (2002) argue that administrative guidance was never really just guidance but actually an authoritative command system that firms not only could not disregard but also saw as crucial to their survival and success. Nevertheless, the actual influence of administrative guidance in particular circumstances and issue areas has been variable, is widely debated and is to some extent changing under the sorts of pressures discussed in this chapter.

Brown (1999) argues that administrative guidance has to a large extent been a two-way street. Financial businesses supplied the MOF with extensive information on their operations because they *trusted* the bureaucrats not to give away their proprietary competitive secrets; non-transparency was actually a *source* of strategic effectiveness, co-ordinative capacity and competitive expansion. They also trusted the bureaucrats to take the national interest into account. Such a role can only be played in a system of governance co-ordinated through hierarchical intermediary institutions like banks, operating in close network relationships with equally hierarchical bureaucracies. Market-led systems demand the opposite, especially transparency and competition. But the uncertain future of administrative guidance is a complex feature of the current reform process. It is often argued that the MOF and other ministries, agencies and political groupings today are divided on how far to change the system, with some younger cadres in particular concerned to promote practices compatible with marketization and competitiveness in a more open, global context.

Mikuni and Murphy (2002) argue that bureaucracies and large firms are just as hierarchical and intertwined today as ever. These networks, they say, are still hidden by the lack of transparency and disclosure that continue to exist despite ostensible corporate governance reforms, the huge amount of discretion bureaucrats can call upon in deciding whether actually to enforce existing rules or not, the relative dearth of auditors and accountants and their cosy relationship with firms, and the small size of the legal profession and its lack of an adversarial tradition. Nevertheless, the large extent of piecemeal reforms in all of these areas and their prominence in political debate and the economic and financial press suggests that an internal struggle is taking place *within* the traditional hierarchies and networks as to how to 'modernize' financial governance in Japan. My own interviews in the late 1990s suggest that indeed there are significant 'modernizing' elites within major bureaucratic hierarchies such as the Ministry of Finance, the Bank of Japan, the Financial Supervisory Agency, and so on, especially among younger bureaucrats with experience abroad, seeking to promote regulatory reform and liberalization.

The fourth foundation, already alluded to, involves institutionalized networks of interlocking personnel between politicians, bureaucrats and business elites, cutting across public and private sectors. Although these networks operate at many levels, probably the best known has been the practice of *amakudari* ('descent from heaven'), although the practice is ostensibly in decline in recent years. Top Japanese bureaucrats rise more quickly in their respective career ladders and retire remarkably young by Western standards, allowing them a long second career in the industries they have often supervised. Although practised in other sectors as well, this phenomenon has been particularly notable in the financial sector – with former MOF officials heading the list in 1999 – thus sealing the web of personal and professional relationships between the bureaucracy and financial institutions. Some stronger institutions, such as former *zaibatsu* banks, have always rejected such parachuting, and in today's context when institutions increasingly want to be seen to be independent in a more open financial marketplace, *amakudari* seems to be losing much of its influence and legitimacy, although Mikuni and Murphy (2002) disagree strongly.

The fifth foundation also represents a cultural and ideological attitude more than an economic calculus: the so-called 'convoy system'. This phrase means that change in the financial system is only allowed to proceed at the speed of the slowest ship in the convoy, in order to protect the whole system from being undermined bit by bit. The convoy system led for many years to (among other things) government-managed mergers of unprofitable institutions with (usually) larger institutions with deeper pockets. MOF-sponsored merger activity has often sought to maintain the size, market share, loan portfolio and sometimes even the distinct internal structures of the failing institutions, including jobs. This seemed to work well when the larger Japanese banks were profitable and apparently internationally competitive prior to the bursting of the bubble, but the extent of the bad loans crisis of the 1990s and early 2000s has meant that many mergers are now recognized to have undermined the soundness of the institutions doing the absorbing.

More recent intervention by the MOF and the newer agencies spun off from it such as the Financial Reconstruction Commission (FRC) and the Financial Supervisory Agency (FSA) has at least ostensibly been predicated upon the condition that major restructuring *should* take place but this has been extremely limited. Analysts have generally been highly critical of the practice of pushing troubled banks to merge with more sound ones, on the basis that rather than the sound bank successfully restoring the weak one to health, the result has often been a weakening of the previously sound bank. Weak auditing practices resulting from close links between bureaucrats, banks and accounting firms have also been criticized. For example, controversy in 2003 over the failure of the newly merged Resona Bank and its (ostensibly temporary) quasi-nationalization, for example, has involved a dispute over whether regulators attempted to intervene to stop newly-tough auditors Shin Nihon from declaring Resona bankrupt because of the way it assessed its capital base. Indeed, the head of the Japanese Institute of Certified Public Accountants believes that auditors 'should take on the role of serving the public interest' in identifying and pursuing more such cases and that 'the kind of administrative guidance which gave rise to the convoy system is over' (*Financial Times*, 21 May 2003). Nevertheless, other cases of intervention to save failing banks and 'zombie companies' are continually being discussed in the media and it is still unclear whether Resona constitutes an exception or is evidence of broader changes in attitudes and approach.

At least three aspects of recent restructuring are notable. In the first place, government bailouts of failing institutions have sought to restructure the latters' loan portfolios, for example selling off bad loans at highly discounted market prices or having government agencies take over such loans while seeking partners willing to restructure their own activities in order to ensure both safety and profitability. Indeed, the MOF's approach has involved an uneven blend of old and new Japanese practices, on the one hand, with methods used by the first Bush Administration in the United States during the later stages of the Third World debt crisis (the Brady Plan) and in the Savings and Loans crisis of the late 1980s. Second, the big banks no longer have such deep pockets, being highly vulnerable to the bad loans crisis themselves, and have since the mid-1990s increasingly been forced into so-called 'megamergers', reducing the number of major commercial banks (called 'city banks') from eleven to five, four or possibly three in the near future.

Furthermore, firms outside of the traditional banking sector – foreign banks and financial firms, on the one hand, and certain non-financial firms, too – are playing an increasing role, especially as the 'big bang' reform process has made it possible for financial holding companies to be set up to cut across these boundaries. However, the convoy approach, like much of the cartellized financial system (and other sectors of industry too), has also often been justified not only for its role in ensuring the safety and soundness of the banking system but also as a kind of social policy to protect jobs – both in the banks themselves and in the firms with which they are linked through their loan portfolios. It is this 'stakeholder' facet that is most under threat from financial globalization, because international investors and foreign firms are interested only in 'shareholder value' – i.e. return on capital – and not in subsidizing loss-making activities. Mikuni and Murphy (2002) argue that these restructurings, while more thoroughgoing than previous arranged mergers, are still decided upon and carried out in non-transparent ways through administrative guidance. Nevertheless, there is a growing level of public scrutiny both from the media and from some more active shareholders that makes it more and more difficult to undertake restructurings if they are not justified by market criteria – in other words, if they do not involve real cost-cutting, structural streamlining, labour flexibilization, efficient investment and profit maximization.

The sixth foundation derives from the organizational structure of Japanese industry in general, especially the *keiretsu* system. This is analogous to an endogenous private sector version of the government-industry links discussed earlier. Modelled on the big pre-war *zaibatsu* trading houses, partially dismantled by the postwar occupation authorities, the *keiretsu* are basically very diverse conglomerates made up of firms which are sometimes formally merged, but more often held together by extensive cross-shareholdings. At the core of each of these conglomerate networks has been a main bank which has played various coordinating roles with regard to inter-firm relationships (Horne 1985; Suzuki 1987). These internal governance processes involve not only the supply of investment capital but also other cartel-like inter-firm arrangements on pricing, cross-subsidization of profitable and loss-making activities, dealings with internal and external suppliers, wholesale and even retail distribution, the manipulation of share prices for cross-held shareholdings, and so on.

Although there has been considerable restructuring of the *keiretsu* system because of the bad loans crisis and new government regulations, the outcome has not been so much to unwind shareholdings, spin off subsidiaries and create a more competitive environment as to continue to reshuffle corporate control and to create new, sometimes more powerful oligopolies.

Indeed, this aspect of the Japanese system is one variation on a theme found across East Asia, where complex and loosely coordinated conglomerates are often valued not for their profit potential but rather for their ability to underpin wide-ranging and deeply embedded systems of social control and political influence (Backman 2001).

Restructuring governance: marketization from above and below, or continuing deadlock?

Financial globalization not only threatens the very cohesion of the state–bank–industry nexus at the heart of its capacity to act as a cartel, but also provides a powerful, globally expanding alternative source of capital and transnational systemic organization. At one level, the challenge stems from the sheer *amount* of highly mobile international capital that is available today, dwarfing the capacities of bank-led systems to provide cheap, liquid capital for investment in general. Not only do international capital flows free industry from dependency on bank loans, but state actors find themselves constrained by transnational financial market forces too with regard to macro-economic and micro-economic policymaking, thus limiting available policy alternatives (Cerny 1996). At a time when the Japanese government is becoming more and more indebted, up to 150 per cent of GDP (by far the highest level among developed countries), especially to Japanese banks – the market for Japanese government bonds still being quite restricted, as there is little individual ownership and therefore little liquidity and not much of a secondary market for pricing purposes – government debt, far from being inflationary, is actually taking more out of the money supply than it puts back in, through new spending on politically opportunistic projects and the growing 'structural deficit' stemming from interest payments on that debt. Indeed, should interest rates rise from the current near-zero policy, the government's structural deficit could quickly become crippling.

At a second level, however, the challenge comes from changes that are required in the *structure* of the governance of the financial system itself – that is to say, the process of marketization. For capital to be made available, both foreign market actors *and* internationally linked domestic market actors must be confident that their money will gain a market rate of return and that the financial instruments they have bought can be sold again at market prices ('liquidity'). And finally, investment must be able to flow into uses that are determined in the markets, not by state planners, 'relationship' bankers or oligopolistic industrialists. In the current Third Industrial Revolution, sometimes called the 'new economy', volatile and rapidly metamorphosing high technology industries have been compared with the coming of electricity or the automobile. This process involves a *redirection* of investment away from older industries and towards newer, more flexible, 'post-Fordist' industries.

Indeed, this is exactly what *was* happening, however unevenly and sporadically, in Japan at the end of the twentieth century (Katz 1998, 2003). The internationally competitive export sector – the product of the era of intermediary-led catch-up – is still crucial, but international competitiveness has drawn many of these industries to produce in other parts of East Asia and the world (including the United States and Europe) rather than in Japan. At the same time, the increasingly loss-making protected sector – today including many banks as well as agriculture, distribution, construction and a range of other uncompetitive industries – is still being protected, although it is under increasing pressure to restructure, driven by the need to seek capital from outside traditional channels as well as by growing government deficits. However, the third sector, the so-called 'new economy', while extremely dynamic at the recent turn of the century, has suffered from a severe credit crunch. Banks still do not lend sufficiently to smaller firms despite MOF and Bank of Japan (BOJ) pressure to do so (*Financial Times*, 12 June 2003), venture capital has dried up, initial public offerings (IPOs) of shares are more and more difficult to arrange, and there is a shrinking of new financial markets originally set up to service this sector. Particularly striking is the way the recently established 'Mothers' market has stagnated and Nasdaq Japan has shut down.

As noted earlier, the internationally competitive export sector has for some years grown steadily more independent from its bureaucratic sponsors because it no longer needs their capital. Such firms are in a position to finance many of their investment needs from retained profits, and they have been increasingly willing to direct these investments to production facilities outside of Japan. On the other hand, their very competitiveness, increasing profitability and internationalization mean that they have easy access to international capital, too, without the constraints of bureaucratic 'administrative guidance'. Nevertheless, many firms in this sector also need to restructure, and that restructuring increasingly comes through international channels, as has been the case with Nissan since its effective takeover by Renault. The protected sector, meanwhile, has, if anything, become *more* dependent on traditional domestic channels of support. Restructuring of vast swathes of unprofitable subsectors and firms would lead to extreme consequences for production and employment (Katz 1998, 2003).

At the same time, the volatility of political coalitions in the 1990s made the predominant Liberal Democratic Party much more dependent on support from the protected sector – especially from agriculture and those rural areas where agriculture is declining and which are increasingly dominated by employment in construction – as its urban base has eroded (Pempel 1998a; Kerr 2001; George Mulgan 2002). The level of unemployment, having grown in 2003 to around 5.6 per cent (although it has fallen back in 2004) – less than in much of Europe, but near rapidly rising American levels (although the lack of a social safety net arguably makes Japan's unemployment rate more socially damaging) – would be badly hit by closures in the protected sector, as employment has already carried the burden over the past couple of decades for the hollowing out of the export sector. In this situation, governments around the turn of the century have relied on regular reflationary packages and a very loose, near-zero interest rate monetary policy. However, with the public debt burden far higher than in other industrialized countries, such an approach is unsustainable in the medium term.

In this context, the role of the state and the role of the private sector are both problematic. The state is a split between the political imperatives of maintaining the protected sector (both financial and industrial), on the one hand, and the imperatives – economic *and* political – of restructuring that sector and promoting the development of an internationally penetrated, marketized financial system. Evidence of schizophrenic reactions to this dilemma abound. The 'big bang' programme initiated by the Hashimoto government in 1996 has for the most part been legislated for (Cunanan and Dowling, 1998), but parts of it are variously accelerated and postponed depending on the balance of influence at different times among and within political coalitions and factions, bureaucratic agencies and competing private firms and sectoral interests. At the same time, the stagnation of the Japanese economy through the rest of the 1990s and up to 2003 has made it difficult to implement the reforms. Economic crisis sometimes reinforces reforms, while in good times reforms seem less necessary, like the old saying about how it is easy to forget to fix a leaky roof on a sunny day. Japan's problem throughout the 1990s has been that it has neither been in crisis nor have there been many sunny days, so the reform process has merely stuttered along.

In particular, the high level of non-performing loans in the banking sector – mainly loans to chronically unprofitable firms ('zombie companies') – means that banks have undermined their own performance by sustaining such firms while attempts to confront the issue have stagnated until recently. Although public awareness and disclosure are rapidly increasing, Mikuni and Murphy (2002) among others argue that, given the general stagnation of the Japanese economy over the past decade, nonperforming loans are a major prop and that to take them away would create a ripple-effect crisis across the whole economy. The reform plans of Prime Minister Koizumi Junichiro and Financial Services Minister Takenaka Heizō have been watered down and resisted by politicians, bureaucrats and banks alike (George Mulgan 2002).

Nevertheless, the possibility of progress seems greater in 2004 than in the mid-1990s – when, of course, it petered out, to be undermined more comprehensively by the world slump of 2000–3. Even the big banks' declaration of huge losses in the 2002–3 financial year 'are seen in some quarters as a positive development because they reflect a new-found ability to admit to the true scale of their problems after years of obfuscation' (*Financial Times*, 26 May 2003). At the time of writing in mid-2004, a surge of growth in the Japanese economy produced by rapid export expansion (mainly to China) has led to a profit rebound for three of the four largest banks, both permitting a rise in loan loss provisions and alleviating the position of some of the companies in trouble (*International Herald Tribune*, 25 May 2004). It remains to be seen, however, whether this is just a sunny day and the leaky roof still needs fixing. In contrast, UFJ Holding, the fourth of the big banks, recently declared larger loan loss provisions and decided to sell its trust bank operations, but, in the words of *Financial Times* correspondent David Ibison: 'The management changes at UFJ and its decision to admit to worse-than-expected non-performing loans are, however, signs that the bank is accelerating its reform drive' (21 May 2004).

The state, although it initiated the 'big bang' programme in order to try to *control* the process of financial deregulation liberalization (Vogel 1996), is increasingly being whipsawed by accelerating trends in the financial markets and the Third Industrial Revolution themselves. Some of those trends have come from abroad

– from what the Japanese call *gaiatsu*, or external pressures from both the United States government and international markets themselves. However, many of the most important changes have come from internal pressures – what has sometimes been called *naiatsu* (in a neologistic response to *gaiatsu*: cf. Brown 1994; Kusano 1999). At one level, *naiatsu* comes from within the political system and the bureaucracy, from the growing intergenerational differences noted earlier between more internationalist and more domesticist bureaucrats, especially within the MOF and the Bank of Japan. Second, there are the political calculations which led the Hashimoto government in 1996 to initiate the 'big bang' reforms for fear of missing the liberalization boat altogether as the post-bubble recession dragged on – and which are continuing to dominate both the rapidly changing internal politics of the LDP and the fractionating coalition politics of the Japanese party system.

Third, although the full impact of the recent break-up of the MOF itself has not yet shaken out, there have been growing inter-agency and intra-agency disputes as functions have been spun off through organs such as the FRC and the FSA. Indeed, Katz (2003) argues that although such agencies seemed keen on reform at the start, officials have been discouraged by the depth and breadth of internal resistance from firms as well as from entrenched bureaucratic and political practices. Scepticism about the restructuring of ministries and agencies is rife. For example, Mikuni and Murphy (2002) argue that these bodies are merely spinoffs from the MOF and BOJ and have not changed their practices with regard to poor disclosure, discretionary application of rules, attempts to control outcomes (mergers, etc.), and desire to rescue as much of the existing system as possible. Nevertheless, their work is increasingly in the media spotlight, comparisons are increasingly made with experiences and institutional structures in other countries, intra-agency struggles abound, and the outcomes they seek to impose and control are increasingly market-oriented. Recent progress by the major banks in the reduction of non-performing loans suggests that changes in governance have grown more successful over time.

Finally, there have been political pressures from new constituencies. Individual as well as institutional savers and lenders increasingly seek to invest at market rates and are put off bank or postal savings deposits by the combination of low (virtually zero) interest rates and fear of loss of savings through bank failure as a result of the bad loans crisis. Furthermore, many urban voters are said by analysts to resent the practice of government subsidies for protected sectors. Indeed, the Liberal Democratic Party, out of power for a brief phase in the early 1990s and now only ruling through a volatile coalition, has been losing much of its already weak urban support and today is overwhelmingly a rural party. The LDP is increasingly split between those who see further liberalization as inevitable and those who seek to backtrack on reform for electoral purposes. The ousting of Prime Minister Mori in favour of the current incumbent, Koizumi Junichirō, was squarely rooted in the reform issue. Koizumi has been forced to tack and pull back in many areas. The key issue here is whether reform can be combined with (1) preventing a further credit crunch crisis that will plunge Japan into much deeper recession while banks and unprofitable firms restructure, and (2) dealing with the internal politics of the

LDP, which increasingly seem to entangle Koizumi and his supporters despite their pledges of reform (George Mulgan 2002).

Decompartmentalization, price competition, new technology and the advent of the financial market economy in Japan

Thus although change has been partly leveraged through particular 'big bang' reforms, those reforms are not leading the process but lagging it. Doors set ajar at all levels – by *gaiatsu*, by the 'big bang' reforms, and by the globalization of financial markets themselves – are being levered further both by international firms and by domestic *naiatsu* from Japanese firms seeking to compete for investment funds on a wider international playing field as well as the day-to-day interactions and growing linkages between those international and domestic firms. The key actors here are therefore (1) foreign firms and investors seeking to enter or expand within the Japanese market, (2) domestic firms and investors seeking to get out of the vicious circle of the protected sector, (3) new entrepreneurs seeking to expand venture capital activities especially in new technology sectors such as the internet or to import practices such as hostile takeovers, (4) old firms restructuring and downsizing in the face of international competition whether in industrial sectors like the automobile industry (Nissan) or through bank megamergers, (5) young consumers turning to fashionable high-tech products that are often not reflected in official statistics, and the like.

Comparative analysts of financial system change are likely to identify two specific kinds of public policy reforms as generally crucial for the political management and promotion of financial system restructuring in such a globalization-driven context (for France, see Cerny, 1989), and so it is proving to be in Japan. The first is the decompartmentalization of financial markets themselves. One of the major ways that governments across the developed world have attempted to prevent market failure has been to legally separate different kinds of markets from each other so that the kind of contagion or domino effect across markets like those characteristic, for example, of the 1929 Wall Street crash and its aftermath can be prevented. In Japan, via Article 65 of the Securities and Exchange Law of 1948, as in the American Glass-Steagall Act of 1933, the main regulatory barrier to be erected was the prohibition of commercial banks from dealing in securities and of securities firms and investment banks from engaging in commercial banking activities, i.e. those that involve taking deposits from the public.

It was not until the mid-1990s, especially with the 'big bang' programme, that significant progress began towards lowering compartmental barriers within Japan. As in the United States, a major means to this end has been to allow different firms to merge into federalized *holding companies* made up of partially or wholly owned subsidiaries operating in different market sectors. Holding companies were the basis of the pre-war *zaibatsu* and as such were prohibited in order to prevent their renascence, although that prohibition was easily bypassed in various ways. Today, holding companies have once again been legalized and indeed are the basis for much of the inter-firm restructuring taking place within the Japanese financial sector. Today, in Japan as elsewhere, however, such subsidiaries increasingly have to be characterized by certain levels of *internal compartmentalization*, what the British call 'Chinese walls' and the Americans call 'firewalls' among different market sector activities. Mikuni and Murphy (2002) argue that such Chinese walls in Japan are still a fiction.

However, the acceleration of changes to accounting rules and corporate governance rules, as with other issues, has created a public and media awareness of the problems and specific cases of conflict of interest, and so on, are being targeted. For example, one widely discussed development has been the recent adoption of rules which permit listed companies to adopt American-style corporate governance regimes, including the establishment of separate committees to conduct audits, nominate the board of directors and set executive pay. These changes have come from a combination of indirect *gaiatsu* – the American Sarbanes-Oxley Act of 2002 in particular, with its effectively extraterritorial auditing requirements – and *naiatsu* – including the government-led unwinding of cross-shareholdings within the *keiretsu*, greater foreign ownership of Japanese companies, demands for greater shareholder participation in corporate management, and changing attitudes among managers in the more internationalized Japanese companies. Although originally met with scepticism, thirty-six major companies will adopt these proposals in the near future (*Financial Times*, 16 June 2003). As with the Resona affair, it is difficult to predict whether this is a cosmetic change or represents a broader structural shift. Nevertheless, as with the Enron, WorldCom, Arthur Andersen and New York analyst research issues in the United States – all of which have raised awareness levels across the world, putting corporate governance issues at the forefront of debate in new ways – the links between these questions and ongoing processes of reform are altering patterns of financial system governance.

With different markets opened up to arbitrage, the second key structural reform is to enable market actors to fully compete on price and quality of service across those markets. The first stage of this type of reform was to deregulate interest rates. Although limited forms of interest rate deregulation began in the late 1970s, this was generally restricted to certain sectors of the bond market, and a combination of administrative guidance and the convoy system ensured that Japanese banks basically charged the same interest rates until the mid-1990s. Indeed, the cultural inhibition against breaking ranks is still strong in traditional banking sectors. However, a combination of the bad loans crisis, financial innovation primarily in the securities field, the lack of compartmentalization in global financial markets, and the rapid pace of change in Japanese securities markets has put such traditional practices very much on the defensive, and it is highly likely that they are on their way out except in certain kinds of financial institutions catering to special constituencies such as small regional banks, agricultural cooperatives, credit unions and the like – although even here changes are proceeding surprisingly rapidly because such institutions have also been severely affected by non-performing loans and lack of profitability. At the same time, the question of financing the public sector deficit and the limited scope of the Japanese Government Bond (JGB) market may well be not only crowding out private sector spending and investment but also holding back change through deflation.

Perhaps the most important reform leading to extensive price competition across the entire system is the deregulation of brokerage commissions in securities markets. Given that the most important financial innovations in recent decades have been those in the securities markets – most notably the huge expansion of innovation and trading in so-called 'derivatives' such as futures, options and swaps, originally developed for agricultural commodities and foreign exchange trading – freedom of market actors to negotiate commissions is probably the ultimate means of undermining cartel-like price fixing in the financial services sector. After brokerage commissions were completely liberalized in October 1999 (after having been progressively deregulated over the previous two years), Japanese financial markets were hit by a veritable avalanche of change. Much of it is still inchoate, but it bears a remarkable resemblance to wider trends in financial markets around the world.

The first and most striking manifestation of these changes at the time was the increasingly visible entry of foreign financial firms into Japan. Foreign investors and firms are now welcomed by a growing range of market actors and the business media, as reflected, for example, in the pages of the English-language *Nikkei Weekly*. Even more impressive has been the rush of Japanese financial institutions to take advantage of these firms' experience and skills through joint ventures and the like in areas such as mergers and acquisitions. These developments have also helped catalyse the rapid growth of the venture capital industry in Japan, a sector which virtually did not exist a few years ago, as well as the investment trust and mutual funds sector. Although many joint ventures have been limited in scope (Malcolm 2001), they are increasingly ubiquitous and entrenched, impacting on the way the Japanese financial system itself operates.

However, the stagnation of the Japanese economy along with the financial slump across the developed world has undermined this trend since 2000, with foreign capital rapidly withdrawing from the country, only returning in Spring 2003 – and on a basis which many observers believe may constitute just another fragile and temporary 'bear market rally'. Nevertheless, there has grown an awareness that change will only come when such firms – and their practices – return on a more solid footing. This influx has even had a visible impact on the cultural context of the financial system. Foreign firms have become very fashionable as employers of high-flying Japanese graduates. Changing jobs is more respectable and desired. And in the markets themselves, new forms of demand mushroomed for a while and are beginning to return. However, the new economy boom is still mainly in limbo. Japanese firms, which once dominated new sectors of consumer electronics as they came along, are far less competitive today. Their only technological edge seems to be in the booming domestic mobile phone industry, but the fact that Japanese cell phone technology is not fully compatible with systems in other countries has severely limited their penetration of export markets. In contrast, US cell phone technology, which is also incompatible with other countries (especially the European GSM standard), benefits from a huge internal market that Japan lacks.

Nevertheless, Japanese financial system governance is being increasingly marketized, if at an uneven pace. In the first place, despite a string of politically motivated delays, many of the 'big bang' reforms promised and partially legislated for in 1996–8 are now finally coming on stream of their own accord. Furthermore, at the same time, Koizumi and Takenaka are apparently committed to further, ostensibly far-reaching, measures. However, these measures are being unevenly implemented, with a major (if somewhat watered down) programme presented at the end of October 2002. At the same time, opposition to some of these measures by the powerful Hashimoto faction and others in the LDP – paradoxically led by the man who as Prime Minister in 1996 initiated the 'big bang' programme – has not coalesced around an alternative. *Sub rosa* guerrilla political warfare has been the order of the day. Splits in the opposition parties have played into the hands of the resisters. Public and media opinion, as well as pressures from modernizing sectors amongst some party politicians, bureaucrats and private sector groups has grown stronger in favour of continuing the reform process, and there seems to be a growing momentum for reform and anger at resisters. Whether the current return to rapid economic growth will accelerate or mute the pressure for reform is still to be seen.

Conclusion

Although private sector-led changes have been enabled by bureaucratic shifts and the 'big bang' programme, pressures for them have not come so much from the state *per se* as from a combination of international market developments and changes in technological and market structure working through the private sector and altering the basis of public–private network relationships. Closed public–private and private–private networks based on trust are being overlaid and at least partially contested and replaced by more individualistic and competitive relationships based on marketization. The state, still deeply embedded in and constrained by the practices comprising the failing traditional Japanese model, has made many false starts since the mid-1980s and is still floundering. But those false starts have included and kicked off many real policy and bureaucratic changes that have a life of their own, however contested, in the evolving dialectic of financial market globalization and regulatory liberalization.

Can Japan continue to resist the restructuring pressures coming from the 'structural *gaiatsu*' of the global financial marketplace (Pempel 1998b) and the 'structural *naiatsu*' of rapidly mutating domestic economic and political interests? Part of the price to pay may be the 'creative destruction' of the protected sector, further political instability, and growing social dissatisfaction. In this context, the current rapid growth of the economy in 2004 may have contradictory consequences. On the one hand, growth may simply soak up pressures for change. Export-led growth, after all, was the core of the developmental state. Additional growth may permit more firms with non-performing loans to start to pay some of them back, ostensibly heading off the need for further structural changes in the banking system. Growing trade surpluses may undercut the credit crunch that has made financial system reform seem urgent. At the same time, reduced unemployment and the revival of consumer spending may decrease potential social dissatisfaction, diminishing political pressure for reform.

On the other hand, recovery, if sustained, may attract more foreign capital, bolster securities markets and venture capital, and reinforce transnational linkages – capital mobility and price sensitivity – in the more dynamic sectors of the economy. Regulatory reform may appear more a political opportunity than a threat, strengthening pro-reform *naiatsu*. In the latter scenario, as the current uneven global recovery gains momentum, neo-liberal norms and practices are likely to become more and more deeply embedded. The Koizumi government is apparently committed to further reform of the financial system and the opposition Democratic Party of Japan seems to favour it, too, although with some differences of emphasis. Changes elsewhere in East Asia, too, are broadly in the direction of neo-liberal re-regulation, even in China. Japan is not yet a 'financial market economy', but it is unlikely that the developmental state can be resurrected; the earlier 'credit-based economy' and the sites of governance that have gone along with that are in structural decay. In a world of financial market globalization and neo-liberal marketization in general, it may no longer be a question of whether Japan becomes a 'financial market economy', but when – and with what consequences for the wider economy, politics and society.

References

Backman, Michael (2001) *Asian Eclipse: exposing the dark side of business in Asia*, Singapore: Wiley.

Brown, J. Robert Jr. (1994) *Opening Japan's Financial Markets*, London: Routledge.

Brown, J. Robert Jr. (1999) *The Ministry of Finance: bureaucratic practices and the transformation of the Japanese economy*, Westport, CT and London: Quorum Books.

Carlile, Lonnie E. and Tilton, Mark C. (eds) (1998) *Is Japan Really Changing Its Ways? Regulatory reform and the Japanese economy*, Washington, DC: Brookings Institution Press.

Cerny, Philip G. (1989) 'The "little big bang" in Paris: financial market deregulation in a *dirigiste* system', *European Journal of Political Research* 17, 2 (March): 169–92.

Cerny, Philip G. (1990) *The Changing Architecture of Politics: structure, agency and the future of the state*, London and Thousand Oaks, CA: Sage.

Cerny, Philip G. (ed.) (1993) *Finance and World Politics: markets, regimes and states in the post-hegemonic era*, Cheltenham, Glos. and Brookfield, VT: Edward Elgar.

Cerny, Philip G. (1994) 'The dynamics of financial globalization: technology, market structure and policy response', *Policy Sciences* 27, 4 (November): 319–42.

Cerny, Philip G. (1996) 'International finance and the erosion of state policy capacity', in Philip Gummett (ed.) *Globalization and Public Policy*, Cheltenham, Glos. and Brookfield, VT: Edward Elgar, pp. 83–104

Cerny, Philip G. (2000) 'Restructuring the political arena: globalization and the paradoxes of the competition state', in Randall D. Germain (ed.) *Globalization and Its Critics: perspectives from political economy*, London: Macmillan, pp. 117–38.

Cerny, Philip G. (2002) 'Webs of governance: national authorities and transnational markets', in David M. Andrews, C. Randall Henning, and Louis W. Pauly (eds) *Governing the World's Money*, Ithaca, NY: Cornell University Press, pp. 194–215.

Chandler, Alfred D. Jr. (1990). *Scale and Scope: the dynamics of industrial capitalism*, Cambridge, MA: Harvard University Press.

Chernow, Ron (1990) *The House of Morgan: an American banking dynasty and the rise of modern finance*, New York: Simon and Schuster.

Coudrat, C. (1986). 'États-Unis: une économie de marchés financiers', in F. Renversez, (ed.) *Les Systèmes Financiers*, Les Cahiers Français 224 (January–February) Paris: La Documentation Française, pp. 26–42

Cunanan, Christian O. and Dowling, Peter (eds) (1998) *Japan's Big Bang*, Tokyo: Kozo System.

Evans, Mark (ed.) (2004) *Policy Transfer in Global Perspective*, Aldershot: Ashgate.

Hartcher, Peter (1997) *The Ministry: the inside story of Japan's Ministry of Finance*, London: HarperCollins.

George Mulgan, Aurelia (2002) *Japan's Failed Revolution: Koizumi and the politics of reform*, Canberra: Asia Pacific Press.

Horne, J. (1985) *Japan's Financial Markets: conflict and consensus in policymaking*, Sydney: George Allen and Unwin.

Johnson, Chalmers (1982). *MITI and the Japanese Miracle: the growth of industrial policy, 1925–1975*, Stanford: Stanford University Press.

Katz, Richard (1998). *Japan, the System that Soured: the rise and fall of the Japanese miracle*, Armonk, NY and London: M. E. Sharpe.

Katz, Richard (2003) *Japanese Phoenix: the long road to economic revival*, Armonk, NY and London: M. E. Sharpe.

Kerr, Alex (2001) *Dogs and Demons: the fall of modern Japan*, London: Penguin.

Kusano, Atsushi (1999) 'Deregulation in Japan and the role of *naiatsu* (domestic pressure)', *Social Science Journal Japan* 2, 1 (April): 65–84.

Loriaux, Michael (1991). *France After Hegemony: international change and financial reform*, Ithaca, NY: Cornell University Press.

Lütz, Susanne (2002) 'Convergence within national diversity – a comparative perspective on the regulatory state in finance', paper presented at the annual conference of the British International Studies Association, London School of Economics (16–18 December).

Malcolm, James D. (2001) *Financial Globalisation and the Opening of the Japanese Economy*, Richmond: Curzon.

Mikuni, Akio and Murphy, R.T. (2002). *Japan's Policy Trap: dollars, deflation, and the crisis of Japanese finance*, Washington, DC: The Brookings Institution.

Morishima, Michio (2000) *Japan at a Deadlock*, London and New York: Macmillan and St Martin's Press.

Pempel, T. J. (1998a) *Regime Shift: comparative dynamics of the Japanese political economy*, Ithaca: Cornell University Press.

Pempel, T. J. (1998b) 'Structural *gaiatsu*: international finance and political change in Japan', paper presented to the annual meeting of the American Political Science Association, Boston, MA (2–6 September).

Renversez, F. (1986) 'France: une économie d'endettement', in F. Renversez (ed.) *Les Systèmes Financiers*, Les Cahiers Français 224 (January–February) Paris: La Documentation Française, pp. 3–25.

Suzuki, Y. (ed.) (1987) *The Japanese Financial System*, Oxford: Oxford University Press.

Thompson, G., Frances, J., Levačić, R., and Mitchell, J. (eds.) (1991) *Markets, Hierarchies and Networks: the coordination of social life*, London and Thousand Oaks, CA: Sage.

Van Wolferen, Karel (1990) *The Enigma of Japanese Power: people and politics in a stateless nation*, New York: Knopf.

Vogel, Stephen K. (1996) *Freer Markets, More Rules: regulatory reform in advanced industrial countries*, Ithaca, NY: Cornell University Press.

Vogel, Stephen K. (1999). 'Can Japan Disengage? Winners and losers in Japan's political economy, and the ties that bind them', *Social Science Journal Japan* 2, 1 (April): 3–21.

Wright, Maurice (2001) *Japan's Fiscal Crisis: the Ministry of Finance and the politics of public spending, 1975–2000*, Oxford: Oxford University Press.

Wright, R. W. and Pauli, G. A. (1987) *The Second Wave: Japan's global assault on financial services*, London: Waterlow.

Zysman, John (1983) *Governments, Markets, and Growth: financial systems and the politics of industrial change*, Ithaca, NY: Cornell University Press.

6 Koizumi's 'robust policy'

Governance, the Japanese welfare employment regime and comparative gender studies

Osawa Mari

This chapter discusses the type, and a possible shift in the type of governance of the welfare-employment regime in Japan, the structures and processes of which are determined by the perceived relative competency, authority and legitimacy of the state, market and family in supporting the reproduction of the labour force at micro, meso and macro levels, as the very basis of any political economy.

What various sides in the current debate on the type of governance agree on is that the Japanese welfare-employment regime belongs to the 'male breadwinner' model. This model entails two fundamental assumptions about the division of labour between the sexes: first, that resources to support livelihood and labour reproduction every day and inter-generationally, in terms of monetary income, are and should be secured by the man as the husband/father of the family primarily through participating in the labour market and earning a 'family wage' as a full-time, long-term employed worker, and exceptionally through receiving social security benefits in unemployment, sickness or retirement; and second, that resources in terms of personal services (care) and readily consumable goods (cooked food and washed clothes, for instance) are and should be supplied primarily by the woman as the wife/mother of the family through unpaid work as a homemaker, and only exceptionally through social welfare services. It is the family assumed as such that has been the fundamental site of governance in the Japanese welfare-employment regime since the rapid economic growth period as the very basis of societal reproduction, and gender relations crosscutting the family, labour and other markets and state institutions are one of the most important elements of its governance.

What should be kept in mind is that the male breadwinner- full-time housewife households have never been an overwhelming majority of families in Japanese society even in its heyday in the late 1970s. The type of governance of the welfare-employment regime is not a mere reflection of the reality of family life or the dominant mode of labour reproduction, but assumptions in and design of the social policy and employment system do condition individual women and men to choose a particular style of work and family life rather than other ways. Governance should therefore be seen as having been practised in both bottom up and top down ways, and as a result is contested.

The performance as well as legitimacy of this type of governance started to be questioned and explicitly contested in the early 1990s, as the recession after the bursting of the 'bubble economy' continued and population ageing, hand in hand with a declining birth rate, accelerated. After the various attempts made by successive administrations to reform the political, social and more generally the governing institutions and structures of Japan, the coalition cabinet of Prime Minisiter Koizumi Junichirō took office in April 2001, calling for an overall structural reform of Japanese society.

Thus, on 26 June 2001, soon after taking office, the Koizumi cabinet launched the so-called *Honebuto no Hōshin* ('Robust Policy') that laid down the fundamentals for a structural overhaul of Japanese society. This 2001 'Robust Policy' was actually based on a proposal, with a blueprint of its own, drafted by the *Naikakufu Keizai Zaisei Shimon Kaigi* (The Cabinet Office's Council on Economic and Fiscal Policy – CEFP, chaired by the Prime Minister himself), led by the Minister of Economy, Trade and Industry (METI), Takenaka Heizō. According to one member of the CEFP, 'Koizumi's reform is hesitantly treading along the path of the *Keizai Senryaku Kaigi* (Economic Strategy Council of Japan, hereafter ESC). 'While progress has been made in some areas, it continues to be a mere extension of its policy recommendation' (*Asahi Shimbun*, 13 June 2001).

The ESC, chaired by Higuchi Hirotarō, a key player in Keidanren and the former president of Asahi Breweries, submitted its final policy recommendation in February 1999, titled 'Strategies for Reviving the Japanese Economy'. It concluded that, in order to revive the economy in the twenty-first century, Japan must totally transform its social system, 'which has heretofore placed excessive emphasis on the equality of results'. The report also refers to the mounting anxiety over Japan's future, saying 'these fears are attributable to [the] eroding sustainability in the Japanese-style wage and employment systems and the generous social security system'. It concludes that Japan should aim to build 'an environment of "creative competition" by ensuring equality of opportunity to all [those] who wish to enter into private activities' under transparent and appropriate rules. To do this, 'provisions of renewed safety nets are urgently needed' (ESC 1999a: 17, 3).

In short, the ESC concludes that in Japan, the equality of results is stressed to such an extent that it has become detrimental, and thus assumes Japanese society to be fairly egalitarian. Based on these premises, it proposes to use 'equal opportunity' as a lever in order to proceed with an overall reform of the social safety nets. Let us call this notion of the Japanese-style social system the concept of 'fair discrepancy'. Thus, can we say that Koizumi's social reform is 'an extended version' of the plan for Japan's social reform based on this 'fair discrepancy' theory?

The ESC recommendation characterized Japan as overly egalitarian and called for social reform by introducing '"small government-type" safety nets rather than "big government" intervening in private activities and guaranteeing total life'. It states that ' . . . the desirable safety nets are to provide a civil minimum to all citizens in need who understand self-responsibility, by assisting them to "re-challenge" their lives' (ESC 1999a: 25).

With regard to social security in particular, the ESC concludes that the prolongation of stagnant economic growth, the sharp decline in the birth rate, and the rapid ageing of the population have further widened the inequality between generations and are eroding the sustainability of the social security system itself. Thus it states, first, that the national minimum should not be set too high for social security benefits since 'too *generous* a standard will cause moral hazards and result in bloated government', and proposes to limit the social services to 'the socially desirable minimum' (ESC 1999a: 28, 30 my emphasis). Second, the report is critical of past attempts at social security reform led by the Ministry of Health and Welfare (from 2001, the Ministry of Health, Labour and Welfare), which the Council considers as having repeatedly raised the insurance premiums and reduced the benefits. As a result, 'households and enterprises have lost confidence in future sustainable growth. Moreover, they have given less credence to government policies' (ESC 1999a: 28).

While criticizing past reform attempts by the former Ministry of Health and Welfare, the direction that the ESC points at in order to 'build a sustainable, confidence-based social security system' is to 'actively mobilize private initiatives and keep public intervention to a minimum'. In other words, what the ESC wants is a 'small, inexpensive government'. Thus the ESC's emphasis on privatization, deregulation and liberalization of choice and the way it trusts market functions and lays stress on 'self-responsibility' based on strict selectivity seems to allow us to interpret its prescription as a neo-liberal, commodification-oriented one in both intent and measures. The dichotomy such as commodification versus de-commodification, efficiency versus equity, or small versus big government, however, is too simplistic to understand how contested governance is in Japan. Despite the ESC's repeated criticism of past reform attempts by the Ministry of Health and Welfare, it will be clearly shown by a comparative gender analysis that its proposals have not parted with Japan's previous model of social policy and the overall governance of the welfare-employment regime. Even if the ESC proposals were to materialize, the co-ordinates of Japan's social policy system and governance structures dominant since the rapid growth period, i.e. the big-company oriented 'male breadwinner' model, would not be easily transformed.

Although there are some valid criticisms of the notion of 'fair discrepancy', few analyses have been made of the ESC report from the viewpoint of the governance of welfare-employment regimes in general, and of comparative gender studies in particular. In this chapter, let us first touch upon the recent debate regarding social discrepancy and equality in Japan to examine the validity of the conceptualization of 'fair discrepancy' and 'equality of opportunity' itself by the ESC (Section 1), then analyze the ESC recommendation in view of the Japanese social policy system and governance structure from a comparative gender analysis (Section 2), and re-examine Koizumi's 'Robust Policy', which is called a 'mere extension' of the ESC's recommendation (Section 3).

Blind spots in the debate on inequality

The concept of 'fair discrepancy' is not an invention of some academic at the ESC. Rather, it is a concept that has been deliberated among various sectors of society during the latter half of the 1990s, and mainstreamed since. As early as the mid-1990s, in fact, employers' associations such as *Nikkeiren* were calling for a 'new Japanese-style management system' based on multiple tracks, diversification and increased flexibility in employment. Multiple tracking implied a further widening of the wage gap between workers through rigid personnel assessment and wage control upon assessing the professional skill and job performance of each employee. It is alleged that this kind of differential treatment has now gained popular approval. For instance, in March 2000, the *Sangyō Kōzō Shingikai* (Industrial Structure Council) of the Ministry of International Trade and Industry (MITI, from 2001 the Ministry of Economy, Trade and Industry, METI) presented a paper titled *Kyōsōryoku aru Tasankaku Shakai* ('Building a Competitive, Participatory Society') to set the direction of the nation's economic and industrial policy with a view to 2025. It upheld the vision of a society that offers multiple choices and diverse ways of living, where 'those who take on challenges will be valued and where appropriate assessment will generate a "fair discrepancy" between those who do not make effort and those who create meaningful values' (Tsūsanshō 2000: 60–1).

As the 'fair discrepancy' theory came into the mainstream from the mid-1990s onward, arguments about social inequality and the widening of the economic gap within Japanese society also came into focus, particularly as the Japanese economy suffered a sharp decline from the latter half of 1997. The two major advocates are Tachibanaki Toshiaki, whose book *Nihon no Keizai Kakusa* (Economic disparity in Japan) won (1998; see also 2000) the 1998 Economist Prize, and Satō Toshiki, whose book *Fubyōdō Shakai Nippon* (Japan, the unequal society) (2000b) attracted substantial attention.

As Tachibanaki pointed out in his 1998 book based on an examination of the trends in the gini coefficient, the income distribution in Japan has become significantly unequal from 1973 onward. While more egalitarian than the US, income distribution in Japan around 1990 had become equivalent to the United Kingdom, France and Germany, which are considerably more unequal in comparison to the Scandinavian nations (Tachibanaki 1998: 5–6). Thus he questions the concept of 'fair discrepancy' which posits that Japanese society is placing 'excessive emphasis on the equality of results'.

On the other hand, Satō reviewed the nation-wide survey on Social Stratification and Social Mobility (hereafter referred to as the SSM Survey) held once every decade for over fifty years now. The latest survey results of 1995 showed that, in the white-collar employees bracket, the ratio of sons reaching the father's occupational status has increased among male employees in professional or managerial posts grouped as 'white-collar/employed/managerial (WEM) (born between 1936 and 1955). The index is the 'odds ratio' between the father's main occupation and the son's occupation at the age of 40. In this case, the 'odds ratio' refers to the odds of the son becoming a 'WEM' himself if the father is a 'WEM', as compared to sons of 'non-WEM' fathers. Until 1985, the 'odds ratio' was on the decline at around 4.3, but in the 1995 survey, the trends reversed and the odds jumped to 8. These figures, Satō concludes, come close to that of males born during the last decade of the Meiji era (Satō 2000a, b).

It should be noted that Satō reassures us that the 'odds ratio' of WEM is found to decrease when measured by the son's initial occupation or at age thirty (Satō 2000c: 95–6). The point he wants to make is that, while the status of 'the privileged white collar employee' has been consistently open to Japanese males in their 20s (an indication of equal opportunity among them) since the Meiji era, this does not automatically mean that their 'effort/performance' will always be duly compensated. When looking at the occupation a man holds at age 40, 'the birth factor' appears to be increasingly more influential in recent years as compared to 'individual effort'. Satō expresses his concerns that, if the 'equality of results' is rejected in favour of 'equality of opportunity' under these conditions as advocated by the 'fair discrepancy' theorists, what he calls the *gambaru kiban* or the 'basis for making greater effort' would be a virtual candle in the wind.

Arguments on increased social inequality and the widening of the economic gap have already been criticized by various sectors of society. Rebuttals of Tachibanaki's theory, to cite an example, were made by the bureaucrats of the Economic Planning Agency as well as by Ōtake Hideo, professor of labour economics at the University of Osaka (Ōta 1999, *Nihon Rōdō Kenkyū Zasshi* 2000*)*, to which Tachibanaki duly replied (Tachibanaki 2000). Above all, let us look at how Tachibanaki responded to those who considered the widening of the economic gap to be a welcoming sign.

In his rebuttal, Tachibanaki initially points out that inequality of results could be tolerated as long as equality of opportunity is fully guaranteed. In Japan, however, where 'such factors as parent's occupation and income levels are becoming increasingly more influential', a 'yellow light' is already flashing for equal opportunity in general, and a 'red light' for Japanese women in particular (Tachibanaki 2000: 81). Second, he considers the social safety nets to be insufficient, especially in the fields of unemployment, medical insurance and livelihood protection (public assistance). This, he argues, ends up in too large an inequality of results, even if the equality of opportunity is ensured.

In response to Satō's argument, Seiyama Kazuo, who was one of the leaders of the 1995 SSM Survey, examined the same data and raised some additional issues (Seiyama 2000). According to Seiyama, the odds ratio did not rise sharply in the 1995 survey among professional workers (including the self-employed) and white-collar employees of large enterprises. Neither does the 'odds ratio' rise among the 'WEM' bracket if 'current occupation' rather than 'occupation at age forty' is adopted as an index. Thus he concludes that the reality of the so-called 'erosion of the middle class' merely consists of 'having to apply the principle of competition to male white-collar college graduates', and that 'most high-school graduates and women have long before been cast into this kind of harsh competition' (Seiyama 2000: 91).

Referring to the ongoing debate on growing inequality and discrepancy within Japanese society, Kariya Takehiko compares the Japanese situation with that of the US as a way to point out the limitations of Japan's 'warped notion of equality'. According to Kariya, the principle of 'equality of results' in the US encompasses the idea of guaranteeing an opportunity to develop individual skills and talents, and focuses more on inter-group equality, whereas in Japan, there is no such notion as 'equality among groups'. This has led to the uniform treatment of individual members in such closed circles as corporations, schools or industry in a fairly obsessive manner. None of the current debate that proposes to transform the 'equality of results' into an 'equality of opportunity', however, takes this aspect into full account. Their mind-set is to simply scrap the 'keep up with the neighbours' mentality and practises of uniform treatment within a closed communal sphere (Kariya 2000). Whichever – the equality of results or opportunity – is in question, the crucial viewpoint of inter-group equality remains ignored.

In relation to the above, let me also point out the fact that Satō stresses the essential difference between the equality of opportunity and that of results. 'While equality of results is fairly visible, equality of opportunity is not so . . . until much later' (Satō 2000b: 167). With the 'distribution of status and wealth' in mind, Satō goes on to stress the following: 'Equality of opportunity can only be assessed by conducting a survey after people have attained a certain social status to see whether the past situation for which the person is not responsible (i.e. whether or not one's father's occupation is WEM) is related in any way to the status one attains (i.e. whether or not one is WEM at age forty) (Satō 2000c: 95).

In fact, for the generation born between 1926–45, not much difference was noted in social status or income whether one's father was a WEM or not, while among those born between 1936–55, the mean annual income of a son with a 'WEM' father was ¥8.41 million against ¥6.05 million for a son with a 'non-WEM' father. Thus Satō concludes that a discrepancy of 1.4 times has emerged due to attributes the individual has no control over, such as the father's occupation (Satō 2000a: 74; Satō 2000b: 124–5).

Satō goes on to develop his original theory on the social safety net. He advocates that, in a society that upholds equal opportunity as a principle, we need a machinery to keep constant watch over unfair practices that are not apparent until much later on, and a system of compensation (e.g. redistribution of income) in case unfair practice is spotted, as 'systems inherent to a society of equal opportunity' (Satō 2000b: 173–5). By showing that things are not all that simple, Satō's argument contains some criticism of the ESC-type mind-set that full enforcement of 'equality of opportunity' should lead to a 'small government'.

As we follow the ongoing debate on the issues of economic disparity and equality in Japanese society, it becomes apparent that it has taken place within a severely limited arena. On the one hand, those who 'welcome the widening of fair discrepancy' ignore the considerable wage disparity between groups based on gender, with men earning more than women, and the size of the enterprise, with the employees of large corporations earning more than those in small-and medium-sized enterprises, that have long existed in Japan. These advocates tacitly limit the scope of the debate to the male labour market (and of large enterprises), which they assume to be a peculiarly non-competitive environment.

Meanwhile, Satō seems to jump to conclusions when he says that 'Japan has turned into a society in which no son can surpass the status of the father' simply because the odds ratio of passing on a privileged occupation from father to son has risen to 8. Seiyama's comment on the situation of male high school graduates and women in general is a valid criticism of Satō's argument. This author still disagrees with Seiyama's argument, however, that college-graduate white-collar male workers 'who, until now, had been well sheltered by the seniority wage system and lifetime employment' are now faced anew with 'competition and commodification' (Seiyama 2000: 91) – that is, a struggle for survival and their valuation in market terms.

Studies on management, corporate society and labour issues have already revealed that, inside the internal labour 'market', Japanese white-collar male college graduates are indeed subjected to severe 'competition' (Iwata 1977; Watanabe 1990; Kumazawa 1997). And there is no sign that either the 'fair discrepancy' theorists or Seiyama himself has taken into account these existing studies on the subject.

The reason Satō focuses on the son's occupation at age 40, rather than their 'current occupation' at any age, is precisely because he takes into account the harsh on-going competition within the internal labour market. In reply to Seiyama's criticism, Satō explains the reason he focuses on the occupation of male workers at the age of 40, rather than at the age of 20, when about to start their career, or at the age of 50, just before many in Japan's large enterprises move on to a second career in a smaller company. This, he stipulates, is because, for a white-collar male college graduate, the outcome of the promotion race is determined by whether he can reach a managerial post by the age of 40 (Satō 2000: 94, 97). In any event, Satō's 'WEM' bracket only accounts for somewhat over 20 per cent of all Japanese males born between 1936 and 1955 (Satō 2000b: 73). How Satō is able to respond to Tachibanaki's view that a symbolic red light is flashing for Japanese society with regard to the equality of opportunity for women remains to be seen.

'Thatcherism twenty years late': the report of the ESC

So far, we have reviewed the current debate over social disparity and equality in Japan, along with the different arguments on the provision of 'social safety nets'. It seems clear that the concept of 'fair discrepancy' advocated by the ESC is hardly based on solid data regarding the actual state of inequality in Japan and fails to analyse in enough depth the notion of 'equality of results' versus that of 'equality of opportunity'. Meanwhile, both the 'fair discrepancy' theory and the 'social stratification' concept advocated by Seiyama and Satō, despite their conflicting views, share common ground – the data they marshal only apply to male white-collar college graduates. Neither is there any evidence that they have examined recent research findings in the field of welfare-employment regimes in formulating their 'safety net' concepts, at a time when comparative gender analysis can provide the most valid data within the study of comparative social policy.

As Esping-Andersen, the author of *The Three Worlds of Welfare Capitalism* (1990), mentions in his 'Preface to the Japanese Edition', Japan is a difficult case to classify, to the extent that it has served as a touchstone for his typology. The Japanese welfare state, as of 1980, exhibited the lowest expenditure among OECD countries, and was of a 'liberalistic' nature in the sense that its 'highly selective' social policy offered insufficient family support, and that its low degree of 'de-commodification' compelled the individual to participate in the labour market. Meanwhile, the division of its social insurance services by occupation and social stratification (due to disparity created by the size of the enterprise, etc.) demonstrate its more 'conservative' nature. Japan's similarity to Switzerland, Spain and Greece cannot be mapped out until such gender index as gender equality in employment is added on to create a more precise and multi-dimensional measure of their similarity and difference (Siaroff 1994).

Another typology of welfare state regimes exists, in which gender is used as an axis to focus on the subject of rights in social policy and the unit of contribution/ benefit, thereby setting off the 'male breadwinner' model against the 'individual' (Sainsbury 1994). In terms of the burden of taxation/social insurance premiums, however, dependant/co-residency deductions remain important as a type of unit of assessment. While Japan's current taxation system is based on individual units of assessment, large deductions can be claimed for dependants and co-residency (Danjo Kyōdō Sankaku Kaigi Eikyō Chōsa Senmon Chōsakai 2002: 10–12).

What various sides agree on is that Japan belongs to the 'male breadwinner' model characterized by insufficient public support for the family and compelling participation of the individual male in the labour market (due to a low degree of 'de-commodification'). As we have seen so far, the viewpoint of comparative gender studies plays a crucial role in characterizing Japan. In the following section, let us review the changes that have taken place in Japan during the past two decades – the 1980s and the 1990s.

Among the several hypotheses on the recent direction taken by welfare state regimes, Esping-Andersen, who is the primary three-model advocate, emphasizes their 'divergence'. As for the first model, the social democratic regime adopted the 'welfare as investment' strategy and promoted more balance between work and family life for both women and men through public family support and vocational training (the Scandinavian route). In the Anglo-Saxon regime, deregulation in the labour market was promoted and the selectivity of social services was reinforced (the neo-liberal route). Finally, the conservative regime intensified the dual structure of the labour market, and allowed for an overall decline in the labour force rate (the labour force retrenchment route) (Esping-Andersen 1996, 1999). We share his view of these three routes as the best way to understand the different type and trajectory of welfare regimes.

In the case of Japan, which as mentioned above is a difficult case to typify, under the slogan of 'building a Japanese-style welfare society', the Japanese government made extensive 'reforms' in all social security service sectors during the 1980s, thereby intensifying the big company-centred 'male breadwinner' model. These reforms went against both the 'de-commodification' route that regards the security of livelihood as an individual's social right and thus discourages dependency on the labour market (the employer), and the 'work/life balance' route that promotes equal employment legislation, individuals as the unit of assessment, and support for double income households. For instance, the annual income ceiling of a spouse to become eligible for Spouse Tax Deduction was repeatedly raised (in 1984, 1987, 1988 and 1989). There was also the introduction of a Special Tax Deduction for Spouse (1987), which allowed tax cut/exemption to the household of a worker whose spouse's annual income remained below a fixed ceiling. Moreover, the 1985 Pension Reform introduced the 'third class insured person' category to the basic pension system, which exempted a worker's dependent spouse from insurance premium payments. The annual income limit to become eligible as a dependant is equivalent to that of a 'dependent family' member, as defined by the Health Insurance Schemes.

Although financial adjustments have been made since in both pension and medical security systems in an attempt to bridge the separately formulated social insurance programmes, there is still a long way to go for Japan to establish a unified system similar to the Scandinavian states. Moreover, no significant moves have been made throughout the 1990s to either improve the gender-based wage inequality or increase the ratio of women in managerial positions. Increase in female employment has been due to the rising number of non-regular, mostly part-time, workers (Osawa 1994, 1998).

For Japan, the 1990s may have been the 'lost decade' not only in terms of structural reform and economic growth, but also as far as social security reform is concerned. Neither the 'Five-year Plan to create a Lifestyle Superpower' advocated by the Miyazawa Kiichi cabinet nor the 'Welfare Vision for the Twenty-first Century' presented by Hosokawa Morihiro's non-LDP Cabinet went beyond a mere retouching of the 'Japanese-style welfare society' of the 1980s. From the end of 1996 to early 1997, then Prime Minister Hashimoto Ryutarō launched the 'Six Major Reforms' (of the administrative, financial and educational systems, and of economic, fiscal and social security structures). Among them, only administrative reform (reorganizing of ministries and agencies and de-centralizing power) and economic structural reform (deregulation of employment/labour) had born some fruit by the early 2000s.

Some legislation regarding the promotion of a gender-equal society, however, deserves our attention. Promoting a gender-equal society was deemed 'the key' and 'one of the pillars' of Hashimoto's Six Major Reforms (Osawa 2000b). The Child/Family Care Leave Law was enforced (in 1991, 1995 and 1997), and the 'ILO 156 Convention regarding the equal opportunity/treatment of women and men with family responsibilities' was ratified in 1995. And in 1997, the Long-term Care Insurance Law was enacted on the one hand (effective as of April 2000), and on the other hand, 'Protection Provisions for Women' were abolished from the Labour Standards Law with the call for the deregulation of employment, which thereby led to the Equal Employment Opportunity Law being reformed and strengthened (effective as of April 1999). The Basic Law for a Gender-Equal Society, which contained the fundamental philosophy that 'no person shall be discriminated against on the basis of gender', was enacted in June 1999. These legislative measures are illustrative of Japan's social transition towards the 'Work/ Life Balance' model by promoting equal opportunity between women and men and encouraging individuals with family responsibilities to join the labour force. This, aside from the scale of the budget and the robustness of policy enforcement, parallels the 'Scandinavian route'.

Compared to gender equality laws and anti-discrimination laws on the basis of sex in other countries, Japan's 'Basic Law for a Gender-equal Society' is significant in terms of Articles 4, 15 and 17 that highlight gender mainstreaming, and the role of the Council for Gender Equality of the Cabinet Office, which is the promoting machinery (Osawa 2000a: 73–83).

Article 4 stipulates that 'care should be taken so that social systems and practices have as neutral an impact as possible on the selection of social activities by women and men', which is one of the fundamental tenets of the Basic Law. Article 15 states that 'the state and local governments, when formulating and implementing policies recognized as influencing the formation of a gender-equal society, shall consider formation of a gender-equal society.' The policies to be considered here potentially extend over all sectors, for those policies with goals/measures that seem to be quite unrelated to gender equality or women's social advancement may, as an outcome, have considerable effects.

Article 17 stipulates the provisions on handling complaints and redress of human rights violations. It declares that 'the State shall take necessary measures for handling complaints in regard to policies implemented by the government which are related to promoting the formation of a gender-equal society or which are recognized as influencing the formation of a gender-equal society, and, necessary measures intended for relief of victims whose human rights have been infringed through factors impeding the formation of a gender-equal society, including gender-based discriminatory treatment' (Article 17). Note that the 'complaints' here include not only direct policies/measures to promote the formation of a gender-equal society, but also those 'policies recognized as influencing'.

As part of the administrative reforms led by Prime Minister Hashimoto, the central government offices switched over to a new system starting 6 January 2001, as seen in the reorganization of a range of key ministerial functions. Along with it, the Council for Gender Equality became the centre in the national machinery of the Basic Law for a Gender-Equal Society, and the Bureau for Gender Equality was set up within the Cabinet Office.

According to Articles 21–28 of the Basic Law, the Chief Cabinet Secretary heads the Council, which is composed of twelve relevant cabinet ministers and twelve academics. Their major tasks are: (1) 'to monitor how government measures are being implemented with regard to promoting the formation of a gender-equal society, (2) to evaluate and assess the impacts of government measures on the formation of a gender-equal society'.

Meanwhile, within the Council for Gender Equality, five specialist committees had been set up as of May 2001 on 'basic issues', 'the implementation of measures to support the balancing of work and child rearing', 'violence against women,' 'handling/monitoring complaints', and 'gender impact evaluation and assessment'. (The Specialist Committee on 'the implementation of measures to support the balancing of work and child raising' was dissolved after submitting a report in 2001.)

While some trace of the Scandinavian route can be found in the above reforms, changes with regard to social security were far from the Scandinavian strategy of 'welfare as an investment'. As was clear from both the 1993 and 2000 reforms, the government continued to undermine the credibility of its pension schemes by stressing the onset of a fiscal crisis and repeatedly increasing premiums while reducing benefits. Radical reform of the Medical Insurance System had also been planned in parallel with the establishment of public Long-term Care Insurance. In 1994, the Health Insurance Act was revised for the purpose of 'raising the efficiency' of medical care by expanding such services as in-home medical care. While several proposals for reform were made between 1995 and 1997, substantial reform was suspended due to the tenacious objection of the Medical Association, with the exception of the 1997 revision that reduced the provision to the insured from 90 to 80 per cent (Tsuboi and Takagi 2000).

In summary, the Long-term Care Insurance Law, enacted in December 1997 and enforced in April 2000, was the only major reform in the social security field during the 1990s. Despite its many problems, the introduction of public long-term care insurance for the elderly can be considered a step towards the 'Scandinavian route' or 'balance of work and family life' since it is moving in the direction of 'support by the entire society' rather than relying on the unpaid care provided by female members of the family. A revision made by the coalition government parties in the latter half of fiscal year 1999, however, undermined the very core of the Long-term Care Insurance system even before it took effect.

More specifically, the Long-term Care Insurance Law had initially been designed to provide benefits in services and not in cash payments. Some members of the *Iryō Hoken Fukushi Shingikai* (Advisory Council on Medical Insurance and Welfare), however, repeatedly insisted on providing benefits in cash. In August 1999, conditions for dispensing cash benefits were submitted to the *Kaigo Kyūfu Bukai* (Committee on Long-term Care Benefits), allowing family members engaged in long-term care to be considered as providing in-home visit services. As a result, conditions that can quite likely expand the payment of cash benefits were approved.

In the autumn of 1999, the Liberal Democratic Party's policy chief, Kamei Shizuka, contended that long-term care insurance services could destroy 'Japan's admiral (*utsukushii*) tradition of children taking care of their parents'. Based on this viewpoint, the government adopted 'special measures for the smooth implementation of the long-term care insurance system' on 5 November 1999. This exempted people in the Class 1 insured category (65 years and over) from paying premiums for the first six months, and reduced their payment to 50 per cent for the following twelve months (Osawa 2000b: 16). Kamei made a further call to impose restrictions on the provision of housework services for elderly people who are residing with their family. As of June 2000, the Ministry of Health and Welfare adopted a policy to restrict housework assistance when providing in-home visit services (*Nikkei*, 20 June, 2000).

As explained above, the fact that Long-term Care Insurance was introduced under the terms that insurance premiums would not be collected from the insured was a decision that could jeopardize the very foundation of the social insurance system in Japan. While the measure was adopted with the primary aim of reducing the financial burden on the elderly with a view to the general elections to be held by October 2000 with the ending of the term of the House of Representatives, it no doubt slowed down the work to build the infrastructure needed to provide services. This meant the efforts to reduce the actual burden of family caretakers, who were mostly women, were again put off. In effect, the measure stood in the way of social transition towards the 'work/life balance' model by clinging to Japanese-style welfare that relied on unpaid family (i.e. female) welfare provision on the premise of the traditional family model.

To sum up, the governance of the Japanese welfare-employment regime as manifest during the 'lost decade' of the 1990s saw the introduction of all three routes in a partial and indecisive way. First, it adopted elements of the 'work/life balance' model or the 'Scandinavian route' by promoting the participation of women and men in the labour force and socializing long-term care; second, it adopted elements of the 'neo-liberal route' by promoting deregulation of labour; and third, it adopted elements of the 'conservative route' in the sense that the restructuring and deregulation of employment further deepened the dual structure of the labour market. Ikegami Takehiko, a specialist in fiscal studies, made a comparative analysis of the expenditure and burden of taxation/social insurance premiums in the industrial democracies from 1970 to the latter half of the 1990s (Ikegami 2001), and concluded that Japan is 'a minimal welfare state' and 'a maximum construction state'. While the ESC Report called Japan's social security 'generous', Japan's social security system, in reality, is far from being either 'generous' or 'excessive'.

Against this backdrop, how can we assess the proposals made by the ESC on social security reform? Its concrete measures of reform were (1) Pension Reform: restructure public pensions to limit their role to basic pension (and privatize the earnings-related portion), to be financed solely by tax revenues in the future. Initiate a defined contribution-type pension scheme for individuals and enterprises. (2) Medical Services and Long-term Care Reforms: long-term care and medical services for the elderly are to be financed solely by tax revenues in the future. Services should be offered either by publicly set up facilities run by the private sector, or 100 per cent private enterprises. Introduce a voucher system and encourage more market competition in the field of medical services. (3) Measures to cope with the declining birth rate: introduction of childcare vouchers to offer a wider choice of childcare services. Diversify childcare services, make tax cuts in child rearing, expand child benefits, introduce a more open-door immigration policy (ESC 1999a: 29–31).

Above all, privatization of the earnings-related portion of the public pension and recommendation of personal/corporate pension with a defined contribution plan bear a close resemblance to the pension reform carried out by the Thatcher Government in the UK in the mid-1980s. Thus the ESC proposals were wryly described as 'Thatcherism twenty years late', (available on-line at: http://www.eda-jp.com/satsuki/2001/010330.html, accessed 30 June 2003), in apt criticism of the deregulation as well as of the social security reform belatedly taking place in Japan.

What is more problematic, however, than the 'intent' and 'measures' of these policies is their 'outcome' when we look at the by-products of Thatcher's 1986 pension reforms. As a result of these reforms, the conditions for contracting-out of the earnings-related public pension scheme were eased, and the number of insured decreased by 20 per cent in five years. And it is known that 75 per cent of the new policyholders of certified personal pensions during these years were male. While a majority of the policyholders taking out what were viewed at the time as the advantageous private personal pension plans were men, women remained in the public pension scheme with reduced terms of provision (information on the current crisis in UK pensions, available on-line at: http://www.pensionsorter.co.uk/pensions_in_crisis.html, accessed 2 July 2003). Not only that, but as tax expenditures were granted to various personal pensions in the form of tax breaks, the total sum of pensions in the early 1990s well exceeded the sum of various income-tested benefits to the elderly. And there is no doubt that the majority of the elderly who receive income-tested benefits are women (Sainsbury 1996: 208, 211).

As shown above, as long as social security systems function within a welfare-employment regime and more broadly a society with gender disparity in terms of wage and/or years in the labour force, a system of governance that apparently has no concern for gender issues often widens the gender disparity of income security for the aged. The ESC Report fails to take systematic gender bias into consideration and lacks what is needed in order to transform Japan into the 'work/life balance' model. Furthermore, the two-year provisional measure to ease the anxiety of unemployment includes a proposal to extend the 'unemployment benefits to dependants in a family' in case 'the head of a household' is unemployed. This is blatantly based on the 'male breadwinner' model in the sense that it fails to consider the number of 'dependants in a family' as 'self-responsibility'. Moreover, it overlooks the fact that members other than the 'head of the household' – overwhelmingly the male breadwinner – is often responsible for supporting the family to limit the target of 'expanded provisions' to only the 'head of household'.

While most politicians by no means welcomed the ESC's recommendation, its concrete proposals were studied by relevant government offices from early April through the end of May 1999. As a result, 'most recommendations' related to pension, medical care, and long-term care were classified as 'issues with too many obstacles to be carried out', an action which the ESC later called 'regrettable' (ESC 1999b). One top bureaucrat in the Ministry of Finance allegedly remarked 'Well, it's another one of those academic essays' available on-line at: http://www.asahi-net.or.jp, accessed 1 April 1999).

And yet, despite the cold welcome given by the relevant ministries and the ESC's repeated criticism of past reform attempts by the Ministry of Health and

Welfare, we should not presume that the proposals have parted with Japan's traditional model of social policy and the overall governance of the welfare-employment regime. Even if the ESC proposals were to materialize, the conventional co-ordinates of Japan's social policy system and governance structures, i.e. the big-company oriented 'male breadwinner' model with a low degree of de-commodification, would not be easily transformed. It is hard for many to believe that a report advocating individual freedom of choice and self-responsibility should include blatantly male-centred proposals.

In contrast, in its proposal released in October 2000 titled 'Social Security towards the Twenty-first Century', 'The Academic Council on Rethinking the Future of the Social Security System' (*Shakai Hoshō Seido no Arikata ni tsuite Kangaeru Yushikisha Kaigi*), set up by the Prime Minister, took up the treatment of the spouse in the taxation/social insurance system and called for a re-examination with a view to creating 'a system neutral in view of individual choices'. Also, the coalition government parties' Negotiation Committee on Social Security Reform compiled 'The General Principles of Social Security Reform' at the end of March 2001. The paper stated that, in employment and labour, they would duly 'promote measures to establish a gender-equal environment by prohibiting gender-based discrimination and encourage women's active participation, so that women can make full use of their ability'. And in regard to the social security system, it clearly calls for a 're-examination of the system in response to such diversified employment forms as part-time workers, and create a gender-neutral system that allows room for individual choice including that of women's participation in the labour force'. Apparently, these statements reflect the 'care to be taken in social systems/practices' as stipulated in Article 4 of 'The Basic Law for a Gender-Equal Society'. As we have seen so far, in comparison with other government proposals that indicated some shift, albeit ambiguously, from the 'male breadwinner' model towards a 'work/life balance' model, the ESC proposals are far more 'conservative' despite their 'reformist' posture.

A reform friendly to working women?

In the preceding section we have seen that the ESC Report, which is a prototype of Koizumi's 2001 'Robust Policy', is not the type of proposal that would shift Japan's conventional stance regarding the social policy system and the overall governance of the welfare-employment regime. In this next section let us turn to examine whether the 'Robust Policy' is really moving towards the 'work/life balance' model.

The '*seikatsu ishin*' ('life restoration') programme presented at the beginning of the Robust Policy states as follows: (1) In order to create 'a society friendly to working women', we will promote moving to the individual unit of assessment for computing tax/social insurance premiums and eliminate 'discrimination on the basis of sex' in employment; (2) We will promote a programme to make 'zero-waiting' a reality in nursery/day-care centres, and will establish facilities for after-school care of children (Cabinet decision '*Kongo no Keizai Zaisei Unei oyobi*

Keizai Shakai no Kōzō Kaikaku ni kansuru Kihon Hōshin' 2001: 4). But nowhere does it stipulate in concrete terms how taxation and social security programmes will be re-examined.

Chapter 3 of the 'Robust Policy' – 'Reforming the Social Security System', is replete with abstract, ambiguous and hard to grasp terminology. The repeated use of 'self-support and self-discipline', 'efficient' and 'private' implies the aim is one of reducing public responsibility.

With regard to the pension scheme, the 'Robust Policy' does not provide any blueprint for government reform and simply states that the intention is to 'establish a sustainable system', so how the government intends to redesign the system remains unclear. Moreover, it has carefully chosen the term 'eliminate' in reference to gender discrimination in employment, rather than 'prohibit' as declared in 'The Outline of Social Security Reform' presented in March 2001 by the coalition government parties' Advisory Council. Certainly, the government's intention of achieving 'zero-waiting to be accepted in nursery/day-care centres' can be praised as a move towards supporting the 'work/life balance' model. Yet, the aim is to promote GOCO (Government-Owned, Contractor-Operated) arrangements rather than increasing public services. If the government relies on the increase of private nurseries/day-care services, without proper regulation and oversight, tragic incidents of death by child abuse and neglect, as occurred in such day care facilities as 'Smile Mom Yamato', and elsewhere, may no longer be limited to a few non-certified childcare services (details of the case available on-line at: http://www.mainichi.co.jp/english/news/archive/200007/21/news03.html, accessed 1 July 2003).

While not exactly government policy, the 'Women and Pension System' Study Group (chaired by Sodei Takako, Professor of Family Sociology at Ochanomizu University) under the Ministry of Health, Labour and Welfare, presented a report in December 2001 with regard to pension reform.

Here let me review the more controversial issues regarding women and pensions. First, basic pension premiums should not be collected from the 'third class insured person', who is a dependent spouse (i.e. a full-time housewife whose annual income is less than ¥1,300,000). These costs are to be shared collectively by all 'second insured persons' who are employed. In other words, relatively low double-income households and single households are providing a 'reverse subsidy' to a household with a full-time housewife headed by a well paid salaried worker. This system, along with the Income Tax Exemption for Spouse, encourages married women to choose limited labour force participation with an approximate annual income of about one million yen or less. It not only curbs the supply of labour by married women and their earning power, but also hinders the improvement of working conditions for women in general.

The second issue is related to the Survivor's Pension. If the husband of a woman who has been participating in the labour market during her working life dies, the wife has to 'give up' either her own benefits (to receive the Survivor's Pension) or the husband's benefits (to receive her own pension). Moreover, the amount of Survivor's Pension benefits is often less than that of a full-time housewife with no history of contribution. The 1994 Pension Reform paved a third path for working women by totalling the Employees' Pension benefits for the wife and husband, and making the wives eligible to receive one half of it. Still, 80 per cent of working women choose to 'give up' their own benefit. Third, whereas a wife can receive a generous Survivor's Pension in case of separation due to her husband's death, if separated by divorce, the ex-spouse is guaranteed no benefits from the husband's earnings-related pension. Besides, Survivor's Pension, which appears advantageous, is not provided in cases of the spouse's remarriage, and thus obstructs the freedom of marriage.

In response to these issues, the 'Women and Pension' Study Group under the Ministry of Health, Labour and Welfare proposed that the government apply the Employees' Pension to part-time workers (thereby moving some people from the category of third insured persons to that of second insured person by lowering the standard working hours and annual income eligible for pension) (Shakai Hoken Kenkyūjo 2002). While this proposal reflects recent views and is oriented towards the 'work/life balance' model, it has been criticized as a lukewarm and far from radical solution.

From the end of 2001 to the beginning of 2002, Prime Minister Koizumi instructed the government's Tax Commission to study 'readjustment and cuts in spouse deductions among others' from the perspective of a 'wider and lighter' share of the tax burden. It coincided with the time the CEFP also took up taxation reform.

As a result, in June 2002, both the basic policy of the Tax Commission and 'the Robust Policy-Stage Two' of the CEFP proposed to abolish the 'special spouse deduction' and re-examine the spouse deduction. 'Robust Policy-Stage Two' further demanded the establishment of a pension system that 'met the principles of a gender equal society'. Concrete measures for pension reform, however, were not specified, except for 'the expanded application of social insurance to part-time workers and the re-examination of the Third Insured Person System'.

Both the CEFP and the Tax Commission advocated a gender equal society as a point of reference in re-examining the spouse deduction and creating a 'neutral' tax system in terms of a 'non-biased' policy in sharing the tax burden and labour force participation. While Koizumi's 'Robust Policy' merely proposed 'to study it', the Council on Tax System took the discussion further.

Indeed, the Council on Tax System came up with a basic policy to abolish the Special Spouse Deduction as a part of the efforts to 'simplify and consolidate dependant deductions' of personal income tax. The grounds are unfair preferential treatment in view of 'care' given to the taxpayer as well as other dependants, as the tax deduction system allows the head of a household to apply for double deduction along with spouse deduction.

While the intention lies in the expansion of the tax base in order to promote a 'wider and lighter' share of the burden, it is epoch-making for the government's Council on Tax System to step in for the first time to re-examine the tax system, which has, until now, embraced the 'male breadwinner' model. And yet, the Council on Tax System remains cautious about abolishing the spouse deduction system itself, though it is still alive as one of their proposals.

In May 2001, the 'specialist committee on gender impact evaluation and assessment' set up under The Council for Gender Equality began its discussions on neutral systems of taxation, social security and employment in order to offer more lifestyle choices to women, including the choice to work. The Committee submitted a mid-term report on 24 April and a final report on 20 December 2002. The Committee's reports can be said to have put pressure on the government to make a shift in the governance of the welfare-employment regime of Japan.

Conclusion

As the chairperson of this Specialist Committee, let me summarize some of our key recommendations. With regard to spouse deduction and special spouse deduction, our report proposed their reduction or abolishment based on a shift towards an individual unit of assessment. For academic studies have shown that these deduction systems had placed restraints on wages, annual income and working hours, and thus, were not neutral in terms of the choice to participate in the labour force. With regard to the pension scheme, the proposals made by the Specialist Committee, based on a shift to an individual unit of assessment, are far more concrete than those of 'Robust Policy-Stage Two'. The key proposals are: (1) To divide the income between wife and husband, require the third insured person to pay premiums, and provide an earnings-related pension (division of pension between wife and husband). (2) To eliminate Survivor's Pension of the Employees' Pension Scheme by dividing the pension between wife and husband (*Danjo Kyōdō Sankaku Kaigi/Eikyō Chōsa Senmon Chōsakai* 2002)

In the studies made by the LDP's Tax System Research Committee since November 2002, and with the preparation of the government budget, it was decided that the special spouse deduction would be abolished as of January 2004. And since January 2002 heated discussions on pension reform are being held by the Pension Group of the Social Security Advisory Council of the Ministry of Health, Labour and Welfare. The moment has come for the Koizumi government to take a clear political stance, resolve the contest over the different ways of governing the welfare employment regime and make decisive moves to adopt the 'work/life balance' model and to part with the 'lost decade'. It is only in this way that a shift in the type of governance of the welfare-employment regime in Japan will take place.

References

Cabinet decision (2001) '*Kongo no Keizai Zaisei Unei oyobi Keizai Shakai no Kōzō Kaikaku ni kansuru Kihon Hōshin*' (available on-line at:
  http://www.kantei.go.jp/jp/kakugikettei/2001/syakaihosyou/syakaihosyou.html, accessed 30 June 2003).
Danjo Kyōdō Sankaku Kaigi Eikyō Chōsa Senmon Chōsakai (2002) '*Raifusutairu no Sentaku to Zeisei, Shakaihoshō Seido, Koyō Shisutemu ni kansuru Hōkoku*, Tokyo: Danjo Kyōdō Sankaku Kaigi Eikyō Chōsa Senmon Chōsakai.

ESC (1999a) (Keizai Senryaku Kaigi) *Nihon Keizai Saisei e no Senryaku (Tōshin)*,Tokyo: Keizai Senryaku Kaigi.

ESC (1999b) *Keizai Senryaku Kaigi Teigen ni taisuru Seifu no Kentō Kekka ni tsuite*, Tokyo: Keizai Senryaku Kaigi.

Esping-Andersen, Gosta (1990) *The Three Worlds of Welfare Capitalism*, Cambridge: Polity.

Esping-Andersen, Gosta (1996) 'After the Golden Age? Welfare state dilemmas in a global economy', in Gosta Esping-Andersen (ed.) *Welfare States in Transition: national adaptations in global economies*, London: Sage, pp. 1–31.

Esping-Andersen, Gosta (1999) *Social Foundations of Postindustrial Economies*, Oxford: Oxford University Press.

Ikegami, Takehiko (2001) 'Wakufea gainen to fukushi kokkaron no tenkan: bunkenteki "fukushi seifu" e mukete', in Shakai Seisaku Gakkai (ed.) *Fukushi Kokka no Shatei*, Kyoto: Minerva Shobō, pp. 43–58.

Iwata, Ryushi (1977) *Nihonteki Keiei no Hensei Genri*, Tokyo: Bunshindō.

Kariya, Takehiko (2000) ' "Chūryu hōkai" ni te o kasu kyōiku kaikaku', *Chūō Kōron* (July): 148–63.

Kumazawa, Makoto (1997) *Nōryoku Shugi to Kigyō Shakai*, Tokyo: Iwanami Shoten.

Nihon Rōdō Kenkyū Zasshi (2000) 'Tokushu: Shotoku Kakusa' (July).

Osawa, Mari (1994) 'Bye-bye corporate warriors: the formation of a corporate-centered society and gender-biased social policies in Japan', *Annals of the Institute of Social Science* 35 (March): 157–94.

Osawa, Mari (1998) 'The feminization of the labour market', in Junji Banno (ed.) *The Political Economy of Japanese Society, Volume 2: internationalization and domestic issues*, Oxford: Oxford University Press, pp. 143–74.

Osawa, Mari (2000a) (ed.) *'21 Seiki no Josei Seisaku to Danjo Kyōdo Sankaku Shakai Kihonhō*, Tokyo: Kabushikigaisha Gyōsei.

Osawa, Mari (2000b) 'Government approaches to gender equality in the mid-1990s', *Social Science Japan Journal*, 3, 1: 3–19.

Ōta, Kiyoshi (1999) 'Nihon no fubyōdō wa kakudai shiteinai', *Ronsō* (July): 172–83.

Sainsbury, Diane (ed.) (1994) *Gendering Welfare States*, London: Sage.

Sainsbury, Diane (1996) *Gender, Equality and Welfare States*, Cambridge: Cambridge University Press.

Satō, Toshiki (2000a) '"Shin chūkan taishū" tanjō kara nijūnen: "bambaru" kiban no shōmetsu', *Chūō Kōron* (May): 68–75.

Satō, Toshiki (2000b) *Fubyōdō Shakai Nippon: sayonara sōchūryū*, Tokyo: Chūō Kōronsha.

Satō, Toshiki (2000c) 'Soredemo susumu "fubyōdo shakaika": senbatsu to kikai to kaikyū', *Chūō Kōron* (November): 92–100.

Seiyama, Kazuo (2000) 'Chūryū hōkai wa "monogatari" ni suginai', *Chūō Kōron* (November): 84–91.

Shakai Hoken Kenkyūjo (2002) *Josei to Nenkin: josei no raifu sutairu no henka nado ni taiōshita nenkin no arikata ni kansuru kentōkai hōkokusho*, Tokyo: Shakai Hoken Kenkyūjo.

Siaroff, A. (1994) 'Work, welfare and gender equality', in Diane Sainsbury (ed.), *Gendering Welfare States*, London: Sage, pp. 82–100.

Tachibanaki, Toshiaki (1998) *Nihon no Keizai Kakusa: shotoku to shisan kara kangaeru*, Tokyo: Iwanami Shoten.

Tachibanaki, Toshiaki (2000) 'Kekka no fubyōdō o doko made mitomeruka', *Chūō Kōron* (May): 76–82.

Tsuboi, Eitaka and Takagi, Takeshi (2000) 'Gekiron: Nihon ishikai wa ōbōka', *Ronsō* (May): 172–89.

Tsūsanshō Daijin Kambō Kikakushitsu (ed.) (2000) *Kyōsōryoku aru Tasankaku Shakai*, Tokyo: Zaidan Hōjin Tsushō Sangyō Chōsakai.

Watanabe, Osamu (1990) *'Yutakana Shakai': Nippon no kōzō*, Tokyo: Rōdō Jumpōsha.

Part II

Issues of governance

7 Japan and global environmental governance

Miranda A. Schreurs

For much of the last decade, the environment has been a very important issue in Japanese foreign policy. During this period numerous changes have been made in Japan's approach to environmental policymaking that have made it a far more visible and proactive player in matters of global environmental governance. In the early 1990s, the Japanese government determined that environmental protection should become an important pillar of its foreign policy. Given that at the time Japan was being widely criticized by environmentalists for its role in global environmental degradation, especially in relation to tropical deforestation, depletion of marine and wildlife resources, and destructive development assistance programmes, the changes in Japan's foreign environmental policy deserve attention. This chapter examines changes in Japan's environmental foreign policy and its approach to environmental governance, the reasons behind those changes, and the obstacles that remain to Japan being recognized as a global environmental leader.

There are many signs of a more proactive Japanese environmental foreign policy. Japan is now among the world's largest donors of official development assistance (ODA) targeted for the environment. It is also a major supporter of the United Nations Environment Programme, Asian Development Bank, and World Bank environmental and energy programmes in developing countries. The Japanese government has established environmental research and training centres and helped set up environmental monitoring networks across East and Southeast Asia. Japanese companies lead the world in obtaining the International Standard Organization (ISO)'s 14001 environmental management certification and are beginning to require suppliers in developing countries like China to obtain the certification as well (Welch *et al.*, 2002; Welch and Schreurs forthcoming). Japan leads the world in the export of air pollution control technologies and large numbers of Asian scientists and engineers are trained in environmental science and management in Japan and abroad.

The Japanese government is signatory to a wide range of global environmental agreements, including the Convention on International Trade in Endangered Species, Agenda 21, the Montreal Protocol on Substances that Deplete the Ozone Layer, and the Kyoto Protocol on Global Warming. Japan is actively promoting greater environmental cooperation with its Asian neighbours by setting up bilateral environmental cooperative agreements and participating in multilateral environmental dialogue (Yoon 2001; Schreurs and Pirages 1998). At the World Summit for Sustainable Development in Johannesburg, South Africa (hereafter, the Johannesburg Earth Summit), Prime Minister Koizumi Junichirō announced that Japan would provide 250 billion yen in support of education for sustainable development in low-income countries (*Africa News*, 27 September 2002). Japan was host to the World Water Forum in March 2003 and is promoting the exchange of best practices among developing nations in an effort to address the water crisis that environmentalists warn will face many parts of the world this century.

Yet, despite these many efforts, Japan is still struggling to achieve international recognition as a leader in environmental protection. While there is wide-spread admiration of Japan's success in bringing its energy efficiency levels up to among the highest of any Organization for Economic Cooperation and Development (OECD) member (OECD 2002; Jänicke and Weidner 2002) and considerable interest elsewhere in Asia in how Japan managed to sustain high economic growth levels while simultaneously reducing air and water pollution levels in its major cities (Rock 2002), Japan continues to have a mixed environmental image globally.

In part, this is because of Japan's continued involvement in controversial activities, such as whaling (Miyaoka 2004), consumption of hard wood from the tropical forests of Southeast Asia (Japan is the world's largest consumer of hard woods) (Dauvergne 1997; 2001), heavy fishing of the world's oceans (Japan is the world's number two consumer of fish after China), and support for nuclear energy. Within Southeast Asia, there is also a perception that Japan shifted its most polluting industries to developing countries, thus, effectively shifting the pollution burden abroad.

Japan's perception problems also have much to do with governance issues. Japan stands out among industrialized countries for the relatively weak position of its environmental non-governmental organizations (NGOs) and think tanks in the policymaking process. Until quite recently, there were sizeable legal and institutional hurdles making it difficult for environmentalists to organize as NGOs and there are still substantial restrictions on making tax deductible donations to NGOs (Pekkanen 2000; Schreurs 2002; Schwartz and Pharr 2003). While the number of NGOs in Japan has risen dramatically in recent years, only slowly are these groups being accepted among decision making circles. Japanese NGOs pale in comparison to their European Union (EU) and United States (US) counterparts in terms of membership size, administrative resources, personnel and policymaking experience. As a result, the voice of civil society in decision making in Japan is far more restricted than is the case in Europe or the US, leaving bureaucrats and industry to shape policies with only limited input from civil society. The result is that Japan approaches environmental protection technologically. It is far weaker in policy areas that require non-technological solutions or that challenge powerful vested interests, such as the construction industry.

Also problematic is Japan's international negotiating style. The need to achieve a degree of consensus among vertically fragmented ministries with contested views on environmental matters makes it difficult for Japan to present an assertive image in international negotiations. It is not uncommon for Japan to wait in stating its own negotiating position until the positions of both the EU and the US are made clear and then to seek some kind of middle ground that too often leaves Japan looking indecisive. This is further complicated by the fact that in the past decade a rift has emerged between EU and US approaches to international environmental protection with the EU favouring multilateral approaches and the US selectively favouring more unilateral or independent approaches. On issues ranging from climate change to biodiversity preservation and genetically modified organisms, there are strong differences in policy perspectives across the Atlantic (Vig and Faure 2004). Japan has tried to take on the role of international broker between the EU and the US, but at the cost of being criticized in the international press for failure to exhibit stronger leadership (particularly the case in relation to the Kyoto protocol). Frequently, the debates between the EU and the US internationally are mirrored by debates between the Environment Ministry and the Ministry of Economics, Trade, and Industry (METI) within Japan. The Environment Ministry tends to take positions closer to that of the Europeans and METI to the position of the US with the Ministry of Foreign Affairs (MOFA) concerned both with Japan's international policy role and its dominant relationship with the US. The division among key ministerial players results in contested and time-consuming inter-ministerial policy negotiations that can make it difficult for Japan to take an assertive stance in international negotiations.

Finally, Japan is simply not very good at publicizing its policy successes and is less likely than European countries to present environmental targets internationally that it will not be able to implement domestically. Combined these differences in governance styles influence policy outputs and public perceptions.

Making the environment a foreign policy priority

For years, Japan has struggled to find ways to enhance its foreign policy visibility. As the world's second largest economy, Japan has been under considerable pressure to do more to contribute to the global community. This pressure was particularly strong throughout the 1980s when the Japanese economy still appeared invincible. Yet, constitutional restrictions on the use of the Japanese Self Defence Forces in military and some peace keeping operations overseas made it difficult for Japan to act as a 'normal' state in the international arena (Inoguchi 1993; Green 1995). This reality forced Japan to seek other avenues whereby it could exert greater international influence.

At the same time that Japan was being pushed by the United States and other nations to do more in the foreign policy realm, internationally awareness began to grow regarding the deteriorating state of the global environment. The dying of forests and lakes from acid rain in Europe and North America, the discovery of a 'hole' in the protective stratospheric ozone layer above Antarctica, suggestions by scientists that the burning of fossil fuels was causing global warming, large-scale tropical deforestation, ocean resource depletion, and the rapid loss of biological diversity, began to garner greater popular and political concern. Initially, Japanese policymakers were slow to react to this growing international concern about global environmental degradation. An analysis of Japan's Environmental White Papers in the 1980s shows that there was only very limited attention to international environmental matters by the Environment Agency prior to 1987 (Schreurs 1996).

In the late 1980s, Japan was criticized for pursuing policies abroad that badly damaged the environment in developing countries. Japan had the dual image of being an international leader in domestic pollution clean up and an international 'outlaw' for policies it pursued overseas that contributed to large-scale environmental degradation outside of the Japanese archipelago.

Given that there was no domestic ground swell in support for a change to Japan's environmental policies and none of the opposition parties rose to champion environmental issues, it is quite remarkable that, at the end of the 1980s, Japanese policymakers (and in particular, Prime Minister Takeshita Noburu) began to look at environmental protection in a new way. By the early 1990s environmental protection was being turned into one of the pillars of Japan's foreign policy (Kameyama 2003; Schreurs 1996; 2002).

There were many reasons for this. The Japanese bureaucracy and industry began to see the possibility of exporting to the developing world lessons learned both from Japan's painful experiences with allowing pollution to get so bad during its high growth years that it resulted in debilitating diseases and death, and from its belated, but eventually relatively successful, efforts with urban air and water pollution clean-up and energy efficiency improvements. The potential for developing new environmental technology industries was not missed by Japanese industry. Japanese industry was eager to find a way to improve its image internationally (Imura and Schreurs forthcoming).

Japan was being heavily criticized in another area marked for foreign policy leadership – that of ODA. In the early 1980s, Prime Minister Nakasone Yasuhiro designated ODA as one of the key pillars of Japanese foreign policy. The huge growth witnessed by Japanese ODA in the 1980s was supposed to win Japan praise and to some extent this praise was forthcoming. But the praise was mitigated by criticism because of the harmful effects of some ODA programmes on the environment in developing countries. Japan's support for large-scale infrastructure projects, including roads cut through heavily forested areas and dams built in developing countries that resulted in large-scale population displacement and environmental damage, resulted in some harsh criticism from the environmental community and other countries. Indeed, 'victims' of a dam project (those that were forced to relocate) completed in 1996 in Sumatra, Indonesia and funded by Japanese ODA currently are suing the Japanese government for destroying their lives (*Japan Times*, 4 July 2003). Promoting 'greener' aid, thus, could help Japan's broader ODA image as well.

Japan also became aware and increasingly concerned about being downwind from China. China's environmental problems are enormous. During Mao's reign, China's natural resources were plundered and the environment left badly scarred because of misguided growth campaigns (Shapiro 2000). Economic reform initiated under Deng Xiaoping and continued by Jeng Zemin has shifted China towards a new model of growth that is premised on entrepreneurship. While this has had a number of positive environmental effects, such as the shutting down of some of the most-heavily polluting state-run industries, rising living standards are creating greater individual demand for resources. As energy demand grows, in the next twenty years or so, China is expected to be the world's largest producer of greenhouse gases. It is already a major source of acid rain in East Asia that causes not only great damage to Chinese agriculture, but is starting to be felt in neighbouring North and South Korea and Japan as well. In an influential book, Vaclav Smil (1993) warned that China was facing an ecological crisis that could greatly restrict its national growth potential. Elizabeth Economy (2004) suggests that China's future will depend on how it deals with expanding deserts and rivers that run black from ecological destruction and pollution. China's environmental problems at the beginning of the twenty-first century are of a magnitude even more serious than those experienced by Japan in the 1960s. For Japan, this is both a threat and an opportunity.

Signs of policy change in Japan

In the late 1980s, when the country's political leaders were considering making environment a foreign policy priority, Japan had a rather mixed environmental image. Over the course of the 1970s and 1980s the country had achieved substantial success domestically in improving energy efficiency and making the air breathable once again. At the beginning of the 1970s, after more than a decade of blatant disregard for the environmental degradation and health problems caused by Japan's rapid economic growth policies, the Liberal Democratic Party introduced a series of sweeping changes to the country's environmental laws and administrative structures. Japan went from having very few protective measures to adopting a series of framework environmental regulations that gave it among the most extensive environmental regulatory requirements for industry of any industrialized country. Although many of the ideas behind specific laws were borrowed from the United States and Great Britain, Japan introduced some innovative regulatory ideas and practices as well – best known among them is the Pollution Victims Compensation Law. Also of great interest is the extensive use of voluntary pollution agreements reached at the local level among government and industries (Matsuno forthcoming). The environmental regulations introduced in Japan between 1967 and 1974 combined with the impact of the 1973 Organization for Petroleum Exporting Countries (OPEC) oil embargo helped to transform Japanese industrial practices, making them far less resource intensive and more energy efficient. By the end of the decade, Japan's environment had noticeably improved. Japan became a world leader in the production of air pollution control technologies. In the late 1970s the OECD (1977) conducted an assessment of Japan's environment. The report concluded that Japan had done much to clean up its environment and that its success with pollution control should serve as an example to other developing countries.

Yet, internationally, in the 1980s Japan was being criticized for its role in the destruction of the global commons. One target was Japan's reliance on drift net fishing, a practice whereby huge nets are strung between two fishing vessels and then dragged through the ocean catching everything that comes in their path. Another was Japan's catching of several hundred whales each year for 'scientific' purposes despite the International Whaling Commission's moratorium on whaling (Miyaoka 2004). Environmentalists were quick to point out Japan's status as the world's largest importer of tropical hard woods. Japanese trading companies (*sōgo shōsha*) purchased huge quantities of lumber from Southeast Asia for use in the construction industry and helped line the pockets of officials in the region that were willing to allow huge swaths of virgin rain forest to be clear cut (Dauvergne 1997; 2001). Japan's importing of products from endangered species for use in traditional crafts as well as for purely decorative purposes also attracted environmentalists' ire. Examples include the use of ivory from African elephants in *hanko* (signature seals) and tortoise shells for making decorative combs (Mofson 1996). The Japanese government and industries further were accused of exporting their most polluting industries to countries with weaker environmental standards and foot dragging in international efforts to regulate ozone depleting chlorofluorocarbons.

If Japan were to be taken seriously as a global environmental leader, it would have to address the many policies for which it was being criticized. With the 1992 United Nations Conference on Environment and Development (UNCED), or commonly the Earth Summit, in Rio de Janeiro as a motivation, the government agreed to ban the use of drift net fishing and cracked down on the importation of animals and animal products from species protected under the Convention on Trade in Endangered Species. The importation of ivory was banned despite its use in a number of traditional crafts. Other practices, such as clear cutting in tropical forests, were targeted for study and reform and Japanese trading firms began to experiment with reforestation efforts.

In 1987, Japan signed the Montreal Protocol on the Protection of the Stratospheric Ozone Layer and in 1990 agreed to an amendment that would accelerate the phasing out of the production and use of chlorofluorocarbons. In 1990, the government established a non-binding target to stabilize Japan's emissions of carbon dioxide (a major greenhouse gas) at 1990 levels by 2000. It also added a global climate change division to the Environment Agency and established a new portfolio of Minister for Global Environmental Affairs. The Ministry of International Trade and Industry (from 1991 Ministry of Economy, Trade and Industry) launched a Green Aid Plan to promote environmental capacity building and technology development in (and exports to) neighbouring China and elsewhere in Southeast Asia. The Environment Agency initiated an Acid Rain Monitoring Network in East Asia (Brettell and Kawashima 1998; Wilkening 2004). And, at the UNCED, Japan with much fanfare pledged to spend billions of yen for environmental projects internationally. It also signed Agenda 21, an international action plan for promoting sustainable development.

Mirroring the changes made to environmental programmes in the early 1970s, the early 1990s became a period of sweeping changes to Japan's environmental laws. The new laws reflected a greater appreciation of the importance of global perspectives on environmental protection. A new Environmental Basic Law was formed replacing the Environment Basic Law of 1967 (as amended in 1970). The new framework legislation places a responsibility on the government to protect the global environment. This was followed in 1994 with the passage of an Environment Basic Plan, which established concrete policies and measures to be taken by the Japanese government to reduce Japan's environmental footprint. In 1997, Japan hosted the Third Conference of the Parties to the Framework Convention on Climate Change where the Kyoto Protocol on Global Warming was formulated. Other noteworthy initiatives include Japan's 1998 Global Warming Prevention Law, its new Recycling Law, and the extensive revisions made to the Law Concerning the Rational Use of Energy.[1] By the turn of the century, Japan was also a key player in efforts to improve environmental conditions in China. Kurt Tong, the Councillor for the Science, Technology, and Environment Division of the US Embassy in China noted that it is not the US, but Japan and Germany, which are the biggest foreign players in environmental protection in China (Lecture, Beijing, 22 January 2003).

By the end of the decade, Japan's approach to environmental protection internationally was far more proactive than it had been a decade earlier. In many ways Japan succeeded in making the environment a pillar of its foreign policy. Its approach to particular environmental issues, however, still provokes some critical reactions and the policymaking process is still less open than liberal critics desire.

Moves to pluralize environmental policymaking in Japan

When global environmental issues first began to gain more attention internationally in the 1980s, there were few actors in Japan concerned with tackling these new kinds of problems. Although Japan had some environmental groups, like the World Wide Fund for Nature, working on species conservation, and the Citizens' Alliance for Saving the Atmosphere and the Earth (CASA) working to phase out chlorofluorocarbons, the number of national environmental groups in Japan was extremely small. Few groups had more than several dozen members and even the largest ones only a few tens of thousands (compared with membership sizes in the hundreds of thousands and even millions for some US and EU groups). Moreover, because of their very weak financial status what few groups that did exist in Japan could do little more than focus on environmental education or local environmental projects, such as the greening of the urban landscape. They were not in a position to advise policymakers or present policy alternatives on global environmental pollution issues. Unlike the many environmental think tanks that existed in Europe and the US, in the 1980s there were no major private environmental research institutes in Japan and universities had but a handful of scholars focusing on environmental law or politics. There were also few Japanese scientists engaged in research on global resource issues or atmospheric or marine pollution. The Environment Agency had a largely domestic focus and few employees followed global environmental matters in any kind of serious way. Only a small number of politicians had any familiarity with environmental matters. In the 1980s, Japan's environmental policy community was remarkably weak for a nation that had achieved such notable success with cutting waste and emission flows in production processes, reducing reliance on oil as a percentage of its total energy supply and cleaning up health-threatening pollution.

Unlike in many Western European countries where environmental groups and Green Parties helped to push sustainable development concerns on to national policy agendas, Japan's decision to become a major environmental player internationally was largely a top-down decision made by a conservative leadership. Because of the West's vocal criticism of Japan as a free-rider on the international system, in the late 1980s the LDP was looking for ways to strengthen its foreign policy contributions. The fact that global environmental issues were suddenly hot international topics in the late 1980s provided the LDP with a potential new international role. Japan could take advantage of its domestic expertise in pollution control and export this know-how to developing countries. This was an idea that proved amenable to many Japanese industries as they saw the possibility to develop new markets in environmental protection internationally, to develop greener images that would be good for sales domestically and internationally, and as a way of engaging in more philanthropy. Being green internationally was also likely to win praise rather than the kind of criticism that much Japanese ODA was receiving.

In order to play a larger global environmental role, however, Japan's leaders quickly discovered that they needed to strengthen their environmental governance capacity. Within the bureaucracy, this meant establishing global environmental departments and offices. Almost overnight all of the major ministries established offices with a global environmental focus. When the government was restructured in 2001, the only new ministry to be created was an Environment Ministry. Within the Diet, politicians also began to go green. A new *zoku* focused on environmental issues formed and quickly became popular among both LDP and opposition party members (Ohta 2000). While their numbers have decreased somewhat in the last few years, environmentally-oriented politicians can be found in all the political parties. Japan has a large contingent of politicians involved in the Global Legislators Organization for a Balanced Environment (GLOBE), an international network of parliamentarians concerned with environmental matters.

There also were some unintended consequences from Japan's largely top-down policy decision to become more engaged in environmental protection overseas. Most impressive has been the rapid growth of Japan's environmental NGO community. Although there is no doubt that social movement groups helped to transform Japan's environmental policies and institutions in the early 1970s, by the end of that decade, the environmental citizens' movements that had formed to protest pollution problems and to promote quality of life concerns had dissipated. Some groups were still active, but they remained focused primarily on local environmental concerns, like the damming of Japan's rivers, the loss of marsh lands, and the paving over of Japan's coastlines (Karan and Suginuma forthcoming). Thus, in comparison with the US and Europe where environmental groups in the 1980s and early 1990s helped to force governments to pay greater attention to problems of acid rain, marine pollution, tropical deforestation, stratospheric ozone depletion, climate change and sustainable development, in Japan there were almost no groups in a position to force such demands on the Japanese government. Indeed, when the Japanese government first began to attend international negotiations dealing with stratospheric ozone depletion and global climate change, it was embarrassed because it was the only advanced industrialized country that had almost no NGOs that could participate in the negotiations as observers. Official delegations from Europe and the US were accompanied by dozens of environmental groups. In contrast, the newly established Green Peace Japan and CASA were among the only organizations attending the first rounds of negotiations on these important issues.

One of the key documents to come out of the 1992 UNCED was a plan for achieving sustainable development called Agenda 21. A key element of Agenda 21 is promoting the participation of civil society in environmental decision making. In most advanced industrialized societies, NGO participation is seen as a critical component of democratic governance as NGOs present societal perspectives into policy debates. If Japan was to become a global environmental player and be recognized as such, the government needed to do something to develop an NGO community. The great irony in this is that government officials had little appreciation for environmental groups and no real desire to open decision making processes to them.

There has been considerable attention in the literature to the obstacle course citizens groups have had to traverse in order to gain legal status as not-for-profit organizations (NPOs) (e.g. Yamamoto 1999; Schwarz and Pharr 2003). Obstacles included the need to win ministerial approval to obtain NPO status and sufficient start up funds (estimated to be in millions of yen). So bad was the situation that many groups simply did their best to exist without even trying to obtain NPO. Even with NPO status, most groups were not eligible to receive tax deductible donations making it difficult to build up any kind of financial basis for their operations. Thus, the incentive to create an NPO also was not strong.

While Japan's bid for global environmental leadership status may have been initiated from above, it did not take long for activists in Japan to recognize that a window of opportunity had been opened for them to participate in some way in environmental governance nationally and internationally. New groups began to form and to take on global environmental causes. The Japan NGO Center for International Cooperation and the Japan Tropical Action Network formed in 1987. Greenpeace Japan and the Rainforest Foundation Japan formed in 1989. A Seed Japan and the Japan Association for Greening Deserts formed in 1991.

These and many other groups dealing with health care, ageing, and education concerns began to mobilize and to demand change to the laws governing NPOs. They won some support for their demands from politicians sympathetic to their cause. Their efforts received a great boost as a result of the efforts of large-scale citizens' groups to help victims of the tragic Hanshin earthquake in 1995. Civil society emerged from this tragedy as the hero while the government was criticized for its slow and inept response to the disaster. Demands for a change to Japan's NPO laws intensified after this time (Pekkanen 2002).

The government initially took some small steps to improve the funding opportunities available to environmental groups in the early 1990s. In 1993, for example, the Japan Fund for the Global Environment was set up to provide funds for NGO activities in the fields of environmental protection and sustainable development. The Ministry of Foreign Affairs also set up a special assistance fund for NGOs doing work in developing countries. More significantly, in 1998 the Diet unanimously approved a new NPO law, which makes it much easier for groups to obtain non-profit status and in 1999 a Public Information Disclosure Law, similar to the US Freedom of Information Act, was passed (Schreurs 2002: 225). In August 2002 in connection with the Johannesburg Earth Summit, the Foreign Ministry budgeted 2 billion yen in support for NGOs working on development assistance. For the first time, the funds are allowed to be used to cover some NGO administrative expenses, including personnel expenses, conference costs and leasing and repair fees for computers and photocopy machines. This is a major policy change since in the past NGOs had to rely on their own resources to cover overhead expenses. Still, notes Harada Katsuhiro, 'the new system requires NGOs to go through cumbersome procedures, such as filling in time sheets every day, as [a condition] to receive overhead subsidies' (*The Nikkei Weekly*, 26 August 2002).

Another interesting development has been the creation of environmental networks that bring together activists from the environmental community with individuals working in companies and in the bureaucracy to brainstorm policy alternatives. One such group is Kiko Forum, established in 1995, to critique the government's climate change policies and to present policy alternatives (Reimann 2001).

Japanese NGOs recognize the importance of networking to enhance their ability to influence the direction of international negotiations. Hayakawa Mitsutoshi, managing director of CASA, noted that Japanese NGOs have come a long way since the 1992 Earth Summit in Rio de Janeiro when they had little impact on the inter-governmental negotiations. 'The network of citizens and international solidarity has certainly changed from that of before, and the key from now on is how to develop that further . . . how to make that network function to have citizens' views reflected' (Kyodo News Service, *Japan Economic Newswire*, 16 August 2002). Interestingly, NGO networks are beginning to emerge linking activists in Japan, South Korea, and China (Yoon 2001). The East Asia Environmental Information Express Messenger launched a web-site (Enviroasia) to share information among NGOs in the three countries (*Nikkei Weekly*, 9 December 2002).

While environmental groups are still not well integrated in policy decision making, they now have at least some voice in the process of environmental governance. The media also have been strong supporters of Japan's new environmental groups and have worked to push governmental acceptance of the positive role that can be played by NGOs not only in policy implementation, but also in its formulation. Many Japanese journalists with whom I have spoken are not shy about admitting that they have an agenda with their reporting – they want to help promote the power of civil society in Japan.

The changes in the institutional structures governing civil society in Japan are quite remarkable and the growth of civil society organizations astounding (Tsujinaka, 2002). While many of these groups are still very small and their level of professionalization still far behind that of their western European and North American counterparts, there is growing acceptance of NGO activities by the broader public and many young people are eager to be involved in voluntary groups. Slowly, the Japanese government also is warming to the presence of NGOs.

At the September 2002 Johannesburg Earth Summit, for instance, the government set up a liaison office for NGOs near the convention centre in order to support their activities. Hundreds of NGO representatives attended the meeting. Even more significantly, in a major change from the past when Japanese government officials would do their best to avoid Japanese NGOs at international negotiations, five NGO members were invited to join the Japanese government's delegation to the Johannesburg Earth Summit in August 2002. This was the first time that NGOs officially joined a Japanese governmental delegation to an international event. They included the executive director of Friends of the Earth Japan, a researcher at the Kitakyushu Forum on Asian Women, the director of the domestic programme division of the Japanese Organization for International Cooperation in Family Planning, the president of the Africa-Japan Forum, and a member of the Japan Forum for Johannesburg (*Japan Economic Newswire*, 31 July 2002).

Still, the relatively closed culture of decision making in Kasumigaseki remains the norm. Only a relatively small number of NGOs are invited to participate in *shingikai* (government council) or to otherwise advise the ministries. An external advisory panel on reforming the MOFA recommended in April 2002 that the ministry deepen its relationship with NGOs and enhance transparency in its foreign aid programme (Kyodo News Service, *Japan Economic Newswire*, 17 April 2002).

Japan's ministries remain at the centre of international environmental policy-making. Key ministries in international environmental decision making include the Environment Ministry; METI; the MOFA; and the Ministry of Agriculture, Foresty and Fisheries. Depending on the issue, other ministries may also be involved. Conflicts of interest among the ministries often lead to contest over policy and policy stalemate. In these instances, prime ministers have been known to apply pressure on the ministries to reach consensus or to formulate more proactive environmental positions. Hashimoto Ryūtarō, for example, pressured the ministries to come to a compromise and announce internationally Japan's negotiating position in the lead up to the Kyoto Protocol negotiations. Environmental groups also have applied pressure on the ministries to move beyond their traditionally conservative policy stances.

Comparing Japan with Germany, the EU and the US

In considering Japan's approach to environmental governance, it is useful to put Japan into a comparative perspective with other advanced industrialized regions. Here Germany, the EU and the US are considered. The US is widely regarded as the force behind the transformation of environmental policies that occurred throughout the industrialized world in the 1970s. Although Great Britain was the first to adopt framework air and water pollution controls, the power of the US environmental movement in the 1960s and 1970s led to sweeping environmental regulatory changes that not only established new restrictions on polluters, but also created new institutional rules governing the relationship among government, industry and civil society. Civil society was greatly empowered through legislative and judicial rulings that gave NGOs new rights and protections, including expanded rules of standing in the courts and the right to engage not only in educational activities, but a degree of lobbying activity as well without losing tax exempt status. NGOs were similarly greatly empowered by the Freedom of Information Act. Also important was the introduction of requirements for projects receiving federal funding to undergo environmental impact assessments. US leadership in environmental policy formulation continued through the 1970s with new regulations governing the release of toxic chemicals and efforts to regulate ozone depleting chemicals.

Interestingly, while Japan followed the US in the introduction of many pollution control laws, these mainly dealt with air, water, noise and soil pollution. There were important initiatives in the US that did not get picked up by Japanese policymakers. In particular, Japan did not adopt environmental impact assessment legislation, a freedom of information act, nor rules empowering civil society groups at this time. It took another 30 years before these kinds of legislative changes were made in Japan. These differences reflect the power of economic interests in Japan, which although they were required to accept emissions control standards and to make energy efficiency improvements, they were able to inhibit for decades the formulation of laws that would fundamentally alter approaches to governance by empowering civil society.

Where Japan did excel was in the implementation of the environmental regulations adopted in the early 1970s. This was done through a combination of regulations, incentives, and voluntary agreements that reflected the close relationship among government and industry and the use of administrative guidance and national and local government levels. By the end of the 1970s and early 1980s, European governments that were suddenly being confronted by a need to address acid rain problems were looking to Japan to learn about its approaches to environmental governance, and in particular the practices that led to major improvements in energy efficiency and air pollution control. More recently, European governments have taken notice of Japan's extensive use of voluntary pollution control agreements at the local level as an innovative form of environmental governance that could potentially be applied to global climate change mitigation.

While US leadership in the formulation of new environmental regulations in the 1970s is generally agreed upon, there are many who argue that since the 1990s, the US has lost its leadership role to the EU (Vig and Faure 2003). In the 1970s, most EU member states were far behind the US in the introduction of new environmental regulations and environmental protection was not as high on the political agenda as it was in the US. In the 1980s that began to change as Green Parties emerged across continental Europe. By the beginning of the 1990s, it was the EU rather than the US or Japan that seemed to be leading the world in pushing for major changes in approaches to environmental governance. This can be seen in terms of EU leadership in relation to climate change, renewable energy policies, and sustainable development initiatives. In recent years, many of the more intriguing new ideas about environmental governance have emanated from Europe. These include such ideas as the formation of Green Plans whereby environmental considerations are brought into all aspects of governmental decision making, policies to promote ecological modernization such as the shifting of tax burdens to the heaviest polluters as is being done in Germany, and efforts to bring concerns about a nation's 'ecological footprint' into planning decisions. The loss of a US leadership role can be explained in large part by the growth in the influence of business interests in Washington DC and a Republican agenda to reduce the size of government, including in the environmental realm. In Japan's case, the lack of a substantive role in environmental governance in relation to national and international issues for Japanese NGOs may explain why in the 1990s the most innovative environmental governance ideas have emanated from Europe rather than Japan, despite the government's intention to play a leadership role globally. Still, Japan is due some credit as normative change has led to some major policy changes. Now, for example, it has one of the world's most complex waste disposal programmes to enhance recycling levels and reduce waste generation. Similarly, Japanese government and industry are working to promote a zero emissions society in which all resource outputs are recycled back into the production process. Japan has followed the European example of introducing renewable energy portfolios mandating that utility companies buy a percentage of their electricity from renewable energy sources.

Japan and the global climate change negotiations: sandwiched between the EU and the US

The negotiations over climate change have been described in great detail (e.g. Grubb 1999; Oberthür and Ott 1999; Harris 2000; Schreurs 2002) and thus are only recounted here to make a point regarding Japan's environmental negotiating style and role in international environmental governance. While Japan is far more proactive than it was during the 1980s in global environmental negotiations, bureaucratic fragmentation and differences in the policy perspectives and governance concerns of the Environment Ministry and METI often result in contentious debates between them over the policy course that Japan should pursue (Ohta 2000; Kameyama 2003). When there are major differences between ministries in policy perspectives, it is difficult for Japan to lead during international environmental negotiations. Such differences are not infrequent. The climate change case is a fascinating one for observing this phenomenon as well as the role that can be played by politicians to force bureaucratic compromise. Three particular decision points are briefly examined: the 1992 Earth Summit; the formulation of the Kyoto

Protocol in 1997; and the Japanese and EU response to the US decision to pull out of the Kyoto agreement.

Diplomatic efforts to address global climate change began in the late 1980s in the preparatory meetings for the 1992 Earth Summit. Already at this early stage in the international negotiations, rifts emerged between the EU and the US in their approaches to climate change mitigation. The EU called for the establishment of concrete targets for carbon dioxide emissions reductions to be included in the Framework Convention on Climate Change. The US baulked at this initiative and announced that it was opposed to the establishment of concrete reduction targets and timetables and instead proposed a 'no regrets' policy in which the government would promote taking action that would not cause any regrets if climate change turned out to be less serious a problem than what scientists claimed. This meant promoting only actions that would be good for greenhouse gas emissions reductions if they were good for other reasons as well (e.g. energy conservation that could be a cost-cutting measure for industry).

An inter-ministerial debate raged within Japan about how to react with the Environment Agency and the Ministry of International Trade and Industry (MITI, now METI) taking different policy positions and winning different policy battles. The Environment Agency favoured the EU approach and with the backing of Takeshita Noboru succeeded prior to the Rio meeting in getting MITI to agree to the idea of a non-binding domestic stabilization target for carbon dioxide emissions as several European countries had already adopted. They failed at this stage, however, in convincing MITI to agree to a binding target. MITI was concerned about isolating the US in the negotiations at Rio and generally was more amenable to the US approach. Indeed, largely because of the influence of MITI, Japan was a member of a coalition going into the Earth Summit that was labelled: JUSCANZ, for Japan, the US, Canada and New Zealand. These were the nations opposing stringent commitments on carbon dioxide reductions. At the Earth Summit in Rio de Janeiro a Framework Convention on Climate Change (FCCC) was formulated that recognized the responsibility of developed states to act to address a problem they had largely created, yet because of US opposition (and Japanese support of that position) no concrete emissions reduction targets were established.

The negotiations leading up to the formulation of the 1997 Kyoto Protocol exhibited a similar kind of rift between the EU and the US, with Japan again taking a middle position between the two. By this time, the US position had softened somewhat and the Clinton administration announced its willingness to consider concrete targets and timetables but also demanded differentiated targets for countries as well as maximum flexibility in how states could achieve their reduction commitments. The US championed the use of market mechanisms (and in particular, emissions trading) and joint implementation and the clean development mechanism (mechanisms whereby a nation can gain credit for reducing emissions in another state since it may be more cost effective to reduce emissions abroad than at home). The EU argued for a common target for all industrialized nations and that a cap be placed on how much credit a country could gain for reducing emissions using these flexible mechanisms and calling upon countries to take action at home to reduce greenhouse gas emissions. Japan attempted to find compromise ground between the EU and the US by proposing a plan whereby nations would be able to set their own reduction emissions targets and timetables but commit internationally to meeting them.

Several months prior to the start of the negotiations, the EU stated it was prepared to reduce its 1990 greenhouse gas emissions by 15 per cent by 2008 – 12 per cent based on a basket of three greenhouse gases. Although Japan was host to the Third Conference of the Parties to the FCCC where the Kyoto Protocol was to be worked out, because of inter-ministerial disagreement and a desire to see what the US negotiating position would be, Japan was slow to announce its position and had to be urged to hurry up and do so by the Conference Chairman Estrada and to take on the leadership role expected of a host country of a major international conference. Japan announced its position and proposed a 5 per cent reduction in greenhouse gas emissions relative to 1990 levels by 2012 for countries allowing for differentiation based in their national circumstances. Formulating this position proved difficult because of a disagreement between the Environment Ministry, the MOFA, and METI over what Japan could really obtain (METI's initial negotiating position was simple stabilization) and it took the intervention of Prime Minister Hashimoto Ryūtarō to work out a compromise among them. Interestingly, Japan announced its position still not knowing what the US position would be largely because of Hashimoto's intervention.

In early October, the US finally announced its bottom line. The US demanded that six, not just three gases should be addressed, and argued that a stabilization target for this basket of six gases at 1990 levels by 2012 was the best it could do. At the December conference, the US succeeded in getting others to agree to address six greenhouse gases, rather than the three the EU and Japan originally sought to address. As a result, the EU announced that a 15 per cent reduction would no longer be feasible. In the end, the EU agreed to an 8 per cent reduction in its emissions of a basket of six greenhouse gases by 2008 – 12 per cent relative to 1990 levels, the US to a 7 per cent reduction, and Japan to a 6 per cent reduction. MITI was apparently pushed by Hashimoto to agree to the 6 per cent reduction goal upon Albert Gore's urging so that internationally an agreement could be formulated. Decisions on how these reductions were to be met, including decisions regarding how much of the reductions could be met through the use of flexible mechanisms, was left for future meetings of the Conference of the Parties to the FCCC.

When the George W. Bush administration pulled the US out of the Kyoto Protocol in March 2001, the EU reacted with anger and an intense lobbying campaign to pull the US back into the agreement. The EU announced soon after Bush pulled out of the agreement, that they had every intention of moving forward with ratification of the agreement even without the US. Japan initially sent mixed signals in reaction to the Bush administration's pull out.

On the one hand, it joined the EU in criticizing the US for pulling out of the agreement without even consulting with other nations about its plans. The Japanese Upper House passed a resolution in April 2002 urging the US to return to the agreement and Environment Minister Kawaguchi Yoriko travelled repeatedly to the US to urge the White House to change its mind. Yet, at the same time, Prime Minister Koizumi made statements when he visited the US to meet with President Bush in April 2002 that raised doubts about whether Japan would move forward with the Kyoto Protocol without the US being on board.

In the end, Japan did decide to side with the EU in moving forward with Kyoto. Japanese public opinion was strongly in favour of staying with the agreement and with an upcoming election, Koizumi did not want to do something that could adversely impact the LDP's performance in the election. Thus, when push came to shove, Koizumi chose to work with Europe in keeping the Kyoto Protocol alive. But, at the same time, he tried to influence the direction of negotiations in a way that would be amenable to the US should the US choose to return to the Kyoto framework. At the Sixth Conference of the Parties to the FCCC held in Bonn where the technical details for implementing the Kyoto Protocol were negotiated, Japan took up the negotiating positions that had been held by the US up until this point in time calling for maximum flexibility in how states were to achieve their emissions reduction targets. The EU had little choice but to give in to Japan's demands or risk losing Japan's support for the agreement as well.

In sum, Japan worked with the EU to help keep the Kyoto Protocol alive. There are now over 110 states that have ratified the agreement and, if Russia joins, then there will be sufficient involvement for the agreement to go into force.[2] In saving the agreement, however, Japan did its utmost not to offend the US by sculpting an agreement that the US might be able to one day join again. Japan remains far more beholden to the US than European countries. Its decision to move forward without the US on the Kyoto Protocol, however, suggests that Japan is perhaps interested in crafting a more independent foreign policy.

The three decision points examined here suggest several additional important points regarding governance in Japan. First, is that bureaucrats are key players in decision making and that the oft-noted bureaucratic fragmentation in Japan is highly evident in the environmental policy realm. METI, which is in close consultation with industry, tends to favour more conservation policy positions than the Environment Ministry, which tends to adopt positions more similar to those supported by European green interests. MOFA wants a strong international presence for Japan in international negotiations but like METI is wary of alienating the US. Second, is that politicians are exerting a good deal of influence on Japan's foreign policymaking. On numerous occasions politicians weighed in on the bureaucratic negotiations and influenced policy outcome. Third, as the Japanese public becomes more and more concerned with global environmental protection and environmental groups become more active, they are pressuring politicians to be greener. As a result, environmental governance in Japan is becoming more pluralistic.

Conclusion

Environmental policy took on a new importance in Japan beginning in the 1990s and, despite continued rises and falls in public and policymakers' attention, remains an important element of Japanese foreign policy. In the 1990s, Japan transformed its legal and institutional structures in order to deal more effectively with global environmental issues. Paralleling or complementing these changes in the legal framework have been changes in Japanese approaches to environmental governance. In part intentionally, and in part as a result of forces beyond its control, by picking up on the environment as a foreign policy priority in the late 1980s, the LDP unleashed a process that is slowly, but noticeably, changing environmental governance in Japan. The process has become more open with greater debate and political input than was the case throughout the 1980s. The environmental policy changes of the 1990s and early 2000s are in some ways reminiscent of the major environmental policy changes that occurred in Japan in the early 1970s. What is different between these two periods is the approach to environmental governance. In the late 1960s the LDP was unwilling to address pollution issues until it was forced to do so by public pressures. This was a period of intense citizen mobilization and a highly contentious political atmosphere in which desperate citizens turned to the courts for redress. In the early 1990s, it was the LDP that picked up the environment as a foreign policy issue. By this time, moreover, environmental decision making already was a regular component of government policymaking. In fact, in the 1980s it had become highly bureaucratized with little public or political input. This changed in the 1990s as environmental issues began again to garner greater societal interest and citizens once more began to show interest in environmental movements. Furthermore, compared with 30 years earlier, environmental issues are far less contested between government and citizen movement (NGO) and interaction is more consultative and cooperative.

Despite the many changes of the last decade, it is interesting to note that the Japanese public remains highly dissatisfied with the government's environmental performance. A cross-national survey conducted in 2000 found that 70 per cent of those surveyed thought that their government did 'too little' to protect the environment (compared with 20 to 50 per cent in most Western European countries) (Vosse 2002). This public dissatisfaction may mean that, in the future, as environmental norms become even more deeply embedded in society and environmental groups become stronger, there will be even more pressure on Japanese politicians to pursue environmental protection causes and push the ministries to go beyond their primarily technologically-oriented approach to pollution control.

According to the World Economic Forum's international environmental sustainability ranking, Japan comes in 78th of 142 countries.[3] The break down of the index suggests that Japan is performing relatively well in terms of its social and institutional capacity for environmental protection and protecting human health domestically, but its environmental systems are stressed and Japan contributes significantly to global environmental problems because of its large population, high population density, and relatively high consumption levels. While progress has been made by Japan in environmental protection and Japan is in a position to share many of its environmental experiences with developing countries in East and Southeast Asia, clearly Japan must still achieve much if it wants to truly be a global environmental leader.

Notes

1   For recent developments in Japanese environmental regulations and policies see the Ministry of Environment website. Available on-line at: http://www.env.go.jp/en/, accessed 4 June 2004.
2   The latest status of the Kyoto Protocol is available on-line at: http://unfccc.int/resource/kpthermo.html., accessed 6 June 2004.
3   See World Economic Forum, Environmental Sustainability Index. Available on-line at: http://www.ciesin.columbia.edu/indicators/ESI/rank.html, accessed 6 June 2004.

References

Brettell, Anna and Kawashima, Yasuko (1998) 'Sino-Japanese relations on acid rain', in Miranda A. Schreurs and Dennis Pirages (eds) *Ecological Security in Northeast Asia*, Seoul: Yonsei University Press, pp. 89–113.

Dauvergne, Peter (1997) *Shadows in the Forest: Japan and the politics of timber in Southeast Asia*, Cambridge, Mass: MIT Press.

Dauvergne, Peter (2001) *Loggers and Degradation in the Asia-Pacific: corporations and environmental management*, New York: Cambridge University Press.

Economy, Elizabeth (2004) *The River Runs Black: the environmental challenge to China's future*, Ithaca, NY: Cornell University Press.

Green, Michael (1995) *Arming Japan: alliance politics, defense production and the postwar search for autonomy*, New York: Columbia University Press.

Grubb, Michael with Vrolijk, Christian and Brack, Duncan (1999) *The Kyoto Protocol: a guide and assessment*, London: Royal Institute of International Affairs, Earthscan.

Harris, Paul G. (2000) *Climate Change and American Foreign Policy*, New York: St. Martin's Press.

Imura, Hidefumi and Schreurs, Miranda (eds) (2005) *Environmental Policy in Japan*, Cheltenham, UK: Edward Elgar.

Inoguchi, Takashi (1993) *Japan's Foreign Policy in an Era of Global Change*, New York: St. Martin's Press.

Jänicke, Martin and Weidner, Helmut (eds) (2002) *National Environmental Policies: a comparative study of capacity-building*, Berlin: Springer Verlag.

Kameyama, Yasuko (2003) 'Climate change as Japanese foreign policy: from reactive to proactive', in Paul G. Harris (ed.) *Global Warming and East Asia*, London: Routledge, pp. 135–51.

Karan, Pradyumna P. and Suginuma, Unryu (eds) (manuscript forthcoming) *Grassroots Environmental Movements in Japan and the United States*.

Matsuno, Yu (manuscript forthcoming) 'Local government, industry, and pollution control agreements', in Hidefumi Imura and Miranda Schreurs (eds) (manuscript) *Environmental Management: lessons and recommendations from Japan*.

Miyaoka, Isao (2004) *Legitimacy in International Society: Japan's reaction to global wildlife preservation*, Basingstoke: Palgrave Macmillan.

Mofson, Phyllis (1996) 'The behavior of states in an international wildlife conservation regime: Japan, Zimbabwe and CITES', unpublished Ph.D Dissertation, University of Maryland.

Oberthür, Sebastian and Ott, Hermann (1999) *The Kyoto Protocol*, Berlin: Springer Verlag.

OECD (1977) *Environmental Policies of Japan*, Paris: OECD.

OECD (2002) *Environmental Performance Review: Japan*, Paris: OECD.

Ohta, Hiroshi (2000) 'Japan's global environmental policy', in Takashi Inoguchi and Purnendra Jain (eds) *Japanese Foreign Policy Today*, New York: Palgrave Macmillan, pp. 96–121.

Pekkanen, Robert (2000) 'Japan's new politics: the case of the NPO Law', *Journal of Japanese Studies* 26, 1: 111–48.

Reimann, Kim D. (2001) 'Building networks from the outside in: international movements, Japanese NGOs and the Kyoto climate change conference', in Jackie Smith and Hank Johnston (eds) *Globalization and Resistance: transnational dimensions of social movements*, Lanham, MD: Rowman & Littlefield, pp. 173–90.

Rock, Michael T. (2002) *Pollution Control in East Asia*, Washington, DC: Resources for the Future.

Schreurs, Miranda (1996) *Environmental Politics in Japan and Germany*, Unpublished PhD dissertation, University of Michigan, Ann Arbor.

Schreurs, Miranda (2002) *Environmental Politics in Japan, Germany, and the United States*, Cambridge: Cambridge University Press.

Schreurs, Miranda and Dennis Pirages (eds) (1998) *Ecological Security in Northeast Asia*, Seoul: Yonsei University Press.

Schwarz, Frank J. and Pharr, Susan J. (eds) (2003) *The State of Civil Society in Japan*, New York: Cambridge University Press.

Shapiro, Judith (2000) *Mao's War on the Environment*, Cambridge, Mass: MIT Press.

Smil, Vaclav (1993) *China's Environmental Crisis: an inquiry into the limits of national development*, Armonk, NY: M. E. Sharpe.

Tsujinaka, Yutaka (2002) *Gendai Nihon no Shimin Shakai, Rieki Dantai*, Tokyo: Bokutakusha.

Vig, Norman J. and Faure, Michael J. (eds) (2004) *Green Giants? Environmental policies of the United States and the European Union*, Cambridge: MIT Press.

Vosse, Wilhelm (2002) 'Japan a disaffected democracy? On political trust, political dissatisfaction, political activity, and environmental issues', in Manfred Pohl and Iris Wieczorek (eds) *Japan 2001/2002*, Hamburg: Institut für Asienkunde, pp. 254–77.

Welch, Eric, Mori, Yasufumi and Aoyagi-Usui, Midori (2002) 'Voluntary adoption of ISO 14001 in Japan: mechanisms, stages, and effects', *Business Strategy and the Environment* 10, 1: 43–62.

Welch, Eric and Schreurs, Miranda (forthcoming) 'ISO 14001 and the greening of Japanese industry', in Michael Hatch (ed.) *Evaluating Alternative Policy Instruments for Environmental Protection*, New York: SUNY Press.

Wilkening, Kenneth (2004) *Acid Rain Science and Politics in Japan*, Cambridge, Mass: MIT Press.

Yamamoto, Tadashi (ed.) (1999) *Deciding the Public Good: governance and civil society in Japan*, Tokyo: Japan Center for International Exchange.

Yoon, Esook (2001) 'Environmental cooperation in northeast Asia: political economy of transboundary pollution regime', unpublished PhD dissertation, University of Maryland.

8 Governance, Asian migrants and the role of civil society

Hatsuse Ryūhei

The aim of this chapter is to analyze the governance of Asian migrants in Japan, focusing on the issue of the unskilled labour force in the period from the 1980s to the present. The governance of such migrants embraces aspects of both immigration and of residence as well as the contestation between the two. Immigration and residence are closely connected as the former necessarily leads to problems with the latter of those migrants who establish residency in a new country. The illegal residence of unskilled foreign workers forms a particularly important area of overlap between the governance of immigration and that of residence. In other words, whether legal or not, as foreigners both come under the legal control of the Japanese state (see Figure 8.1).

Although a wide variation exists among foreigners resident in Japan in terms of their time of arrival, motives for immigration, nationality, lineage, legal status, status of residence, and so on, foreigners can none the less still be divided into two basic categories: old comers and new comers. The former are those resident Koreans and Chinese who came to Japan from the empire's former colonies or their descendants. The latter are those who came to this country from Asia and other parts of the world since the middle of the 1980s, most of whom work in manufacturing, the manual or service sectors, or study at language schools, technical training colleges or universities. With nearly two million foreign residents officially registered at the end of 2002, the number has nearly tripled over the last three decades. In terms of nationality, until the middle of the 1980s Koreans formed the overwhelming majority (over 80 per cent), but now account for only a third (33 per cent). *Kokusaika* (internationalization, or more correctly globalization) has served to increase the number of foreigners, as entertainers from the Philippines and Thailand (mid-1980s), manual workers from Pakistan and Bangladesh (late-1980s), and manual and service workers from China, South Korea, Thailand, Iran, the Philippines, Malaysia and Sri Lanka (early 1990s), have headed for Japan. Many of these foreigners have worked illegally. Since the early 1990s, moreover, *Nikkeijin* (Brazilians and Peruvians of Japanese ancestry) have entered Japan in the wake of a change in immigration policy (1990). In this way, the impact of *kokusaika* has been to not only increase the number of foreign residents in Japan, both legal and illegal, but to make their composition much more complex. The Asian migrants referred to in this chapter belong to the category of new comers.

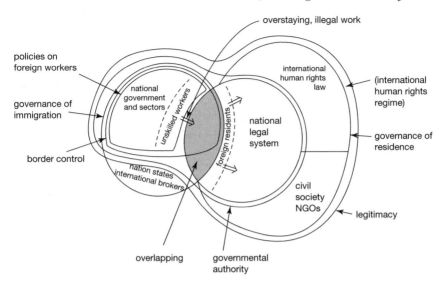

Figure 8.1 Governance of immigration and residence.

Two Japanese laws relate directly to the legal control of foreigners: the Immigration Control and Refugee-Recognition Act (henceforth abbreviated as Immigration Control Act), and the Alien Registration Law. The former decides the legality or illegality of immigrants by stipulating the legal conditions of their entry and sojourn or residence, and the visa status for sojourners and residents, while the latter ensures foreign residents are kept under the surveillance of the Japanese authorities by requiring them to register as aliens when the period of stay is over ninety days. In addition, laws on nationality, enfranchisement, health insurance, pension, employment, labour, education and so forth, are indirectly related to the control of foreigners, as these laws are applied selectively or do not apply to them. Such an indirect system of legal control may infringe their human rights, or deprive them of social and economic benefits, thereby devaluing the life of resident foreigners.

Immigration and residence control policies, which are based on or derived from these two laws, are implemented by both the national and local governments. At the national level, the Ministry of Justice takes the lead role, with other ministries, such as the Ministry of Health, Labour and Welfare, dealing with specific issues within the ministry's remit; at the local level, sub-national political authorities (i.e. 'local governments' such as prefectures, cities, municipalities, etc.) enjoy a degree of autonomy in deciding or implementing policy in respect of foreigners. In terms of social policy, for instance, the general principles are decided by the national government, with the local government being charged with the drafting and implementation of the practical rules governing foreign residents. In other cases, local governments often take policy initiatives in advance of the national government, as with employing foreign residents as civil servants as opposed to no foreigners being employed in national ministries, offering urgent medical attention to foreign patients without health insurance, or providing a monthly subsidy – albeit, far less than the amount of national pension – to foreigners who are over 60 and not eligible for a national pension (Yamada 1993: 142–5; Nakao 1997: 98–100). As residents of their localities, foreigners obviously come into regular contact with the local government, not least when registering their residency, and in particular the clerical officers in charge of alien affairs. They have their own demands at the local level, as in the need for Japanese language education, which calls for a response by the local authorities.

Apart from these representatives of the Japanese state, both big business associations as well as Non-Governmental Organizations (NGOs) and Non-Profit Making Organizations (NPOs) play a role in policymaking and implementation and hence in the governance of foreigners: the former, particularly at the stage of making national law and policy; the latter, particularly at the stage of implementation at the local level. As with other advanced industrial democracies, the treatment of foreigners can emerge as a contested political issue, as when legal and illegal immigrants capture the national spotlight.

Discrimination and prejudice against foreigners, especially Asians, stubbornly persists in Japanese society today. Many Japanese still oppose marriage to Asians, renting them a house or room, or hiring them in big business or the public services. In this respect, there are numerous social problems that need to be resolved: labour conditions, social benefits, medical care, legal status, divorce procedures, exploitation of women, education, desertion of children, naturalization, refugee status, deportation, interpretation at the police station or in court as well as local suffrage, marriage, habitation and job hunting. In the face of these difficulties, foreign, mainly Korean activists, along with sympathetic Japanese, have sought to change government policy. In this way, old comers play an important role in improving the livelihood of new comers and are thus crucial in their governance.

The first section in this chapter outlines the system of immigration control as part of the governance of immigration, paying particular attention to the entry and overstay of Asians. The second section goes on to analyze the situation of foreigners who enter the country legally and engage in unskilled labour (or close to unskilled labour). The third section, focusing on the governance of residence, examines how the domestic implementation of international human rights regimes and civil society protect the rights of foreigners in Japan. Finally, in the Conclusion, the argument as a whole is summarized.

Governance of immigration

Until the mid-1980s, the policies of post-war Japanese governments had in principle denied entry to unskilled foreign labour at immigration control, on the one hand, and discriminated against foreign residents, both socially and politically, through nationality qualification or clauses for various types of public services, infringing their human rights, on the other. It was at the start of the new decade that these two principles began to break down domestically. Legally, in terms of immigration control, the 1990 amendments to the Immigration Control Act were a response to the new situation.

However, looking back, modern Japan has never lived up to the declared principle of eschewing the use of foreign unskilled labour. Thus, during the Second World War, to make up for the shortage of labour brought about by the youth of the land being drafted for military service after the Sino-Japanese War of 1937, the Japanese government and industry conscripted or rounded up one and a half million Koreans and forty thousand Chinese in Korea and Taiwan to feed the homeland war effort. Their forced labour was used in the coal mines of Kyūshū and the construction sites dotted around Japan. In contrast, the post-war Japanese state was to profess measures to deny the introduction of unskilled foreign labour. However, there were between 590,000 and 660,000 Koreans (North and South) from the former colony living in Japan during the period of rapid economic growth (from the mid-1960s to the 1970s) (available on-line at http://mindan.org/toukei. php, accessed 6 July 2004). Excluded from work as civil servants or as teachers at public schools, due to the nationality clause, and denied the opportunity to join the staff of big companies, they became engaged in unskilled labour, as scrap merchants, in independent small businesses or in the management of the pachinko (pin ball) parlour business. It is also even possible to regard the seasonal labour that migrated to big city areas in Kantō and Kansai from the Tōhoku and Kyūshū regions in the 1960s and 1970s as having arisen due to the shortage of this Korean labour. Despite the pivotal role of Korean labour in the nation's postwar economic development, many Japanese have come to think that rapid growth in the 1960s was achieved without the use of foreign labour. From the mid-1980s, as described above, Chinese, Bangladeshis, Pakistanis, Iranians, Filipinos, Koreans, Malaysians, or *Nikkeijin* from Brazil or Peru, were engaged in unskilled labour.

Central to the governance of foreigners is immigration control, although a range of bureaucratic and non-bureaucratic actors contest the issue. The objectives of the Ministry of Justice (MOJ), the Ministry of Education, Culture, Sports, Science and Technology (MEXT), the Ministry of Foreign Affairs (MOFA) and the Ministry of Health, Labour and Welfare (MOHLW) all differ. The intentions of big business associations and small-and-medium sized business associations are similarly at odds with one another, as in the case of the companies these associations represent. Subcontractors of big companies as well as small-and-medium sized firms have been more interested in the introduction of Asian unskilled workers than the giants. NGOs are more concerned with the infringement of the human rights of foreigners than their introduction into Japan itself. Thus the implementation of the legal system for immigration control is quite often a product of finding a balance, or some form of compromise, between and among each these differing interests. What is more, a significant possibility exists, with the exception of special permanent residents or permanent residents (mainly Korean and Chinese), of those on any type of visa staying on after its expiration and becoming illegal residents (so-called 'overstayers'). Under the present immigration control system, both illegal entry by foreigners (relating to landing or entry and effective for three years) and that of overstaying and illegal residence (with no time limit to effectiveness) is a criminal offence. Both of them carry a prison sentence of up to three years, or a fine of ¥300,000 or less. As long as no other crimes are involved, however, probation is normally granted and the offender is handed over to the immigration authorities and forcibly repatriated. In many cases, the above measures are applied to those illegal workers, engaged in unskilled labour, who have been detected at work or who voluntarily declare themselves, although, as discussed below, the treatment is not uniform.

Since the 1960s, the government, particularly the MOJ, has grown increasingly wary of the danger that foreign workers, on having entered the country, might settle down permanently once their contract has expired, as in the case of the former West Germany or France, where contract workers from other countries settled permanently. From January 1989, with the mutual visa-exemption agreements between Japan and both Bangladesh and Pakistan being temporarily suspended, and again in April 1992, when the mutual visa-exemption agreement between Japan and Iran was temporarily suspended, an immediate and sudden fall occurred in newly-arrived Bangladeshi, Pakistani and Iranian entrants (Sōgō Kenkyū Kaihatsu Kikō 1993; Yamagishi and Morita 2002).

While the peak number of new Bangladeshi immigrants was in 1988, with 13,994, this number suddenly decreased to 2,742 in 1989. The peak for Pakistanis was in the same year, 1988, at 19,106; in 1989, this figure dropped to 5,938. In a similar vein, the peak for new Iranian entries was 47,976 in 1991, dropping to 14,314 in 1992 (Table 8.1). In addition, the requirement for entrance visas from Malaysia was tightened in June 1993 when prospective entrants were required to gain permission prior to exiting the country. This change might have had some impact on the reduction of Malaysian new arrivals from 1993 to 1994. However, as the peak for Malaysians was 78,019 in 1991, with a drop to 57,245 in 1992, factors outside Japan probably explain the Malaysian case.

As the above cases suggest, the suspension of mutual visa-exemption agreements proved effective in limiting the number of new entrants from Bangladesh, Pakistan and Iran, although this obviously did not prevent nationals of these countries already in Japan from becoming overstayers. However, once a passport holder of one of these countries stepped outside Japan, it removed the prospect of re-entry. In the short term, then, the government was left with the problem of how to deal with overstayers – in fact, as Table 8.2 makes clear, it took almost a decade for the government to reduce the number of overstayers from these countries by half. In this sense, over the longer term the measures the government adopted in order to curb immigration has had a certain degree of effect.

If we treat the Peruvian case as an exception, Table 8.2 also shows a sharp contrast in the rate of decline for overstayers between those countries to which visa-exemption was temporarily suspended, and others (South Korea, the Philippines, China, Thailand and Taiwan). This implies that the continuation of mutual visa-exemption agreements has had a positive effect on the number of overstayers in the latter group. Conversely, the Peruvian case suggests that the lawful introduction of unskilled labour from 1990 increased the number of overstayers in the 1990s and on to the present. If mutual visa-exemption had been lifted for Japan's close

Table 8.1 The number of new arrivals from selected Asian countries

	1982	1983	1984	1985	1986	1987	1988	1989	1990	1991	1992	1993	1994	1995	1996	2002
Bangladeshi	1,028	1,211	1,490	2,192	4,214	5,660	13,994	2,742	2,427	3,366	2,278	2,178	2,356	2,335	2,350	3,236
Pakistani	4,969	5,404	7,014	8,886	12,881	11,605	19,106	5,938	4,293	6,185	4,768	4,170	3,920	3,754	4,257	4,051
Iranian	1,493	4,006	10,302	23,610	15,904	19,818	14,090	16,282	31,289	47,976	14,313	3,419	2,673	2,091	2,181	3,440
Malaysian	23,578	51,823	63,853	69,867	44,341	38,601	43,726	51,653	54,849	78,019	57,245	42,263	38,923	43,636	47,533	59,269

Source: Hōmudaijin Kanbō Shihōhōsei Chōsabu 1983–2003.

Table 8.2 The estimated number of overstayers, by nationality (selected) and sex (1990–2002)

	01-Jul-90	01-Jul-91	01-Jul-92	01-Jul-93	01-Jul-94	01-Jul-95	01-Jul-96	01-Jul-97	01-Jul-98	01-Jul-99	01-Jul-00	01-Jul-01	01-Jul-02
Total	106,497	159,828	278,892	298,646	293,800	286,704	284,500	282,986	276,810	271,048	251,697	232,121	224,067
M	66,851	106,518	190,996	192,114	180,060	168,532	160,836	155,939	149,828	145,225	134,082	123,825	118,122
F	39,646	53,310	87,896	106,532	113,740	118,172	123,664	127,047	126,982	125,823	117,615	108,296	105,945
Korean	13,876	25,848	35,687	39,455	43,369	47,544	51,580	52,387	52,123	62,577	60,693	56,023	55,164
M	8,793	17,977	22,312	20,998	20,801	21,662	22,549	21,669	20,792	24,434	23,150	21,356	20,747
F	5,083	7,871	13,375	18,457	22,568	25,882	29,031	30,718	31,331	38,143	37,543	34,667	34,417
Filipino	23,805	27,228	31,974	35,392	37,544	39,763	41,997	42,547	42,608	40,420	36,379	31,666	29,649
M	10,761	12,905	14,935	15,861	15,933	16,056	16,081	15,818	15,489	14,722	13,235	11,593	10,456
F	13,044	14,323	17,039	19,531	21,611	23,707	25,916	26,729	27,119	25,698	23,144	20,073	19,193
Chinese	10,039	17,535	25,737	33,312	39,738	39,511	39,140	38,296	37,590	34,800	32,896	30,975	27,582
M	7,655	13,836	19,266	23,630	27,152	26,013	24,789	23,762	22,778	20,748	19,361	18,182	15,749
F	2,384	3,699	6,471	9,682	12,586	13,498	14,351	14,534	14,812	14,052	13,535	12,793	11,833
Thai	11,523	19,093	44,354	55,383	49,992	44,794	41,280	39,513	37,046	30,065	23,503	19,500	16,925
M	4,062	6,767	20,022	25,624	22,611	19,866	17,811	16,839	15,542	13,552	11,082	9,281	8,020
F	7,461	12,326	24,332	29,759	27,381	24,928	23,469	22,674	21,504	16,513	12,421	10,219	8,905
Malaysian	7,550	14,413	38,529	30,840	20,313	14,511	11,525	10,390	10,141	9,989	9,701	9,651	10,097
M	5,023	10,099	27,832	21,250	13,266	8,942	6,537	5,589	5,340	5,195	4,984	4,954	5,280
F	2,527	4,314	10,697	9,590	7,047	5,569	4,988	4,801	4,801	4,794	4,717	4,697	4,817
Taiwanese	4,775	5,241	6,729	7,457	7,871	7,974	8,502	9,409	9,430	9,437	9,243	8,849	8,980
M	2,080	2,356	3,427	3,867	4,032	3,987	4,128	4,328	4,346	4,394	4,330	4,227	4,346
F	2,695	2,885	3,302	3,590	3,839	3,987	4,374	5,081	5,084	5,043	4,913	4,622	4,644
Peruvian	242	487	2,783	9,038	12,918	15,301	13,836	12,942	11,606	10,320	9,158	8,502	7,744
M	172	339	1,904	6,469	8,869	10,066	9,067	8,513	7,721	6,885	6,132	5,723	5,277
F	70	148	879	2,569	4,049	5,235	4,769	4,429	3,865	3,435	3,026	2,779	2,467
Iranian	764	10,915	40,001	28,437	20,757	16,252	13,241	11,303	9,186	7,304	5,824	4,335	n.a.
M	645	10,578	38,898	27,630	20,151	15,762	12,853	10,964	8,883	7,024	5,569	4,158	
F	119	337	1,103	807	606	490	388	339	303	280	255	177	
Bangladeshi	7,195	7,498	8,103	8,069	7,565	7,084	6,500	6,197	5,581	n.a.		n.a.	
M	7,130	7,429	8,003	7,940	7,411	6,910	6,278	5,951	5,326				
F	65	69	100	129	154	174	222	246	255				
Pakistani	7,989	7,864	8,001	7,733	6,921	6,100	5,478	5,157	4,688	n.a.		n.a.	
M	7,867	7,731	7,862	7,562	6,735	5,915	5,294	4,968	4,505				
F	122	133	139	171	186	185	184	189	183				

Source: Kokusaijinryū May 1994: 29, December 1997: 25, November 1999: 26–27, May 2001: 23, May 2002: 19.

Asian neighbours, overstayers, especially female 'entertainers', would have been dramatically curbed, but this was not attempted (Table 8.2). This implies the probable shortage of female labour, especially women engaged in the 'entertainment' industry. In this sense, although the governance of immigration can be said to function more or less effectively on the basis of the immigration control system, the system can be seen to respond to economic needs.

In total, the number of overstayers has doubled between a July 1990 figure of 106,497 (66,851 men and 39,646 women) and 224,067 in January 2002 (118,122 men and 105,945 women), but has recently declined, with the peak of 298,646 (192,114 men and 106,532 women) in May 1993. The number of male overstayers from those countries with the benefits of mutual visa-exemption agreements have gradually decreased since the mid-1990s up to the present, while the number of female overstayers has stayed rather constant during the same period (Table 8.2). This suggests that factors other than a change in legal measures are influencing the number of overstayers in Japan. Two spring to mind: first, economic stagnation, which has reduced the need for the labour supplied by overstayers; and second, the introduction of legal unskilled workers, who have replaced the illegal overstayers as part of the labour force. It is no doubt the introduction of *Nikkeijin* from the 1990s that explains the stable number of overstayers in recent years, although the increase in trainees and pre-college students as well as the establishment of technical internships also have played a role.

Lastly, looking at the breakdown of overstayers in 2002, there are 163,271 temporary sojourners (72.9 per cent of the total), 11,154 entertainers (5.0 per cent), 9,953 pre-college students (4.4 per cent), 4,442 college students (2.0 per cent) and 3,264 trainees (1.4 per cent) (Kokusai Kenshū Kyōryoku Kikō 2002: 109). However, even if these entertainers, pre-college students, technical trainees, and technical interns are not in Japan as illegal overstayers, in reality, many of them are becoming a source of unskilled labour.

Lawful entry and unskilled labour

Although the Japanese government continues to deny the introduction of unskilled labour into the country, this has been the de facto policy from the 1970s onwards, as seen in the case of 'entertainment' visas. The gate was also opened slightly as a result of the 1990 amendments to the Immigration Control Act, when pre-student, trainee or long-term residence visas were newly established or clarified by the 1990 amendments. In other words, even though the legal status of entry into Japan is determined by their entertainment, pre-student, or trainee visas, or their status as *Nikkeijin*, many of them end up being engaged in unskilled labour.

Foreigners (excluding long-term resident Koreans and Chinese) who are engaged in unskilled labour in Japan at present include, (1) people both whose entry and employment are legal but whose working conditions are humiliating (resident Filipino women who entered on 'entertainment' visas), (2) those whose entry is legal and who are allowed to work for fixed time periods, but who end up working under poor labour conditions (pre-college and college students), (3) those who entered legally on the condition that they do not work, but who end up working under poor labour conditions after entry (technical trainees and interns), (4) people both whose entry and employment are legal but whose working conditions are below what should be expected (*Nikkeijin*), (5) those who enter on temporary visas and immediately begin working illegally (illegal workers from the outset), and (6) those who work in poor or inferior conditions as overstayers (originally one of types 2–5 above).

The 1990 amendments established penalties for any employers and/or brokers involved in introducing or employing illegal foreign workers (up to three years imprisonment or a fine of two million yen or less). The amendments also ratio-nalized the visa qualifications for foreigners with a high level of knowledge or specialism, categorizing them as investors and business managers, legal or accounting service specialists, engineers, specialist in humanitarian or international services, or intra-company transferees. As far as pre-college students and trainees are concerned, the amendments made their status clear-cut, removing them from the category of 'miscellaneous' visas. In addition, the long-term resident's visa was newly established in order to enable those who have 'links to Japanese society' and, in particular, 'blood links to Japanese society' (Hōmushō Nyūkoku Kanrikyoku 1998: 96) to be granted such visas. This opened the way for second and third generation *Nikkeijin* to stay legally in Japan, and as the government decided not to impose any restrictions on the kind of work that they could take on, they could engage in unskilled labour.

As far as entertainment visas are concerned, many are granted to female singers or dancers from the Philippines (Ballescas 1992). The annual number of visas granted fluctuates, but from the late 1980s up until the present the number has been 20,000–50,000. The problem here is the actual content of the work carried out: whereas formally these women are employed as hostesses in bars and clubs, prostitution is often expected of them, and in reality many are actually employed as prostitutes. Prior to the arrival of Filipino women in the mid-1980s, Japanese men had visited the Philippines to fill the same needs. From the perspective of the Filipino women, even though their status in Japan is legitimate, their role in the entertainment industry means they may be faced with the possibility of becoming prostitutes. Legal entry leads directly to illicit labour, and indirectly to overstaying. Both the Japanese and Filipino governments have turned a blind eye to this problem for the last twenty years: presumably the former, due to an interest in 'employment' and hard currency; and the latter, due to interest in 'entertainment'. From the perspective of this chapter, this lack of concern for the human rights of Filipino women displays the limits (or the real intent) of the governance systems of both countries. Rather than the government, NGOs, as illustrated by the Asian Women's Shelter founded in Tokyo in 1986, have actually assisted some of these women. Many Thai women, engaged in the 'entertainment' industry and often overstayers, face a similar plight (Caouette and Saito 1999).

Second, pre-student visas are issued to high school or Japanese language school students before entry into university, junior college, or technical college (Asano 1997; Tsuboya 2002). These visas were systematically issued following the 1990

Amendments, but had been issued before this as a special case under the 'miscellaneous' residence qualification. The genesis of this type of visa was the plan of prime minister Nakasone Yasuhiro to boost the number of exchange students from 10,000 in 1983 to 100,000 by the year 2000. This motivated the MOJ in 1984 to simplify the procedures for the acquisition of 'pre-students' status under the 'miscellaneous' visa category (Tsuboya 2002: 140). As a result, the numbers jumped from around 3,500 new entrants in 1983 to more than 35,000 in 1988, particularly amongst Chinese students: from 160 in 1983 to 28,256 in 1988. In 2002, the number of those pre-college students was 47,198 (of which 35,450 were Chinese) (Hōmushō Nyūkoku Kanrikyoku 2003: 180). Although they are presently allowed to work part-time for up to 28 hours (originally 20 hours) per week, they have become a source of unskilled labour and often work beyond the legal time limit. The government recently has begun to tighten the practical requirements for pre-student and student visas, in part because the goal of 100,000 foreign students was reached in 2003 (available on-line at http: //www.mext.go.jp/b_menu/houdou/ 15/11/03111102.html, accessed 24 May 2004) and partly because the government is trying to prevent the recurrence of crimes committed by foreign, especially Chinese, students (available on-line at http://www.jpss.jp/news/tuutatu.html, accessed 24 May 2204).

Third, the government has permitted the introduction of unskilled workers in the form of trainees. In 1993, the five ministries of Justice, Foreign Affairs, International Trade and Industry, Labour, and Construction set up the jointly managed JITCO to operate the system of foreign trainees. The trainees include (1) trainees that governmental institutions (such as Japan International Cooperation Agency (JICA) or the Association for Overseas Technical Scholarship (AOTS)) have invited from developing countries, (2) trainees who are invited by Japanese multinational companies mainly from their foreign subsidiaries, or by Japanese small-and-medium enterprises, and whose acceptance is supported by JITCO, or (3) trainees who apply directly to the immigration authorities. The total overall figure for 2001 was 59,064. Breaking the figure down, there were 12,626 (21.4 per cent) accepted by the government, 37,423 (63.4 per cent) accepted by the private sector who were supported by JITCO and 9,015 (15.3 per cent) direct applicants to the immigration authorities.

The number and nationality of the 37,423 trainees supported by JITCO is 26,837 (71.7 per cent) Chinese, 4,155 (11.1 per cent) Indonesians, and 2,090 (5.6 per cent) Filipinos. In terms of age and gender, male aged 25–29 and female aged 20–24 predominate. Most are being trained for a period of a year or less to work in textiles and sewing, food processing, mechanics, metal treatment, construction, and agriculture. None receive a salary, but the trainees are provided with an average of 75,031 yen per month as an allowance.

In 1993, the government introduced an intern system for technical training. This is a system in which trainees who have passed an evaluation test (which almost no-one fails) are able to work for a limit (set in April 1997) of up to two years after their training is completed. For fiscal 2001, the number of companies which applied to switch to technical training internship was 7,459, and the number of applicants,

22,268. Their breakdown is 15,846 Chinese (71.2 per cent), 3,355 Indonesians (15.1 per cent) and 1,891 Vietnamese (8.5 per cent). Looking at the size of the businesses, up to 70 per cent have less than fifty employees and are overwhelmingly small-and-medium sized enterprises. The average amount paid is 121,000 yen per month (the average monthly wage in Japan in 2001 was 351,335 yen, excluding bonuses. Available on-line at http://www.jil.go.jp/laborinfo-e/q_and_a/costs1.shtml, accessed 3 July 2003). In spite of being 'workers', many of these technical training interns are not signed up to health insurance, social security pensions, workmen's accident compensation insurance, or unemployment insurance – a fact even pointed out in a JITCO white paper (Kokusai Kenshū Kyōryoku Kikō 2002). Quite clearly, these interns are merely a source of unskilled and cheap labour with a time limit attached that meets the demands of small- and medium-sized businesses.

Furthermore, the Basic Plans for Immigration Control (2nd edition) of March 2000 proposes the extension of the scope of the definition of trainees or technical interns (to include hotel staff), and the introduction of foreigners as nursing staff for the elderly or as highly-skilled experts in information technology.

Finally and most importantly, as a result of the 1990 Amendments, the increase in *Nikkeijin* was most salient among foreign residents in the 1990s. The number of overwhelmingly *Nikkeijin* Brazilians has increased markedly from 1987 to 2002 (Table 8.3). In terms of visa category, the number of those Brazilians newly entering on the 'spouse or child of a Japanese' visa qualification clearly dropped from 1992 to 2002, whereas the number of those with a 'long-term resident' qualification rapidly rose from 1992 to 1997, although it then began to fluctuate. The number of Brazilians resident in Japan on the 'spouse or child of a Japanese' visa qualification remained rather constant, whereas the number of Brazilians living in Japan with 'long-term resident' status, increased markedly from 1992 to 2002. Similar trends can be observed in the Peruvian case (Table 8.4). Of those with the 'spouse or child of a Japanese' visa qualification, many are second generation *Nikkeijin*, and of those with 'long-term resident' status, many are third-generation *Nikkeijin*. Among the latter are those related to Japanese nationals, not through blood, but through their family membership (spouse, child, dependant, etc.). The second generation *Nikkeijin* is starting to be overtaken by the third. This also means that the issue of fourth generation *Nikkeijin* will arise in the future.

Whether the long-term resident qualification was established with the aim of introducing unskilled *Nikkeijin* labour or not remains unclear (Ninomiya and Tanaka 2004: 128). Publicly, the aims are explained as being elsewhere, as a measure to bring things into line for Korean special permanent residents in Japan, and those with a Japanese blood line, such as *Nikkeijin* or returnee Japanese women and children left behind in China right after the Second World War. Whatever the intention, however, the establishment of the 'long-term resident' visa and the 'spouse or child of a Japanese' visa were politically adroit in two respects. First, there were 1.2 million *Nikkeijin* in Brazil, and there seemed to be a fixed limit to the number. Second, the national belief that the *Nikkeijin* shared the same blood line as Japanese in Japan could be utilized, although the third or fourth generations,

Table 8.3 The number of Asian and South American residents from selected countries, legally registered, in Japan (at the end of each year)

	1983	1987	1988	1989	1990	1991	1992	1993	1996	1999	2002
The total number of all foreign residents	817,129 100.0%	884,025 100.0%	941,005 100.0%	984,455 100.0%	1,075,317 100.0%	1,218,891 100.0%	1,281,644 100.0%	1,320,748 100.0%	1,415,136 100.0%	1,556,113 100.0%	1,851,758 100.0%
Korean	674,581 82.6%	673,787 76.2%	677,140 72.0%	681,838 69.3%	687,940 64.0%	693,050 56.9%	688,144 53.7%	682,276 51.7%	657,159 46.4%	636,548 40.9%	625,422 33.8%
Chinese	63,164 7.7%	95,477 10.8%	129,269 13.7%	137,499 14.0%	150,339 14.0%	171,071 14.0%	195,334 15.2%	210,138 15.9%	234,264 16.6%	294,201 18.9%	424,282 22.9%
Brazilian	1,796 0.2%	2,250 0.3%	4,159 0.4%	14,528 1.5%	56,429 5.2%	119,333 9.8%	147,803 11.5%	154,650 11.7%	201,795 14.3%	224,299 14.4%	268,332 14.5%
Filipino	7,516 0.9%	25,017 2.8%	32,185 3.4%	38,925 4.0%	49,092 4.6%	61,837 5.1%	62,218 4.9%	73,057 5.5%	84,509 6.0%	115,685 7.4%	169,359 9.1%
Peruvian	432 0.1%	615 0.1%	864 0.1%	4,121 0.4%	10,279 1.0%	26,281 2.2%	31,051 2.4%	33,169 2.5%	37,099 2.6%	42,773 2.7%	51,772 2.8%
Thai	2,233 0.3%	3,817 0.4%	5,277 0.6%	5,542 0.6%	6,724 0.6%	8,912 0.7%	10,460 0.8%	11,765 0.9%	18,187 1.3%	25,253 1.6%	33,736 1.8%
Malaysian	1,337 0.2%	2,649 0.3%	3,542 0.4%	4,039 0.4%	4,683 0.4%	5,639 0.5%	5,744 0.4%	5,461 0.4%	5,544 0.4%	7,068 0.5%	9,487 0.5%
Bangladeshi	n.a.	1,291 0.1%	2,130 0.2%	2,205 0.2%	2,109 0.2%	2,542 0.2%	2,905 0.2%	3,319 0.3%	5,856 0.4%	6,574 0.4%	8,703 0.5%
Pakistan	518 0.1%	1,435 0.2%	2,063 0.2%	1,875 0.2%	2,067 0.2%	3,741 0.3%	4,124 0.3%	4,443 0.3%	5,112 0.4%	6,550 0.4%	8,225 0.4%
Sri Lankan	n.a.	n.a	n.a.	1,064 0.1%	1,206 0.1%	1,658 0.1%	2,097 0.2%	2,375 0.2%	3,225 0.2%	5,052 0.3%	7,312 0.4%
Iranian	394 0.1%	818 0.1%	918 0.1%	988 0.1%	1,237 0.1%	3,419 0.3%	4,516 0.4%	6,754 0.5%	8,418 0.6%	6,654 0.4%	5,769 0.3%

Source: Hōmudaijin Kanbō Shihōhōsei Chōsabu 1984, 88–94, 97, 2000, 03

Table 8.4 (a) Visa status of Brazilian and Peruvian residents in Japan; (b) Visa status of newly-arrived Brazilians and Peruvians in Japan

(a)

	1992	1993	1994	1995	1996	1997	1998	1999	2000	2001	2002
Brazilian national:											
Spouse or child of a Japanese	91,816	94,870	95,139	99,803	106,665	113,319	98,823	97,330	101,623	97,262	90,732
Long-term resident	51,759	55,282	59,280	69,946	87,164	111,840	115,536	117,469	137,649	142,082	139,826
Peruvian national:											
Spouse or child of a Japanese	10,455	10,692	10,784	11,222	11,293	11,309	10,522	10,303	9,978	9,643	8,923
Long-term resident	14,845	14,274	14,718	15,544	16,526	18,746	19,953	20,454	21,369	22,047	21,538

Source: Hōmushō Nyūkoku Kanrikyoku 1998: 97, 277; 2003: 183, 184.

(b)

	1992	1993	1994	1995	1996	1997	1998	1999	2000	2001	2002
Brazilian national:											
Spouse or child of a Japanese	16,815	12,111	8,859	9,049	9,600	13,945	7,382	9,274	14,544	8,627	6,978
Long-term resident	247	435	594	605	4,505	23,456	12,543	15,110	29,264	19,103	14,014
Peruvian national:											
Spouse or child of a Japanese	456	438	399	675	813	894	959	618	844	979	441
Long-term resident	110	180	218	576	1,178	1,848	1,796	1,593	2,573	2,835	1,572

Source: Hōmushō Nyūkoku Kanrikyoku 1998: 277, 279; 2003: 182, 183, 184.

which have less 'Japanese blood', are going to take over the second. However, through this unquestioning consensus, attention was turned away from the real problems of the immigration and permanent settlement of foreigners in Japan.

In the late 1980s, the pros and cons of either hoisting or lowering the national drawbridge to foreign labour was, for a time, widely debated in Japanese society. When the bubble economy burst in the early 1990s, however, social interest in the issue of foreign workers waned under the ongoing recession. Behind this was a strong feeling that, with the economic downturn, the necessity for labour would disappear. Nevertheless, as described above, even in the recession, Brazilians, Chinese, Filipinos and other Asian nationals have not withdrawn from the unskilled labour market. One of the reasons for this is the reliance of the service industry on the cheapest possible labour from Asian residents as well as temporary flexible Japanese workers, and part-time work by students and housewives.

Another reason is more fundamental. Even though there is an economic recession, not all categories of business are facing the same dire situation. *Nikkeijin* are involved in work in areas such as the car industry and electronic parts manufacturing in Ota City, Gunma Prefecture, Hamamatsu City, Shizuoka Prefecture and Toyota City, Aichi Prefecture. They are usually employed indirectly by big businesses through contractors in charge of a certain section in a plant, existing at the bottom end of Japan's two-tiered structure of labour. Many *Nikkeijin* accept night shifts and are a flexible workforce that satisfies the changing demands of business. Adult members of the family, as dependants, also work in the factories that produce packed lunchboxes for convenience stores, agricultural cooperatives, fisheries cooperatives or industrial-waste disposal units. There are also those among them who manage ethnic businesses such as restaurants, small shops, or tourist agencies. In this way, *Nikkeijin* are now becoming established in local society, and are gradually beginning to seek more rewarding lives (Ikegami 2001).

In sum, the actual introduction of unskilled labour under the visas discussed above can best be understood as a political compromise of the government responding to the economic necessities faced by small- and medium-sized businesses. This is the bridge which connects the governance of immigration with that of residence.

Governance of residence

What inevitably follows international migration is a range of problems in the work and life of the migrants. Yet in terms of both its legitimacy and capacity the system of immigration control does not extend as far as jurisdiction over the lives of resident foreigners. This will emerge, in future, as human rights issues, which will lead to the necessary introduction of international human rights regimes and the implementation of a social policy for foreign residents, as discussed below.

Japan's decision to join up to the International Covenant on Economic, Social, and Cultural Rights (1978), the International Covenant on Civil and Political Rights (1978), the Convention on the Elimination of All Forms of Discrimination against Women (1980), and the Convention Relating to the Status of Refugees

(1981) exerted a major domestic impact on foreign residents in Japan. Here is a case of the domestic application of international human rights regimes. International human rights regimes are functioning more or less effectively when it comes to securing the human rights of foreigners. For that purpose, human rights treaties have a significant impact in securing those rights through the provisions of Japan's legal system. The government, however, has been reluctant to introduce into Japan the international legal framework for coping with migrant workers, and, along with those of other industrially advanced countries, has not so far signed the International Convention on the Protection of the Rights of All Migrant Workers and Members of Their Families (effective in July 2003).

As far as illegal foreign residents are concerned, the issue is how to improve their working and living conditions, and how to rescue certain of them from an illegal existence. In this case, the problem concerns how to move from an illegal to a legal status. In general, the problem is one of asylum, but in the case of Japan, it boils down to the problem of granting a special dispensation in each case. Whatever the legal status of foreigners on entering Japan, many will establish themselves in Japanese society through reunion with their families, which also migrate to join them, or by creating families with Japanese nationals (through marriage or the birth of children). Of course, this is not a trend limited only to foreigners resident in Japan, and can be seen in general amongst foreigners who live in all countries. For that very reason, the Japanese government has been wary of accepting foreigners as unskilled workers, although foreigners have started to settle down permanently in Japan.

As is often pointed out, Japanese society discriminates against foreigners. Under these circumstances, the Koreans resident in Japan, being old comers, have acted as the driving force behind the growth of social movements, demanding equal rights with Japanese, with the support of other foreigners as well as Japanese nationals. Tracing this history briefly, in the 1970s this campaigning led to a number of successes: a suit for the employment of a Korean worker at Hitachi Ltd, the opening up of scholarships to foreign, mostly Korean, residents by the Japan Scholarship Association, the employment of foreign workers at Nippon Telegraph and Telephone Public Cooperation (now NTT), the acceptance of legal interns at the Legal Training and Research Institute, and the abolition of nationality clauses in examinations for employment at local authorities mainly in the Kansai region. In the 1980s, beginning with the abolition of the legislative ban on foreigners taking up residence in public municipal housing, semi-national public housing, and on loans from the People's Financial Corporation and the Housing Loan Corporation, the system was changed to allow foreigners to join the national pension and national health insurance schemes, the provision of children's allowances, and the opening up of employment as members of the faculty at national or municipal universities (Tanaka 1995: 130–49). In the 1990s, the fingerprinting of permanent foreign residents when registered as aliens was abolished, and, with the exception of a few firemen's positions, the legislated ban on foreigners taking up employment was lifted from almost all positions in big cities. Under the 1999 reforms to the Alien Registration Law, moreover, the fingerprinting system was completely abolished. Meanwhile, the all-Japan high-school athletics tournaments and the Japan high-school baseball championships have been opened up to international or Korean national schools, which are the equivalent of Japanese high schools (Hatsuse 2001:183–4). However, in March 2003, MEXT determined to continue the present system of not permitting students who had graduated from Korean national schools located in Japan to sit the examination for entry into Japanese universities, in spite of attempts in 2002 to change the situation. This decision was reflective of the worsening of the national feeling towards North Korea following the admission of kidnapping a number of Japanese nationals from Japan to North Korea decades ago. Eventually, MEXT agreed to allow the qualification of those students for the entrance examination on an individual academic basis from the academic year 2004, still refusing to give Asian national schools the eligibility as an educational institute.

While it should be noted that the above successes resulted from the combined efforts of resident foreigners and Japanese nationals to promote the rights of foreigners, international human rights regimes actually had the greater effect. It was in line with the signing of the International Covenant on Economic, Social, and Cultural Rights and the International Covenant on Civil and Political Rights (1978), that the legislative ban on foreigners entering public housing and taking out housing loans was abolished. As a result of joining up to the Convention Relating to the Status of Refugees (1981), the legislation keeping foreigners out of the national pension scheme and preventing their off-spring being granted a children's allowance was repealed. After the introduction of the Convention on the Elimination of All Forms of Discrimination against Women in 1981, moreover, the principle of equality between fathers and mothers concerning Japanese nationality was established through the 1985 reforms of the Nationality Law. One of the results of this change is that now the parents of the off-spring of Korean fathers and Japanese mothers usually opt to give them Japanese nationality, with the child being able to make the final choice between Japanese and the nationality of his or her father by 22 years of age (Tanaka 1995: 158–69). The International Convention on the Elimination of All Forms of Racial Discrimination was signed in 1995, and became legally effective within Japan from 1996. The Convention on the Rights of the Child came into force in 1994, and through the decision on application for a special resident's permit described below, can be seen to have exerted a major impact on the legal judgment made.

Foreign residents can promote their own public campaigns in order to acquire their own rights, and this is something in which Japanese citizens are also able to participate. But this only generally holds true for legal immigrants. In the case of people who are regarded as illegally resident under the Immigration Control Act, they are unable to appear in public spaces to promote their own rights. This is because they fear that, through being seen in public, they will be repatriated to their home countries by the authorities. In these instances, the cooperation of Japanese and legally resident foreign nationals becomes decisive, and the introduction of international human rights regime is essential for the guarantee of the human rights of such foreigners.

On 1 September 1999, twenty-one overstayers, made up of five families (four from Iran and one from Myanmar) and two individuals (from Iran and Bangladesh), voluntarily appeared before the Immigration Bureau in Tokyo seeking special residents permits, as did seventeen other overstayers from five families (all Iranian) on 27 December of the same year, and twenty-six others made up of seven families (two from Iran and one from the Philippines, Peru, Myanmar, Columbia and China respectively) and one individual from Bangladesh on 12 and 13 July 2000 (APFS 2002).

The granting of special residence permits is decided upon approval by the Minister of Justice. The results of the hearings were that sixteen members of four families (all Iranian) at the first hearing, four members of one Iranian family at the second hearing, and twenty-one members of five families (two from Iran and one from the Philippines, Peru and Myanmar respectively) at the third were granted special residence permits. In the decisions, special residence permits were to be granted to families that, even though no blood links with Japanese people existed, had been resident in Japan for long periods of time, were leading stable lives, and, as a basic rule, had children enrolled in schools above middle school (Komai *et al.* 2000). The effect of the children's rights treaties can be considered to be behind the approval of the rights of children to an education. In addition, four members of an Iranian family were judged to be eligible for the permits in September 2003 by the Tokyo district court, having once been refused by the Ministry of Justice (available on-line at: http://cgi.sainet.or.jp/~ikumi/mishuk/news/03919.html, accessed 24 May 2004).

Up until now, special residence permits have been granted, on the whole, to two types of foreigners. One of these, which until the 1980s made up about 80–90 per cent (from several hundred to one thousand per year) of the successful applicants, were resident Koreans. A significant proportion of these Koreans were people who had received special consideration from a 'humanitarian standpoint' when on the point of being forcibly repatriated after violating punishable laws. The other type is that of overstayers who, since the 1990s, have been granted special residence permits because of a real relationship through marriage with a Japanese or permanent resident. Their numbers have increased from 1,281 (84.8 per cent), of a total 1,511, for 1996, and 1,251 (87.4 per cent) of a total 1,431, for 1997, to 2,267 (90.8 per cent), of a total 2,497, for 1998 (available on-line at: http://www.isc.meiji.ac.jp/~yamawaki/yamawaki1.htm, accessed 26 May 2003). Moreover, the fact that the enforcement of the deportation of special permanent residents has been significantly eased has led to a dramatic decrease in the cases of resident Koreans.

It was the NGO, Asian People's Friendship Society (APSF), that gave practical support to these foreigners in pursuing their legal cases, and a group of researchers with interest in the rights of foreigners and issues of immigration (one of whom was Professor Komai Hiroshi of Tsukuba University), that supported the NGO. The group supported the overstayers who were seeking special resident's permits and penned a joint declaration which it submitted to the Minister of Justice on 11 November 1999. The names of 112 researchers from outside Japan and 481 from Japan itself had been added to the declaration in a month. In summary, the declaration stated that those appearing, (1) had already created a basis for their life in Japanese society and established bonds with Japanese society as upright citizens, and were members of their workplace and of local society, (2) that with eight children included among those appearing, measures based on the Convention on the Rights of the Child were necessary, and (3) that the children could speak only Japanese, and had established friendships with Japanese children (Komai *et al.* 2000).

The policy of the Basic Plans for Immigration Control (2nd edition) states that (1) because, even with a one-off amnesty policy, an influx of illegal residents and a lengthening of the time period of that residence can be expected, it is not an effective solution for dealing with the problem, (2) foreigners who have been granted special dispensations are those who have 'intimate social relations with Japanese or others' (actual marital relationships) and have established the basis for life in Japan, (3) that dispensations be granted in cases where it is accepted that, with deep links between the foreigner and Japanese society, there are major issues from a 'humanitarian standpoint' in forcibly repatriating him or her, and (4) in the case of illegal residence where 'intimate social relations with a Japanese citizen, permanent resident, or special permanent resident' exist, and it is accepted that there are sufficient 'links between the foreigner and Japanese society', the matter should be dealt with appropriately, sufficiently taking into account that 'humanitarian standpoint'.

These policies are in line with the results of rulings up until the 1990s. However, it is not clear whether or not the rights of the child are to be included in 'links between the foreigner and Japanese society'. In spite of this, the decision of the MOJ on the foreigners discussed above was interpreted as an acceptance of the rights of children at junior high school and above to continue receiving an education (denied to elementary children of the sixth grade and below). In this way, the dispensations are gradually changing from a form of general asylum to one of partial asylum. Here, the effects of international human rights regimes, beginning with the Convention on the Rights of the Child, have begun to take hold. Meanwhile, the International Convention on the Elimination of All Forms of Racial Discrimination can in the future be expected to increase in effectiveness in Japan. Finally, the Japanese government can be expected at some point to follow South Korea, Taiwan and Thailand in offering general amnesty (Komai *et al.* 2000: 57; Hayase 2001: 10, 12).

The fact that overstayers who are also illegal workers are suffering in terms of labour conditions, the non-receipt of salary, serious work-related injuries, and in terms of treatment for injuries or illness, has become a social problem since the 1980s. From the late 1980s onwards, these overstayers have been helped by NGOs such as Asian Women's Shelter HELP (Tokyo), Karabaw No Kai (Yokohama), Arusu No Kai (Nagoya), Asian Friends (Osaka), Asian People's Friendship Society (APFS, Tokyo), and The Forum on Asian Migrant Workers (Tokyo), and, since 1995, The Foreigners' Earthquake Information Center (Osaka, established at the time of the Hanshin-Awaji Great Earthquake and later changed to The Center for

Multicultural Information and Assistance) (Ōshima and Francis 1988; Gaikokujin Jishin Jōhō Sentā 1996; NGO-katsudō Shien Sentā 1998). There are now innumerable groups from all over the country involved in giving one form of assistance or another to these foreigners. There are also a significant number of instances in which cooperation with overstayers on human rights, daily life and medical care has occurred at local municipalities and regional international centres. Some local governments (villages and towns) have implemented social policies in order to assist Asian brides to settle down smoothly in the region by assuring them of a good social life, language services, and medical care (Kuwayama 1993; Shibata 1997).

Of course, prejudice and discrimination towards foreigners have not disappeared from Japanese society. Even *Nikkeijin* are foreigners. Taking Hamamatsu City as an example, there were 11,716 *Nikkeijin* in 2001 (out of a total population of 590,000). They are said to be 'faceless', because they have little contact with local people in everyday life. There is a significant mental and social rift between them and local society. In a large apartment-house complex in Toyota City in May 1999, there was even an incident in which a major confrontation unfolded between Japanese and Brazilian residents. Recently, relations between Brazilians and Japanese have, however, become routine and normalized in both Hamamatsu City and Toyota City (Ikegami 2001). Newly arrived Chinese and Koreans have started settling in the Shinjuku and Ikebukuro wards of central Tokyo, due to the cheap housing or proximity to their workplaces. This has led to the revitalization of depopulated metropolitan centres. Many Japanese nationals are becoming attracted by the ethnic atmosphere of the restaurants opened there. Thus, newly created ethnic networks, in addition to bringing together people from similar ethnicities, can also attract more Japanese to the same area (Tajima 1998).

Demands for greater political rights, coming mostly from Korean residents, are also now on the agenda. A representative example is the campaign to gain voting rights for foreigners in municipal elections. In 1993, Kishiwada city council (in Osaka) passed a resolution to ask the national Diet to extend the right to vote to foreigners settled in the municipalities. By July 2002 the city councils of 1,503 local municipalities had passed the same resolution to extend the franchise (available on-line at: http://www.mindan.org/sidemenu/sm_sansei27.php, accessed 25 May 2003). In the background is the Supreme Court decision of 1995 stating that the granting of local suffrage to (settled) resident foreigners was not forbidden by the Constitution. However, for the last year or two, the atmosphere in the National Diet has prevented amendment to the Local Election Law.

A recent example that has caught public attention is the approval, through local referendum ordinances, of the participation of permanently settled foreign residents in referenda concerning the amalgamation of cities, towns or villages. This has occurred in Maibara Town, Shiga Prefecture, Iwaki Town, Akita Prefecture, Matsuoka Town, Fukui Prefecture, Kitagata Town, Gifu Prefecture, Nabari City, Mie Prefecture, Nagi Town, Okayama Prefecture, Takaishi City, Osaka Prefecture and Kitano Town, Fukuoka Prefecture. In Takahama City, Aichi a local referendum ordinance (effective September 2002) was passed which sought to approve the standing participation of permanent foreign residents in all referenda, not only those concerning the amalgamation of municipalities.

In summing up, the domestic application of international human rights regimes has resulted from human rights movement of resident Koreans, supported by Japanese nationals and other foreigners. In the governance of residence, human rights specialists and activists, NGOs, and NPOs play such a significant role as to bring together international human rights regimes with the actual realization of an individual's human rights. This indicates a clear role for civil society in the governance of international migration. For that purpose, the vitalization of civil society through the activities of NGOs and NPOs is essential.

Conclusion

This chapter has analyzed the employment of unskilled labour provided by Asian residents in Japan from two perspectives: the governance of immigration and the governance of residence. What we have learned about the Japanese governance of these Asian immigrants can be summarized as follows.

First, the governance of immigration functions through the immigration control system, but the effects are somewhat limited due to the contested nature of governing immigrants. Especially the temporary lift of mutual visa-exemption treaties has proven very effective in stopping the increase in overstaying, but its use is limited to a few countries. The measure cannot be generalized as a way to curb illegal overstaying, and besides, overstaying can in a sense be considered to be a way to respond to social demands from Japanese government and society. This contradiction illustrates the way the governance of immigration is contested in Japan.

Second, while officially denying the introduction of an unskilled labour force, the Japanese government is in actual fact promoting its introduction as a way to meet the wider needs of the Japanese economy. In this way, the governance of immigration is in tension with the wider needs of the Japanese political economy.

Third, international human rights regimes have profound implications for domestic governance in Japan: indeed, through the governance of residence, these regimes can be said to repair the gap in the governance of immigration. From the late 1990s, the crack in the immigration control system seems to have begun to be filled through these governance regimes. What is more, the role of Japanese civil society has grown in importance and is itself becoming part of the governance system.

Fourth, once the domestic implication of international human rights regimes become clear, NGOs and other civil actors can function even more effectively as part of the overall governance regime for foreigners. Without cooperation between Japanese citizens and foreigners in promoting human rights, this role would be left in the incomplete hands of the state.

Finally, two points become clear from the above analysis. First, the governance of immigration and the governance of residence are complementary in terms of function. Second, human rights regimes are necessary in order for the Japanese immigration system to function in the future. It is in this that the connection between the international and the domestic can be seen in the governance of immigrants and foreign residents in Japan.

References

APFS (ed.) (2002) *Kodomotachi ni Amunesutii o*, Tokyo: Gendai Jinbunsha.

Asano, Shin'ichi (1997) *Nihon de Manabu Ajiakei Gaikokujin: kenshūsei ryūgakusei, shūgakusei no seikatsu to bunka henyō*, Okayama: Daigaku Kyōiku Shuppan.

Ballescas, Ma and Rosario, P. (1992) *Filipino Entertainers in Japan: an introduction*, Quezon City: the Foundation for Nationalist Studies.

Caouette, Therese and Saito, Yuiko (1999) *To Japan and Back: Thai women recount their experiences*, Geneva: International Organization for Migration.

Gaikokujin Jishin Jōhō Sentā (ed.) (1996) *Hanshin-daishinsai to Gaikokujin*, Tokyo: Akashi Shoten.

Hatsuse, Ryūhei (2001) 'Japanese responses to globalization: nationalism and ultranationalism,' in Glenn D. Hook and Hasegawa Harukiyo (eds), *The Political Economy of Japanese Globalization*, London: Routledge, pp. 173–87.

Hayase, Yasuko (ed.) (2001) *Ajia Taiheiyōchiiki ni okeru Kokusai Jinkō Idō*, Tokyo: Nihon Bōeki Shinkōkai Ajia Keizai Kenkyūsho.

Hōmudaijin Kanbōshihō Hōsei Chōsabu (ed.) (1983–2003) *Shutsunyūkokukanri Tōkeinenpō*, Tokyo: Ōkurashō Insatsukyoku.

Hōmushō Nyūkoku Kanrikyoku (1998) *Shutsunyūkokukanri 1998*, Tokyo: Ōkurashō Insatsukyoku.

Hōmushō Nyūkoku Kanrikyoku (2003) *Shutsunyūkokukanri 2003*, Tokyo: Ōkurashō Insatsukyoku.

Ikegami, Shigehiro (ed.) (2001) *Burajirujin to Kokusaika suru Nihonshakai*, Tokyo: Akashi Shoten.

Kokusai Kenshū Kyōryoku Kikō (ed.) (2002) *2002 Nendoban Gaikokujin Kenshū Ginō Jisshū Jigyō Jisshi Jyōkyō Hōkoku JITCO Hakusho*, Tokyo: Kokusai Kenshū Kyōryoku Kikō.

Komai, Hiroshi, Watado, Ichirō and Yamawaki, Keizō (eds) (2000) *Chōkataizai Gaikokujin to Zairyūtokubetsukyoka*, Tokyo: Akashi Shoten.

Kuwayama, Norihiko (1993) 'Ajia kara no hanayome e no sōgōteki keā no jissai to tenbō', in Gekkan Shakai Kyōiku Henshūbu (ed.), *Nihon de Kurasu Gaikokujin no Gakushūken*, Tokyo: Kokudosha, pp. 120–35.

Nakao, Hiroshi (1997) *Zainichi Kankoku – Chōsenjin mondai no kiso chishiki*, Tokyo: Akashi Shoten.

NGO-katsudō Shien Sentā (ed.) (1998), *NGO Dairekutorī*, Tokyo: NGO-katsudō Shien Sentā.

Ninomiya, Masato and Tanaka, Aurea Christine (2004) 'Brazilian workers in Japan', *University of Tokyo Journal of Law and Politics* 1 (Spring): 121–43.

Ōshima, Shizuko and Francis, Carolyn (1988) *HELP Kara Mita Nihon*, Tokyo: Asahi Shimbunsha.

Shibata, Gisuke (1997) 'Kokusaikekkon no shinten ni yoru nōsonshakai no kokusaika', in Komai, Hiroshi and Watado, Ichirō, (eds), *Jichitai no Gaikokujin Seisaku*, Tokyo: Akashi Shoten, pp. 369–89.

Sōgō Kenkyū Kaihatsu Kikō (1993) *Nihon e no Dekasegi Banguradeshu Rōdōsha no Jittaichōsa*, NIRA Research Project No.930025, Tokyo: Sōgō Kenkyū Kaihatsu Kikō.

Tajima, Junko (1998) *Sekai Toshi Tokyo no Ajiakei Ijūsha*, Tokyo: Gakubunsha.

Tanaka, Hiroshi (1995) *Zainichi Gaikokujin (Shinpan)*, Tokyo: Iwanami Shoten.

Tsuboya, Mioko (2002) 'Nihon "Ryūgaku" "Shūgaku" no Imi', in Ogura Mitsuo and Kanō Hirokatsu (eds) *Higashi Ajia to Nihon Shakai*, Tokyo: Tokyo Daigaku Shuppankai, pp.135–63.

Yamada, Takao (1993) 'Seikatsu e no enjo ga hitsuyō nara', in Ebashi Takashi (ed.) *Gaikokuji wa Jūmin desu*, Tokyo: Gakuyō Shobō, pp. 140–9.

Yamagishi, Tomoko and Morita, Toyoko (2002) 'The Iranian experience of Japan through narratives', *Islamic Area Studies Working Paper Series* 30, Tokyo: Islamic Area Studies Project.

9 Corruption and governance in Japan

J. Babb

We can never know the full 'truth' about the issue of corruption in Japan or anywhere else. Past and present cases that have been revealed to public scrutiny may not be the only nor the most significant cases. Even the pursuit of allegations of corruption may be insufficient to supplement empirical data on those cases brought to trial. The alternative to a purely empirical study is a hermeneutic and perspectival (though expressly not a cultural relativist) approach which aims at understanding the internal logic of corruption. That is, concretely, this chapter examines the theoretical and pragmatic perspectives of corruption as the basis for understanding the issue of corruption in Japanese governance.

There is an inherent perspectivism (Poellner 2001: 85–117) in any analysis of corruption because some may view certain practices as corrupt that others view as simple interest intermediation or a rationally calculated choice. What is legally defined as corrupt practices varies from one historical period to another and one country to another. Even if one accepts that there may be certain fixed notions of what is corrupt, the degree to which this inhibits corrupt practices also varies according to perceptions of the situation by the individuals, organizations and institutions involved. Thus, it would be a mistake to judge Japan using seemingly objective but instead flawed empirical models or economic arguments over the rationality and costs of corruption.

This chapter suggests that it is best to try to look at the manner in which the Japanese themselves have constructed their political understanding of and attempts to cope with corruption. In doing so, the political must be highlighted as a contrast to fixed notions of culture and/or 'good governance'. In the end, it is possible that the changing nature of political corruption may be as much a part of Japanese governance as the attempts to eliminate it.

Judging corruption and governance

The considerable writing on corruption in Japan by outsiders seeks to explain and critique Japan while implicitly holding the absent discussion of Western political ethics as a higher standard. This must provoke a variety of feelings in those who read this literature: salutary warning, reassurance that it is possible to comprehend corrupt behaviour and other such sentiments. A consciously non-judgemental narrative of Japanese political practice, in this context, would be seen as 'failing to engage the relevant literature' or 'not providing a coherent narrative strand to aid the Western reader'. It is easier to disdain, attack or even whitewash corrupt practices because it is the best way to be seen as relevant, coherent and engaging the subject in an accepted and predictable manner.

We cannot avoid looking at the existing literature on corruption, but this chapter will also contemplate the possibility that corruption is secondary, a distraction or even necessary and desirable. This should not be seen as a relativist argument though it may be necessary to 'bracket' the implicit negative connotation of corruption to reveal the other possibilities of such practices. This can be accomplished through a hermeneutic exploration of the meaning of corruption in Japan. What we hope to show is that corruption can be interpreted as part of a constellation of fate, moral character and democratic action that escapes our conventional understanding of the issue.

To view the issue in the context of governance discourse is to raise and reveal key problems. Governance as a concept is loaded with a range of implications. In some sense, it seems to embody the hope of drawing attention to a wider range of actors, sites of contestation and processes than are often accommodated by conventional theories. At the same time, governance discourse may lead to a realization of the archaic meaning of the word: to control.

The origin of the recent revival of governance as a word can be found mainly in the notion of corporate governance. This has been extended by international organizations in a bid to legitimize rule-creation at the international level in a manner that would be understood and acceptable to business which has adopted governance rhetoric. Adoption of the term by international relations scholars seeks to expand this legitimizing process further to embrace the exploration of a range of related issues while at the same time subtly (or not so subtly) contesting or subverting the concept.

The corporate governance provenance of the concept immediately raises problems. Unspoken or not, corporate governance suggests norms and rules to modify the behaviour of the range of actors involved with the corporation, including executives, managers, workers, stockholders, consumers and those affected by the 'externalities' of corporate actions. Corporate governance is created for the benefit of the corporation as a whole. It inculcates ethics and social norms to help the corporation avoid obvious pitfalls to the corporation's long-term benefit. In doing so, it avoids divisive and damaging confrontation, and diffuses and manages social and political claims on the corporation (see Chapter 11).

In a generic notion of governance, it is unclear who (or what) the beneficiary is. The removal of clearly drawn lines of conflict, desirable to profit-making entities, threatens the de-politicization of politics by making it a question of 'good' management. The attempts to diffuse norms raises the potential for the internalization of norms that both makes citizens into subjects and invades their personal self-definition with externally imposed norms to be internalized as appropriate to the governance structure.

The issues raised in a discussion of corruption in Japan challenge the easy notion of established norms simply in need of adoption and/or internalization. None the less, placing a consideration of corruption in the context of thinking about governance potentially aids our understanding of both concepts. This chapter will focus primarily on thinking about corruption before turning to its relation to governance in the conclusion. It will first review conventional scholarly thinking on the subject, but given the above discussion, the main focus must be the sources of Japanese understanding of the concept.

The conventional approaches

There are several literatures on corruption. The largest and growing body of literature focuses on the economic rationality of corruption. It is also a literature that closely approximates the concerns of conventional definitions of governance with its implicit assumptions about the value of economic rationality. The relationship of economic rationality to ethics is complex. The implicit assumption of the literature is an a priori moral argument that corruption is inefficient, economically harmful and, thus, bad. Of course, these studies are backed by impressive empirical evidence (Treisman 2000; Jain 2001; Mo 2001), though operationalization of measures of corruption are complex (Lancaster and Montinola 2001), and the validity and universality of indicators are epistemologically contentious. Moreover, this literature has been criticized for its implicit assumptions about the ideal model of modernity and efficiency on which it is based (Theobald 1999). It is possible that corruption might be politically necessary or even beneficial in some ways. On the contrary, it may be those actors whose ideals most closely approximate the model of economic rationality that are most prone to corruption (Hopkin 1997; Frank and Schulze 2000).

There is also an implicit democratic ethical argument in much of the commentary on corruption that must also be addressed. 'Undue' influence, especially as a result of unseen and unmonitored influence, the sale of influence and distortions of public priorities, are all contrary to the egalitarian ethics of democracy. Of course, this unequal influence exists even in situations not considered to be corrupt. Those who are wealthy, organized, and even passionate, for example, can exert a disproportionate influence on the democratic political process. This is a perennial debate in democratic theory and one that has been practically resolved, for example, by an emphasis on transparency in political finance or the prohibition of contributions of a specific type. This process of transparency laws and prohibitions creates new crimes and criminals, however, as the violation of the transparency maintaining laws and blanket prohibitions, rather than the undue influence, are criminalized. Indeed, Japanese electoral and campaign finance law contains strict reporting requirements, limits on contributions and spending and even a prohibition on door-to-door canvassing and severely limited use of the posters and the mass media that would seem unnecessarily restrictive elsewhere.

At its worst, corruption involves a diversion of public funds for narrow private purposes, or in effect, embezzlement against the people and a distortion of democratically determined priorities. There must be a sense, however, that the public is harmed by this diversion rather than benefits from it. For the narrowest gain accruing to an individual or limited group of people, the criminal law is in theory brought to bear. In the case of diversion to a social group or coalition of interests in society, the decision over the appropriateness of the use of funds is largely political and not one for the law and the criminal prosecution service. If the public objects to systematic diversion of funds, then the only recourse is a political one: vote those responsible out of office. In Japan, they have very often not done so, though the law and political action has had to respond to 'public opinion'. Moreover, systematic corruption, in public works for example, has had redistribution effects that make their impact more similar to public policy than corruption.

Western social science research on Japan has tried to grapple with the paradox of both seemingly high levels of democracy and corruption for many years. One solution is to deny that Japan has a real democracy with part of the evidence being the existence of corruption itself (Hertzog 1993). One of the earliest solutions, however, was to attribute the problem to the traditions of Japanese political culture. Bradley Richardson's (1974) early work, for example, used public opinion surveys to explore the attitudes of the Japanese which led them to fail to reach the norm of civic culture as exemplified by the US and the UK drawn from the seminal work of Almond and Verba on the civic culture (1965). The focus was often on Japan 'particularism' where the democracy was based on personal exchange (as in clientelism) rather than the more open, universalistic West. The problem is that the categories used in this research are inevitably misleading because they are created by the social scientist themselves for their own theoretical purposes. They do not provide a very deep insight into the internal logic of the Japanese, especially Japanese politicians, in terms of how they construct their understanding of corruption. In addition, they posit a static notion of culture where change only can come as a result of the modernization of the culture.

Institutional arguments are often used in contrast to cultural arguments. Curtis has made the clearest institutional arguments: this is implicit in his earlier work (1988: 160–9) but explicit in his most recent. 'Although an image of Japanese politics as hopelessly corrupt is widespread, there is far less corruption now than there was in the past. . . . Experience suggests that the way to reduce corruption is to pass and enforce laws that are targeted directly at corrupt practices rather than by changing the electoral system' (1999: 165). Similar arguments have been presented by this author, but these were less optimistic: 'any laws are enacted based on the assumption that the authorities have the will to enforce them' (Babb 2001: 63, 47–63). Enforcement is difficult due to the political control of the judicial institutions by the corrupt politicians they are meant to monitor and prosecute. Therefore, institutions matter but only insofar as they are created and used effectively, and that is not always politically possible.

In recent years, a rational choice approach to Japanese politics has become popular. In many ways rational choice arguments are also institutionalist arguments but with a greater emphasis on simple relationships. Interestingly, corruption in

Japan is not identified as a focus for research given that it is absent from indexes of the key works in the field, Ramseyer and Rosenbluth (1997) and Kohno (1997). In these volumes, fundraising and even scandal are raised as part of the narrative but corruption is not considered to be a phenomenon that must be explained. At the same time, there is an implicit justification of corruption as a process of exchange and 'side payments' that fits well with models of rationality. As with all rational models, however, the values (matrixes of payoffs) are created *ex post facto* as consistent with the predictive power of the models in terms of how they accommodate the data. Indeed, given the complexity of the values involved – which in any case are not explored in any depth – it is easy for researchers to pick and choose data (statements and actions) that confirm the models.

What is the existing data on corruption? Surprisingly, few scholars working on the subject seem to be operating with anything approaching a comprehensive database. Of course, a truly comprehensive database is impossible given that some corruption successfully evades detection because those involved are determined not to get caught. Even so, not all the allegations in the literature are used by scholars researching the subject. The tables in this chapter are probably not complete, but they are the most comprehensive available to date. From these known cases, certain patterns do emerge.

First of all, the cases have been divided into those in which prosecution was initiated (Table 9.1) and those in which it was not (Table 9.2). In both cases, a significant number of cases of bureaucrats and local government officials implicated or prosecuted for corruption have been omitted to place the focus on members of parliament (MPs). There are slightly more cases of allegations of corruption (41) than those which have resulted in the prosecution of an MP (35). The clusters of prosecutions and gaps between them are telling in themselves. There are many cases in the late 1950s and early 1960s, but there is a large gap between 1968 and 1976. The reason was not a sudden decline in corruption but simply that the career of one individual prosecutor was so severely damaged by his pursuit of the Kyōwa Sugar case that subsequent prosecutors became wary of pursing cases involving government politicians (Uozumi 1997: 67–9).

The data in Table 9.1 indicate those cases in which the prosecution was successful and those in which it led to the removal of the MP from office. This is an issue because political control of the judicial system and the unwillingness of the ruling Liberal Democratic Party (LDP) to use parliamentary means to expel indicted MPs has meant those implicated are able to avoid removal from office indefinitely. This is noticeable in the cases in which the defendant dies prior to the outcome of the appeal, most famously in the case of former Prime Minister Tanaka Kakuei in the Lockheed scandal. It is interesting, however, that in recent years more MPs have begun to resign and two have taken their lives. Either the will or ability of politicians to fight corruption cases and remain in office may have declined. The current exception is Nakamura Yoshirō who was convicted as part of one of the *Zenecon* construction scandals but still refuses to resign. This may be one of the reasons that prosecutors have begun to pursue politicians for tax evasion because it is often easier and more damaging to be convicted for not having

Table 9.1 Postwar prosecutions for corruption involving MPs (1945–2003)

Year	Scandal	Prosecuted?	Convicted?	Removed?
1947	Tsuji Karoku	yes (2)	no	no
1948	Showa Denkō	yes (8)	yes (2)	died (2)*
	Coal Nationalisation	yes (8)	yes (3)	no 1 died
	Tōyō Seifun	yes	yes**	no
1950	Kyoto Keirinjō	yes	no	died
1951	Excise Tax Law	yes	yes	nk
	Kanonji Kyorinj	yes	no	died*
1954	Shipbuilding	yes (3)	no (3)	no
	Rikuun Transport	yes (2)	no	no
	Nikkōren	yes (2)	yes (2)	yes (1)
	Workers Fund Misuse	yes	yes	nk
1956	School Library Law	yes	no	died
1957	Marine Products	yes	yes	nk
	Prostitution Law	yes (3)	yes (2)	nk
	Shintsūkawa Dam	yes	yes*	no
1961	Bushū Tetsudō	yes	yes	died
1966	Tanaka Shōji	yes	yes	yes
	Construction Gift	yes	no	no
1967	Kyōwa Sugar	yes	yes	died
	Osaka Taxi	yes (2)	yes (1)[†]	died
1968	Nittsū	yes (2)	yes (1)[††]	yes
1976	Lockheed	yes (3)	yes	no[†††]
1986	Yoriitokōren	yes (2)	yes (2)	yes (2)
1988	Zenjiren	yes	yes	yes
1989	Recruit	yes (2)	yes (1)	yes (1)
1991	Kyōwa	yes	yes	yes
	Zenecon	yes	yes	no
1995	Two Credit Associations	yes	yes	yes
1997	Orange Kyōsai Kumiai	yes	yes	yes
1998	Nisshō Securities	yes	no	yes (suicide)
	Defence Agency	yes	yes	yes (suicide)
2000	Construction	yes	yes	yes
	KDS	yes (2)	yes (2)	yes (2)
2001	P.O. Managers	yes	on-going	yes
	Foreign Ministry	yes	yes	yes

Sources: Fujita (1980), Murobushi, (1981), Iwai (1990), Gendai Seijika Jinmei Jiten (1998)

Notes:
nk   = not known
*MP   being prosecuted died during appeal.
**   no on appeal.
†   The second politician died during the trial.
††   One politician died during trial. Second was first conviction upheld against a sitting MP.
†††   Two died before appeal completed.

Table 9.2 Postwar allegations of corruption involving MPs (no prosecution) (1945–2003)

Year	Scandal	Year	Scandal
1949	MCI Textiles	1966	Banokon
1950	Goi Industries		Shinanogawa Kasenjiki
	Nippon Hassōden		Sahkalin Smuggling
1953	Reiyūkai		Tokyo Taishō
1954	Hōzen Keizaikai		Arafune Transport Minister
	Nisshoku	1968	Next Generation
	Nippei		Badge System
1955	E. German Imports	1987	Land Co.Finance
1957	Zenkōren	1974	Tanaka Kakuei Finances
1958	Chiba Bank	1977	Seoul Underground
	Grumman	1979	Airliner
1959	Indonesia Reparations	1980	Zeiseiren
1961	New Tōkaidō Line		KDD
1962	Bullet Train Land	1984	Sankō Steamship
1964	Kōmeigaike	1986	Marcos Rebate
	Toranomon Land Sale		Peace Mutual Bank
1965	Kutoryū Dam	1992	Sagawa Kyūbin*†
	Fukuhara	1997	Fuji HI
	Second Airport Land	2000	Uzui Donation

Sources: Fujita (1980), Murobushi, (1981), Iwai (1990), Gendai Seijika Jinmei Jiten (1998)

Notes:
*   (MP tried on other charges)
†   The allegations that led to the resignation of Prime Minister Hosokawa in 1994 were indirectly connected to this case.

Table 9.3 Postwar prosecutions for tax evasion involving MPs (1945–2003)

Year	Scandal	Prosecuted?	Convicted?	Removed?
1990	Inemura Tax Evasion	yes	yes	yes
1993	Kanemaru Tax Evasion	yes	no (died)	yes*
1994	Ōtani Tax Evasion	yes	yes	yes
	Kondō Tax Evasion	yes	yes	yes

Sources: Fujita (1980), Murobushi (1981), Iwai (1990), Gendai Seijika Jinmei Jiten (1998)

Note:
*Resigned before died.

reported suspicious contributions as income than the mere allegation of receiving them. Such cases have been isolated in Table 9.3.

We have been forced to omit important recent cases of scandal involving secretaries of MPs (affecting former Agricultural, Forestry and Fishery Minister Ōshima Tadamori and former Foreign Minister Tanaka Makiko among the most prominent cases) due to the fact they do not fit into an established category. The use of both public and private secretaries in questionable activities has been a frequent issue in political reform, but space limitations do not permit a detailed discussion in this chapter. Moreover, minor prosecutions of MPs from such things as minor election law violations have been also omitted because they generally result only in a small fine being paid despite being much more numerous than well-known cases of serious allegations of corruption.

The existence of a continuing number of cases of corruption despite changes strengthening the laws in 1975 and 1994 may mean that corruption is detected and dealt with more effectively rather than that the laws have no effect. It is difficult to say given we can never know the true data set of corruption incidents given their nature. Anecdotal evidence suggests that little changed after 1975. Indeed, the situation may have become worse at the height of the bubble economy in the late 1980s and early 1990. None the less, the persistence of corruption scandals after changes in the law in 1994 may only be indicative of a lower tolerance of corrupt practices, and therefore, a higher likelihood that it is revealed. Again, we can never know.

There is a limit to all the theories and empirical evidence. All these approaches define the problem of corruption in Japan from without. The economic approach seems to make simplifying assumptions that, at best, are simplistic, and beg the question of the origin of values and implicit moral assumptions or consequences. Even the cultural approach, with some claim to be exploring the Japanese definition of politics, is so dependent on assumptions and categories drawn from the Western social science tradition that it is less than useful. Rational choice models accept the priority of value preferences but then also arbitrarily simplify them to fit their models. Institutional approaches, where sufficiently historical, can begin to enhance our understanding and there is much that can be learned from a review of the empirical evidence which can be collected. None the less, it is the richness of the lived experience of Japanese with corruption that must be revealed in its full complexity before we can begin to understand what corruption means to governance. Therefore, it is the broader Japanese hermeneutic context itself to which we must now turn.

Hermeneutics and the genealogy of corruption in eastern tradition

The alternative to the social science model for studying corruption can be found in a hermeneutic approach such as that advocated by Gadamer (1989). Gadamer argues that we cannot avoid our pre-judging of concepts and situations because we are too influenced conceptually by them in how we approach a problem. Indeed, the literature review above suggests that our theoretical starting point often determines in advance the conclusions. As an alternative, Gadamer embraces the idea of the influences of tradition on the thinking of the researcher and the research. His exploration of the hermeneutics itself suggests that an exploration of the rich traditions of use and change in use of a concept is one way to approach the problem.

The problem in the Japanese case is that the tradition is not Western and this would imply a larger gap between the Western observer and Japanese thought. However, Japanese thought is not simply non-Western either. There should be no false dichotomy between non-Western and Western. Japan has a deeply rooted and rich non-Western or East Asian heritage but has also confronted Westernization and assimilated Western thought in many areas. We cannot avoid examining all forms of thought in the Japanese tradition as they impinge on this issue.

It is best to start with the deepest layer of hermeneutic understanding which is bounded by language. Without intending to bog down the discussion in philology, the words used to denote corruption in Japanese, drawn primarily from Chinese, are instructive of the conceptualization of the concept(s). The most commonly used words are *oshoku, fuhai* and *wairo*. The words are old but do not appear in the earliest Chinese classics in their current form. A full discussion of how these words have come to be used in Japanese and applied to the situations we now describe as corruption is beyond the scope of this chapter, but there are two important points to be made none the less.

One is that corruption as a dirty but necessary task, as action leading to dire consequences and as a way to get special treatment all remain in the discourse of corruption. Second, none of these words is used in any of the classic Chinese texts that form the basis of Japanese political thought – which instead focuses on fair taxation and the correct behaviour of rulers in ritual and custom. Funds were raised by officials in various ways for both private and public uses. The methods of fund-raising and the use of these funds for gifts is a secondary issue in the classic literature but is made the main focus by a modern reader looking for corruption as we conceive it today. The level of taxation and the giving of gifts to officials did not violate any law except a sense of propriety. A state that heavily taxes is in moral and physical danger (of revolt and the attentions of predatory states) and not one in which officials receive 'gifts' *per se*.

In fact, all histories and conceptual analyses of corruption have been written to have an effect on an audience. Authors have intended to moralize, and thus often to titillate as well as explain and isolate the subject. The terminology of corruption in both English and Japanese is filled with religious implications. Corruption is a chief characteristic of this sinful world in Christianity, but the filth and decay of Japanese terms for corruption also resonate with Buddhist and Shintoist implications. As a result, discussion of corruption is immediately involved in moral considerations. It is important to note, however, that these innate implications of terminology and judgement emerge slowly and fitfully in the historical process. Even today, the meaning can be seen as in the process of being revealed rather than as a fixed truth.

As we approach Japan, we must be aware that the Tokugawa regime (1603–1868) domesticated Buddhism and promoted Confucianism as the alternative moral order to support the political order. There was no independent church as in Europe to impose exacting moral standards independent of political leaders and Confucian scholarship was initially constrained by dependence on the Tokugawa house and that of local *daimyō*. In any case, corruption by officials, in the sense of diversion of tax resources, would be seen as theft against the *daimyō* or *bakufu* and punished as such. None the less, it was exploitation of peasants, not corruption that was the primary concern due to the increased danger of revolt and thus invoking the pragmatic prohibitions of exploitation in the classic Chinese literature.

The rise of a Tokugawa merchant class raised new and difficult problems, however. To the extent that they profited from transactions involving *daimyō* and *bakufu* authorities, they were in danger of being accused of theft. Corruption in the modern sense of the word is not a concern of the political theorists of the Tokugawa era. For example, the main focus of Sorai Ogyū's *Seidan* (Discourse on Government) (1987), one of the most direct treatments of political economy in the period, is the role of money, including the quality and quantity of the money supply. As Najita writes: 'It is important to note here that while these commentators saw the money economy as falling squarely within the vision of the ancient sages, especially the idea that cash was a necessary ingredient in the maintenance of social well-being, they also couched their views in such a way that the usurious handling of money by merchants was seen as a corruptive influence that undermined society' (Najita 1987: 228).

Care must be taken not to fall into the trap of viewing contemporary depictions of Tokugawa corruption on Japanese television as similar to that of today because these programmes are made as a not-too-subtle commentary on modern problems. The problem for Tokugawa merchants was that even charging interest on loans could be construed as usurious in a way that is perfectly legal today. Any profit, especially profits that led to ostentatious wealth, would be viewed as a theft from society. These beliefs among Japanese, elite and common alike, meant that the existence and role of merchants in any form was questionable and the formation of merchant academies in the Tokugawa era was intended precisely to grapple with this problem and create an appropriate ethics to justify the merchant's role (Najita 1987).

This situation changed with the Meiji Restoration (1868) which led to the formation of a modern state in Japan. The new imperial Japanese state was formed based on laws that were recognizable to the Western powers to facilitate trade and Japan's acceptance into the family of nations. Yet, even in this period the focus was not corruption but the powers of the aristocracy versus merit in government. In Nakae Chōmin's *Discourse of Three Drunkards on Government*, the focus of playful discussion is the extreme contrast between a hereditary aristocracy, in Japan the samurai class, and popular government. Nakae recognizes that the samurai have given up their swords, but long to have a chance to use them again (Nakae 1984: 109). None the less, ambitious samurai took up the cause of political struggle through democratic (or popular) means. In fact, Meiji politicians and merchants were among the first to adopt the old samurai values as a standard for all gentlemen, high born or not. The values of these individuals focused on discipline, compassion and decisiveness but with no mention of corruption as something to be avoided. The lack of democracy and the domination of political power by an unaccountable elite was more of an issue than corruption.

Corruption and democracy in Japan

It was only when dissenting groups, including disgruntled former samurai, were incorporated into politics through the representative institutions of imperial Japan that the problem of corruption became prominent. Scalapino cites corruption as a major problem and cause of the failure of prewar democracy and party politics but it may be that corruption and democracy were inseparable (1953: 247). Democratic governance is more likely to be associated with corruption than with the conditions that militate against it. It would not be surprising if this is also the period in which the discourse of corruption has its beginnings in Japan. It is easy to forget that democracy is also associated with corruption in Jacksonian democracy in the United States, and that corruption became more of an issue in Regency England with rising demands for political reform. In fact, bribery itself is a relatively new notion that is associated with modern political practice (Noonan 1984).

In response to the rise of the idea of corruption, there were various strands of opposition to corruption in prewar Japan. One not often noted was the female suffrage movement. For example, in 1928 on the occasion of the first general election under universal manhood suffrage, a Vote for Women Alliance issued a demand that those with the right to 'vote cleanly for true representatives without being misled into inappropriate behaviour such as selling votes and abstaining' (Ichikawa 1980: 194). The key role played by Christians and Christian church organizations in this alliance suggests why it might have helped to introduce moral discourse into the debate on corruption in Japan

New laws had been implemented prior to the passage of universal manhood suffrage legislation in anticipation of problems involving corruption, but the extent of the expansion of corruption in the first election under universal manhood suffrage exceeded all predictions. One response from the Hamaguchi government (1930–1) was the establishment of a special parliamentary commission to study the problem which concluded that greater education of voters was required. However, one member of the commission, the constitutional scholar Minobe Tachikichi, dissented by arguing that it was flaws in the electoral law rather than ethics of voters that gave rise to corruption. The problem could only be solved by shifting the focus of elections away from voting for individual candidates towards a party-based system of proportional representation (Fujita 1980: 45–6). The problem was that institutional solutions were not only politically difficult to implement, but also many groups gained politically from their attacks on party government corruption.

One important source of vocal opposition to corruption in politics came from violent groups and those associated with the military. Military radicals advocated a 'Showa Restoration' to revive a decaying Japan and explicitly raised ideals of purity in politics and contrasted them with corruption scandals that undermined public trust in politicians. This approach took its most violent form when Prime Minister Inukai Tsuyoshi was assassinated in 1932 by terrorists claiming to be fighting political corruption. Importantly, these individuals were strongly influenced by Nichiren Buddhism, which not only is traditionally nationalistic, but this sect's scriptures also contain powerful images of decay caused by misrule, and these can easily be transformed into anti-corruption arguments.

Yet, it was not just oppositional and extremist forces in prewar Japan which made these arguments. The Saitō cabinet formed in the wake of the Inukai assassination made the issue of political corruption a key issue to be addressed by the government. It gave the legal reform commission (*hōsei shingikai*) headed by a leading politician, Hiranuma Kiichirō, the responsibility for examining the issue. This commission immediately dropped the issue of electoral system reform. It has been suggested that this was the beginning of an emphasis on spiritual enlightenment as the solution to corruption rather than institutional solutions (Fujita 1980: 47–55). This view is supported by the role the right-wing Hiranuma later played behind the scenes in the prosecution of the Teijin Incident of 1934. The Teijin Incident involved the sale of shares in Teijin Ltd, a rayon manufacturer, which appeared to have been manipulated for the benefit of key politicians, including cabinet ministers. Saitō decided to dissolve his cabinet prior to any arrests, but sixteen men were charged with corruption. Even though the defendants were found not guilty of wrong-doing, the image of widespread party political corruption lingered. This image was fed by groups such as the National Foundation Society (*Kokuhonsha*) formed by Hiranuma who were suspicious of democracy (people-based or *minpon* rule) and advocated nation-based (*kokuhon*) spiritual ideals.

Even after right-wing approaches to politics were discredited by Japan's defeat in 1945, the connection between party politics and corruption persisted. Indeed, the war and immediate postwar chaos expanded opportunities and experience in corrupt practices. Democracy and corruption once again seem to have been positively related. The main legacy of the Allied occupation may have been more democracy, but also more corruption, and more moralizing over the problem of corruption. Commentary by journalists, former occupation officials and US scholars formed the early discourse on corruption in Japan which in turn informed later scholarship in Japan and abroad.

Corruption became an obsession not just of foreign commentators but also the Japanese media and the major organizations of civil society. Everyone was against corruption. In the wake of a number of scandals in 1954, the Clean Election Alliance (*Kōmei Senkyō Renmei*) was formed by a coalition of forty-one organizations including business, women's, local government organisations (Fujita 1980: 160). The Alliance gathered together the leaders of the four main parties in late 1954 and had them pledge to clean up election practices. Immediately afterward, 112 media organizations including all the major and local newspapers, news agencies and broadcasters announced their support for the Alliance movement. For the media, which enjoyed their role as an informal opposition and were keen to protect their newly won freedoms, corruption was a useful subject to critique those in power, though they were careful not to directly alienate politicians who could provide individual reporters with access to information.

The importance of the Alliance in promoting a set of ideals and suspicions in early postwar Japan should not be underestimated. It monitored campaign violations and the attitudes of the Japanese towards democracy and corruption, and issued reports with its results which were duly reported by the media and taken up by scholars. The surveys of the Alliance formed the basis for the political cultural analysis of Richardson (1974: 23–5). The political attractiveness of the movement can be demonstrated by the fact that when the Buddhist religious lay organization, *Sōkagakkai*, established its political party, it appropriated the *Kōmei* name for the party. As the largest group in the Nichiren sect, *Sōkagakkai* and *Kōmeitō*, continued the Nichiren prophetic and apocalyptic tradition of criticism of the failure of leadership in the Age of *Mappō* (Decline of Law) in Buddhist thought. In order to put these ideals into practice in a largely democratic context, an image of opposition to political corruption was natural.

In fact, corruption was a useful issue for the opposition and the media to attract attention and support though this occasionally backfired when one of their own was also implicated in scandal. The fact that one can openly criticize and pursue the corrupt practices of ruling politicians must count as one of the key features of Japanese democracy. It continues to be important in Japanese politics as Stockwin's chapter in this volume demonstrates. The problem is that all that remains in the public perception from years of political debate on the issue is the belief that Japanese politics is inherently corrupt, and thus potentially undermines democratic practice. Any attempt to substitute notions of 'good governance' for existing political practice, however, will also have its own problems. This is because criticism of corruption stands in stark contrast to how the problem of corruption has come to be understood in Japan by those who engage in politics in the post-war period. It is important to see how past history and political ideals are taken by and used by politicians because it will also help to explain the persistence of what is commonly perceived to be corrupt behaviour.

The political virtues of corruption

Corruption has been a persistent problem in Japan throughout the postwar period. It has dogged the major factions in the ruling Liberal Democratic Party, and as noted above, it has also involved MPs from the opposition parties – the Japanese Socialist Party, Kōmeitō and the Democratic Socialist Party – with only the Japan Communist Party relatively untouched by serious allegations of corruption. As part of the party in power, LDP politicians have enjoyed more opportunity to engage in graft compared to their opposition counterparts. Moreover, the corruption has been directed at general political fundraising and the protection of a traditional way of life that might have been threatened by post-war economic growth and modernization.

Most seemingly corrupt politicians could argue that they have acted in ways that were completely honourable. They could dismiss criticism of their methods by arguing that they were a necessary evil, and stressed their loyalty to their supporters and to Japan itself. Not only did scandal not damage their self-understanding of their roles and values, it may in fact have reinforced it and certainly did not stop them from teaching their methods and justifications to others. The main evidence for the discussion used in this section in order to obtain an understanding of Japanese politicians' views on corruption are the words used by the politicians themselves, and that of their biographers and the main pundits who construct the wider understanding of their ideals. A careful reading of Japanese political texts would be more useful to the understanding of corruption in Japanese governance than any number of interviews, ethnographic or otherwise, given the difficulties inherent in the study of corruption.

In these texts, politicians and their supporters are not oblivious to the problem and confront it in their autobiographies and the biographies that seek to promote them. Many of these sentiments are consistent with, if not derivative of, classical thought on the appropriate behaviour for political leaders: benevolence, loyalty and determination. Note that these virtues are not inconsistent with what may be seen as corrupt practices. Of course, there is both the influence of Japanese conceptualization drawn from customary social relations and a heavy dose of self-justification. None the less, their ethics have sustained their behaviour against vocal and persistent criticism. The sincerity and strength of these convictions should perhaps not be doubted.

While politicians rarely overtly defend corrupt behaviour, the use of the corruption issue is often seen as politically motivated, especially the most celebrated cases. One of the earliest and most important, the Showa Denkō scandal (1948), was used by the Liberal Party under Yoshida Shigeru to attack the Socialist and Democratic Parties coalition policies associated with a controlled economy. A similar furore arose in the ship-building scandal (1954) when a senior government politician, Satō Eisaku, was implicated but given immunity from prosecution by his fellow cabinet ministers. Opponents used the situation to vigorously attack the government and certainly damaged its reputation. Not surprisingly, corruption became an issue again when Satō became prime minister in the 1960s, with the so-called 'black mist' scandals creating the atmosphere of widespread corruption but with few actual prosecutions. Even the Lockheed scandal is not defended by supporters of former Prime Minister Tanaka Kakuei but seen as a plot against him by the United States which is alleged never to have forgiven his independent foreign policy, especially in the Middle East.

The most recent scandals (i.e. since 1990) were also used politically by government opponents but with more success. It might be argued that the most important reason for this is the unravelling of the political machine created by former Prime Minister Tanaka and sustained by his successors until 1992. The main financial brain behind the machine, Kanemaru Shin, was arrested in that year and his supporters within the LDP, particularly those MPs associated with Ozawa Ichirō, were isolated within the party. Ozawa choice was to bolt the party and attack it from the outside on the very issue of corruption that had been the main source of his influence. Even when the LDP returned to power under Prime Minister Hashimoto Ryūtarō, also a former Tanaka faction member, the attempt was made to divert attention from politicians by making an issue of corrupt bureaucrats which was an effective if cynical political move by a politician who had taken full advantage of these tendencies in the bureaucracy in the recent past.[1] The political use of the corruption did not change but the stakes were now higher.

Since recent trends in corruption and Japanese governance in general seem to turn crucially on the arrest of Kanemaru in 1992, it might be worth ending with a discussion of the case. It is crucial to remember that at first only Kanemaru's personal secretary, Haibara Masahisa, was implicated in the Sagawa scandal. However, rather than allow him to take the blame, Kanemaru called Haibara and insisted that he needed to tell the truth: 'I do not want you to end the same as Aoki', referring to Takeshita's personal secretary who committed suicide after he and Takeshita, among others, were implicated in the Recruit scandal. He continued, 'you saw what happened to Miyazawa [Kiichi] when he tried to lie during the Recruit scandal' and so, he concluded 'We must be honest' (Mukaidani 1993: 146–8). Those who focus on Kanemaru's decision not to let his personal secretary take the blame could be seen as compassionate because a more cynical approach might have saved his political career and prevented the fall of the LDP from power in 1993.

Kanemaru's reasons for obtaining the money are also important. He was the financial brains behind the Tanaka-Takeshita political machine that effectively ran Japan, many might say successfully, for twenty years. The benefits provided by Tanaka, his successors and allies to supporters throughout Japan were warmly received and created intense political loyalty, especially in rural areas of Japan, such as Kanemaru's home prefecture of Yamanashi, where the economic benefits of years of high levels of economic growth had not come directly. Even Kanemaru's political intrigues in the years prior to his resignation were spent in trying to break down the old political divisions in Japanese politics to unite the country in an effort to deal with the rise of Japan as an economic superpower. It is difficult to see Kanemaru as an evil figure. Indeed, his fate is somewhat tragic. One might also contrast the respect given to Takeshita when he died in 2000 to the treatment of Kanemaru who died in disgrace and whose memory has not been rehabilitated. Could one really say that Kanemaru was more culpable than Takeshita in the corruption that characterized politics under the influence of the Takeshita faction? The moral lessons are multitudinous and depend on the perspective you want to adopt.

Therefore, politicians such as Kanemaru do not think they are bad but they have needed money to get things done. When they are caught obtaining the money in questionable ways, they can explain it away or try to divert attention by focusing on their role as a loyal superior, friend, colleague and patron. They are simply doing what they need to do to get things done, and to get things done in Japanese politics requires money. It is a dirty business but someone has to do it. The amounts of money that Japanese politicians handle are enormous but they see very little of it personally. Indeed, it might be useful to contrast corruption for the gain of particular individuals and fundraising for general political purposes. The least celebrated cases of corruption in the Tables most often involve individual politicians seeking what might be perceived to be personal gain. The most celebrated suggest the presence of deeper rooted 'structural' corruption at the heart of the Japanese system of governance. However, since these scandals are involved with their need to raise money to act effectively as politicians, it is seen as simply an occupational hazard to be caught in the act.

Second, seemingly corrupt politicians are engaged in constituency service, particularly the protection of groups that are potentially disadvantaged. In Japan, it has been the rural communities at the heart of the LDP support base which have benefited from corruption. In a sense, this process has distorted democratic priorities as the flow of funds to rural constituencies has enabled the LDP to remain in power, but it could also be seen as a response to democratic priorities that the LDP has remained in power as a series of democratically elected governments who systematically used the powers of government to enhance their interests and the interests of their supporters. The process is suspect to many because the defence given for their practices by the politicians themselves focuses on maintaining a network of what would be described in the political literature as patrons and clients. In contrast, they perceive it as a network of those who can help others and those who need help. Seemingly corrupt politicians have been known for their fundraising abilities and the power to get things done by those in need. The two aspects are intimately connected. Wealthy and urban Japan complains most vigorously about corruption but it is also the least in need of assistance and protection in the same sense.

Conclusion

Competing conceptions of political virtue have not and perhaps will not go away. As we have seen, the meaning of corruption is contested and malleable. To demonize corruption in the context of a discussion of governance could also create new problems. In fact, it is interesting that corruption is intimately connected with the growth of democratic governance in Japan, and one could even argue corrupt politicians are engaged in governance of a sort. Moreover, models of economic rationality implicit in established notions of governance may themselves promote questionable ethical standards.

In its positive sense, governance focuses on decentralization of control and valorization of difference. At the same time, governance can be viewed as negative in that it holds out the danger of a newer and subtler form of control. Ironically, it is possible to conceive of corrupt behaviour as consistent with the positive and negative meanings of governance. On the positive side, corruption has often been engaged in as a means to keep politicians in power primarily based on the protection of potentially disadvantaged groups in Japanese society. On the other hand, side payments can be and have been used to diffuse political confrontation and 'manage' problems rather than confront them. Decentralization and recognition of the claims of those fighting modernization and globalization can easily serve as the justification for corrupt practices in the absence of an alternative form of ethics.

Indeed, human feelings in politics are not unethical by themselves and protecting people from the ravages of modernism is often laudable. If the 'corrupt' methods of political bargaining and adjustment in Japan were to be replaced by formal and efficient methods which ignored fears of threatened groups and refused to permit inefficiency in the name of a particular style of life, then the corrupt methods might still seem attractive. Political ethical ideals will be interpreted in a way that accommodates corruption so long as there is dirty business that needs to be taken care of and that one must find a route to the powerful to exercise influence. This can even further be justified if it can be argued that it helps the nation avoid decay or defeat by protecting important social groups.

These arguments are not intended to be a 'defence' of corruption. It is simply that an unreflexive 'governance' approach to politics is also unattractive and may be even more bereft of virtue. Governance is often set up as a panacea but it is more likely to be a means of legitimizing the definition of social and political reality of the scholars, politicians, officials and powerful organizations that attempt to control the concept. None the less, precisely because governance is contested, those who engage in and benefit from systemic corruption will resist these norms, especially when they conflict with other ideals they hold dear, even at the price of a moral battle within themselves and with society, not to mention the rule making and enforcing institutions of the state. It is useful to go beyond blame in order to understand politicians when they make and remake their own norms, and attempt to manipulate the institutions and laws of the state to protect their supporters, which is exactly what Japanese conservative politicians have done. Redefining politics as governance would not remove this problem and might even make it worse.

Note

1   This chapter has avoided a discussion of bureaucratic corruption because it raises a slightly different set of issues, but those who suggest that bureaucratic corruption is a new phenomenon are incorrect. Bureaucrats have been prosecuted and convicted in a number of scandals throughout the postwar period, including most of the scandals involving politicians listed in Table 9.1. See Murobushi 1981: 211–14 for post-war data up to 1981.

References

Almond, Gabriel and Verba, Sidney (1965) *The Civic Culture*, Boston: Little Brown.

Babb, James (2001) *Business and Politics in Japan*, Manchester: University of Manchester Press.

Curtis, Gerald (1988) *The Japanese Way of Politics*, New York: Columbia University Press.

Curtis, Gerald (1999) *The Logic of Japanese Politics*, New York: Columbia University Press.

Frank, Björn and Schulze, Günther G. (2000) 'Does economics make citizens corrupt?' *Journal of Economic Behavior and Organization* 43, 1: 101–13.

Fujita, Hiroaki (1980) *Nihon no Seiji to Kane*, Tokyo: Keisō Shobō.

Gadamer, Hans-Georg (1989) *Truth and Method*, 2nd ed. London: Sheed and Ward.

Hertzog, Peter (1993) *Japan's Pseudo-Democracy*, Folkstone: Japan Library.

Hopkin, Jonathan (1997) 'Political parties, political corruption and the economic theory of democracy', *Crime Law and Social Change* 27, 3–4: 255–74.

Ichikawa, Fusae (1980) *Sutopu Za Oshoku Gün!* Tokyo: Shinjuku Shobō.

Jain, Arvin K. (2001) 'Corruption: a review' *Journal of Economic Surveys* 15, 1: 71–121.

Kohno, Masaru (1997) *Japan's Postwar Party Politics*, Princeton: Princeton University Press.

Lancaster, Thomas and Montinola, Gabriellar (2001) 'Comparative political corruption: issues of operationalization and measurement', *Studies in Comparative International Development* 36, 3: 3–28.

Mo, Pak Hung (2001) 'Corruption and economic growth', *Journal of Comparative Economics* 29, 1: 66–79.

Mukaidani, Susumu (1993) *Chiken Tokusōbu*, Tokyo: Kōdansha.

Murobushi, Tetsuro (1981) *Oshoku no Kōzō*, Tokyo: Iwanami Shinsho.

Najita, Tetsuo (1987) *Visions of Virtue in Tokugawa Japan*, Chicago: University of Chicago Press.

Nakae, Chomin (1984) *Discourse of Three Drunkards on Government* (Tsukui, Nobuko trans.) Tokyo: Weatherhill.

Nichigai Associates (eds) (1999) *Gendai Seijika Jinnmei Juten*, Tokyo: Nichigai Associates.

Noonan, John T. (1984) *Bribes: the intellectual history of a moral idea*, Berkeley: University of California Press.

Ogyū, Sorai (1987) *Seidan* (Tsuji Tatsuya ed.) Tokyo: Iwanami Shoten.

Poellner, Peter (2001) 'Perspectival truth', in J. Richardson and B. Leiter (eds) *Nietzsche*, Oxford: Oxford University Press.

Ramseyer, J. Mark and Rosenbluth, Francis McCall (1997) *Japan's Political Marketplace* 2nd ed. Cambridge, MA: Harvard University Press.

Richardson, Bradley (1974) *The Political Culture of Japan*, Berkeley: University of California Press.

Scalapino, Robert (1953) *Democracy and the Party Movement in Prewar Japan*, Berkeley: University of California Press.

Theobald, Robin (1999) 'So what is really the problem about corruption'? *Third World Quarterly* 20, 3: 491–502.

Tomoaki, Iwai (1990) *Seiji Shikin no Kenkyu*, Tokyo: Nihon Keizai Shinbun Sha.

Treisman, Daniel (2000) 'The causes of corruption: a cross-national study', *Journal of Public Economics* 76, 3: 399–457.

Uozumi, Akira (1997) *Tokubetsu Kensatsu*, Tokyo: Iwanami Shinsho.

10 Whose problem?

Japan's homeless people as an issue of local and central governance

Tom Gill

Japan is often portrayed as a highly centralized state, in which national government tends to dictate policy to the regions (Johnson 1995). This view has been contested, for example by Muramatsu Michio (1997), whose reassessment of relations between central and local governments lays particular stress on the importance of welfare programmes as manifestations of that relationship (1997: 90). This study of recent homeless policy broadly supports Muramatsu's position on Japanese-style governance: here is an awkward issue that the central government has traditionally been more than happy to leave to cities and prefectures to sort out, but which now demands a national response.

Background

Until about 1999 the government of Japan largely ignored the issue of homelessness. Article 25 of the national constitution, backed up by the 1950 Livelihood Protection Law (*Seikatsu Hogo-hō*), guaranteed every citizen of Japan a 'minimum standard of civilized living'.[1] The government's position was that anyone unable to provide for themselves was eligible for livelihood protection (*seikatsu hogo*) and that consequently there was no need for anyone to become homeless. Faced with the steadily mounting evidence of tents, shacks and cardboard boxes around the major cities, the government would argue that homeless people fell into one of two categories: (1) people who had not applied for welfare, out of pride or ignorance of the benefits available; and (2) people who had applied for welfare but had been turned down on the judgement of their local welfare office. Hence the problem was transferred to the individuals themselves or to local authorities.

In the last few years, however, homelessness has risen high enough to trigger a modest media boom.[2] The TV and print media have tended to focus on 'new homeless' – laid-off white-collar workers, young people, women, and so on. However, it has been argued elsewhere (Gill 2001b) that the media's search for novelty has obscured the fact that even today most homeless people are in fact of the 'old homeless' type – middle-aged to elderly working-class men. This perception is regularly confirmed by quantitative research (Kanagawa-ken 2001; Tamaki and Yamaguchi 2001), and most recently by the national government survey of 2003, briefly discussed below.

Why does the livelihood protection programme not cover these people? Usually because of rules invented at ground level by the officials implementing the programme. In many cities applications are still turned down unless the applicant can prove that s/he is (1) over the age of 65; or (2) too ill or injured to work. Just being unemployed is not enough. In some districts, too, applicants must have a bank account and a permanent address – the latter a particularly harsh requirement for a homeless person.

Violent attacks on homeless people have become a regular occurrence, and people are clearly becoming desensitized to them. Murders get four or five paragraphs in the newspaper and lesser incidents barely merit a paragraph. According to my own coverage of the Japanese press, the two years from 1 July 2001–30 June 2003 saw at least twenty murders of homeless people, eight of them by fellow homeless people. These incidents have strengthened negative associations with homeless people and fuelled 'not in my backyard' (NIMBY) opposition to any attempt to construct homeless shelters near the homes of 'ordinary folk'.

In 1998, the Ministry of Health and Welfare (MHW; Kōseishō) at last acknowledged the problem, issuing an estimate for Japan's national homeless population: 16,000. Subsequent surveys in 2000 and 2001 generated headline figures of 20,000 and 24,000 (Table 10.1). These figures were totalled from a haphazard collection of regional counts. In early 2003, the first attempt at a co-ordinated national survey generated a figure of 25,296. This included 20,661 men, 749 women and 3,886 people of 'unclear' gender (reflecting sloppy counting practices, especially in Osaka). Homelessness remains a predominantly male phenomenon in Japan.

Trends in government homeless statistics do not necessarily have anything to do with trends in the actual number of homeless people. Until 2003 a large part of the statistical increase was directly attributable to more cities, towns and villages making counts; while the relatively small increase shown in the first unified national count in 2003 must be treated with scepticism, since the count was held in winter, whereas most of the cities had until then been counting in summer months, when warmer weather tends to swell the visible homeless population. Counting methods have not been consistent either. Note also that these statistics cover only narrowly-defined street homelessness, omitting the growing numbers living in shelters. Activists and social workers often say that a truer figure would be roughly double the official figure.

Recent developments in homeless policy

Launch of countermeasures; expansion of budget

The year 2000 saw a significant development as the Ministry of Health and Welfare announced a formal policy for the support of homeless people (*hōmuresu jiritsu shiensaku*), consisting mainly of a shelter construction programme and deployment of employment counsellors from the public employment exchange at the shelters. For the first time, too, a specific item on homeless support was included in the national budget. The policy continues to hold prefectures and the thirteen major

Table 10.1 Statistics on homelessness in Japan

Location	1998	1999	2001	2003 (Jan/Feb)
Tokyo (23 wards)	4,300 (Aug)	5,800 (Aug)	5,600 (Aug	5,927
Yokohama	439 (Aug)	794 (Aug)	602 (Aug)	470
Kawasaki	746 (Aug)	901 (Jul)	901 (Jul)	829
Nagoya	758 (May–Jul)	1,019 (May)	1,318 (May)	1,788
Osaka	'8,660' (Not surveyed)	8,660 (Aug)	'8,660' (Not surveyed)	6,603
Sapporo	18 (Dec)	43 (Nov)	68 (Dec 2000)	88
Sendai	53 (Mar)	111 (Oct)	131 (Aug)	203
Chiba	104 (Aug)	113 (Aug)	123 (Aug)	126
Kyoto	200 (Mar 99)	300 (Oct)	492 (Jun)	624
Kobe	229 (Aug)	335 (Aug)	341 (Aug)	323
Hiroshima	98 (Feb)	115 (Nov)	207 (Feb)	156
Kitakyūshū	80 (Mar 97)	166 (Nov)	197 (Aug)	421
Fukuoka	174 (Oct)	269 (Aug)	341 (Aug)	607
Major provincial cities	288 (numbers and dates unclear)	706 (24 reports)	1,684 (38 reports)	1,476 (30 reports)
Other towns and villages	Not surveyed	1,119 (73 reports)	3,425 (347 reports)	5,655*
Total	*16,247*	*20,451*	*24,090*	*25,296*

Source: MHLW statistics.
Most recent surveys available on-line at: http://www.mhlw.go.jp/houdou/2003/03/h0326-5.html, accessed 28 June 2004.

Notes:
* The 2003 survey did not give this figure. It was generated by subtracting the other sub-totals from the grand total. Apart from major cities, the data was presented by prefecture.

metropolises designated as special cities (*shitei toshi*) responsible for their own homeless people, but guarantees 50 per cent of the necessary funding from the national coffer. Since then the policy has been expanded and budget appropriations have risen accordingly (Table 10.2).

The 2002 Homeless Self-reliance Support Act

The doubling of the budget in FY 2003 reflected another important development: the passing of the Homeless Self-reliance Support Act on 31 July 2002.[3] This is Japan's first piece of legislation designed specifically to deal with homelessness. Officially entitled the 'Special Law on Temporary Measures to Support the

Table 10.2 National budget for homeless support measures (2000–2004)

FY2000	0.97 billion yen	–
FY2001	1.08 billion yen	+ 11%
FY2002	1.35 billion yen	+ 25%
FY2003	2.70 billion yen	+100%
FY2004	3.00 billion yen	+ 11%

Source: MHLW statistics.

Self-Reliance of Homeless People' (*Hōmuresu no Jiritsu no Shien na do ni kan suru Tokubetsu Sochi-hō*), it was drafted by a team of young Dietmen in the Democratic Party of Japan, submitted as a private member's bill, accepted by the governing coalition headed by the Liberal Democratic Party and passed unanimously on 31 July 2002 – the last day of the ordinary Diet session. It was promulgated a week later, on 7 August.

The key items in the new law are as follows:

1   The government recognizes that many people have become homeless through no fault of their own and that this is 'causing friction with local society' (Art. 1).
2   The act sets an objective of providing housing and stable employment to homeless people and those at risk of becoming homeless to enable them to maintain personal autonomy (Arts 3, 5) and pledges adequate funding (Art. 10).
3   People in charge of parks and other public spaces are empowered to remove homeless people's dwellings where 'appropriate use of the facilities is being obstructed' (Art. 11).
4   The government pledges to carry out a unified national census of the homeless population (Art. 14).[4]
5   All the provisions are temporary and will lapse after ten years.

Reaction to the new law among homeless people and activists has been sharply divided. Some welcome the law as a long-overdue public commitment to act on homelessness; others condemn it as an underhand way of enabling the government to evade its constitutional duty to provide livelihood protection to all who need it. Critics point out that the cost of housing people in homeless shelters is far less than putting them on livelihood protection, which entails paying the rent on a small apartment and supplying cash for independent everyday living. Livelihood protection payments vary with individual circumstances and region, but usually a single person can hope to receive around 80–90,000 yen a month plus up to 40,000 yen in rent support – 130,000 yen a month is an often quoted all-in figure. By contrast, even if the government figure of 25,000 homeless happened to be accurate, the expanded budget of FY2003 works out at roughly 100,000 yen per capita – about 6 per cent of the cost of putting all those people on *seikatsu hogo*. So there is a risk that the new law could lower the bar as to what constitutes a 'minimum standard of civilized living' in Japan. Article 11, on 'returning public spaces to their proper uses' is particularly hated, out of concern that it could eventually become a pretext for mass expulsions of people living in tents and shacks from parks in urban areas.

Against this, supporters of the law and neutrals argue pragmatically that the sad fact of the matter is that the national and local authorities simply are *not* going to put everyone on livelihood protection, and that under the circumstances as they are, the provisions of the new law are better than nothing.

Ultimately the positive or negative impact of the new law will depend on how it is implemented – and particularly on the entrance and exit strategies of shelters in the various cities. How many people, chosen on what basis, will be able to use, or want to use, the shelters; and where will they go after leaving the shelters? These key issues are discussed below.

National bureaucratic structures

The MHW was merged with the Ministry of Labour (MOL; *Rōdōshō*) on 6 January 2001, to form the Ministry of Health, Labour and Welfare (MHLW; *Kōsei Rōdōshō*). In the long term this should be a good thing for homeless policy, since welfare used to be handled by the MHW and employment by the MOL, and these two central pillars of homeless policy are now handled by the same ministry.[5] However, a look at how the budget for homeless support breaks down (Table 10.3) shows that a bureaucratic fault-line remains. Of the seven items covered, the first three are ex-MHW policies and the last four are ex-MOL policies. In terms of personnel, too, as of late 2002 there were nine MHLW officials detailed to homeless policy, of whom four were in the Regional Welfare Section of the Social Support Bureau

Table 10.3 Homeless support budget breakdown, FY2002 and FY2003 (Unit: millions of yen).

Item	FY2002	FY2003 (request)
1. General consultation	–	306 (382)
2. Self-reliance support	837	1,204 (1,035)
3. Emergency shelters	180	446 (983)
4. Activating homeless people's abilities	8	44 (44)
5. Employment counselling	114	– (206)
6. Training for day labourers, etc.	212	463 (463)
7. Test employment	–	240 (240)
Total	1,351	2,703 (3,353)

Source: MHLW home page available on-line at:
http://www.mhlw.go.jp/topics/2003/bukyoku/syakai/1-j2.html, accessed 24 June 2004.

Notes:
1   In FY2003 the 'employment counselling' item was incorporated into the 'self-reliance support' item – hence the rarity of an allocation figure higher than the amount requested.
2   In addition to the above, 500 million yen was allocated to homeless policy in a supplementary budget for FY 2002: 300 million yen for emergency shelters and 200 million yen for 'emergency support enterprises' (*kinkyō enjo jigyō*), defined as 'provision of everyday necessaries to homeless people in a condition of deteriorating health'.

(*Shakai Enjo-kyoku Chiiki Fukushi-ka*; ex-MHW) and five were in the Planning Department of the Elderly and Handicapped People's Employment Counter-measures Section (*Kōrei Shōgaisha Koyō Taisaku bu Kikaku ka*; ex MOL). There is a working group that combines members from both departments but it remains to be seen how effective this *cohabitation* will be. The restructuring of the budget in 2003, to shift employment counselling costs to the self-reliance support budget (Table 10.3 note 1) represents a first small erosion of the old bureaucratic barriers, with a traditional MOL item being moved to a budget sector associated with the MHW.

A second fault-line may be discerned within the ex-MHW part of the budget, between items 2 and 3 – which between them accounted for 60 per cent of the 2003 budget. Both items essentially are money for building and running shelters for homeless people, but 'homeless self-reliance support projects' (*hōmuresu jiritsu shien jigyō*) involve shelters which are supposed to be staging places on the way back to mainstream society, generally known as self-reliance support centres (*jiritsu shien sentā;* SSCs) whereas 'emergency shelter projects' (*hōmuresu kinkyū ichiji shukuhaku [sherutā] jigyō*) are supposed to provide temporary havens *in extremis*. These shelters are most frequently referred to as emergency temporary shelters (*kinkyū ichiji hinanjo;* ETSs). Hence we have the germ of a two-tier system here. As we shall see, how in practice these two kinds of shelter should relate to each other is an issue now being contested in Japan's major metropolises.

Elsewhere in the budget, the new item for 'general consultation' means counselling to inform homeless people of the various services available to them, including an element of outreach work, a relatively new concept for Japan, though well established in other industrialized countries (Rowe 1999). Item 4, which translates in full as 'projects for activating homeless people's abilities' (*hōmuresu nōryoku katsuyō suishin jigyō*) means employment projects using task forces of homeless people to carry out tasks such as cleaning, weeding, recycling of magazines and so on. There were two such projects in operation as of July 2003, and three more were provided for in the FY2003 budget. Still, this important aspect of homeless policy looks remarkably under-funded at just 44 million yen, less than 2 per cent of the budget.

Two further items reflect the close relationship between homelessness and the declining Japanese tradition of day labouring (*hiyatoi rōdō*). As discussed elsewhere (Gill 2001b), casual labour markets called *yoseba* have traditionally served as a last-resort place of employment preventing many men without regular employment from slipping into homelessness. In the last two decades, factors such as economic recession, the decline of the construction industry and increasing automation of work once done by unskilled labour have crippled the casual labour market, and the *yoseba* have gradually changed from 'workers' towns' to 'welfare towns' (Stevens 1997). In Osaka, Tokyo and Yokohama, many homeless shelters tend to be located near one of the three famous *yoseba* – Kamagasaki (Osaka), San'ya (Tokyo; see Fowler 1996) and Kotobuki (Yokohama; see Stevens 1997; Gill 2001b). Hence item 6: training for day labourers. The idea is to get men away from the uncertain lifestyle of the day labourer by imparting skills. As for item 7, early experiments with putting homeless men in employment have often failed as a result of men inured to casual employment quitting shortly after starting a regular job. Hence the idea of paying employers to take a chance on such men for a trial period of employment.

Homeless policy as applied in major cities

We will now examine how various themes discussed above play out at ground level by taking a look at the operation of homeless support policy in the five major cities of Osaka, Nagoya, Yokohama, Kawasaki and Tokyo.[6] The FY2003 budget statement called for increasing the number of homeless SSCs from eleven (with a combined capacity of 1,400) to sixteen (1,900); and for increasing ETSs from nine (2,500) to eleven (3,100). However, as of June 2004, there were only nine SSCs (944) and five ETSs (1,050) actually in operation (Table 10.4). These are early days, but so far bureaucratic inertia in some cities and intense NIMBY opposition from residents in all cities has kept actual provision lagging some considerable way behind the central government blueprint. The struggle to appease the citizenship has also led city governments to specify time limits for homeless facilities – three years in Osaka, five in Tokyo and Kawasaki, and ten in Nagoya. Osaka would actually have had to start *closing* shelters at the end of 2003 in order to keep that promise. In fact, when the deadline came, the city Welfare Office (*Fukushi Jimusho*) made an informal decision to keep the shelters open 'for the time being'. According to a city official, consent was obtained from local citizens' groups.[7]

Table 10.4 SSCs and ETSs operating and planned as of June 2004

Except for the SSC in Yokohama, all facilities are for men only.

Tokyo

Location	Capacity	Status
Self-reliance Support Centres (*Jiritsu Shien Sentā*)		
Taitō ward	104	Open since FY2001
Shinjuku ward	52	Open since FY2001
Toshima ward	80	Open since May 2001
Sumida ward	110	Open since March 2002
Shibuya ward	72	Open since March 2004
Emergency Temporary Shelters (*Kinkyū Ichiji Hogo Sentā*)		
Ota ward	300	Open since December 2001
Itabashi ward	100	Open since March 2003
Edogawa ward	100	Open since March 2004
Chiyoda ward	100	Scheduled to open FY2004
Arakawa ward	100	Scheduled to open FY2004

All Tokyo facilities are scheduled to close five years after opening.

continued

Table 10.4 continued

Osaka

Location	Capacity	Status
Self-reliance Support Centres (*Jiritsu Shien Sentā*)		
Ōyodo (Kita ward)	80	Open since October 2000
Nishinari (Nishinari ward)	100	Open since November 2000
Yodogawa (Higashi-Yodogawa ward)	100	Open since December 2000
Emergency Temporary Shelters (*Kasetsu Ichiji Hinanjo*)		
Nishinari Park	200	Opened December 2001
Osaka Castle Park	300	Opened November 2002

Another temporary shelter, in Nagai Park, opened in December 2000 and was closed in March 2003. All Osaka facilities were scheduled to close three years after opening, but when the three-year period for the SSCs expired in late 2003, the city government made an informal decision to keep them open 'for the time being'.

Nagoya

Location	Capacity	Status
Self-reliance Support Centre (*Jiritsu Shien Sentā*)		
Atsuta ward	92	Opened November 2002
Emergency Temporary Shelter (*Kinkyū Ichiji Shukuhaku Shisetsu*)		
Wakamiya Ōdori Park	150	Opened November 2002

Nagoya facilities are temporary structures but with no scheduled closing date. Theoretically they will last as long as the 2002 Homeless Support Law (10 years).

Yokohama

Location	Capacity	Status
Self-reliance Support Centre (*Jiritsu Shien Sentā*)		
Kotobuki-chō (Naka ward)	226 (206 men, 20 women)	Permanent facility opened May 2003, replacing temporary facility operational since 1993 with capacity of 204.

Emergency Temporary Shelters: None

Kawasaki

Location	Capacity	Status
Self-reliance Support Centre (*Jiritsu Shien Sentā*): None. One planned for FY2005		
Emergency Temporary Shelter		
Tsutsumine-chō (Kawasaki ward)	250	Temporary facility opened May 2004.

Administrative structures

This fault-line between housing policy and employment policy is also very much in evidence in local government: traditionally, housing and welfare have been handled by cities, but employment by prefectures. Communication does not appear to be very good. In Nagoya, for instance, Nagoya City Hall and Aichi Prefectural Hall are on opposite sides of the same road, yet a city official ruefully admitted that it was very difficult to get prefectural officials to pay much attention to what the latter tended to view as a strictly city issue.

Tokyo has a unique administrative structure: since 2000, homeless policy has been handled by the city's 'Special Ward' (*tokubetsu-ku*), sometimes called 'the 24th ward of Tokyo'. This is a kind of 'virtual ward' – it has no geographical existence, but manages facilities that are the responsibility of the wards but are too large and expensive for each ward to have one of its own. The twenty-three wards have been divided into five blocs, and each bloc is supposed to have one SSC and one ETS. Every five years both types of facility are supposed to be closed and replaced with equivalent facilities in another ward in the same bloc.

A second important feature of regional homeless administration – one shared with many other branches of welfare provision – is the apparently universal practice of farming out projects (*itaku jigyō*) to 'external organizations' (*gaikaku dantai*). These are usually Non-Profit Organizations (NPOs), funded by the city and/or prefectural government but not technically part of the government. Most of them have the status of *shakai fukushi hōjin* ('social welfare juridical person'). Some have surprisingly long histories: management of the Nishinari SSC is entrusted to Osaka Jikyōkan, a sizeable welfare corporation with ninety years of history that also runs a dozen other welfare facilities. The Yokohama SSC (called *Hamakaze* – 'Yokohama Breeze') is run by an NPO called the Keiseikai, which was founded in 1918, initially to help out down-on-their-luck sailors, and which also runs a range of welfare institutions. By contrast, the Nagoya facilities are run by a brand-new NPO – the Hōryū Welfare Association – established for that particular purpose.

Arrangements that seem similar at first glance often prove to be very different on closer inspection. Thus, for example, the other two SSCs in Osaka, and both the ETSs there, are run by an NPO called the Miotsukushi Welfare Association (Miotsukushi Fukushi-kai). Many members of this NPO's staff are serving or retired members of the city government. The Nishinari ETS has a staff of fifteen, of whom four, including the director, are on secondment from the city government's Public Welfare Bureau (*Minseikyoku*), one is recently retired from the same bureau, and the other ten are temporary staff (*rinji*), hired from the general public through recruitment advertising. Hence it is really only on paper that the city government is entrusting management of the shelter to the Miotsukushi-kai. In fact there is not a single officer of that welfare corporation on the staff, which instead consists of present and former city officials and temps hired from outside the Miotsukushi-kai. The latter appears to be providing little more than a cost-saving flag of convenience.

The extensive use of NPOs has many advantages for regional governments:[8]

1 Their staff need not be paid as highly as government officials, nor need they be given the same job security, pension rights, and so on. Hence NPOs are a cheaper and more flexible way of providing welfare than direct government provision.

2 Sometimes the NPO can be jointly funded by city and prefecture, neatly hopping over the bureaucratic rift mentioned above.

3 If anything goes wrong, blame can generally be attached to the NPO, and the government can respond by canceling the contract and getting a new NPO to take over the project.

4 The NPOs often have more specialized know-how in their field than government officials, who are often moved to totally different responsibilities in personnel reshuffles before they have a chance to build up experience.

5 Since they are not officially part of the government, the NPOs are slightly less bound by the formal rules and informal customs that hamper much government activity.

6 The NPOs can in some cases be a useful source of *amakudari* and secondment postings for retired or surplus government officials.

The two-tier system

The bipartite system of Self-reliance Support Centres and Emergency Temporary Shelters seems to be a fairly recent development, although a similar pattern may be observed in other branches of welfare policy, such as treatment of single-parent families and victims of domestic violence.

Self-reliance Support Centres

'Self-reliance support' *(jiritsu shien)* has become a popular welfare buzzword in Japan in recent years. The term is included in all government policy documents on homelessness and in the title of the new homeless support law. It has a pleasantly progressive ring to it, implying that recipients are not hopeless social failures but are merely in need of a helping hand to regain their self-reliance. At the same time it creates a third conceptual category, in between the traditional ones of 'self-reliant' (with a living income) and 'dependent' (in need of livelihood protection payments), which may have ominous implications depending on how it is interpreted in practice.

The first SSCs opened in Osaka in autumn 2000. Tokyo followed suit in 2001 and Nagoya in 2002. The Yokohama shelter opened in May 2003 is officially designated an SSC today, although its predecessor had opened in 1993 before the term had been coined. The shared objective of all SSCs is to take homeless people off the street, sort out their health and hygiene problems, restore a spirit of self-respect, and help them to return to mainstream life: through employment and independent living where possible; by arranging livelihood protection payments where that is not possible.

The Nishinari SSC in Osaka is a two-storey brick building (formerly a nursing home) on the outskirts of Kamagasaki, surrounded by a high wall with three strings of barbed wire above. The only door in the wall is permanently locked and access may only be gained by requesting admission through an interphone linked to the shelter's office. The shelter's name is written in tiny characters on a small card pinned to the door.

The Nishinari Centre has eighty beds and a full-time staff of eight supplemented by two part-timers. Twice a week three employment counsellors come to the Centre from the nearby public employment exchange. There are also weekly visits from nurses and legal advisers. The former conduct examinations for a range of health problems, of which tuberculosis is the most feared and alcohol disorders the most common. The latter provide legal advice on debt rescheduling and declaration of personal bankruptcy for those who have got into financial trouble, often with *sarakin* loan sharks.

In principle users are allowed to stay for three months, extendable to a maximum of six or occasionally seven. Getting the extra months is conditional on finding regular employment: the idea is to use the three months to recover one's health, composure and appearance, attend job interviews and get a job. Then one can stay three or four more months, commuting to work from the SSC, in order to earn and save enough money to leave the shelter and move into an apartment. One culture-specific aspect of homelessness in Japan is the high cost of rejoining main-stream society: the need to pay roughly six months' worth of rent upfront means that there is usually a considerable time lag between finding employment and being able to move into an apartment. The time schedule at the Nishinari SSC reflects this fact of life.

One of the Tokyo SSCs is Taitōryō, located very close to Ueno Park, facing the famous Kan'ei-ji temple. It has 104 beds and an annual budget of 180 million yen. There was powerful NIMBY opposition to opening the Centre. Consequently it has no nameplate to reveal its function, is surrounded by fences, and outside stairs are concealed behind plastic covers. As one of the staff dryly remarked, people do not want to be reminded of gloomy matters like homelessness when attending funerals at the temple.

There are two crucial differences between this SSC and its counterparts in Osaka. First, the permitted stay is shorter: two months in principle, and a maximum of four if work is obtained (against three and six in Osaka). Residents are strongly encouraged to attend job interviews in their first three weeks at the Centre, which assists by keeping a wardrobe of interview suits and an ironing board for loan, and by taking photos to put on job application forms. The aim is to get the resident in a job within a month or so, leaving three months to build up savings.

The second crucial difference is that SSCs in Tokyo provide a considerable amount of financial support to residents who get jobs and move into apartments. On receipt of a letter confirming employment the SSC will pay 31,000 yen to buy work clothes and tools; the SSC will also pay half the initial costs of moving into an apartment (key money, deposit, realtors' fees, etc.), up to a maximum of 139,200 yen; plus 19,800 yen to buy a futon and 25,000 yen to buy household necessaries.

The men also get a modest allowance of 400 yen a day while they are still in the Centre. To the best of my knowledge no other city will hand over sums of cash, large or small, to homeless people. The Taito SSC staff estimate that even with this assistance, the project of rejoining mainstream society requires the man himself to save at least 300–350,000 yen.

Officials spoken with in Osaka were deeply sceptical of the Tokyo approach. Homeless men were generally irresponsible with money, and handing them cash was only likely to cause more trouble – like giving booze to an alcoholic. The men would be better off with the extra time in the SSC, which was the advantage offered by the Osaka system in lieu of the Tokyo cash handouts. Tokyo officials admitted that there had been quite a few cases where the cash handouts had been abused, but pointed out that they maintain a strict one-chance-only policy: people who squander the goodies from the SSC are not allowed to use the SSC a second time. The restriction is resented: on 9 April 2003, a coalition of homeless support activists submitted a petition to the Tokyo authorities whose demands included permission for repeat visits to SSCs.

The newly opened SSC at Atsuta in Nagoya is based closely on the Osaka approach; the Yokohama SSC, named *Hamakaze*, resembles the Osaka model in having a six-month maximum stay and not providing financial support, but should properly be regarded as a hybrid institution, including some elements of the ETS (see below). It is located in the middle of the Kotobuki yoseba, and there is a pragmatic recognition that many homeless men are career day labourers who are unlikely to settle down in permanent employment. Many men cycle between the SSC and the street at intervals of about one month – the maximum stay if one does not find employment – and this is tolerated. If a man does succeed in getting a job, he is transferred to a different room on the top floor of the seven-storey building and his stay is extended to six months.

Nearly all homeless shelters in Japan are male-only institutions, reflecting the overwhelmingly male homeless population. However, *Hakamaze* does have twenty places for women. Elsewhere, women tend to be categorized outside the homeless care system – as single parents if they have children, or as victims of domestic violence. Also women tend to be far more successful than men at applying for livelihood protection: a homeless woman is viewed as considerably more shocking than a homeless man, and so patriarchal attitudes tend to work in women's favour in this particular instance.

Emergency temporary shelters

The emergence of the ETS as a bureaucratic category stemmed from the success of the first of its kind, opened in Nagai Park, Osaka in December 2000 and closed in March 2003. In what will be called the 'Osaka Model', the SSCs are classified under 'Self-reliance Support Centre Enterprises' (*Jiritsu Shien Sentā Jigyō*), and the ETSs under 'Park Normalization Policy' (*Kōen Tekiseika Taisaku*). This two-sided policy reflects the contrasting concerns of homeless people and non-homeless park-users respectively.

Over the last decade, large shanty-towns have developed in major metropolitan parks around Japan. The one in Nagai Park had 458 assorted shacks and tents in it when the ETS opened at the end of 2000, and by August 2002 only eight tents and shacks were left.[9] These impressive figures encouraged the Osaka authorities to open the Nishinari and Osaka Castle Park ETSs, and Nagoya followed suit.

However, a look at the official data for the Nagai Park shelter reveals some underlying problems. In the twenty months from December 2000 to August 2002, 206 men entered the shelter, of whom 184 exited, leaving twenty-two still in residence at that time. Clearly then, not all the 450 tents and shacks were vacated because of the shelter. Out of the 184 who left the shelter, some 45 per cent went into livelihood protection institutions, 20 per cent went to an SSC, and 10 per cent into hospital. Only 7 per cent exited to jobs, while 18 per cent voluntarily discharged themselves (*jishu taisho*), probably to return to homelessness. In short, three-quarters left the shelter only to enter some other welfare institution. Ironically, people who had been living self-reliantly – often in quite well-constructed shacks, some with petrol-driven electricity generators, often with incomes from recycling tin cans or magazines – emerged from the shelter to state-dependent lifestyles in various welfare institutions.[10]

The figures for the Nishinari Park shelter are rather different. By the end of October 2002, after nine months of operation, 142 tents and shacks were still standing in the park out of the 251 counted in December 2001, and the shelter was more than half empty, with just seventy-five men in residence. Just eighteen men had used and then left the shelter in those nine months, and half of them were voluntary discharges. By the end of April 2004, the city government still counted ninety-six improvised dwellings in Nishinari Park.[11]

This is hardly surprising if one looks at the situation in Nishinari Park. The makeshift dwellings of the homeless people are shabby but sometimes quite comfortable-looking. Many of the men there have pet cats or dogs, and have acquired quite a large collection of personal possessions over the years. Moving into the shelter means abandoning communal park life and a lot of the possessions and animals. In exchange you get 2 *jō* (6.6 square metres) of personal space in a bunk bed, which you are supposed to vacate after six months.[12] Moreover, unlike the SSC where you get three meals a day, at the shelter you get just the rice for the evening meal – you must supply your own accompanying dishes, and all the food for breakfast and lunch. This aspect of shelter life, particularly resented by residents, is supposed to point up the strictly temporary nature of the accommodation. Nor are there any legal or employment counsellors at the shelter.

On the other hand, the shelter is extremely clean and hygienic; showers and laundry are free; there are plenty of televisions; and there is no ban on drinking. This last, along with the non-enforcement of the six-month limit, is on the initiative of the director, who has also thought up several modest income-generating schemes for residents. Even so, the question of what happens after you leave the shelter remains without a convincing answer. The director tends not to refer them to the Nishinari SSC because he feels that their background and personality would make it difficult for them to fit in with the more controlled regime there. He points out that the shelter's proximity to Kamagasaki, the great Osaka yoseba, means that a lot of hardy men, used to periods of unemployment and homelessness, are sleeping in the park.

The Nagoya ETS is closely modelled on the Osaka pattern, being located inside a major city park, and with a very similar regime, including the provision of just rice for the evening meal. In Tokyo, by contrast, the ETSs are formally portrayed as feeder institutions for the SSCs. They are not located in parks; they supply three meals a day; and conduct regular assessments of the physical and mental condition of inmates, before deciding whether to pass them on to an SSC, put them on livelihood protection, or send them to hospital. The stay is limited to one month in principle and two months at most. Only three of the five planned were actually open at the time of writing, however, in Ōta, Itabashi and Edogawa wards. Of these the one in Ōta ward (called Ōta-ryō, or Ōta Lodge) is by some way the biggest homeless shelter in Japan, with a capacity of 300. It has an annual budget of 480 million yen, and is run by a welfare corporation called the Yūrin Kyōkai. Before the launch of the homeless support policy, it had been used for twenty-five years as a temporary shelter for San'ya day labourers during the New Year holidays (when conventional welfare facilities are closed). It is located on a large piece of otherwise unused land in a warehouse district far from any residence, factors making this a natural site for the shelter. Whether it will really be relocated to affluent Setagaya ward in five years as planned under Tokyo's bloc-rotation system is rather doubtful.

Staff at Ōtaryō say that in practice roughly 50 per cent of residents exit to SSCs, 25 per cent to livelihood protection, and 25 per cent fail to make progress and go back to the streets.

Another variation in ETS management emerged in May 2004, when the city of Kawasaki finally opened its *Wan Naito Sherutā* (One Night Shelter), after a lengthy battle against NIMBY-minded citizens. This shelter uses a registration system; men who register can apply every night for permission to use the centre, being admitted at 6 p.m. and expelled at 6 a.m. This seems to be the first case of an American-style night shelter in Japan. A month after opening, the shelter had 140 registered users, of whom roughly half were sleeping there on the average night.[13]

Entrance and exit strategies

Getting In

One of the key differences between ETSs and SSCs is in admission policy. In the park-based ETSs of Osaka and Nagoya, anyone showing a willingness to abandon his shack or tent can be admitted to the ETS, and indeed easy admission is part of the park clearance strategy. By contrast, people cannot enter an SSC without a referral from the local welfare office (*fukushi jimusho*). Usually this is obtained by the homeless person visiting a welfare office and persuading a caseworker that he would be a suitable candidate for an SSC. In addition some referrals are made by outreach workers who tour homeless districts looking for suitable people.

The situation in Tokyo is rather different. In theory at least, ETSs are supposed to lead to SSCs, and SSCs to a job or livelihood protection. Hence getting into the system carries rather more significance – especially in view of the tempting cash benefits available to those who can last the course. The downside of this is that wards are reluctant to refer people to the SSCs, since they know from experience that few of them will get a job and many will end up on livelihood protection – part of the costs of which must be borne by the referring ward. Hence Tokyo SSCs are often operating well below capacity, and those who do get referred tend to be 'elite homeless' with a better than average chance of getting employed. Even the ETSs operate a referral system, reflecting their feeder role for the SSCs and their geographical distance from homeless districts.

Getting out

As mentioned above, the Osaka and Nagoya ETSs have no clear exit strategy, which is a major disincentive to abandoning an ad hoc residence in a park to enter one. In Tokyo the ETS is supposed to lead to the SSC, then – perhaps via a third institution, the 'group home', a shared group residence in which lifestyle skills and employment training are provided – to independent living and a steady job. A simplified version of the Tokyo government's flow diagram is shown in Figure 10.1; unfortunately, at the time of writing the 'group homes' still do not physically exist[14] and the final transition to independent living is proving hard to make. The missing arrow – from the SSC to livelihood protection – in fact accounts for many real cases.

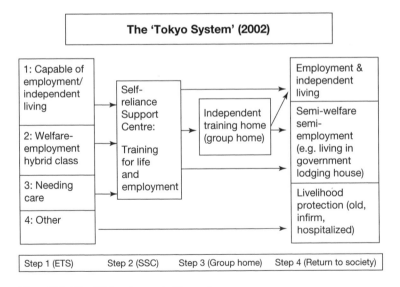

Figure 10.1 The 'Tokyo System' of homeless governance.

Note: Simplified translation of Tokyo Metropolitan Government Welfare Dept. press release at http://www.fukushi.metro.tokyo.jp/press_reles/2002/pr0221.htm, accessed 24 June 2004.

Formidable barriers face formerly homeless people seeking employment. With unemployment around 5.5 per cent there are plenty of non-homeless people ahead of them in the queue. Social prejudice is strong, and the question of how honestly to answer questions on application forms about 'current place of residence' is a tricky one since admitting to living in a shelter will often ruin one's chances of being taken on. Inevitably the kinds of job that ex-homeless people do acquire tend to be tough and badly paid, making it very hard to stick at it, especially if one has been away from regular employment for many years, as with many of the day labourers in the Yoseba districts. Men used to earning their living by the day are often habitually or even ideologically disinclined to work regularly or save money, yet the 'return to mainstream society' requires them to do just that. SSCs attempt to overcome these problems through employment and lifestyle counselling, but seldom with much success.

For example, in its first twenty-one months of operation (to the end of August 2002) the Nishinari SSC 'graduated' 356 men (it is a male-only institution). Of those 356,140 (about 40 per cent) got jobs, fourteen went into hospital, thirty-four entered other institutions (mostly livelihood protection hostels), and 168 were listed as 'other', which SSC staff said generally meant they had failed to get work and gone back to the street. Unfortunately, as SSC staff themselves admit, the true figure for successful employment is nowhere near the 40 per cent officially claimed. Men are listed as entering employment on their own say-so, and many who really do get work are known to quit very quickly. The one method used to confirm continued employment is the sending of a questionnaire a few months after the man has departed. Further inquiries are ruled out on privacy grounds. Staff tentatively stated that no more than 30 per cent of the cards came back. Similar admissions were heard of gross discrepancies between statistics and reality at SSCs in Tokyo and Yokohama.

Role of the private sector

With a total capacity of around 2,500, the system is clearly inadequate as it stands – an inadequacy that represents a business opportunity for private enterprise. The biggest and most notorious 'homeless business' is SSS (Social Security Service), which is now housing far more formerly homeless people in the Tokyo area than the public system.

The SSS approach is very simple. The firm – officially a non-profit organization under the 1998 NPO Law – contracts with a homeless person to supply an apartment or at least a bed in some shared accommodation, along with meals and other daily necessities. Once the homeless person has moved in, SSS helps him to apply for livelihood protection. Now that he has a *bona fide* permanent address, the homeless person tends to succeed. Once the payments start coming, SSS charges the person a monthly sum that amounts to almost the entire livelihood protection payment, to cover rent, meals, utilities, and so on. The man is left with a token amount of pocket money. SSS is based in Tokyo, where it is said to have over 100 hostels and apartment buildings, housing some 3,000 people, and is moving into other areas with varying degrees of success.

SSS and its activities provoke very mixed reactions from activists and social workers. On the one hand, they strongly suspect that this organization that enjoys NPO status is in fact making profits out of the welfare payments of people who are often poor and weak. On the other hand, there is no denying that without SSS there would be several thousand more homeless people on the streets of Tokyo. Essentially, SSS and similar outfits are forcing city governments to meet their constitutional obligation to provide livelihood protection payments to those who cannot support themselves – an obligation that the emerging public shelter system sometimes seems designed to evade.

Hence some activists are trying a new approach to housing homeless people that may briefly be described as 'SSS minus the exploitation'. An early pioneering example is the Tabidachi no Ie (Journey's Start House), a communal dwelling at Chigasaki, Kanagawa prefecture, run by a Christian NPO that has rented a disused company dormitory to house forty formerly homeless people.[15] It assists in making livelihood protection claims, and leaves them a much larger proportion of the monthly payment after deducting rent and other expenses. It opened in 2002 and has had a successful first two years. A similar enterprise in Ichikawa, Chiba prefecture, is also up and running. A hospice recently opened in San'ya using the same principle (*Mainichi Shimbun*, 3 June 2003). In the long run, projects like this may prove very significant for homeless people in Japan.

Conclusion: everyone's problem, no-one's problem

What does the case of homelessness policy tell us about governance in Japan? First of all it sheds light on relations between central and local government. In contrast to the highly centralized, top-down style of governance described in many studies, this case shows a negligent central government, keen to leave the issue to the regions but reluctantly drawn into the fray as the issue escalates. Even now, the national policy largely boils down to providing matching funds for local initiatives – which vary considerably across the country.

Second, the administrative structures implementing homeless policy appear not as a smoothly contoured chain of command but as a threadbare patchwork of systems, with responsibility contested, divided and diffused at every level – between ministries, between bureaux, between prefectures, cities and wards, and between welfare officials and park/public space officials at every level. The net result is to make it radically unclear who is in charge. Here Japan may have something to learn from the British experience, where the Blair government's 1999 appointment of Louise Casey as 'homeless tsar' appears to have been quite effective in reducing homelessness (Casey's Rough Sleepers' Unit claimed on 3 December 2001 to have reduced the number of people sleeping to about 550 from 1,850 in 1998). At any rate in Britain it has been possible to answer the question 'who is in charge?' with a single person's name, whereas in Japan the same question can only be answered by a lengthy academic paper like this one. Prime Minister Koizumi Junichirō has shown some interest in the concept of policy tsars in other fields, and perhaps something similar would be effective here.

Third, any analysis of governance in action must take account not only of the big administrative structures but also of the individual personnel who work within those structures and the processes by which they are appointed, rotated and promoted. My impression is that the officers who deal directly with homeless people, such as the managers of shelters, are often seasoned veterans with a good understanding of the issue. By contrast, those based higher up the chain of command, in city halls and the MHLW, tend to be relatively young and inexperienced men who will be switched to some other appointment before they can acquire much experience dealing with the issue. Indeed, one official at the MHLW told me that his introduction to homeless policy had taken the form of a couple of hours' conversation with his predecessor.

Japan is in urgent need of bold thinking that can rapidly translate into action. The present system of governance holds out little prospect of such a thing happening. The ultimate answer to the question in this chapter's title is that right now, while homelessness may well be 'everybody's problem' in a philosophical sense, it is not clearly any particular person or organization's problem in the sense of administrative responsibility. Ironically, cities that make an effort to combat homelessness attract more homeless people, while those that shirk their responsibilities are rewarded with smaller homeless populations as those at threat move away to cities with better provision.[16] Clearly this is one social problem that needs to be tackled at the national level.

Notes

1 An earlier version of this Occupation-era law was passed in 1946. The 1946 version excluded applicants deemed able but not willing to work, those who had people (e.g. spouse, parents) responsible for their welfare, etc. These exclusions were removed from the 1950 version.
2 For example, a May 2004 search of the Amazon Japan home page found sixty-five books with the word *hōmuresu* in the title, of which thirty-six had been published in the three years from April 2001 to April 2004. Documentaries about homeless people have become a mainstay of early evening TV.
3 An unofficial English translation of the law is available on-line at: http://member.nifty.ne.jp/nojuku/english/eng_idx.html, accessed 24 June 2004.
4 This was duly carried out in Jan/Feb 2003, generating the figure of 25,296 mentioned earlier.
5 Another branch of the central bureaucracy is also concerned with homeless people in a different way: the Ministry of Land, Infrastructure and Transport (*Kokudo Kōtsūshō*), which is in charge of policy on national parks and public spaces. For the MLIT the *ad hoc* dwellings of homeless people represent an obstacle to running parks for the general public.
6 The field-trips were made to Osaka and Nagoya in October 2002, Tokyo in November 2002, and several in Yokohama up to June 2004. A total of five shelters have been visited and numerous local and national officials interviewed.
7 Telephone interview with Yamada Yoshiro, Homeless Independence Support section, Osaka City Welfare Department, 10 June 2004.
8 See Nakamura (2002) for a perceptive account of the tactical game between NPOs and government in another welfare field – provision of services to deaf people.
9 By the end of April 2004, the number of improvised dwellings had crept back up to 20.

10 Note, too, that Nagai Park had one exceptional factor at play – the use of the stadium located in the park as the venue for several matches during the 2002 World Cup. Concern to avoid football fans from around the world seeing the Nagai Park shanty town may well have encouraged the local authorities to accept applications for livelihood protection from the Nagai ETS.

11 Available on-line at: http://www.city.osaka.jp/kenkoufukushi/sonota/sonota_20.html, accessed 24 June 2004.

12 In practice the six-month rule is not enforced, in view of the low level of demand for places in the shelter, but even so the prospect of the shelter being closed after three years means that life there is still correctly viewed as temporary.

13 Telephone interview with Inoue Hideomi of the Kawasaki City Regional Welfare Bureau, 10 June 2004.

14 Two group homes, each with twenty places, are planned. Formally they are called 'self-reliance training homes' (*jiritsu kunren hōmu*).

15 The facility opened in November 2001. Available on-line at http://www.cam.hi-ho.ne.jp/noguchi/tabi.html, accessed 24 June 2004.

16 The situation in the Kansai is a good case in point. Kyoto's relatively small homeless population partly reflects the fact that Kyoto provides very poor services for homeless people, who therefore tend to drift to Osaka with its gradually expanding system of shelters, employment programmes, etc.

References

Fowler, Edward (1996) *San'ya Blues: laboring life in contemporary Tokyo*, Ithaca and London: Cornell University Press.

Gill, Tom (2001a) *Men of Uncertainty: the social organization of day laborers in contemporary Japan*, Albany: SUNY Press.

Gill, Tom. (2001b) 'Chūryū hōmuresu to iu sakaku: saikin no hōmuresu rupo o yonde', *Yoseba* 11: 180–7.

Johnson, Chalmers (1995) *Japan: Who Governs? The rise of the developmental state*. New York and London: W.W. Norton.

Kanagawa-ken Toshi Seikatsu Kenkyūkai (2001) *Kanagawa kenka Nojukusha Chōsa Chūkan Hōkokusho*. Yokohama: Kanagawa Toshi Seikatsu Kenkyūkai.

Muramatsu, Michio (1997) *Local Power in the Japanese State*, Berkeley and Los Angeles: University of California Press.

Nakamura, Karen (2002) 'Resistance and cooptation: the Japanese Federation of the Deaf and its relations with state power', *Social Science Japan Journal* 5, 1: 17–35.

Rowe, Michael (1999) *Crossing the Border: encounters between homeless people and outreach workers*, Berkeley and Los Angeles: University of California Press.

Stevens, Carolyn (1997) *On the Margins of Japanese Society: volunteers and the welfare of the urban underclass*, London: Routledge.

Tamaki, Matsuo and Yamaguchi, Keiko (2001) 'The employment structure of homeless people: preliminary findings from the Eastern Tokyo homeless survey', *Journal of the Faculty of International Studies, Utsunomiya University* (March): 83–99.

11 The political economy of Japanese 'corporate governance'

A metaphor for capitalist rationalization

Hasegawa Harukiyo

This chapter aims to shed light upon 'corporate governance' as an issue in the rationalization of Japanese capitalism. Its focus is on the current domestic debate on how Japanese corporate governance should be reformed. While the focus of attention in this debate is the improvement of governance based on the strengthening of 'external' monitoring, there is no guarantee that this will solve most current corporate problems. The reason for this is straightforward: the current debate ignores an important aspect of Japanese capitalism, namely, corporate restructuring. Indeed, this chapter argues that in the current debate 'corporate governance' is actually a metaphor for large-scale corporate restructuring in response to the 'external' constraints of globalization. That is, the real strategy of corporations is to carry out large-scale restructuring taking advantage of the debate on corporate governance. Such restructuring may be taken as a response of capital to the combined forces of the internal logic and necessity of Japanese capitalism and of the pressure from the United States and other members of the Organization for Economic Cooperation and Development (OECD).[1]

Thus, in contrast to the functional approach of the existing 'corporate governance' literature (Fukao and Morita 1997; Keizai Kikakuchō 1998; Kubori *et al.*, 1998; Keidanren 2000; Lorsch 2000), the approach adopted here is related more to political economy – that is, it aims to examine structural change in Japanese capitalism and redefine the issue of 'corporate governance' as reforms in top management and hence as part of a major restructuring of Japanese capitalism. By addressing the issue from this perspective we can go directly to the heart of the problem and locate the discourse of 'corporate governance' in a broader context – that of the governance of an enterprise. We also thereby place the discussion firmly in the context of how governance has been contested in the Japanese political economy.

The major part of this chapter rests on data compiled in 1999 and interviews conducted in the same year, when the debate was at its most intense among journalists and academics, and major companies were engaged in large-scale restructuring. Of course, various reforms have been made since then and are still in progress. The year 1999, however, remains a crucial turning point in the corporate restructuring scenario; and although the information in Figure 11.1 and the interviews come from that year, the overall discussion herein derives from information collected both before and after that time.

The chapter consists of three sections. The first considers the meaning of 'corporate governance' and governance in an enterprise. We classify governance into types, actors, objectives, methods and relationships. The second section looks at the scope and extent of top management reform, and discusses the issue of 'corporate governance' in relation to 'internal' necessity. This section pays particular attention to the correlation, if any, between the degree of reform, industrial sectors and ownership structure. The third section examines more specific cases of corporate restructuring, and explains why so-called 'corporate governance' reforms can be understood as part of large-scale corporate restructuring. The changes in governance taking place, however, do not necessarily emulate the Anglo-American model;[2] rather their aim is to 'redefine' existing management, namely to take advantage of 'external' constraints and deal with internal necessity, thus pursuing capitalist rationalization.

Meaning of governance and 'corporate governance'

When 'corporate governance' is discussed as an issue of 'transparency' and 'accountability' (Hamada 2002; *Nikkei*, 24 October 2002; *Nikkei*, 13 and 15 November 2002) or 'responsibility' and the 'function' of top management (Osano 2001; *Nikkei*, 23 and 24 October 2002), two issues tend to be conflated and the real meaning of 'corporate governance' remains opaque.

The first, rooted in a shareholder approach, is the demand from institutional investors for profitability and market capitalization (Committee on the Financial Aspects of Corporate Governance 1992; OECD 1999; Harvard Business Review 2000; Keidanren 2000). The second issue is democracy in general, more specifically a questioning of whether or not top management is taking proper account of the needs for welfare and justice in society in carrying out its business operations (Carroll and Buchholtz 2002; Wheeler and Sillanpaa 1997; Rengō 1999; Jacoby 2001; Post *et al.* 2002; Rahman *et al.* 2002;). This harks back to a stakeholder approach. Though contested, these two issues are frequently conflated in discussion of 'corporate governance' in Japan.

A political economy approach, however, alerts us to the diverse genesis of these two approaches. The shareholder approach views a company as a means for private profit based upon private ownership, which gains ultimate legitimacy from the tenets of capitalist society. The stakeholder approach, in contrast, regards a company as a public institution serving the broader needs of society, and as such adopts a socio-democratic perspective. The advocates of the shareholder approach consider 'external monitoring' to be both effective and necessary, and view the internal monitoring unique to Japan as being in need of replacement by an Anglo-American style of external monitoring. We ask here whether this is the case or not; and if there are changes, how should they be understood?

A survey by Japan's leading economic newspaper, the *Nikkei* (26 July 1999), which was published at the time the debate on 'corporate governance' was at its peak in the journalistic and academic worlds, indicated a correlation between the scale of corporate reforms, the size of corporations and the increase of their market capitalization. It reported that, of the top twenty-four companies with the largest corporate reforms, twenty-one recorded an increase in market capitalization in June 1999 compared to the previous year, despite a virtual lack of correlation with current profitability or other performance indicators. In effect, the *Nikkei* legitimized large-scale reforms as effective for corporate governance.

The basic logic of this approach is the structure–function–performance hypothesis; more specifically, the ownership–control–performance hypothesis. Under this logic, the assumption is that external monitoring (the Anglo-American model) is more effective than the internal monitoring characteristic of Japanese companies. Reforms are thus necessary to replace Japan's traditional 'corporate governance' with that type in place under Anglo-American capitalism. The discussion then proceeds to the question of how and to what extent top management systems in Japan should be reformed.

Before we go into the detail of the reforms now taking place, let us first define 'governance' as an order between two parties in an organization. Thus, the issue of who governs whom, and to what end, needs to be clarified. In a capitalist economy, enterprise governance is an issue of order, which implies it is a system of control as well as a process to achieve capital accumulation. Owners of capital, either directly or indirectly, delegate the authority of capital to govern the whole process of capital accumulation to various categories of employees: first to hired directors, next to managers, and finally down to the staff. In this sense, employees in business are agents working at different levels of governance in order to optimize capital accumulation. The authority of capital is manifest as the power to govern, which is transformed into a control and management system and the subsequent relationships binding employees to the corporate order set in place under capitalism.

Table 11.1 shows how the authority of capital is manifest as power from shareholders to the board/chief executive officer (CEO); from management to employees; from management to trade unions; and from management to community. The authority of capital is embedded in relationships throughout business, as shown by the various levels of order in business organizations. The boardroom and CEO is where shareholder benefit is discussed, while for stakeholders 'corporate governance' is part of the whole governance of an enterprise and includes community relations. The methods of governance, however, differ according to the level, such as 'monitoring', 'human resource management (HRM)', 'industrial relations' and 'corporate citizenship'.

As this hierarchical logic of capital is not always compatible with the interests of labour and the community, 'corporate governance' is contested by the counter-balancing forces of labour and the community, i.e. the forces of stakeholders in and around the company. Owners of capital will assert their rights of private ownership, and exert authority in order to enhance their own system of governance, while labour and society may confront it and seek instead a more socially oriented type of governance through the influence of unions, government policies and sometimes

Table 11.1 Governance in enterprise: types, actors, objective, methods and relations

Types of governance	Actors	Objective of governance	Methods of governance	Relationship
Governance of board and CEO	Shareholders, governing board and CEO	Profitability, accountability	External/internal monitoring	Shareholders vs. board and CEO
Governance of employees	Management, governing employees	Efficiency	Management methods (HRM)	Management vs. employees
Governance of industrial relations	Management, governing trade unions	Assimilation/ compliance	Industrial relations management	Management vs. labour unions
Governance of community relations	Management, governing community	Symbiosis	Company as member of the community (corporate citizen)	Management vs. community

citizen movements. In this case, rather than the tenets of capitalism, the authority of labour and the community is derived from and is legitimized by universalistic human rights and the shared values of the community.

As Table 11.1 suggests, governance is thus essentially an issue of order or the social relations that exist between capital and labour, which is manifest in terms of various types, actors, objectives, methods and relationships. 'Corporate governance' can thus be understood as a crucial element in the holistic functioning of capitalism, though the countervailing dynamics arising from labour and the community also need to be taken into account.

Let us now turn to the origins of the current debate on 'corporate governance'. It dates back to Berle and Means' *The Modern Corporation and Private Property* (1932). Their major finding and point of debate was the 'divorce of ownership from control', which provides the foundation for the current debate – that a company must govern itself in a way that will satisfy shareholders.[3] This discussion sought an ideal relationship between shareholders and board members; the central concerns being efficiency, profitability and market capitalization.

More recently, in the US, the 1980s saw attention given to these issues against a backdrop of changes in US capitalism in the previous decade – in particular, the increasing influence of institutional investors (such as pension funds) upon corporate boards and CEOs and their accountability to shareholders. Peter Drucker commented as early as the mid-1970s on this new phenomenon, calling it 'pension-fund capitalism' (Drucker 1993: 74). This change in the structure of capitalism was a focus of academic attention, for it was seen as having important implications for American democracy, reflecting as it did the pension funds of ordinary citizens. It also had important academic implications for major issues affecting the corporation, such as 'ownership', 'control' and 'governance' (Yoshimori 1996; Scott 1997; Shibuya 1999; Uetake and Nakata 1999). The work of Shibuya (1999), in particular, deserves mention, as his investigation of the detailed discussions held in the US Senate committee on the operation of governance in 1974 was important in highlighting how this structural mechanism of ownership, control and governance has much to do with the current issue of 'corporate governance'.

These discussions of 'corporate governance' expanded into a debate on how to reform corporations in the US and wider afield. Mostly this was in order to increase profitability, productivity and market value, and was in this sense an effective discourse for enhancing 'shareholder value'. It was especially so in Japan, which was faced with US-led globalization and the long recession of the 1990s (Keizai Kikakuchō 1998; Keidanren 2000; Harvard Business Review 2000).

Such discussions have of course been supported by neo-classical principles (market orientation), while the stakeholder approach, which includes the interests of various shareholders such as employees, suppliers, trade unions, and communities, is supported by those who regard companies as answering social need, in other words, those who hold social democratic values (Drucker 1993; Kelly *et al.* 1997; Scott 1997; Wheeler and Sillanpaa 1997; Korten 1999; Rengō 1999). Although 'corporate governance' as discussed in the US can be dealt with as an issue of democracy, in essence this would be no more than 'sophistry', simply because institutional investors never act with democratic intent, but rather on behalf of a small number of investors playing a major role in such pension funds.

When the discussion emerged in Japan as a means of enhancing market capitalization, reforms in top management took place; but, more fundamentally, the discourse was used to legitimize large-scale restructuring. Various proposals and reports, as listed below, were issued in the latter half of the 1990s, spurred on by frequent corporate corruption scandals and encouraged by various reports issued in the US and Britain:[4]

- 8 September 1997: 'Draft plan for a revision of the Commercial Law concerning 'corporate governance', offered by the Sub-committee for Commercial Law, the Committee of Legislation in the Liberal Democratic Party (LDP);
- 10 September 1997: 'Urgent Proposal on methods of 'corporate governance' by a special committee on 'corporate governance', Keidanren;
- 30 October 1997: 'Principles of corporate governance: to consider new Japanese-style corporate governance, by the Japan 'corporate governance' forum of the Japan Committee for Economic Development;
- February 1998: 'Report from the Committee on Corporate Systems in the 21st century' by the Ministry of International Trade and Industry (MITI).

However, if we examine the content of these reports we see differences in emphasis depending on the objectives of the respective institutions (Takahashi 1999). Each report expresses its own role and position. For example, Keidanren and the LDP put emphasis on the function of auditors and legal procedures to sue directors, while the use of external directors (for transparent and sound business operations), the increased independence of external auditors and the adequate provision of an infrastructure for the effective functioning of markets are put forward by MITI (from 2001 METI, Ministry of Economy, Trade and Industry). Comparing these Japanese reports with that of the OECD (1999), we can see how the latter acknowledges the necessity of keeping a balance between various stakeholder interests, while the Japanese reports are more shareholder-oriented. Of course, the extent to which the balance proclaimed by the OECD can be realized in reality remains to be seen.

'Corporate governance' as a metaphor for corporate restructuring

The above examined the current discussions on 'corporate governance' in the US and Japan, and defined 'corporate governance' as an issue of relations between capital and labour. We now come to analyze the structural change in Japanese capitalism and consider its relationship to top management reforms, which is an issue of 'corporate governance'.

Table 11.2 shows that Japanese capitalism has indeed gone through a trajectory of structural change from the high to the stable and the low growth periods. This structural change also implies a shift in capital accumulation, namely, from labour-intensive to capital-intensive industries, manufacturing to services, and then from exports to foreign direct investment (FDI).

Table 11.2 Economic growth, 'corporate governance' and paradigm of technology

Period	Average percentage GDP growth	Pattern of growth	Model (ethos) of 'corporate governance'	Paradigm of technology
1956–73 (18 years)	9.2	High growth	Top management: internal Employees management: collective Industrial relations: conflictual 'compromise'	Mass production (Fordism)
1974–91 (18 years)	3.9 (−5.3)	Stable growth	Top management: internal Employees management: collective/individual Industrial relations: compromise/accommodation	Mass/multi production/ New technology
1992 – 2001 (10 years)	0.9 (−3.0)	Stagnant growth	Top management: internal/ 'redefined' internal Employee management: collective/individual HRM Industrial relations: accommodation/dissatisfaction	Mass production/ Information Technology

Source: GDP growth rates from National Accounts and Economic Planning Agency.

This change in the structure of capitalism went hand in hand with different models of 'corporate governance' as well as technological paradigms. In essence, the change was from an internal/collective/conflictual model in the high-growth period to a 'redefined' internal/individual/accommodation model of 'corporate governance' today. The technological paradigms also shifted from mass production to information technology.

Table 11.2 also shows that governance in an enterprise consists of top management, employee management and industrial relations management. Organizational adjustment is inevitable to accommodate external constraints. It is for this reason that governance at each level has changed. 'Corporate governance' has changed – but not to an 'external' governance model – i.e. convergence, so much as a 'redefined' model of existing 'internal' governance. The governance of employees has undergone a more drastic and real change from a 'collective' – to a more 'individual' – oriented model, as shown by the case studies below. The governance of industrial relations has also changed from a conflictual/compromise model to one based on cooperation/accommodation, and then to accommodation/dissatisfaction. Thus, although journalists and academics have discussed 'corporate governance', reforms at top management level seem somewhat modest compared to the other levels of enterprise governance.

Tables 11.3 and 11.4 show a report from the Tokyo Stock Exchange on reforms in top management by listed large companies. Almost 60 per cent claim to have made some reform to their top management system. The breakdown of such reforms is shown in Table 11.4. As can be seen, the biggest reform is the reduction in the number of board members (contrary to our case studies). In many cases this was achieved by the introduction of a system of Executive Officers (*Shikko Yakuin-Sei*). External Board Directors were also introduced and reviews of remuneration systems were carried out, but such measures were less in evidence than board downsizing. External Board Directors have been mostly introduced not for the purpose of external monitoring, but to complement the functions of existing board members. It is therefore difficult to conclude that a large shift is emerging from 'internal' to 'external' 'corporate governance'. Rather, the real import of reform at the level of top management is the rationalization of board membership, which became too large during the high-growth period. To a certain extent rationalization

Table 11.3 Reforms designed to enhance the function of the board

	Number of companies	*Percentage (%)*
'Reforms already made'	785	59.9
Reforms not made	520	39.7
No reply	5	0.4
Total	1,310	100.0

Source: Arata 'Kōporeito Gabanansu Reitingu' (Rating of 'corporate governance'), in *Nissei Kiso Ken Report*, 2002/6, p. 8.

Note: Total companies surveyed was 785.

Table 11.4 Specific reforms carried out by companies who responded 'reforms already made'

Specific reforms	Number of companies	Percentage (%)
Introduction of external directors	261	33.2
Reduction of board members	363	46.2
Introduction of *Shikko Yakuin-Sei*	279	35.5
Review of remuneration system	131	16.7
Others	219	27.9

Source: Arata 'Kōporeito Gabanansu Reitingu' (Rating of 'corporate governance'), in *Nissei Kiso Ken Report*, 2002/6, p. 8.

Note: Total companies surveyed was 785.

of directors may lead to speedy and individual decision-making, but this has nothing to do with 'external'-oriented 'corporate governance'.

The *Nikkei* survey of July 1999 on corporate reforms in 910 major Japanese companies (excluding financial institutions) (*Nikkei*, 26 July 1999) showed that the so-called reform of 'corporate governance' is actually only a part of general company restructuring. Figure 11.1 was compiled by the author based upon the *Nikkei* survey, which shows the degree of reform by industrial sector – it is noteworthy

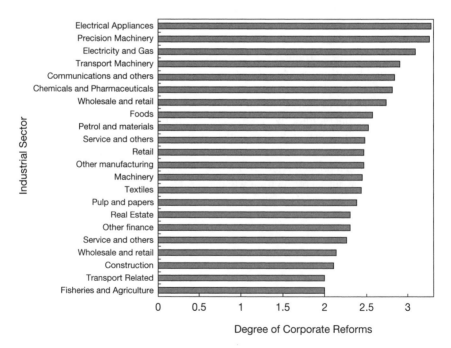

Figure 11.1 Degree of corporate reforms by industrial sector.

Source: Compiled from the *Nikkei* Corporate Reforms Survey (*Nikkei*, 26 July 1999)

that the most extensively restructured industrial sectors are concentrated in manufacturing, where companies are well known for their proactive stance in responding to global competition.

The criteria for 'corporate restructuring' were degree of merger and acquisition (M&A) activity, reform of organization, reform of employment practices, use of information technology (IT), and reform in attitudes and corporate values. Sony, Fujitsu, Honda, Canon, Komatsu, Toshiba, Matsushita Denkō, Matsushita Denki Sangyō, Ricoh and Asahigarasu were assessed as having achieved the most corporate restructuring, including top management reforms.

A non-manufacturing exception is the electricity and gas industries; but the electric industry is now facing government pressure to de-regulate and thus faces potential global competition. Conversely, fisheries/agriculture, transport-related, construction, wholesale and retail, services and others, non-bank financials and real estate are among the least reformed sectors.

We can see from Figure 11.1 that only a handful (about 100–150 companies) of listed companies are pursuing large-scale restructuring. In this context, reform in 'corporate governance' cannot be said to have been achieved in both scope and depth among all Japanese companies.

Many proposals and reports have been made, as shown in the previous section, and usually the US model is taken as a universal model for 'corporate governance', but in reality it is a metaphor for large-scale restructuring to deal with the competitive global market. This may imply that corporate restructuring for global companies like Sony has created governance closer to the Anglo-American model, but as detailed later, even Sony remains a Japanese model in many respects. As in the case of Matsushita, Honda and others, their restructuring can be seen as a 'redefined' Japanese model.

This is not to deny the potential for institutional convergence. Indeed, one factor which points in the direction of convergence towards the Anglo-American model is the change in the composition of ownership. Japan's 'internal'-oriented 'corporate governance' was created by mutual/aligned ownership among major conglomerates (*keiretsu*) and main banks, i.e. the system of Japanese *keiretsu*. How far has this been undermined by the forces of globalization? Table 11.5 shows the decline in the number of individual owners, while financial institutions and corporations remain the dominant shareholders (59.9 per cent). The relative importance of foreign owners has, however, increased to 18.5 per cent as a consequence of globalization and also pension funds. On the other hand, that of non-financial corporations has decreased noticeably from 30.0 per cent to 22.3 per cent, reflecting a dissolution of mutual holdings (i.e. sales of shares) among non-financial corporations.

Also, if we compare the composition of major shareholders between Japan and the United States, institutional investors claiming the need for effective 'corporate governance' account for 71.7 per cent in the United States, but only 12.9 per cent in Japan. However, so-called *keiretsu* shareholding (main banks and affiliated corporations) is much smaller for the US, accounting for only 3.8 per cent, as against 66.3 per cent for Japan (Fukao 1999).

Table 11.5 Recent changes in ownership of listed companies (per cent)

	2000	1990
Financial institutions	36.8	42.7
Deposit dealing banks	(11.8)	(14.8)
Life insurance	(7.7)	(9.3)
Non-life insurance	(2.7)	(3.8)
Pension funds	(7.2)	(3.7)
Investment funds	(3.0)	(3.8)
Dealer/broker	0.8	1.7
Non-financial corporations	22.2	30.0
Individuals	19.9	20.8
Foreign	18.5	4.8
Government	2.4	1.6

Source: Adapted from Shimada (2003).

A conceptual consideration of ownership-control-governance of capitalist firms suggests that major shareholders have the right to a 'voice', i.e. a 'monitoring' role. In the US it is external institutional investors and in Japan it has been internal *keiretsu* shareowners which have performed this role. This characteristic has not yet changed much, although some say that the increased percentage of foreign shareholders may play the role of increasing 'external' monitoring. It may be true to some extent, as in the case of Sony and some other corporations, but they are still far off the Anglo-American model.

Cases of corporate restructuring

This section investigates individual cases of corporate restructuring in two industrial groups, manufacturing and services. These two groups were chosen in order to compare the scope and extent of corporate restructuring and reforms in terms of the Anglo-American model of 'corporate governance'. In the manufacturing industry two companies from each of the electro-electric and automobile companies – Sony and Matsushita, and Toyota and Honda – were chosen as typical cases for such comparison. In the service industry, Tokyo Electric, Mitsubishi Estate, Sumitomo Bank and Kinki Nippon Tourist were also deemed representative of their respective service industries. Globalization in the service industry is much less than in manufacturing, suggesting a lower perceived need for restructuring in the Anglo-American direction.[5]

While these specific cases may not necessarily exemplify the typical circumstances of Japanese corporate reform activities overall, they do provide information of value in assessing the issue of 'corporate governance' and its meaning to Japanese companies, since the selected companies are themselves broadly representative of major industries. The survey was conducted in September 1999 using semi-guided interviews. The information on the state of restructuring for each company is therefore as of September 1999. Interview results show some reforms had already been made, while others were either in process or scheduled, depending upon the company. Table 11.6 shows a summary of such reforms identified from the interviews and compares these representative companies in six major areas in order to show the degree and scope of the reforms. Although further restructuring has occurred since the interviews, the author is of the opinion that the direction and type of restructuring made in this period was crucial in determining the path of major corporations for the ongoing restructuring. In this regard the information presented below remains of crucial importance for understanding the issue of corporate governance and its relation to restructuring.

Corporate restructuring in manufacturing: Sony, Matsushita, Honda and Toyota

Sony Corporation

Sony is said to be the most modern of Japanese companies in the sense that it is the closest to the Anglo-American model of 'corporate governance'. The board has become relatively small with ten directors (seven internal and two external directors) compared to average large Japanese corporations; external board members do not function as external monitors, so stock options are just an additional bonus for top management. HRM is individualized and rationalized, but the hierarchical management structure remains traditional.

At least in appearance, Sony is the Japanese company that has moved closest to the Anglo-American model. It has a global strategy, taking into account the pressures of globalization, and continues to grow, even while many others are struggling. Sony is unique in that it does not belong to any *kigyō-shūdan* (*keiretsu* group). Seventy per cent of sales are now overseas and foreigners own as much as 45 per cent of the total number of issued shares. Head office organization has been rationalized and the concept of networking introduced into management. The style of management has shifted towards greater attention to 'market capitalization'. It declares itself to be a 'shareholder active investor' as well as a 'stakeholder active agent'. The headquarters acts as a cost centre, while the affiliated companies, located throughout the world, are profit centres.

Sony's total workforce increased from 173,000 to 177,000 employees in 1998–9. Affiliated companies have now exceeded 1,000, and human resources for top management in the US and Europe are being localized.

As strategies for developing a global business, they seek network-oriented business, digitalization and a global supply of parts from the most appropriate markets. Parts numbering is now standard all over the world. Sony's research and development (R&D) centres are located in the US, India and Europe, with a division of labour and functional co-ordination. A sophisticated information architecture is in use for global production and sales, and analysis of global information is available on-line.

In finance, capital is supplied through the US financial market and the procedures of the Securities and Exchange Commission (SEC) are being used. The company seeks to enhance corporate value in the stock market. M&A is not considered as a means for growth and development.

Employment has shifted towards a more individual and diversified style. There are twice-annual recruitments of new graduates and also mid-term recruitment whenever necessary. An annual salary system is in place for all employees above deputy section chief. Seventy per cent of the annual salary is determined by basic pay, with the remaining 30 per cent performance related. In-enterprise recruitment/transfer is practised, with about 200 employees changing jobs annually. There are short-term contract employees and also about fifty foreign employees working on a contract basis in Japan. There are, however, no part-time workers.

The company has a stock option scheme for board members and has also introduced *Shikko Yakuin-Sei*, a system practised on an annual contract basis. The hierarchy of positions, however, remains very traditional, with position titles such as general manager, deputy general manager, section chief, deputy section chief, assistant section chief, group chief and deputy group chief, staff.

Matsushita Electric Industrial Company Limited

Matsushita is a global company, with certain key differences to Sony, in that it is still 'traditional', which may derive from its lower dependence upon ownership and financial structures.

Although no great change has occurred in the number of Matsushita employees, there has been re-organization within the company. Sales break down into 50 per cent domestic and 50 per cent overseas. Production shifted in 2001 to 70 per cent domestic and 30 per cent overseas. The overseas transfer of labour-intensive work has led to a relative decline in the numbers of female employees.

The style of management, in particular in decision-making, has shifted to a more individual-oriented style, although in keeping with existing Matsushita custom. Significantly, more attention is now paid to profitability than overall market share.

As a business strategy, the evolution of DVD and a shift from analogue to digital products is now well underway at Matsushita. In this sense, 'thin', 'related' and 'less energy' are concepts being translated into product development. Matsushita also now needs to factor social and environmental costs into product cost, to comply with legislation on recycling industrial products in effect since 2001. The division of labour between Japan and Asia has shifted from a vertical mode, in which Japan provided materials and parts and Asia carried out manufacturing or assembly, to a horizontal mode, in which each region or locality produces the most appropriate products, representing a shift towards symbiotic development.

In finance, Matsushita does not depend upon capital markets like bonds markets. The standards of SEC are applied and CCM (Capital Cost Management) is used to assess the performance of each business division.

In employment, job-oriented employment has become more popular. Mid-career/term employment has been introduced and employees in managerial positions are all on an annual salary system. The percentage of the salary determined by seniority is now 30 per cent, with the rest being determined by job and other individual-oriented elements, thus creating a pay difference of about 3 million yen per annum at section chief level and 4–5 million yen at that of general manager. There are contract employees as well as part-time employees. There are still social gatherings, including parties, trips, and so on.

The top management organization has not changed in number (32 board members) and there is no *Shikko Yakuin-Sei*, although there is a stock option scheme and some external members were invited onto the board.

Honda Motor Company Limited

Profitability is considered most important and reforms in HRM have been made, but Honda's 'corporate governance' *per se* remains traditional.

Honda's business as a whole has made good progress since 1993, but shifted from expansion of market share to profit-orientation with a return on equity (ROE) rate of 18.1 per cent in 1999. Overseas now exceed domestic sales and, since 1999, production has reflected this change in the pattern of sales.

The style of management is characterized by seniority orientation in the workplace, but other parts of the company focus on ability and job performance. The decision-making style has shifted from *Wai Gaya* culture (Japanese-style collectivism) to 'top-down' individual orientation. However, meetings remain as numerous as before.

In terms of business strategies, independence, technology and product marketability are considered sources of competitiveness. Strategies to enhance the integrated strength of R&D, production and sales, and improvement in cost and design, are seen to be vital. Japan is the R&D centre and products are made wherever consumer demand exists. Seventy per cent of materials and parts are now procured from outside the company.

In finance the standards of the SEC are applied and the relative importance of funding capital in the US has increased.

Employment style is characterized by individual orientation, in that employees are supposed to work not for the company but for themselves. No internal recruitment system exists and ability and performance determine salary. The volume of dispatched labour has increased. The same wage system is applied to both direct and indirect workers.

There is no *Shikko Yakuin-Sei* and board members number forty. External board members exist, but do not represent institutional investors. There are no stock options and no holding company. There is some relationship with Mitsubishi but this is limited to consultation and an exchange of views.

Toyota Motor Corporation

Toyota is an outstanding company in terms of performance and profitability, but its structure is far from what may be called the ideal Anglo-American model of 'corporate governance'.

Toyota has been forced to scale back automobile production from 4 to 3 million units following the collapse of the bubble economy and is suffering from over-capacity. Competition in both market and R&D has increased since then. There have, however, been no plant closures or organizational changes in departments and sections. Since the bursting of the bubble economy, sales of high-value cars have declined, but an increase in the production of low-cost cars has helped to offset this. Management aims to create a global image of the company by strengthening technological alliances rather than by increasing M&A and capital alliance.

Business strategies are shifting from export orientation to production wherever there exists a market for localization. The company aims at a 10 per cent share of the world market of 60 million cars. In terms of sales, it aims to sell 2.5 million in the domestic market and 3.5 million in overseas markets. R&D is centred in Japan (10,000 employees), while R&D in the US is focused on areas relevant to marketing (485 employees), and in Europe on design and market research (fifty employees).

In finance, global funding is pursued, such as the issue of Euro bonds and stock market listing in New York and London. However, the relative emphasis is not on drumming up extra cash, but on strengthening corporate power/ability. Toyota has decreased its own stock and is paying more attention to investor relations. The ownership of shares by foreigners is around 7–8 per cent and the possibility exists of an increase in institutional investors.

In employment, individual ability is more than ever considered important. Reflecting this, two types of recruitment, regular and mid-career, are utilized. Employment still involves entering the company and receiving in-enterprise education and training to become a professional staff member. The use of female workers on production lines has increased, and the emphasis is on the creation of specialist, rather than generalist, staff, and individual ability assessment is applied. An annual salary system has not been introduced. In-enterprise recruitment is not in use, while interviews are used for the assessment of promotion. Position titles have not changed, but two types exist, one for external purposes and the other for internal purposes. Externally, there are general managers, deputy general managers, managers, section chiefs, deputy section chiefs and staff, and internally there are general managers, room chiefs and staff leaders.

The company has no affiliation with *kigyō shūdan* (*keiretsu* group), which creates its organizational character. Toyota's division system is not absolute, as each division tends to share parts and equipment. Parts are commissioned from the most suitable suppliers around the world, but affiliated suppliers are committed to the design of these parts. Parts specification is determined by first acquiring a global standard, either in Japan or abroad, as shown in the case of the battery used for electric cars.[6]

The board structure has not changed, but stock options were introduced in 1997. Internal seniority is in principle maintained. There is no system of external board members but there are external advisers. No institutional investors are major shareholders.

Corporate reforms in non-manufacturing industry

The Tokyo Electric Power Company Incorporated

The company seems to be restructuring without change to the so called 'corporate governance'. Company objectives are currently to reduce costs and pursue rationalization of the organization, establishments and personnel, and to develop new areas of business.

In management style, this company pays more attention to shareholders, investors, customers and communities, rather than operate based on its own internal logic. Decision-making has shifted from bottom-up to top-down style and individual responsibility is now emphasized.

The company aims to develop overseas business, such as consulting services for electric-related projects, the development of uranium mines and the establishment of finance companies to supply funds for overseas business, in order to deal with economic stagnation at home and increased competition. Reduction of excess human resources, debts and equipment, while increasing returns to investors, is a particular focus of attention. A typical overseas business project is its participation in optical communications with Softbank and Microsoft.

In finance, Tokyo Electric aims to raise funds by issuing bonds overseas. Foreign ownership has increased and investor relations (IR) is of greater concern. The time may come when some investors start to exert their rights at the annual shareholders' meeting, but this has not yet occurred. The percentage of shares owned by banks is decreasing.

In employment, assessment of individual ability and performance is to be enhanced in the area of employment management. The scope of the annual salary scheme is to be expanded. Diversified employment schemes, such as part-timers, mid-career recruitment and in-enterprise recruitment (transfer), have now been introduced.

With regard to organization, the company is moving towards the network business paradigm, transferring authority to create autonomous management at a lower level. In-enterprise accounting, business divisions and in-enterprise companies have been adopted and authority is now delegated to these units. Two external members and two external auditors have been invited to join the board. A report on environmental issues has been published and was evaluated highly as a good example of the company's social awareness.[7] Positions in the managerial hierarchy have been reduced to general manager, deputy manager and group manager. The number of board members has not, however, changed, and neither *Shikko Yakuin-Sei* nor a stock option scheme have been introduced.

Mitsubishi Estate Company Limited

In contrast to what is said and Mitsubishi's own desire, the company remains quite conservative and the change was made but remains small in scale. There has been no variation in the number of and seniority order among board members and external board members, except for the purpose of 'internal' 'corporate governance'.

With its corruption problems (as manifest by the *sōkaiya* and Umino Ie incidents)[8] the company has determined to break with its old practices and culture. The number of businesses and employees has decreased and the focus of business has shifted from land ownership to 'fee business (management business)', due to the collapse of the so-called 'land myth'.

Management style is changing from traditional to market-oriented. However, group cohesion is strong and the maintenance and protection of the 'Mitsubishi brand' is considered very important. Decision-making is still slow and the bottom-up style remains. There are many meetings and the scope of individual responsibility is small. As a means to diversify 'risks', globalization is pursued and overseas businesses are being developed jointly with overseas capital. Management of apartments and outsourcings have become more important and are becoming the core business.

Financially, the company has not been accustomed to raising capital overseas, but for the last eight years has had to devise strategies to satisfy the scrutiny of stock market analysts. The percentage of foreign ownership now accounts for 15 per cent, but the company has not yet adopted global accounting standards.

In employment, performance pay and objective management have been introduced. The company depends only upon the recruitment of new graduates and they are recruited not by job criteria but as general staff. Annual salary schemes have not been introduced and promotion is determined by a combination of the assessment of personnel management and self-assessment. Part-timers are used as regular human resources.

The company is considering restructuring towards a 'company'-based division system, but there is no intention of establishing a holding company. The managerial hierarchy was even previously rather simple, consisting only of general mangers, deputy managers and staff. There are six qualifications for grading employees. The number of board members has not changed and there is no stock option scheme. Seniority is maintained among board members and external directors are from companies of the Mitsubishi group, such as Meiji Life Insurance and Mitsubishi Bank.

The Sumitomo Bank Limited[9]

Although a necessity for change is felt to exist, the company remains traditional. The need for change has been seriously perceived, but the speed of change has been rather slow. Rationalization of overseas and domestic businesses and human resources has been carried out.

Management style has shifted to market-orientation and the evaluation of individual performance. The company's annual athletics meeting was abolished. A review was made of old business practice and awareness of profitability increased. Decision-making remains 'bottom-up' and meetings still involve a large number of people.

Business strategy has shifted to regional strategies. An active approach to IR and the promotion of IT are now considered important. The number of external board members has risen to three and that of monitoring members to two. The *Shikko Yakuin-Sei* was adopted and business policies are now more domestic-oriented.

In finance, the accounting system has become more internationalized.

In employment, some change has been made, but the basic principle of promotion based on seniority has not altered. Competition among those of the same year entry has intensified, but among board members reverse promotion is never seen, and thus the seniority custom remains unchanged. Annual salary and in-enterprise recruitment schemes have not been introduced. Part-timers are recruited from subsidiary companies and more than half of clerical employees are now part-timers.

Kinki Nippon Tourist

This company faces the most serious situation of all those interviewed and has undertaken the most radical restructuring, replacing regular employees with contract workers on a large scale. Kinki Nippon recorded a deficit in 1998 and large-scale rationalization is now in progress. Rationalization at head office and in personnel sought to lower numbers from 7,200 in 1998 to 6,878 in 1999. Early retirement for those over 50 is in progress and will be stepped up to those over 45 years of age.

Management style needs to cope with increased competition, lower prices, the continued recession and a shift from group to individual travel. Internet-based business operations have gained in importance. Business performance in consolidated accounting has been pursued and decision-making has speeded up.

As a business strategy emphasis is laid upon the replacement of as many regular employees as possible with less costly contracted employees, for terms of one year, extendable up to five years. The administration of payment accounts has been outsourced and a scrap-and-build policy implemented in all companies in the group. Products are now more individualized and targeted at middle-aged and older customers. The business has become more profit-oriented than before and domestic and overseas sales account for 64 and 33 per cent respectively.

Neither an employee share nor stock option scheme has been introduced and there is no foreign ownership of shares.

In employment, seniority-based pay increments were terminated and the principle of market and individual orientation adopted, with higher rewards going to those generating more profits. Each branch is now regarded as a company and the head of the company is a regular full-time employee, while all others are contract employees. For regular employees, seniority promotion applies only for the first three years and then promotion becomes more individualized, with large differentials among those who entered the company in the same year. Objective management has been introduced and those who are in management are paid based on an annual salary scheme. Some in-enterprise recruitment has been introduced. Part-timers currently account for 1 per cent, and contract employees for 16 per cent, of all employees.

The organization was rationalized through scrap-and-build: the number of general managers decreased from thirty-one to twenty-four at head office, and section chiefs from fifty-two to thirty-seven. The organization became flatter in shape. A *Shikko Yakuin-Sei* was introduced with a one-year period of service. The merit of this scheme is to make executives exempt from litigation by investors. The number of meetings between sections has increased and seniority among board members remains. An external board member is dispatched from the parent company, Kinki Nippon Tetsudō and Japan Railways.

As seen in Table 11.6 all the above companies agree on three areas of 'corporate governance'; profitability, HRM and external board members. The relative importance of profitability has increased for two reasons, one being 'corporate governance' (market capitalization) and the other the sheer survival of the company. The latter would seem to have more weight, since companies need to secure profitability in order to survive the increased competition in situations of no macro economic growth. This internal necessity is being achieved by the introduction of individual-oriented HRM, of which the foremost objective is to reduce the total labour cost of non-managerial employees, with an annual salary scheme as its counterpart for managers. External board members were introduced not for 'external monitoring' but to 'strengthen' existing board functions. Some companies have introduced *Shikko Yakuin-Sei* in order to reduce the number of board members and deter investors from suing the board. It is, however, only Sony that has reduced the actual number of board members by the introduction of *Shikko Yakuin-Sei*.

In all other companies interviewed the number of board members and seniority among them remain the same. They may say they are creating a new business paradigm, but the reality is still traditional in most of the companies, even Sony. Clearly, however, HRM is the most important target for restructuring, with the aim of redefining enterprise governance.

Conclusion

The dynamics of capitalist development are uneven, requiring constant corrective measures if a company wishes to maintain or improve its position under conditions of global competition. The flux of fortune between countries competing against each other inevitably leads to emulative activity. The process is one of corrective rationalization in the appropriate sphere, either production systems, 'corporate governance' and/or more dynamic corporate restructuring. 'Corporate governance' discourse is also a phenomenon of, and a metaphor used to improve, the workings of the logic of capitalist accumulation. How far such logic is generating dynamics of 'convergence' of different forms of capitalisms along Anglo-American lines remains to be seen.

However, looking at structural change in Japanese capitalism and the specific cases of corporate restructuring detailed above, 'good governance' for Japanese companies implies the continuous growth of the company, rather than a shift from

Table 11.6 Reforms for 'corporate governance' of major companies

	Profitability	Smaller Board	Shikko Yakuin-Sei	Individual oriented HRM	Annual Salary	Stock Option	External Board Members	Total Points
Sony	*	*	*	*	*	*	*	7
Matsushita	*			*	*	*	*	5
Honda	*			*	*		*	4
Toyota	*			*		*	(*)	4
Tokyo Electric	*			*	*		*	4
Mitsubishi R E	*			*			*	3
Sumitomo Bank	*		*	*			*	4
K N Tourist	*		*	*	*		*	5
Total Points	8	1	3	8	5	3	8	

Source: Compiled from interview results. Include a note on interviews at start of section.

Note: (*) means external advisers.

'internal' to 'external' 'corporate governance'. The continuous growth of the company is considered evidence of good 'corporate governance', leading to less corruption, more investment, greater employee satisfaction and more contribution to various stakeholders. For example, both Toyota and Honda, or Sony and Matsushita, are enjoying sound governance with different style/structures of 'corporate governance'. In fact, there seems no 'corporate governance' problem in these companies.

Rather, the issue of 'corporate governance' in Japan can be taken as a catalyst and metaphor for large-scale corporate restructuring in the 1990s and beyond. Indeed, the real content of 'corporate governance' was not so much emulation of the Anglo-American model as the 're-definition' and 'modification' of existing enterprise governance. 'Corporate governance' in Japan also has no relevance to 'fictitious' industrial democracy as has emerged in the United States as an excuse for 'corporate governance'. Indeed, the democratic governance of an enterprise as a reflection of labour and the community remains an important consideration for the Japanese people, ensuring any attempt to impose a 'one-size-fits all' mode of corporate governance will be contested.

Notes

1   US pressure emerged in the 1970s and 1980s in the form of trade conflicts, but thereafter continued in the form of globalization, and is exemplified in the Structural Impediments Initiatives (1989) and the US–Japan Framework Talks on Bilateral Trade (1994–7), as well as the OECD agreement (1994) on labour flexibility. Other aspects of 'external' constraints are global standards for accounting and environmental protection.
2   The term Anglo-American model is defined in this chapter broadly as a governance system which is controlled by external forces (shareholders and external directors), in contrast to the Japanese system, which is governed by mutual holdings, main banks and internally promoted directors. This kind of generalization is made expressly for the sake of our analysis and we regard reality as naturally more varied, both in Anglo-American and Japanese capitalism.
3   This implies that a company is the means by which its owners make profit, but more specifically highlights Berle and Means' suggestion that 'the two attributes of ownership – risking collective wealth in profit-seeking enterprise and ultimate management of responsibility for that enterprise – had become divorced' (Berle and Means 1932: viii).
4   In Britain the Report from the Committee on the Financial Aspects of Corporate Governance (1992), the Greenbury Report (1995) and the OECD Paper (1997) were published, while in the United States there was a report on the principles of corporate governance issued by the American Bar Association (1992) and various statements by the Business Roundtable (Monks and Minow 2001).
5   The restructuring in service industries, which experience less necessity for globalization, offers evidence that the need for restructuring in 'corporate governance' varies from industry to industry reflecting the degree of competitive pressures from globalization.
6   There are two major global groups competing in the fuel cell electric vehicle project; one is the Ford/Daimler Chrysler group and the other Toyota/GM group. This system, if achieved, will become a revolution in the fuel system of the automobile and it will make a 100 per cent environmentally friendly car. It is assumed that the global

standard will be formed by either of these two groups, which will then be able to enjoy a dominant position in the global market.

7   Contrary to this official report, the company was accused on 29 August 2002 of repeatedly compiling false reports on the condition of their seventeen nuclear plants. Thirteen had been kept in operation without repairs and even at the time of this revelation eight such plants were in operation. This was exposed by General Electric inspectors as a classic case of whistle-blowing. As a result of this scandal, five top-ranking management figures, including the then-current chairman and president, resigned. Although this has obvious relevance to issues of corporate governance, such as transparency in business and management, it would also seem to have deeper implications in relation to Japan's future energy policies in terms of the political relationship between industry and civil bureaucracy. (see Yoshioka Hitoshi, available on-line at: http://www.hansen-jp.com/217yoshioka.htm, accessed 22 June 2004).

8   This is a symbolic case revealed in 1997 of corporate corruption, in which major corporations of Mitsubishi Group including Mitsubishi Estate Co. Ltd., Mitsubishi Motors, Mitsubishi Electric Corporation, Hitachi Ltd., and Toshiba Corporation were involved. They were using and paying *Sōkai-ya* (racketeers) in order to run the general meeting of shareholders in their favour.

9   The survey was conducted in September 1999, while in October of the same year the merger plan with Sakura Bank was announced and these two banks were merged in April 2001 forming Sumitomo Mitsui Bank.

References

Arata, Keisuke (2002) 'Kōporeito gabanansu reitingu', in *Nissei Kisoken Report* 2002/6: 8–15.

Berle, Adolf A. and Means, G. C. (1932) *The Modern Corporation and Private Property* (revised edition, 1964), New York: Harcourt, Brace & World.

Carroll, Archie B. and Buchholtz, Ann (2002) *Business and Society: ethics and stakeholder management*, Mason: South Western College Publishing.

Committee on the Financial Aspects of Corporate Governance (1992) *The Cadbury Report*, Basingstoke: Burgess Science Press.

Drucker, Peter F. (1993) *Post Capitalist Society*, Oxford: Butterworth Heinemann.

Fukao, Mitsuhiro (1999) *Kōporeito Gabanannsu Nyūmon*, Tokyo: Chikuma Shobō.

Fukao, Mitsuhiro and Morita, Yasuko (1997) *Kigyō Gabanansu Kōzo no Kokusai Hikaku*, Tokyo: Nihon Keizai Shimbunsha.

Hamada, Yasushi (2002) *Fusei ō Yurusanai Kansa*, Tokyo: Nihon Keizai Shimbunsha.

Harvard Business Review (2000) *Corporate Governance*, Boston: Harvard Business School Press.

Jacoby, Sanford M. (2001) 'Employee representation and corporate governance: a missing link', *Journal of Labor and Employment Law* 3, 3: 449–89.

Keidanren (2000) *Wagakuni Kōkai Gaisha ni okeru Kōporeito Gabanansu ni kansuru Ronten Seiri*, Tokyo: Keidanren.

Keizai Kikakukucho (ed.) (1998) *Nihon no Kōporeito Gabanansu*, Tokyo: Keizai Kikakucho Keizai Kenkyūsho.

Kelly, Gavin, Kelly, Dominic, Gamble, Andrew (1997) *Stakeholder Capitalism*, Basingstoke: Macmillan.

Korten, David C. (1999) *The Post-Corporate World*, West Harford: Kumarion Press.

Kubori, Hideaki, Suzuki, T., Takanashi, T. and Sakai, R. (1998) *Nihongata Cōporeit Gabanansu*, Tokyo: Nikkan Kōgyō Shimbunsha.

Lorsch, Jay W. (2000) 'Empowering the board' in *Harvard Business Review on Corporate Governance*, Boston: Harvard Business School Press, pp. 25–51.

Monks, Robert A. G. and Minow, Nell (2001) *Corporate Governance* (2nd edition), Malden: Blackwell Publishing.

OECD (1999) *OECD Principles of Corporate Governance*, Paris: OECD

Osano, Hiroshi (2001) *Kōporeito Gabanansu no Keizaigaku*, Tokyo: Nihon Keizai Shimbunsha.

Post, James E., Preston, Lee E. and Sachs, Sybille (2002) *Redefining the Corporation: stakeholder management and organizational wealth*, Stanford: Stanford Business Books.

Rahman, Sandra Sutherland, Waddock, Sandra, Andriof, Jorg and Husted, Brian (eds) (2002) *Unfolding Stakeholder Thinking: theory, responsibility and engagement*, Sheffield: Greenleaf Publishing Ltd.

Rengō (1999) 'Rōdō Kumiai kara mita Kōporeito Gabanansu', in *Rengō Sōken Report* 129:11–17.

Scott, John (1997) *Corporate Business and Capitalist Classes*, Oxford: Oxford University Press.

Shibuya, Hiroshi (1999) 'Amerika no kikan tōshika to kōporeito gabanansu: kenkyū shikaku settei no kokoromi', *Shōken Keizai Kenkyū*, 22: 15–28.

Shimada, H. (2003) *Kabushiki Hoyū Kōsei to Kigyō Keiei Kōritsu* (Composition of share holdings and managerial efficiency), p.25. (Available on-line at: http://www.isfj.net/top/report/kinyu/kinnyu_keio_shimada.pdf, accessed 24 June 2004).

Takahashi, Yoshiaki (1999) 'Saikin no Nihon no Kōporeito Gabanansu o meguru Kakushu Hōkoku, Teigen ni tsuite', *Shōgaku Ronsō* 40, 3/4: 255–79.

Uetake, Teruhisa and Nakata, Masaki (1999) *Gendai Kigyō no Shoyū, Shihai, Kanri*, Kyoto: Mineruba Shobō.

Yoshimori, Masauru (1996) *Nihon no Keiei, Ōbei no Keiei*, Tokyo: Hōsō Daigaku.

Wheeler, David and Sillanpaa, Maria (1997) *The Stakeholder Corporation*, London: Pitman Publishing.

12 Governance through the family

The political function of the domestic in Japan

Takeda Hiroko

Describing the transition of the concept of 'governing' from the sixteenth century to the eighteenth century in Europe, Foucault commented that,

> The art of government . . . is essentially concerned with answering the question of how to introduce economy – that is to say, the correct manner of managing individuals, goods and wealth within the family.
>
> (Foucault 1991: 92)

The Foucauldian usage of governing – *governing* linked with *the family* via *economy* – seems to be increasingly focused upon by politicians and other policymaking agents in the new millennium Japan. As rapid demographic changes in the 1990s, in particular, ever-falling birthrates,[1] unprecedented ageing and an increase in the single population, was generally posited as destabilizing the standard profile of the family in Japan, people were inundated with discourse on 'the correct manner of managing individuals, goods and wealth within the family'. This demographic and familial transition was associated with economic stagnation following the bursting of the 'economic bubble', and was viewed as a sign of the dysfunction of the Japanese political, economic and social systems. In order to cope with this situation, the government implemented a series of policies aimed at promoting gender-equality, which would possibly alter the existing familial relations as well as popular recognition of the familial (Ōsawa 2002). This political process in late 1990s Japan suggests that the 'economy' of the family was the very object of national governing, and in this sense, the governance of the family in 1990s Japan appears to be the antithesis of the assumption of the private/public distinction, in which the family, economy and the conduct of governing have been analyzed respectively in different disciplines within the social sciences.

Yet, the view that regards the family as domestic space has also been countered by theoretical developments in the study of governance.[2] First, the development of feminist scholarship within political economy has criticized the gendered assumption of the social sciences which underestimates the role of the family as a site of governance. For instance, a pioneer of feminist political economy, Folbre, argues that neither neoclassical nor Marxian (including socialist-feminist) economic theory has effectively analysed gender issues, in particular, the family as a unit of social reproduction. Accordingly, theories of women's disadvantaged positions in the family and women's disproportionate engagement in household activities, which result in their economic and political disempowerment, have remained underdeveloped (Folbre 1994: 88–90). Responding to the dilemma posited by Folbre, Elson locates the household, along with firms and governments, as an integral part of the macro-economy, in terms of its function in consumption and social reproduction (Elson 2000: 78–80). Such research elucidates how the multi-dimensional reproductive activities play a crucial role in the global and national political economy, and in so doing, makes the family visible in the system of governance. In other words, by critically reviewing the existing paradigms at the base of gendered social science, new insights into the role of the family as a site of governance have been achieved. [3]

Second, such research on the transition in the ways of governing draws attention to the neglected question of political power. Inspired by Foucault's discussion of *biopolitics*, politics regarding our bodies, subjectivities, sexualities and even the 'politics of life itself' (Rose 2001) have started to be addressed.[4] The area in which biopolitics functions is in the management of the population. More specifically, biopolitics is concerned with, first, the 'discipline of human bodies', namely, internalizing norms and patterns of behaviour through institutional disciplines, and second, the calibration of the health, body and sexuality of the population (Foucault 1978: 139–41). Foucault argued that biopolitics has been incorporated into the governing system of modern states as the quintessential principle of governing, and he calls this process the 'governmentalization of the state'. In this governing system, the governing monitors, instructs and takes care of the governed, rather than suppresses the governed as happened in the pre-modern era. By so doing, the governing encourages the governed to 'autonomously' conduct their everyday lives in ways suited to the maintenance and growth of the modern, liberal capitalist state. The family here appears as an essential unit for biopolitics. In the family, various reproductive activities – such as monitoring and taking care of each member of the family – are carried out in cooperation with various 'medium apparatuses', namely schools, medical organizations and social services, and through these activities, biopolitics functions. In Dean's words, '[t]he family is a reality to be taken into account as an instrument and objective of government, rather than the very *a priori* of government itself' (Dean 1999: 108).

The discussion of both feminist political economy and biopolitics suggests that the family is not a politically and economically free zone but is rather a contested site of governance. In fact, the family functions through reproductive activities as a part of the governing system of the national political economy. Within the family, children are procreated, raised and trained, while workers are revitalized for the next day's work, in cooperation with other actors in the political economy. Through these activities, it is not only the family but also national economies and states that are reproduced, sustained and developed. In this respect, if 'in much of the public and political debate, governance refers to sustaining co-ordination and coherence among a wide variety of actors with different purposes and objectives such as political actors and institutions, corporate interests, civil society, and transnational organizations' (Pierre 2000: 3–4), it seems that the reproductive function that the family plays in the political economy calls for an analysis of the family and governance.

The purpose of this chapter is thus to locate the family in an analysis of the political economy of governance in Japan, by taking the 1990s political situation into account. In order to do so, the chapter focuses upon household economy management as an issue at the heart of the intersection of the activities of the family and those of the Japanese political economy. The household economy management of each family initially controls the micro-economy within the family, yet, it is also a part of the national economy that influences and is influenced by trends in the current economy as well as the particular historical conditions of the time (Nakamura 1993: 2–3). Because of the implications of household economy management, the Japanese government and government-related organizations have been conducting numerous surveys on household economy since the 1920s. Furthermore, reacting to the enduring economic setback of the 1990s and ongoing deflation, household economy management seems to be coming to the attention of both policymakers and the Japanese 'middle-class'. Below, the chapter will look in detail at the functions of the household economy in modern and contemporary Japan and the implications for the Japanese political economy. More specifically, the first part of the chapter provides a concise history of household economy management and governmental activities relating to it. The second part examines contemporary Japanese household economy management since the economic setback of the 1990s. Finally, the chapter discusses a case in which household economy management stretched out into the 'public sphere' and channelled some women into the arena of local politics.

Good household management and Japanese families

The political and economic importance and benefit of a well-managed household was already acknowledged by the founding fathers of the Meiji state. In order to achieve the top-priority agenda of 'enrich the country, strengthen the military' (*fukoku kyōhei*), the family was located in the state governing system as part of the foundation of the state. It was the women, wives and mothers of the household, who appeared to be the agents carrying out all of the work within the Meiji household, in contrast to household management in the previous Edo period that was mainly conducted by men. Meiji enlightenment writers such as Fukuzawa Yukichi and Mori Arinori even argued for 'equal rights' for women and the promotion of women's education, in order to turn women into competent agents of household management (Kaneko 1999: 23–40; Koyama 1999: 24).

The statist concern with the good management of the family and household eventually resulted in a variety of governmental interventions into the household economy management of each family. These governmental interventions were conducted through many different channels. First, household economy management was included in female state education. Since its establishment in 1885, the Tokyo Women's Normal School (*Joshi Shihan Gakkō*) taught its students bookkeeping and home economics. Yet, it was in the mid-1890s that an academic subject equivalent to contemporary 'domestic science' began to take shape and the first comprehensive textbook on household economy management was published (Miyokawa 1997: 63). Also, in 1901, a graduate of the Normal School, Ōe Sumi, was sent to Britain for three years in order to study 'domestic science', which was emerging as an independent academic discipline at the time. After she returned from Britain, Ōe was appointed as a tutor in the Normal School, and engaged in the training of future teachers of domestic science and developed the curricula for a new Japanese domestic science education which was based on the natural and social sciences. According to Kashiwagi, the new domestic science education that Ōe promoted was synchronized with the statist policy on national female education that emphasized women's role as competent agents of household management in building a well-governed state (Kashiwagi 1995: 94). Teachers trained by Ōe taught the new 'domestic science' including the management of household economy across Japan.

Second, responding to the serious economic hardship experienced among the working class after the Russo-Japanese War (1904–5), the government embarked on conducting official surveys of the actual situation of each household by keeping track of housekeeping books. Inflation after the war brought about severe hardship for low and middle income families, in particular, those who were tied to a fixed wage such as lower-class bureaucrats, police officers, school teachers and company employees. This 'living expense' issue (*seikatsuhi mondai*) was raised in the Diet, as a potential source of social disorder and public disturbance, and the Ministry of Agriculture and Commerce conducted a series of national surveys on family living expenses in order to provide concrete data for the discussion (Tada 1989: 39–66). The concern with economic hardship among low-income families became more acute during the First World War, and this situation led the national government, subnational political authorities and large private corporations to carry out numerous surveys on the household economy (Tada 1989: 101–8). The first nation-wide survey of household economy, a prototype of the present Family Income and Expenditure Survey, was conducted by the Statistics Bureau of the Cabinet Office (*Naikaku Tōkeikyoku*) in 1926 (Tada 1989: 212).

Third, the government also began to organize a variety of semi-governmental movements, activities and events aimed at the 'improvement of everyday life'. These governmental initiatives, from the holding of national exhibitions to training courses in housework skills for housewives, were meant, again, to educate and train Japanese women to be competent agents within their homes, that is, 'housewives'. The most high-profile example of these attempts was perhaps the Everyday Life Improvement Movement (*Seikatsu Kaizen Undō*) initiated in 1919, in which Ōe Sumi played a central role. This enlightenment movement was to 'introduce science into everyday life at home' and to 'promote the rationalization and streamlining of everyday life' (Koyama 1999: 101). In cooperation with the Ministry of Education, the movement dealt with a variety of issues from time management or economizing to the modernization and westernization of everyday life, and the management of household economy was a particular point of focus. Topics such as budgeting and rationalized consumption were taught through lectures and exhibitions themed on household economy (Koyama 1999: 163–4). Garon maintains that the Everyday Life Improvement Movement was the 'final element in the evolving savings campaigns' in the growing atmosphere of democratization and consumer culture (Garon 2000: 48). According to him, the first governmental savings drive started just after the Russo-Japanese War in order to 'retire foreign debt and finance Japan's military build-up and other projects', and for that purpose, 'diligence' and 'thrift' were promoted (Garon 2000: 46).[5] Yet, the management of household economy promoted by the Everyday Life Improvement Movement emphasized the importance of building up savings, as Koyama also argues, not only through economizing but also through budgeting and 'wise' consumption (Koyama 1999: 195–206). In this sense, the drives for the improvement of everyday life were derived from not only the statist concern with household economy management but also the desire of each family for a 'better life'.

Indeed, the Everyday Life Improvement Movement was a nationwide semi-governmental movement, not a mere governmental campaign, and in this sense, it is important to note the private and grass-roots desires and efforts for improving everyday life evident at the time. In particular, demands for 'tips' on household economy management were acute among low and lower-middle class housewives, and women's magazines, for instance *Fujin no Tomo* (Women's Friend) established in 1908 and *Shufu no Tomo* (Housewife's Friend) established in 1917, swiftly responded to such demands. Reflecting the strong Protestant faith of its main editors, Hani Motoko and her husband Hani Yoshikazu, *Fujin no Tomo* enthusiastically promoted the rationalization and economizing of everyday life based on stoicism. Also, Hani Motoko's writing on household economy management, *Kaji Kakei Hen* (On Housework and Household Economy), circulated widely and became the bible of household management for upper-middle class housewives. In her magazine and book, Hani stressed the budgeting and planning of the household economy and the need for keeping housekeeping books. The Hanis' venture eventually went beyond publishing the magazine, and they organized readers' associations (*Fujin no Tomo Zenkoku Tomo no Kai*) across Japan with support from domestic science professionals. According to Kashiwagi, these ventures introduced modern ideas of engineering, namely, the technologies of planning and management, into Japanese family lives that were facing contradictions brought about by the capitalist economy; namely low income, unemployment, redundancy and other hardships (Kashiwagi 1997: 33). In contrast to the upper-middle-class orientated *Fujin no Tomo*, *Shufu no Tomo* targeted the mass market and lower-middle class housewives, and promoted the economizing and rationalization of everyday life through providing practical housework tips and suggestions on how to manage the household economy. Also, *Shufu no Tomo* and other magazines started a common trend in Japanese women's magazines that can be still seen today, namely, that of providing readers with housekeeping books as an annual supplement.[6] Faced as they were with the economic difficulties caused by inflation,[7] Japanese housewives welcomed these articles regarding housework and household economy management. Through these practices housewives became agents of household economy management and housekeeping books penetrated into Japanese families as a tool of good household economy management (Koyama 1999: 42–9).

The Everyday Life Movement and ventures of women's magazines during the period of Taishō democracy in the 1920s were eventually absorbed into the total war project. As the expense of the war and colonization burgeoned, the purpose of the savings campaign was to mobilize people's small savings to finance the empire's expense: '[t]he nation's capacity to sacrifice and save was touted as Japan's secret weapon' (Garon 2002: 107). Ōe Sumi and Hani Motoko joined in the government's savings promotion campaign as members of the National Savings Promotion Council in 1938. During the next year, the National Saving Promotion Bureau appointed thirty-one women 'saving lecturers' including Ōe, Hani, and Oku Mumeo, who founded the Housewives Confederation (*Shufu Rengō Kai*, abbreviated to *Shufuren*) after the war (Garon 2002: 65). Moreover, Hani's daughter, Hani Setsuko, was appointed to a plurality of posts in the war-support organizations, which included the directorship of the Great Japan Women's Association (*Dai Nippon Fujin Kai*), a subordinate organization of the Imperial Rule Assistance Association (*Taisei Yokusan Kai*). The readers' associations of the *Fujin no Tomo* were utilized for the wartime efforts of 'innovation of life' (*seikatsu kakushin*). Limits on resources during the total war period put economic pressure on each Japanese family, and housewives were forced to conduct further rationalization and economization in everyday life. Existing organizations aiming at the rationalization of everyday life such as *Fujin no Tomo* readers' association were highly useful for the then government that was 'troubled with the planning of guidance on everyday life at home in the wartime' (Suzuki 1997: 77; 76–94 passim).

It is important to note that defeat in the Second World War and occupation by the Allies did not bring about a genuinely 'radical' change to the relationship between household economy management and the government. Domestic science remained a subject taught at primary and secondary schools as well as an academic discipline offered at the tertiary education level, higher education now being open to women, and household economy management was a quintessential part of the course. Domestic science was taught at schools to both male and female students until 1962, and thereafter only female students were assigned to study domestic science at secondary school level until the curriculum change introduced in 1994. At high school, domestic science became a compulsory subject after the change in the 1960 curriculum guideline of the Ministry of Education (Hisatake *et al.* 1997: 109; Yokoyama 2002: 31–4).

The economic hardship resulting from the war also increased demands for accurate sets of data on household economy and consumption, and numerous surveys on household economy and consumer prices were conducted by the Statistics Bureau of the Cabinet Office (*Naikaku Tōkeikyoku*). Such governmental surveys on the household economy were systematized from the 1950s to 1960s. Two major national surveys on household economy, the Family Income and Expenditure Survey and the National Survey of Family Income Expenditure took shape, respectively in 1953 and 1959, and still continue today (Sōmushō Tōkeikyoku 2002).

Finally, the difficulties experienced in everyday life led Japanese housewives to organize voluntary activities and consumer movements aimed at 'protection of everyday life'. In 1946, for instance, readers of the *Fujin no Tomo* gathered in order to set up the 'Housekeeping Books Federation' (*Kakeibo o Tsuketōsu Dōmei*) that still publishes data collected from its members' housekeeping books in every issue of *Fujin no Tomo*. According to the article celebrating the 52nd anniversary of the Federation, housewives joined the venture in order to 'encourage each other and learn from others' housekeeping books' in a situation where economic devastation and inflation drove their household economies into crisis (*Asu no Tomo* 116, 1998: 33). In 1948, two years after the establishment of the Housekeeping Books Federation, one of the largest and most powerful consumer organizations, the Housewives Confederation, was organized under the leadership of Oku in order to tackle the difficulties faced by families in everyday life (Shufu Rengōkai 1998: 29–30).

Furthermore, governmental interventions in household economy management continued through the postwar version of the Everyday Life Improvement Movement, namely the New Life Movement (*Shinseikatsu Undō*). The New Life Movement got underway in the early 1950s. It received encouragement and endorsement from the then government, and in 1955 Prime Minister Hatoyama Ichirō invited 150 guests to the Prime minister's residence to ask for cooperation in the promotion of the movement (*Tokyo-to Shinseikatsu Undō Kyōkai* 1973: 119–21). Just as its prewar predecessor did, the New Life Movement promoted the rationalization of everyday life. In particular, it stressed the importance of family planning and life planning including budgeting and the promotion of savings (Takeda 2005: 132–6). Importantly, many large corporations such as Toyota, Nippon Kōkan, Toshiba Denki, Tokyo Denryoku, and Sumitomo Kinzoku, to name but a few, introduced the New Life Movement into companies' welfare policy and encouraged employees' housewives to join in its activities. Through the activities of the New Life Movement, housewives developed their skills and increased their knowledge of good housekeeping, which included budgeting, keeping housekeeping books and boosting household savings.

The New Life Movement in the 1950s and 1960s was closely related to the major actors in the state's policies, and as regards the management of household economy, the Ministry of Finance, the Bank of Japan and the Central Council for Savings Promotion (*Chochiku Zōkyō Iinkai*) made significant inputs, and lectures and training courses on savings and management of household economy were often organized in cooperation with these actors. Responding to the implementation of the 1949 Dodge line, which sought to stimulate the Japanese economy, the governmental savings promotion campaign was quickly restored, in order to accumulate financial resources for the reconstruction and growth of the Japanese economy: in other words, in order to serve what Garon calls 'economic nationalism' in postwar Japan (Garon 2002: 109–14).[8] The importance of building household savings and the usefulness of housekeeping books for savings purposes were zealously promoted by the New Life Movement, through training courses, public lectures and the mass-media (Tama 1996: 168–76). Large women's organizations such as the Housewives

Confederation and National Federation of Regional Women's Organizations
(hereafter NFRWO) led by Yamataka Shigeri enthusiastically took part in the New
Life Movement. In fact, Oku and Yamataka were members of the directors' board
of the New Life Movement Association (Takeda 2005: 237), and their organizations
made significant contributions to the promotion of the 'rational management of
household economy' through budgeting and housekeeping books.[9]

The New Life Movement changed direction in the 1970s, distancing itself from
the strong emphasis on family planning and life planning laid down by policymakers, and initiated activities closely related to local communities through
organizing 'everyday life schools' (*seikatsu gakkō*). Everyday life schools run by local
housewives were initially study groups dealing with consumer problems and other
life-related issues. However, they eventually developed into civil movements aimed
at preserving the local ecology (Takeda 2005: 135–6).[10] By this time, the economic
boom led to rising family incomes, and consequently, economizing lost its sense of
urgency in Japanese household economy management. The rate of keeping
housekeeping books, according to surveys conducted by the Saving Increment
Central Committee, has declined since the 1970s. Yet, the negative consequences
of economic growth created another set of problems in everyday life, represented
by environmental disasters and the destruction of local communities. These new
situations added a fresh political dimension to household economy management.
In order to challenge governmental policies, for instance, women political activists
used their housekeeping books as evidence at judicial cases on consumer issues and
ecological protection (Miyazaki 1984: 36).[11]

The management of household economy has been, therefore, an issue at the
heart of governmental intervention into the domestic world since the modernization
of the Japanese state was initiated in the late nineteenth century. Positing that
well-organized households and families are the foundation of a prosperous state,
the prewar and postwar governments provided housewives with numerous
incentives and opportunities to obtain skills and knowledge of 'better' household
economy management, and the *modus operandi* of such governmental interventions
remained similar up until the 1970s. In doing this, on the one hand, the Japanese
state could access sufficient financial resources to wage either military or economic
war/competition with other industriously advanced countries, while, on the other
hand, each family 'autonomously' survived economic difficulties and crises in
everyday life. On the whole, the reproduction of the Japanese state was secured
through housewives' conduct of household economy management.

Household account management in the 'lost decade'

In the economic stagnation following the bursting of the 'economic bubble' in
the early 1990s, not only the national economy and large Japanese corporations
but also the household economy has been facing the pressing needs of 'restructuring' and 'downsizing', and this situation has shed a new light on household
economy management. The economic events of the late 1990s, in particular, the
'destabilization' of the lifetime employment system in large corporations and

increase in 'social costs', acted as a red alert for the families of Japanese white-collar workers. First, the sudden down-fall of the Hokkaidō Takushoku Bank and the Yamaichi Stock Company in 1997 shook the confidence of Japanese white-collar workers over their employment security. Both companies occupied leading positions in their sectors, providing their mainstream employees with life-time employment and a good standard of pay. The collapse of such companies signified a fundamental transition in the Japanese employment system of large corporations, and brought about profound anxieties. These anxieties were further deepened, first, when the struggles of ex-employees in their 40s and 50s to obtain new employment were widely reported in the mass-media, and second, when many large corporations implemented downsizing at a time of ongoing economic stagnation in which the unemployment rate was at its highest level in the postwar period.[12]

Second, in 1997, the expenses of each household increased through the rise in the consumption tax, social security contributions and the patient's share of medical expenses. The sum of the increase in this 'social cost' totalled approximately 7.9 trillion yen, which was almost equivalent to 3 per cent of the total income of company employees (Yamada and Itō 1998: 65). Importantly, the increased burden of the social cost in 1997 not only reduced the real disposable income of each white-collar worker's household, but also was recognized as presaging a long-term trend in increases in the social cost of the 'ageing' and 'childless' society. The demographic changes in the 1990s mentioned earlier mean that the Japanese pension and medical insurance system based on inter-generational transfer will be forced either to increase the financial burdens on the workforce or to reduce the welfare standard. In fact, from the Year 2000, the Elderly Care Insurance Law called for an increase in medical insurance on average to 2,500 yen per person per month for those over 40 years old (Yamada and Itō 1998: 89), and insurance payments were raised by an average 13.1 per cent in May 2003 (*Mainichi Shimbun*, 25 May 2003). Furthermore, the starting age for receiving a state pension was raised from 60 to 65 in the revision of the pension system in 2000, and the spouse special tax deduction benefit for company employees' was abolished from FY 2004, thereby increasing the tax burden on households.[13]

The anxieties and uncertainty over the security of employment and the future social security system engendered a sense of 'risk' amongst families of white-collar workers, and resulted in self-imposed restraints in consumer spending and maintaining household savings, despite the unprecedented low interest rate and governmental appeals for the 'promotion of consumption' (Nakagawa 1999: 71–5; Niimi 2001: 27–8; Ide 2002: 20–1).[14] In other words, the situation in the macro-economy in the late 1990s was translated into each household, particularly those of white-collar workers, as a necessity to run a tight household economy. Responding to this, economizing and housekeeping books again appeared as an essential part of household management. Many women's magazines, both old names such as *Fuji no Tomo* and *Shufu no Tomo* and newcomers such as *Suteki na Okusan (Mrs Nice)* and *Orenji Pēji (Orange Page)* started to feature economizing tips, while the activities of the Central Council for Financial Services, a renamed organization of the ex-Central Council for Savings Promotion, [15] were brought to popular attention. Yet, despite the apparent similarities, the revival of economizing and household account books in the late 1990s shows significant difference from the early postwar situation, in particular in terms of their relationship with governance. Reading articles on household economy management in popular magazines, the following five points need to be noted in this regard.

First and foremost, good management of the household economy is regarded as essential to building a good home, as the prewar and early postwar discourses on the household economy management posited. Hani Motoko wrote in the early twentieth century that the well-organized and planned management of the household economy was the foundation for the happiness of the family (Hani 1927: 1–12). Similarly, Yamazaki Eriko, whose book on economizing and savings became a best-seller in 1998 and made the author a media celebrity, also stresses that economizing and a rationally-planned life is a life style that leads to good health and psychological satisfaction, i.e. 'happiness' (Yamazaki 1998: 3–7). Importantly, the 'good' household economy management of the late 1990s also refers to controlling all the dimensions of everyday life, including controlling childbirth, as it did in the activities of the New Life Movement (*Tōyō Keizai* 5656, 2000: 46-7). Furthermore, the moral importance of household economy management has been extended to public 'happiness' through ecological causes. Yamazaki's book also provides a good example of this point. Having lived in Germany, Yamazaki claims the German style ecologically-friendly 'simple life' is the inspiration for her management of the household economy, through which she has managed to pay back a twenty million yen mortgage within seven years (Yamazaki 1998: 48–61). Ecology is a preferred theme for the members of *Fujin no Tomo*'s readers' associations. Since the 1980s, the 'ecology housekeeping books' (*kankyō kakeibo*) that record all the ecological impact of everyday activities as well as expenses have been promoted by the (then) Environment Agency and subnational political authorities. Inspired by the approaching Kyoto International Environmental Forum in 1998, some readers' associations introduced ecology housekeeping books into their activities, claiming a link between their everyday practices and global ecology (*Fujin no Tomo*, December 1997: 54–67).

Second, the promotion of savings and housekeeping books since the late 1990s is, however, primarily recognized as a practical measure for the 'protection of everyday life', in which families that are facing crises in everyday life are forced to adopt. Articles in women's magazines as well as business magazines (usually meant for male white-collar workers) such as *Purejidento* (*President*), *Tōyō Keizai* (*Eastern Economics*), *Ekonomisuto* (*Economist*) regularly ran articles on families in economic crises, including families suffering due to redundancy resulting from the 'restructuring' or even the collapse of companies, those affected by a reduction in salary, changes of jobs and early retirement. These stories are used as incentives for readers to start economizing and keeping housekeeping books. Yamazaki also notes the disabling of her husband in an accident as the turning point which changed their lifestyle from wasteful to stoic (Yamazaki 1998: 4–6). Moreover, as mentioned above, the 1990s economic setback and crisis experienced by Japanese families are recognized not only in contemporary terms but also as a long-term trend that brings about enduring effects. In particular, anxieties and 'risk' over post-retirement life are predominant. For example, the magazine *Arujan* (*Argent*, meaning 'money' in French) published by a major information service publisher, Recruit, repeatedly appealed to its readers in their 30s that the sum of one hundred million yen would be needed for a 'comfortable' retirement life, presuming you live until 84 years of age (*Arujan*, January 2001: 55–67). Post-retirement life, as a motif of savings, seems now to be prioritized over paying for children's education or buying a family home, goals which used to be the primary purposes of household savings (*Tōyō Keizai*, 5764 2002: 30–4). Echoing the rhetoric of 'self-responsibility' (*jiko sekinin*) promoted by the government, Japanese white-collar worker families are attempting to survive the present economic difficulty and future risk due to uncertainty through the tight management of the household economy.

Third, the government's inputs today seem more 'subtle' than in the past, as Garon suggests (Garon 2002: 214). On the surface, today's popular practices of household management seem to contradict the official governmental discourse of 'consumption promotion' for boosting the Japanese economy. Furthermore, compared to the prewar and early postwar period in which the governmental organizations and semi-governmental movements played an enlightening role, the contemporary savings promotion is, at first glance, carried out by mainly private actors (popular magazines, voluntary associations, and individuals), and the role of governmental actors, in particular that of the Central Council for Financial Services, has been reduced to holding some public lectures[16] and an annual public essay competition organized through local branches of the Bank of Japan, a competition which generally collects only around 800 entries.[17] As an effect of the reorganization of the Japanese administrative system in 2001, the 'encouragement of savings' was deleted from the agenda of the new Financial Services Agency (*Kinyūchō*), and this resulted in the reconstruction of the committee as an organization to promote the 'spread of knowledge regarding finance' (*Kurashi to Okane* 212, 2001: 10). Yet, despite its organizational scaleback, the committee seems to retain wide but indirect influence through a number of channels. First, household financial advisers and specialists who frequently contributed to the activities of the committee, for example, Ogiwara Hiroko and Takahashi Nobuko, are also regular contributors to TV programmes and articles on the household economy in the mass media. Second, the annual essay competition held by the committee has become a reservoir for non-professional advisers of the household economy in the mass media. Yamazaki Eriko mentioned above was one of the winners of the 1997 competition, which eventually gave her the opportunity to publish books. Also, other winners often receive media attention. For example, the business magazine *Purejidento* interviewed two 1999 winners in articles themed on survival tips after sudden redundancy (*Purejidento*, 15 October 2001: 102).[18] Finally, the close partnership between the committee and the Housewives Confederation and NFRWO, both of which have firmly established political and social influence as women's lobby groups, remained, and this provided the committee with access to the members and activities of those women's organizations. Furthermore, the committee also keeps a close relationship with organizations such as the Japan Association for Financial Planners, which supervises qualifications and activities of financial planners that provide advice on household economy management, both in the mass media and on a private basis.

Fourth, gender relations in the discourse on the management of the household economy are ambivalent. Household economy management had been considered primarily as a part of housework assigned to women since the late nineteenth century. On the one hand, the 1990s economic setback shook this gendered framework. For example, such major business magazines whose readers are generally white-collar male workers as *Purejidento*, *Ekonomisuto* and *Tōyō Keizai* started to run features on household economy management in order to cope with the contemporary trend of company 'restructuring', pay reduction, early retirement and the other economic uncertainties of the 1990s. Along with the financial information magazine *Arujan*, these newcomers stress the importance of sharing the responsibility of household economy management. On the flip side of male participation in household economy management, women's engagement in paid work is encouraged as a measure to disperse the economic risks that contemporary Japanese white-collar families are facing. By maximizing 'mama's income' (*Tōyō Keizai* 5764, 2002: 34), the bread-winning responsibility can be shared between a couple, along with household economy management responsibility, and in so doing, families can obtain economic security. In an article in *Purejidento* entitled 'Solutions to All the Fifty Five Problems of Businessmen in 2001', an 'economic analyst' advises readers, namely male white-collar workers, to share the responsibility of bread-winning and household economy management in order to build a 'good home' (*Purejidento*, 29 January 2001: 88–99). As such, the conventional image of the nuclear family has become irrelevant, at least for the majority of white-collar worker families, and in this respect, gender relationships within Japanese families have been forced to change due to the economic situation. On the other hand, however, discourses encouraging male participation in household economy management and female participation in paid work seem to simultaneously enhance conventional gender relationships. For instance, male participation is often described as a solution to the shortcomings and problems in the existing household economy run by housewives, as men can introduce accounting and management methods practised at their companies (*Purejidento*, 1 January 2001: 84–91; *Ekonomisuto* 22 June 1998: 8–13; *Tōyō Keizai*, 8 June 2002, 5764: 31–5). While men are coming back home with their specialist skills obtained outside the home in order to 'protect their families in crisis', women's participation in paid work is generally supposed to be a part-time commitment, reflecting the dominant trend in the Japanese labour market and reproductive work. Although some discourses encourage women to earn over the limit of the spouse tax deduction (1.03 million yen per year), no concrete strategies or episodes in which a woman regains a full-time job are discussed, apart from advice to 'keep the present full-time job if you have one' (*Tōyō Keizai*, 8 June 2002, 5764: 33). This suggests that the power relationship in the family has remained as before, in the sense that men are dominant in the control of major issues, decision-making and access to financial resources.

Finally and most importantly, household economy management in the 'lost-decade' after the bursting of the bubble has produced double-edged consequences for the Japanese government. On the one hand, through tight household economy management, Japanese families have autonomously been surviving a time of economic difficulty by economizing, maintaining savings and planning their lives, while even taking care of ecological issues. This suggests that household economy management is still functioning to stabilize the everyday lives of Japanese families, and consequently, allows the government to concentrate economic resources on the recovery of the national economy at the expense of economizing and life planning for those it governs. On the other hand, however, practices of household economy management often appear to be at loggerheads with the government's appeal for an expansion of consumption to ameliorate the present economic deflation. The rational behaviour of Japanese white-collar families to survive the present and future crisis and 'risks' by holding back on consumer spending has caused stagnation in the macro-economy, leading to a delay in economic recovery.

Summarizing the above points, household economy management in the 1990s, therefore, can be seen to be playing a certain role in the contemporary system of governance in Japan. The practice of household economy management has contributed to making Japanese white-collar families autonomous enough to survive economic crises. Yet, such autonomy appears to be at odds with the governing of the national economy, and consequently destabilizes national governance. This function of household economy management countering the governing bodies has been, however, displayed in the most evident way in women's grass-roots activities. Development in local politics since the 1980s demonstrates that household economy management can contribute to governance in an alternative way, one that appears, sometimes, to be antagonistic to public policies. The next section will examine a case in which civil movements have grown out of housewives' practices of household economy management.

Breaking into politics via the domestic

Since the 1980s, Japanese local politics have witnessed the participation of housewives through issues related to problems in everyday life (Takabatake 1993: 150; Shindō 1996: 209–16). Perhaps, the most well-known example of these cases is the activities of the Seikatsu Club Cooperative. The Seikatsusha Net, the political organization of the Seikatsu Club Cooperative, deployed very effective election campaigns and sent their 'proxies' to local assemblies in order to channel their claims on consumer and ecological issues to the political arena. It was a new type of women's movement that exercised a certain influence in Japanese local politics (LeBlanc 1999; Ogai 1999).

The groundwater protection movement in Ōno city in Fukui prefecture led by Noda Yoshie is also a new type of housewives' movement that has had a major impact in the local political arena.[19] Located in Hokuriku, which is known for its heavy snow, Ōno is a place blessed with abundant groundwater that is still used by households as drinking water, as well as being used for industrial production.

In the mid 1960s, the local political authority introduced a policy of using groundwater for melting snow. This policy resulted in an increase in water usage, and hence the exhaustion of household wells, which added to the burden in everyday housework. One housewife, for example, claimed her baby's dirty nappies could not be dealt with. The groundwater protection movement was initiated, first from a small private gathering of readers of *Fujin no Tomo* (Noda 2002). One day, Noda read a short newspaper article on the groundwater level and its connection with the land subsidence in the Hokuriku region, and realized that the problem of the exhaustion of local wells in Ōno was caused by the overuse of groundwater. She raised the issue in the readers' group, and embarked on studying the groundwater problem. Cooperating with local women's and consumer's organizations including the everyday life school of the New Life Movement,[20] Noda eventually organized the Groundwater Protection Association in Ōno (*Ōno no Chikasui o Mamoru Kai*) to protect the groundwater (*Fukuiken Ōno no Mizu o Kangaeru Kai* 2000: 3–14). The movement in Ōno resulted in Noda running for election to the local assembly. She served as a member of the assembly for sixteen years until 1999, and engaged in water and other ecological issues in Ōno. After Noda's retirement, her two successors from the Groundwater Protection Association are currently working as members of the assembly (*Fukuiken Ōno no Mizu o Kangaeru Kai* 2000: 276–8).

Interestingly, household economy management played a crucial role in the groundwater protection movement in Ōno. Noda has been a reader of *Fujin no Tomo* since 1955. She sympathizes with Hani Motoko's thoughts on household economy management, and also enthusiastically keeps her own housekeeping books. As mentioned above, the gatherings of readers of *Fujin no Tomo* provided her with the first opportunity to discuss the groundwater problem. Moreover the methods that she had learnt through keeping the *Fujin no Tomo*'s housekeeping books became the basis for the collection and analysis of data by the Groundwater Protection Association, and hence influenced the legislation for ground water protection. According to email exchanges with her, Noda explains that the influence of the *Fujin no Tomo*'s activities regarding housekeeping books was twofold. First, through keeping housekeeping books, she learnt the importance of accumulating concrete quantified data for making a convincing case. Second, the housekeeping books provided her with practice in analysing data. In her words, 'I would say that my long-term attitude of starting to practice ideas from close surroundings and thinking about issues by collecting data [note: that Noda learned from *Fujin no Tomo* and Hani Motoko's thoughts] helped me in winning people's trust. I have kept this methodology in working for the local water protection movement. Making counter-arguments based on data collected from actual situations was the best method for a housewife, who is neither a professional nor specialist, to contest and persuade the local political authority' (Noda 2002).

As such, the groundwater protection movement in Ōno was profoundly rooted in everyday practices of household economy management. Issues were raised from situations in everyday lives and housewives' practices, and furthermore, domestic skills of household economy management were adopted to create a new set of regulations to which local male politicians, administrative bodies and industries were opposed. In this sense, household economy management conducted within family life contributed to transforming local governance in Ōno, a town which as a result now offers a more adequate environment in which to conduct the reproductive activities of everyday life.

Conclusion

In a sense, both the revival of economizing and housekeeping books in the late 1990s, along with the groundwater protection movement, evolved around different levels of reproduction. On the one hand, the contemporary attention to household economy management is a measure for Japanese families autonomously to survive the present economic crisis and continue their reproductive activities, and a concomitant of this is that those people who fail to successfully implement household economy management are being marginalized through the prevailing rhetoric of self-responsibility. On the other hand, the self-protective reproductive practices of white-collar workers and their families created a negative impact on the national governing of the economy that aims at boosting the economy through the expansion of consumption. Furthermore, the groundwater protection movement in Ōno was designed to recreate a local community in which people's everyday lives had come under severe pressure, in order to secure a sustainable environment for reproductive activities. These cases certainly share common ground in terms of seeking 'protection of everyday life', or, in other words, in seeking the 'security of reproductive activities'. Through these processes, it is not only the reproduction of the family but also that of the Japanese economy and nation-state that are maintained, whilst being modified through a process of contestation. Thus, once the political and economic system turns against reproductive activities, 'autonomous' Japanese families have manoeuvred to survive or even challenge the existing governance system by resorting to the skills of household economy management. That is to say, families and household economy management are still functioning to sustain and develop the national political economy of Japan as part of the governance of the Japanese political economy, but simultaneously, they provide opportunities to alter the system of governance.

Indeed, as mentioned at the beginning of this chapter, rational household economy management in the contemporary era is posing a fundamental threat to the reproduction of the Japanese economy and nation-state due to the falling birth rates. The increasing cost of childcare, particularly the cost of education, and uncertainty over the future, dissuade many Japanese couples from having children or even forming a new family. Furthermore, as Suzuki points out, in a situation where children are not expected to be responsible for the post-retirement life of their parents, the cost performance of children has been reduced, and children have become a 'luxurious commodity' restricted to those who can afford to take some risks to have them (Suzuki 2000: 31–47). In fact, a sociologist specialized in the family, Yamada Masahiro, even argues that forming a family has become a 'risk' in contemporary Japan (Yamada: 2001). While it is certainly a 'rational choice' for an individual person to postpone and indeed give up having children in such a situation, this reproductive practice, rooted in the New Life Movement, undermines fundamentally the foundation of the governing system in Japan. Faced with this new situation, the Japanese government is seeking measures to cope with this reproductive problem. In this sense, governing the family is still a focus point of negotiations and contestation over survival between state, economy and individuals. The connection between household management and governance in modern and contemporary Japan offers a good case study to analyse the entangled relationships between the art of governance, the economy and the family.

Acknowledgements

I would like to thank the Japan Foundation Endowment Committee for a generous research grant that made it possible to conduct research in Japan for this project.

Notes

1 Total fertility rate, representing the number of children that a woman is supposed to bear during her reproductive life, has constantly fallen, and the 2002 figure (1.32) again reached its worst record (available on-line at: http://www.1.ipss.go.jp/tokei/Data/ Popular2004/4_3_2.gif, accessed 3 June 2004). In order to sustain the size of the population, the total fertility rate needs to be above 2.08 (the population reproduction level).

2 For example, Pierre and Peters discuss the importance of the 'role of society' in governance, in particular, in terms of public/private interactions. While they comment that '[t]he most important thing to do if one wants to improve the capacity for steering and management for the government, therefore, would be to strengthen the self-governing capacities of segments of society', in a later part of the paragraph they develop their notion to 'what matters is the generation of organizational capacity and the movement of interest and identification beyond the family' (Pierre and Peters 2000: 33). There is no reason specified why such capacity needs to be 'beyond the family', though the family falls within the term 'segments of society'.

3 Feminist economists such as Folbre and Elson tend to use the term 'social reproduction'. I would argue, however, that the concept of 'reproduction' needs to be better articulated and detailed in order to discuss the function of the family in the political economy. Numerous works on the different levels of reproduction, from childbirth to political socialization, are widely evident in the range of social science disciplines, and their implications for the maintenance and growth of economies and nation-states deserve a more integrated analysis. For the multiple levels of reproduction and their implications and functions in the case of the Japanese political economy, see Takeda (2005).

4 Foucault coined the term 'governmentality' to refer to a governing system in which biopolitics comprises the rationality of governing. Rose suggests that the analytics of governmentality is differentiated from the sociologies of governance in two senses. Firstly, 'analyses of governmentalities are empirical, but not realist', as 'they are not studies of actual organizations and operation of systems of rule', but 'of a particular "stratum" of knowing and acting'. In other words, '[t]hey are concerned, that is to say, with conditions of possibility and intelligibility for certain ways of seeking to act upon the conduct of others, or oneself, to achieve a certain end'. Second, the roles of the analytics of government are diagnostic rather than descriptive' and they 'seek an open and critical relation to strategies for governing', and 'open a space of critical thought' (Rose 1999: 19).

The term govermentality is translated as 'tōchi-sei' in Japanese. The first part of the term, 'tōchi' is a Japanese word used as a translation of the English term 'governance', while the second part 'sei' signifies the nature or tendency. Also see the introductory chapter.

5   Garon notes that bureaucrats who organized the early Japanese 'savings campaign' 'studied the "Thrift Campaign" in the United States', and 'were directly inspired by the model of Britain's National War Savings Committee' (Garon 2000: 46).

6   Prior to this, Hani Motoko had already published her own version of household account books in 1904.

7   The economic difficulties after the First World War culminated in the rice riots of 1918, initiated by wives and mothers in a fishing village in Toyama prefecture in order to protect their family lives.

8   Ikeda Hayato, the Minister of Finance on a number of occasions and the Prime Minister (1960–4) who implemented the income-doubling policy, played a key role in the implementation of the postwar savings campaign.

9   For example, the Housewife Confederation organized public exhibitions on household economy and savings. The NFRWO supervised the activities of local women's association (*fujinkai*), in which training courses for keeping household account books were often held.

10 For example, the everyday life school in Suginami ward in Tokyo played a central role in tackling garbage disposal and smog, both predominant environmental issues in 1970's Japanese cities (Takeda 2005: 150)

11 As Miyazaki also points out, unions used the household account books in their activities. Even today, unions publish data on the household economy collected from their members' household account books every February, just before the annual Spring Labour Offensive (*Shuntō*). This is in order to use them to support their negotiations for securing a family wage.

12 The number of unemployed has increased constantly since the late 1990s. According to surveys conducted by the Statistic Bureau of the Ministry of Internal Affairs and Communications (*Sōmushō*) published in April 2003, the number of unemployment amounted to 3.59 million, which was the worst on record. The number of unemployed among bread-winners also recorded its worst level of approximately 1.00 million (Available on-line at: http://www.stat.go.jp/data/roudou/2.htm, accessed 28 May 2003).

13 The abolition of the spouse tax special deduction was officially advised by the Tax Commission to Prime Minster Koizumi Junichirō in November 2002, and included the FY2003 Tax Reform published by the ministry of Finance, in December 2002 (Available on-line at: http://www.mof.go.jp/english/tax/tax2003/tax2003_tr.htm, accessed 16 May 2003)

14 In order to relieve banks which have been in trouble with accumulated non-performing loans, the Japanese official interest rate has been kept at a record-breaking low level since 1999 as the official policy of the Bank of Japan.

15 The Central Council for Savings Promotion was renamed as the Central Council for Savings Information in 1988, and again as the Central Council for Financial Services Information in 2001 (available on-line at: http://www.saveinfo.or.jp/save/what.html/, accessed 28 May 2003).

16 It is interesting to note that the annual public lecture held by the council for its 'savings and life planning promoters' and members of women's organizations such as the Housewives Confederations and the NFRWO kept its title the 'New Life and Women' up until 2003. This lecture has been a tradition since the time the council functioned as part of the New Life Movement in the 1950s (*Kurashi to Okane* 214, 2002: 6).

17 The results of the annual essay competition were published in the journal, *Seikatsu no Sekkei* (Life Planning), and are now published in its successor from 2001 *Kurashi to Okane*

(Everyday Life and Money) by the Central Council for Financial Services Information. According to the former, the number of total entries since the inception of the competition in 1954 had reached 64,000 by the year 2000 (*Seikatsu no Sekkei* 209, 2000: 54).

18 One of these winners runs a website which provides economizing tips as well as a long list of her media appearances (available on-line at: http://www.hi-ho.ne.jp/hasidate/kakei/, accessed 28 May 03).

19 The information regarding Ōno discussed here is based on two sources; first on private email exchanges between Noda and her successor, Yonemura Teruko, who is also a member of the Groundwater Protection Movement and Ōno City Assembly. Second, it is also based on the publications of the movement by the Groundwater Protection Association (*Ōno no Mizu o Kangaeru Kai* 1988; *Fukuiken Ōno no Mizu o Kangaeru Kai* 2000).

20 The New Life Movement was introduced in Fukui prefecture through the activities of local women's associations in the early 1950s. In 1975, the Fukui New Life Movement Association selected Ōno city as a region of 'community planning' (Yoshida 1982: 26). Some actors engaged in community planning in Ōno also joined the Groundwater Protection Association (*Fukuiken Ōno no Mizu o Kangaeru Kai* 2000: 348).

References

Dean, Mitchell (1999) *Governmentality: power and rule in modern society*, London: Sage Publications.

Elson, Diane (2000) 'Gender at the macroeconomic level', in Joanne Cook, Jennifer Roberts and Georgina Waylen (eds) *Towards A Gendered Political Economy*, Basingstoke: Macmillan, pp. 77–97.

Folbre, Nancy (1994) *Who Pays for the Kids?: Gender and the structure of constraint*, London: Routledge.

Foucault, Michel (1978) *The History of Sexuality Volume 1: an introduction*, Harmondsworth: Penguin Books.

Foucault, Michel (1991) 'Governmentality', in Graham Burchell, Colin Gordon and Peter Miller (eds) *The Foucault Effect*, Chicago: the University of Chicago Press, pp. 87–104.

Fukuiken Ōno no Mizu o Kangaeru Kai (2000) *Yomigaere Inochi no Mizu: chikasui o meguru jūmin undō 25-nen no kiroku*, Tokyo: Tsukiji Shokan.

Garon, Sheldon (2000) 'Luxury is the enemy: mobilizing saving and popularizing thrift in wartime Japan', *The Journal of Japanese Studies* 26, 1: 41–78.

Garon, Sheldon (2002) 'Saving for "my own good and the good of the nation": economic nationalism in modern Japan', in Wilson, Sandra (ed.) *Nation and Nationalism in Japan*, London: RoutledgeCurzon, pp. 97–114.

Hani, Motoko (1927) *Hani Motoko Chosakushū kaji kakei hen*, Tokyo: Fujin no Tomosha.

Hisatake, Ayako, Kainō, Tamie, Wakao, Noriko and Yoshida, Akemi (1997) (eds) *Kazoku Dēta Bukku: nenpyō to zuhyō de yomu sengo kazoku*, Tokyo: Yūhikaku.

Ide, Mitsuru (2002) 'Kakei to kurashi', *Tōkei* 1: 19–23.

Kaneko, Sachiko (1999) *Kindai Nihon Joseiron no Keifu*, Tokyo: Fuji Shuppan.

Kashiwagi, Hiroshi (1995) *Kaji no Seijigaku*, Tokyo: Seidosha.

Kashiwagi, Hiroshi (1997) 'Hani Motoko no atarashii katei seikatsu no teian', *Fujin no Tomo* 4: 30–3.

Koyama, Shizuko (1999) *Katei no Seisei to Josei no Kokuminka*, Tokyo: Keisō Shōbō.

LeBlanc, Robin (1999) *Bicycle Citizens: the political world of the Japanese housewife*, Berkeley and Los Angeles: University of California Press.

Miyazaki, Reiko (1984) 'Onna no sengoshi 50 kakeibo: shufu ga kakitsuzuketa "kateishi" no ayumi', *Asahi Jānaru* 26, 11: 32–7.

Miyokawa, Masahide (1997) *Nihon Kakeibokishi: anāru gakuha o fumaeta kaikeishi ronkō*, Tokyo: Zeimu Keiri Kyōkai.

Nakagawa, Shinobu (1999) '90-nendai irigomo Nihon no kakeichochikuritsu wa naze takainoka? Kakei zokuseibetsu ni mita "risuku" no henzai nikansuru jisshō bunseki', *Nippon Ginkō Chōsa Geppō* 4: 69–101.

Nakamura, Takafusa (1993) 'Kakeibo kara mita seikatsushi: sono ito to gaikan' in Nakamura Takafusa (ed.) *Kakeibo kara Mita Kindai Nihon Seikatsushi*, Tokyo: Tokyo Daigaku Shuppankai, pp. 1–30.

Niimi, Kazumasa (2001) 'Fukakujitsusei to jisuinfurekano shōhi kōzō henka: kakei kōdō eno makuro-semimakuro apurōchi', *Japan Research Review* 11, 4: 11–71.

Noda, Yoshie (2002) 'Ōno no mizu o mamoru undō ni tsuite no shitsumon', Emails (15 November 2002 and 21 November 2002).

Ogai, Tokuko (1999) 'The political activities of Japanese housewives: from "invisible" to "visible" political participation', *The Journal of Pacific Asia* 5: 59–97.

Ōno no Mizu o Kangaeru Kai (1988) *Oishii Mizu wa Takaramono: Ōno no mizu o kangaerukai no katsudō kiroku*, Tokyo: Tsukiji Shokan.

Ōsawa, Mari (2002) *Danjo Kyōdō Sankaku Shakai o Tsukuru*, Tokyo: Nihon Hōsō Shuppan Kyōkai.

Pierre, Jon (2000) 'Introduction: understanding governance', in Jon Pierre (ed.) *Debating Governance*, Oxford: University of Oxford, pp. 1–10.

Pierre, Jon and Peters, B. Guy (2000) *Governance, Politics and the State*, Basingstoke: Macmillan.

Rose, Nikolas (1999) *Powers of Freedom: reframing political thought*, Cambridge: Cambridge University Press.

Rose, Nikolas (2001) 'The politics of life itself', *Theory, Culture & Society* 18, 1: 1–30.

Shindō, Muneyuki (1996) *Shimin no tame no Jichitaigaku Nyūmon*, Tokyo: Chikuma Shobō.

Shufu Rengōkai (1998) *Ayumi: Shufuren 50 shūnen kinen*, Tokyo: Shufu Rengōkai.

Sōmushō Tōkeikyoku (2002) 'Kakei chōsa no hensen', available on-line at: <http://www.stat.go.jp/data/kakei/6.htm, accessed 6 December 2002).

Suzuki, Rieko (2000) *Chōshōshika: kiki ni tatsu nihon shakai*, Tokyo: Shūeisha.

Suzuki, Yūko (1997) *Feminizumu to Sensō: fujin undōka no sensō kyōryoku*, Tokyo: Marujusha.

Tada, Yoshizō (1989) *Nihon Kakei Kenkyūshi: wagakuni niokeru kakeichōsa no Seiritsu ni kansuru kenkyū*, Kyoto: Kōyō Shoten.

Takabatake, Michitoshi (1993) *Sekatsusha no Seijigaku*, Tokyo: Sannichi Shobō.

Takeda, Hiroko (2004) *The Political Economy of Reproduction in Japan: between nation-state and everyday Life*, London: RoutledgeCurzon.

Tama, Yasuko (1996) 'Shōsanka to kazoku seisaku', in Inoue Shun, Ueno Chizuko, Ōsawa Masachi, Mita Munesuke and Yoshimi Shunya (eds) *Kazoku no Shakaigaku*, Tokyo: Iwanami Shoten, pp. 159–87.

Tokyo to Shinseikatsu Undō Kyōkai (ed.) (1973) *Tokyo-to Shinseikatsu Undō Jūgonen no Ayumi*, Tokyo: Tokyo-to Shinseikatsu Undō Kyōkai.

Yamada, Hisashi and Ito, Yūichirō (1998) 'Shinchōkasuru kakei kōdō to shōrai shotoku genshō no inpukuto', *Japan Research Review* 8, 2: 86–94.

Yamada, Masahiro (2001) *Kazoku to iu Risuku*, Tokyo: Keisō Shobō.

Yamazaki, Eriko (1998) *Setsuyaku Seikatsu no Susume*, Tokyo: Asuka Shinsha.

Yokoyama, Fumino (2002) *Sengo Nihon no Josei Seisaku*, Tokyo: Keisō Shōbō.

Yoshida, Shigeo (1982) 'Fukui no shinseikatsu undō no ayumi nonaka kara', *Shakai Kyōiku*, 308: 25–31.

Index